WAVING THE FLAG

Waving the Flag:
Constructing a National Cinema in Britain

ANDREW HIGSON

CLARENDON PRESS · OXFORD
1995

Oxford University Press, Walton Street, Oxford OX2 6DP
Oxford New York
Athens Auckland Bangkok Bombay
Calcutta Cape Town Dar es Salaam Delhi
Florence Hong Kong Istanbul Karachi
Kuala Lumpur Madras Madrid Melbourne
Mexico City Nairobi Paris Singapore
Taipei Tokyo Toronto
and associated companies in
Berlin Ibadan

Oxford is a trade mark of Oxford University Press

Published in the United States
by Oxford University Press Inc., New York

British Library Cataloguing in Publication Data
Data available

Library of Congress Cataloging in Publication Data
Higson, Andrew.
Waving the flag : constructing a national cinema in Britain /
Andrew Higson.
Includes bibliographical references.
1. Motion pictures—Great Britain—History. I. Title.
PN1993.5.G7H54   1995
791.43'0941—dc20   94–30577
ISBN 0–19–812369–8

1 3 5 7 9 10 8 6 4 2

Typeset by Graphicraft Typesetters Ltd., Hong Kong
Printed in Great Britain
on acid-free paper by
Biddles Ltd.,
Guildford and King's Lynn

FOR DAD

who is nearer to Hollywood than I am!

Acknowledgements

This book has been in gestation for an incredibly long period (an earlier version was presented as a Ph.D. thesis at University of Kent), and there are far too many people that I ought to thank to list them all here. I remain indebted to them all the same! In particular, I would like to thank various people who read and commented on the book in one draft or another, including Steve Neale, Ben Brewster, John Hill, Annette Kuhn, Thomas Elsaesser, Sue Winston, and the anonymous OUP readers. I am particularly grateful to Roger Sales and Peter Kramer for their many helpful suggestions (it seems a very long time ago now!), and especially Andrjez Gasiorek, who took valuable time out from his own research to read my typescript most meticulously and to comment on it most encouragingly.

The research for the book would have been virtually impossible without the existence of the British Film Institute, particularly the staff of the Library, the National Film Archive Viewing Service, and Stills, Posters and Designs. Andrew Lockett, Jason Freeman, Vicki Reeve, and their colleagues at OUP have also always been supportive, efficient, and helpful, as have the staff of the Library at the University of East Anglia (UEA).

Over the years, my understanding of British cinema history has benefited invaluably from discussions with many former colleagues and friends, including John Ellis, Mick Eaton, and Nick Burton, who deserve a special mention for making sure that I followed the right paths when I first started researching this area. I am grateful too to students at UEA (and formerly at Leicester Polytechnic and Sunderland Polytechnic) for their insights and enthusiasm.

The School of English and American Studies at UEA has provided a secure and intellectually stimulating base for seven years now, and the friendship and support of my colleagues is greatly appreciated. In particular, Charles Barr, Thomas Elsaesser (now at the University of Amsterdam), and Laura Mulvey have always made sure that to work in Film Studies at UEA is to work in an exciting and enjoyable environment. I am grateful too for the fact that the University granted me a Study Leave in order to complete this book.

Finally, I would like to thank Val, Billie, and Luisa for providing the best possible antidote to the trials and tribulations of working in higher education in the 1990s! Thanks for all your support and affection; I couldn't have written the book without you.

All film stills were supplied by the British Film Institute (Stills, Posters and Designs). For permission to reproduce film stills, I would like to thank Rank Film Distributors Ltd. (Stills 10–16 and 24–35); the Post Office Film Library (Still 23); and Lumiere Pictures Ltd. (Stills 17–22). I have been unable to trace the copyright holders for Stills 1–9.

I would also like to thank the following for permission to re-use material previously published by them:

BFI Publishing for permission to re-use material which first appeared in 'Addressing the Nation: Five Films', in Geoff Hurd (ed.), *National Fictions: World War Two in British Films and Television* (London, 1984), and in ' "Britain's Outstanding Contribution to the Film": The Documentary-realist Tradition', in Charles Barr (ed.), *All Our Yesterdays: 90 Years of British Cinema* (London, 1986).

State University of New York Press for permission to re-use material which first appeared in published form in 'Re-constructing the Nation: *This Happy Breed*', in *Film Criticism*, 16/1–2 (1991–2), and in Wheeler Winston Dixon (ed.), *Re-Viewing British Cinema 1900–1992: Essays and Interviews* (New York, 1994).

The Editors of *Screen* for permission to re-use material which first appeared in 'The Idea of National Cinema', *Screen*, 30/4 (1989).

Contents

List of Illustrations

I

Introduction

At the turn of the century, British film-makers were among the most enterprising in the world. By the First World War, this initiative had been lost to the American film industry and, ever since, British screens have been dominated by Hollywood films. Various measures have been adopted by British film-makers, the film industry, the state, and various self-appointed guardians of the film culture in an effort to establish and maintain a national cinema in the face of this competition. In the pages that follow, I will be exploring some of the more pervasive cultural and economic forms that this construction of a national cinema has taken.

The materials with which I will be dealing include films, the industry which produces and presents those films, and the culture which consumes them—in particular what I call the intellectual film culture. One of my central arguments is that critical discourses do not simply describe an already existing national cinema, but that they themselves produce the national cinema in their utterances. This is not to deny that the film industry has produced a huge range of films over the years. Of course it has, but descriptions of British cinema as a national cinema do not generally attempt to embrace all such activity. On the contrary, they tend to be far more selective in promoting one particular reading of British cinema over others. Similarly, representations of the nation in British films are not reflections of the actual formation of the nation-state, but rather ideological constructions of 'the nation', a publicly imagined sense of community and cultural space. Another of my concerns here will be to examine the sorts of representations which have dominated at least certain traditions of British cinema.

The core of the book is made up of three detailed case-studies which explore different but often interdependent areas of British film practice which have in various ways been interpreted as models for the construction of a national cinema in Britain. The case-studies illustrate different strategies for attempting to secure or maintain a significant and profitable share of the film market. One such strategy has been competition with Hollywood as the international market leader by attempting to emulate its films. Another strategy has been the differentiation of British films from Hollywood, sometimes by drawing on specifically British popular cultural traditions, sometimes by attempting to establish some form of art cinema.

Two of the case-studies deal with key moments in the development of specific traditions of British film-making which have been taken up within intellectual film culture as authentic versions of national cinema. These are the areas of British film practice which have been described most frequently by film critics and historians as distinctive, indigenous, and worthy of serious attention. One of my central concerns here is to explore their similarities with and differences from classical Hollywood. Chapter 3 looks at what I call the heritage film and the role of cinema in the construction of the national past, and examines in detail Cecil Hepworth's period literary adaptation of 1924, *Comin' Thro' the Rye*. This film is often regarded as retarded in comparison with American cinema of the period, but I represent it as an example of a genre which is quite self-consciously developed as a form of product differentiation from Hollywood and an affirmation of established cultural traditions. Chapter 5 deals with the documentary-realist tradition, from its beginnings in the documentary idea and film practices of the 1930s, via the story documentary, to the mainstream feature films of the war period which draw on these ideas and practices. In particular, I examine two celebrated examples of the latter, *Millions Like Us* and *This Happy Breed*.

The case-study in Chapter 4 deals with much more popular and critically less respectable genre films, and looks at the ways in which they have exploited rather different indigenous cultural traditions. The focus here is on two box-office successes of 1934, *Sing As We Go* and *Evergreen*, both musical comedies and starring respectively Gracie Fields and Jessie Matthews, the two biggest British female stars of the period. The films therefore share a great deal, but they also represent two distinct industrial responses to Hollywood's international domination of the cinema. The former exploits the indigenous popular traditions of music-hall and northern English working-class culture to produce a film primarily for the domestic market. The latter is much closer formally to classical Hollywood cinema, being part of its producers' expensive bid for a place in the American market.

All three case-studies relate the cultural analysis of films to the economic context of those films. Detailed analysis of the ways in which the film industry seeks to exploit British cinema as an international cinema through its economic and cultural policies is, however, reserved for the study of popular cinema in Chapter 4. Thus each case-study takes on different aspects of the debates about national cinema, and explores different aspects of British cinema history. Since the first case-study deals primarily, although not exclusively, with the early 1920s, the second with the state of the commercial film industry in the mid-1930s, and the third with the development of the documentary-realist tradition between the late 1920s and the mid-1940s, some sort of chronological history of British cinema and British film culture is produced, although it is not in any way intended to be exhaustive as a history.

Any adequate account of a national cinema must be much more than a history of films and must include, at the very least, some consideration of both the film industry and film culture. Before I move on to the case-studies themselves, I will therefore be establishing a broader context for the discussion, first, by considering the term 'national cinema' in a little more detail; secondly by providing an overview of political and economic responses made by the state and the film industry to the fact of American market domination; and thirdly by providing a brief critical history of British film culture.

2

British Film Culture and the Idea of National Cinema

The discussion of national cinemas has proceeded with great imprecision, not least the discussion of British cinema. To take just one fairly random example, Raymond Durgnat suggests at the outset of his influential account of post-war British cinema, *A Mirror for England*, that, in selecting the films he will discuss, 'our criterion has had to be rather arbitrary and subjective: is it about Britain, about British attitudes, or if not does it *feel* British?'[1] One can, of course, sympathize with Durgnat to some extent, since national identity is by no means a fixed phenomenon, but constantly shifting, constantly in the process of becoming. The shared, collective identity which is implied always masks a whole range of internal differences and potential and actual antagonisms. The concept of national cinema is equally fluid, equally subject to ceaseless negotiations: while the discourses of film culture seek to hold it in place, it is abundantly clear that the concept is mobilized in different ways, by different commentators, for different reasons. In general, one can identify four such uses of the term, although any particular utterance about national cinema will probably mobilize more than one of these.

First, national cinema can be defined in economic terms, with the focus being on the film industry rather than film texts. One is concerned here with the infrastructures of production, distribution, and exhibition within a particular nation-state; the scale of capitalization and integration, the patterns of ownership and control and the size and make-up of the workforce of these infrastructures; the size of the domestic market and the degree of penetration of foreign markets; the extent of foreign intervention; and the relative economic health of the industry. From this point of view, the history of a national cinema is the history of a business seeking a secure foothold in the market-place in order to maximize profits, and/or to keep a 'national' labour-force in full employment.

[1] London, 1970, 5, my emphasis. Parts of this chapter appeared in *Screen*, 30/4 (1989), as 'The Idea of National Cinema'. For a comparable attempt to define the concept and practices of national cinema, see Stephen Crofts, 'Re-conceptualizing National Cinema/s' *Quarterly Review of Film and Video*, 14/3 (1993).

Secondly, national cinema can be discussed in terms of exhibition and consumption. In this case, the major questions are: which films are audiences watching? How many foreign films, and especially American films, are in distribution within a particular nation-state? How do audiences use these films and what are the effects of this diet on their well-being? Should these viewing practices be regulated? Often what is at stake here is an anxiety about the nation's cultural standing, and about the assumed effects of foreign cultural intervention—especially the effects of 'Americanization'.

Thirdly, there is an approach which is much more evaluative from the outset, allowing only certain aspects of the full range of cinematic activity in a particular nation-state to be considered under the rubric of national cinema. In a sense, this approach to the definition of national cinema emerges as a response to the previous approach, since it attempts to privilege the cultural specificity—potential or actual—of a national cinema. This may take the form of a marketing strategy designed to negotiate a place in the international market for a relatively diverse group of films by lending them the brand-name of a national cinema and promising audiences a singular and coherent experience. In general, such a perspective will privilege particular film movements or directors felt to have some connection with the national culture, where the latter is defined in high cultural terms. From this perspective, popular cinema generally becomes something quite separate from national cinema, hardly worthy of critical appreciation; as Geoffrey Nowell-Smith has noted, it has always been something of a struggle to enable 'the recognition of popular forms as a legitimate part of national cultural life.'[2]

Fourthly, national cinema can be defined in terms of representation. This time, the concern is with what the films are about. Do they share a common style or world-view? Do they share common themes, motifs, or preoccupations? How do they project the national character? How do they dramatize the fantasies of national identity? Are they concerned with questions of nationhood? What role do they play in constructing the sense or the image of a nation? One of the most productive ways of exploring national cinema from this perspective is in terms of genre analysis, for the processes of repetition and reiteration which constitute a genre can be highly productive in sustaining a cultural identity. Probably the most common version of this view of national cinema is the argument that 'a nation's films reflect a nation's thoughts', implying that cinema simply reflects or expresses a pre-existing national identity, consciousness, or culture.[3] This argument tends to deny that cinema might actively work to produce

---

[2] 'Popular Culture', *New Formations*, 2 (1987), 80.

[3] Penelope Houston, *The Contemporary Cinema* (Harmondsworth, 1963), 18. The classic example of the reflection thesis is Siegfried Kracauer's study of German cinema, *From Caligari to Hitler* (Princeton, NJ, 1966 [1st pub. 1947]).

such identities through its own textual processes and forms of engagement with the spectator. An alternative view is that national identity is constructed in and through representation: 'a nation does not express itself through its culture: it is culture that produces "the nation".'[4] It is perhaps necessary in the end to draw on both these arguments. Yes, films will draw on identities and representations already in circulation—and often they will naturalize those identities. But films will also produce new representations of the nation.

Common to all assertions of national cinema is the idea of nationhood. One of the most influential recent accounts of this concept is that proposed by Benedict Anderson. He argues that the experience of nationhood, the sense of belonging to a nation, is a question of feeling part of an imagined community. He sees four key elements to this mythic experience of nationhood: the sense of community, 'a deep, horizontal comradeship'; the inherently limited nature of that community as it is imagined, the sense of territorial boundaries to the cultural space of the nation; the sense of sovereignty, of both pre-eminence and independence; and finally of course the process of imagining itself.[5] The imaginative process must be able to resolve the actual history of conflict and negotiation in the experience of community. It must be able to hold in place—or specifically to exclude—any number of other experiences of belonging, whether to a particular class, race, gender, region—or another nation. The extent to which these different social experiences can be transformed into the singular experience of a coherent national community, with boundaries clearly demarcating the 'inside' from the 'outside', is evidence of the power of national sentiment—or rather of the narratives and apparatuses which mobilize it.

Anderson argues that modern nations are forged less through militaristic activity or blood-lines than through more or less organized systems of language, education, and mass communication; it is by these means that the people inhabiting a nation-state come to know themselves as a community and as different to others outside this community. The narratives of belonging which language, education, and mass communication put into circulation are the means by which the community of nationhood is imagined. The communications systems of the twentieth century clearly play a major role in this process of interpellating a heterogeneous mass public as a knowable, self-contained national community (although, surprisingly, Anderson does not consider their role).[6]

---

[4] James Donald, 'How English is it? National Culture and Popular Literature', *New Formations*, 6 (1988), 32.

[5] *Imagined Communities: Reflections on the Origin and Spread of Nationalism* (London, 1983). The quotation is from p. 16. See also Homi K. Bhabha (ed.), *Nation and Narration* (London, 1990).

[6] See Raymond Williams's discussion of the idea of 'knowable communities' in *The Country and the City* (London, 1985), 165 ff.

Cinema, both as a general cultural experience and entertainment form, and as the individual films which contribute to that experience, is of course one of these 'mass' communications systems, one of the means by which the public sphere is constructed on a national scale. Individual films will often serve to represent the nation to itself as a nation. Inserted into the general framework of the cinematic experience, such films will construct imaginary bonds which work to hold the peoples of a nation together as a community by dramatizing their current fears, anxieties, conceits, pleasures, and aspirations. A diverse and often antagonistic group of peoples are thus invited to recognize themselves as a singular body with a common culture, and to oppose themselves to other cultures and communities. Of course this work is never completely achieved: all film texts are the site of ideological tensions, audiences may read a text against the grain, other more critical films exist which serve to challenge the nationalizing myths found in the most resolutely patriotic films.

Even so, many films do explore narratives of nationhood and in many cases they will imbue the experience of a shared culture with a profound sense of tradition and invoke a collective memory of an undisputed national past. Cultural practices which emerged under specific historical conditions are re-imagined as authentic, timeless, and uncontestable national traditions. This produces a rich paradox, for, to the historian's eye, nations are decidedly modern, products of the period since the late eighteenth century, whereas the mentality of nationalism is permeated by a sense of the antiquity of nations and their traditions.[7] In the heritage film, we find cinema explicitly aligning itself with this sense of antiquity.

The concept of national cinema when used in a cultural as opposed to an economic sense, equally involves the assumption that a particular body of films shares a coherent and unique identity and a stable set of meanings, at the expense of other possible identities and meanings. This process of negotiation takes two forms. On the one hand, the potential coherence and unity of a national cinema depends upon an affirmation of self-identity: a cinema is national in so far as it draws on already existing, indigenous cultural traditions. Of course, this will very often mean that the interests and traditions of a specific social group are represented as in the collective national interest.

On the other hand, a national cinema only takes on meaning in so far as it is caught up in a system of differences; British cinema is what it is by virtue of its difference from American cinema or French cinema. A national cinema may appeal only to specific sections of the national community—

[7] See Anderson, *Imagined Communities*, 14 and *passim*; also Eugene Kamenka, 'Political Nationalism: The Evolution of the Idea', in Id. (ed.), *Nationalism* (London, 1976), 3–20; Anthony D. Smith, *Nationalism in the Twentieth Century* (Oxford, 1979), 1–13; and Tom Nairn, *The Break-up of Britain* (London, 1981), 329–41.

that is, it may start to unravel that sense of a shared culture. But it can also be presented in the international arena as part of a strategy of cultural and economic resistance, a means of asserting national autonomy in the face of (usually) Hollywood's international domination. Cinema thus does its part in establishing and maintaining the limits of what is imagined as a shared national culture—it helps to reaffirm the boundaries of the national community. At the same time, however, the film industry has developed within a capitalist economy and certain sectors of the industry have sought to maximize their market potential by addressing international audiences. In crossing national borders, they begin to imagine the social on an international scale. The maintenance of national boundaries is thus increasingly at odds with the potential of the mass media to cross national boundaries and create new, multinational, even global, imaginative territories and cultural spaces.

This of course has been the experience of Hollywood, not only the most internationally powerful cinema in economic terms, but also the cinema which has represented itself most easily as an international culture. It has achieved this position by successfully appealing to fantasies, desires, and aspirations that are not simply of local or national interest and by operating an economic policy which depends upon financial success in foreign markets. As a result, American cinema never functions as simply one term within a system of equally weighted differences; as Thomas Elsaesser has argued, 'Hollywood can hardly be conceived . . . as totally other, since so much of any nation's film culture is implicitly "Hollywood".'[8] American cinema has for many years been an integral and naturalized part of the popular imagination of most countries in which cinema is an established entertainment form; in other words, Hollywood has become one of those cultural traditions which feed into so-called national cinemas: 'America is now within.'[9] Hollywood thus functions as a doubled mode of popular fantasy, being both a naturalized part of national culture, and, at the same time, 'other', visibly different, even exotic,[10] hence its propensity to be dismissed as escapism, while at the same time being so evidently the mode of production, representation, and consumption that has become the international standard.

If Hollywood constitutes the international standard, then in a sense a distinctive national film production is by definition non-standard and marginal. It is certainly the case that the types of British film which have over the years been understood within intellectual film culture as truly national—the documentary-realist tradition or the heritage genre, for

    [8] 'Chronicle of a Death Retold: Hyper, Retro or Counter Cinema', *Monthly Film Bulletin*, 54 (1987), 166.
    [9] David Morley and Kevin Robins, 'Spaces of Identity', *Screen*, 30/4 (1989), 21.
    [10] See Geoffrey Nowell-Smith, 'Popular Culture', *New Formations*, 2 (1987), 81.

instance—have been unable consistently to win popular support. The terms 'national' and 'popular' are therefore not generally equivalent within British film culture, with 'national' tending to indicate bourgeois interests, values, and tastes.[11]

One implication of this scenario is that, for a cinema to be nationally popular, it must paradoxically also be international in scope; that is to say, it must work with Hollywood's international standards. To some extent, this has indeed been the case. But there is also the possibility of working with different standards, whether economic, or cultural, or both. It is to the various ways in which the British film industry has negotiated this minefield of possibilities that I now turn.

INDUSTRIAL AND GOVERNMENTAL RESPONSES TO AMERICAN DOMINATION

It is possible to identify five relatively distinct economic policies adopted by national film industries, and by the state in circumscribing the affairs of those industries, in seeking to come to terms with the greater market control of the American film industry and to maintain reasonable levels of profitability. To some extent, and certainly in Britain, two or more of these policies have tended to operate in tandem at any one time.

First, there is the possibility of collusion with the American film industry in jointly exploiting the domestic market through the distribution and exhibition of American films. For many companies, collusion rather than rivalry with one's American competitors has seemed a far less risky means of securing profits. In the case of the British film industry, many of the major distribution and exhibition companies have been organized primarily to foster, extend, and consolidate the domination of the British market by American popular films. The major American studios have had their own distribution companies operating in Britain for some time, while the major British companies have built up close relationships with American producers and distributors, who often also have substantial financial interests in British companies. British companies have found this sort of co-operation necessary, since the American film industry was much better organized along established capitalist lines well before the British film industry, and was able to pursue imperialist policies with some vigour, undercutting the charges of local distributors, since they could go into the British market in the knowledge that costs had already been recovered from the huge American domestic market. One of the consequences of this

[11] Compare Antonio Gramsci's discussion of inter-war Italian culture in David Forgacs and Geoffrey Nowell-Smith (eds.), *Antonio Gramsci: Selections from Cultural Writings* (London, 1985), esp. 196 ff.

policy has been a developing conflict of interest between producers, on the one hand, and distributors and exhibitors on the other. As Tom Ryall has noted with reference to the inter-war years,

the exhibition sector of the British film industry had established itself substantially on the basis of screening American films and had generated a large audience whose tastes were attuned to Hollywood. This factor was important in defining certain limits within which the production industry was obliged to work. The work of building up a cinema audience and the work of building up a national production industry . . . can be seen to have been in a state of contradiction.[12]

A second policy is direct competition with the American film industry on its own terms by creating a strong domestic economic base with sufficient capital to support production and distribution on the same scale as Holly-wood. In practice, this has generally meant building up a combine power-ful enough to dominate the domestic market by integrating production, distribution, and exhibition interests and reinvesting profits from distribu-tion and exhibition back into production. Ironically, this will in most instances mean some sort of collusion with American companies in ex-ploiting the home market. This has been the case with the virtual duopoly that has existed in the British film industry since the late 1920s, thus reinforcing the conflict between producers and the rest, as noted above, and particularly between small independent companies and the major combines.

The sort of production encouraged by such a policy has tended towards high-budget films with an international appeal to audiences used to Holly-wood production values and pleasures. Invariably, the argument has been that such films must be aimed above all at the huge American market since the domestic market is too small to support expensive productions. In most cases, this has meant seeking some sort of alliance with American distributors in the United States. There is of course a further irony here in that one of the assumptions underlying this policy is that a strong national cinema is one that can compete internationally with Hollywood, on its own terms and its own terrain. I will be looking at this particular strategy for building up a strong British cinema in Chapter 4, when I consider *Evergreen*, the Jessie Matthews vehicle made by Gaumont-British, one of the two vertically integrated combines of the early 1930s.

In contrast to the policy of direct competition, which writes money on the screen in imitation of Hollywood's production values, there is, thirdly, the possibility of product differentiation. This involves producing films with distinctively indigenous attractions and a qualitatively different re-gime of experiences and pleasures, generally on a budget small enough to

---

[12] *Alfred Hitchcock and the British Cinema* (London, 1986), 33.

make it feasible to generate a profit from the home market alone. Creating something different also means building different audiences with different tastes, often recruiting them from pre-cinematic cultural forms such as music-hall or middle-class theatre, given the attachment of mainstream audience taste to American films. This is possible because of the inevitable heterogeneity of audiences and markets, and because companies operating this policy will tend to confine themselves to limited areas of exploitation and cultural appeal, areas considered marginal—that is, marginally profitable—by Hollywood. Despite the familiar accusation that British film-makers have failed sufficiently to differentiate their product from the international standards of the Hollywood model, and thereby to establish a recognizable national cinema with a readily marketable label, it is possible to discern two key forms of market specialization in the history of British cinema, with smaller independent companies dominating the scene in both cases. One is the cheap, popular, but often inexportable genre film or programme-filler—especially those brands of film comedy which draw on established indigenous successes in music-hall, radio, and more recently television. I will be exploring this particular strategy for building a national cinema when I look at the Gracie Fields musical-comedy, *Sing As We Go.*

The other key form of product differentiation, this time at the prestige end of the market, is the production of art cinema for the international arena, or quality films developed for solid middle-class domestic audiences rather than specifically for the export market—an élitism which potentially severs such films from any national-popular success. There have been two relatively sustained and in many ways quite distinct attempts to create an art cinema in Britain, in the form of the heritage genre and the documentary-realist tradition, the subjects respectively of Chapters 3 and 5.

Even those areas of commercial feature film-making which are most strongly and self-consciously differentiated from Hollywood still draw on the traditions of the classical Hollywood film. The popular understanding of cinema is so closely based on the watching of American films that to offer something too different is almost to revolt against the very idea of cinema.[13] The strategy of product differentiation thus always runs the risk of alienating the majority audiences who enjoy Hollywood films. In the case of art cinema, this risk has to some extent been diminished by developing a separate art-house infrastructure of distribution and exhibition—in effect, a further fragmentation of the national market.

Each of these policies of collusion, competition, and product differentiation is a form of economic self-regulation on a national scale. They can

[13] Cf. Edward Buscombe, 'Film History and the Idea of a National Cinema', *Australian Journal of Screen Theory*, 9–10 (1981).

effectively exist alongside each other at any one time, with different sectors
of the industry operating different policies. However, they are in practice
usually carried out in conjunction with a fourth policy, regulation by the
state, conceived as a defence of national cinema on a national scale. This
sort of protectionist interventionism in the form of various legal barriers
to free trade, supplemented by various incentives to domestic production,
plays an important role in determining the parameters and possibilities of
a national cinema. The need for effective propaganda during the First
World War reconciled the British state to the cultural significance of cinema and its capacity to reproduce nationalist ideologies. This paved the
way for peace-time policies a decade later in the form of the Cinematograph Act of 1927 which imposed a quota on the importation of foreign
films. The quota system was justified in terms of the detrimental effects on
both the national culture and the national economy assumed to be the
result of wide circulation of American films. However, as Margaret
Dickinson and Sarah Street have argued, while 'a few remarks about the
cultural importance of film became an almost obligatory element in any
preamble to a statement on film policy', most of the actual regulations
introduced have been of a primarily economic nature without any sort of
quality control or stipulations as to content, and in many cases have been
designed to encourage the introduction of dollars into the British economy.[14]
'Finance and profit have always been the main factors in deciding what
films are made and shown in Britain. The system of State aid was not
designed to replace or compete with commercial finance, and it failed to
reverse the long-standing trends towards monopoly and American control.'[15] As Armand Mattelart and his colleagues have pointed out, even at
its strongest, this sort of economic protectionism relies on a territorial
definition of nationality. It establishes a geographical and politico-judicial
boundary between the nation and its others but 'while it limits foreign
influence, it proposes no other alternative than the limit itself.'[16] Cultural
tradition, national identity, and cultural energy are assumed, negatively,
rather than planned for and fostered. In fact, the state did help to foster
a tradition of art cinema in Britain through its involvement in documentary film practice from the late 1920s, and more recently through the
system of arts subsidies, local government cultural funding, and the establishment of Channel 4. The state's provisions in these cases made possible
various generally élitist types of independent production, distribution, and
exhibition.

[14] *Cinema and State: The Film Industry and the British Government, 1927–84* (London,
1985), 2, and *passim*.
[15] Ibid. 248.
[16] Armand Mattelart, Xavier Delcourt, and Michèlle Mattelart, *International Image Markets* (London, 1984), 17–18.

A major problem with all of these policies, whether they take the form of industrial self-regulation or regulation by the state, is that they conceive an international problem on a national scale.[17] A fifth policy recognizes that Hollywood's dominance is precisely international, not confined to individual nation-states, and that to resist that dominance successfully requires some sort of international co-operation. The British film industry has been involved in two concerted efforts to promote such a policy with its European neighbours, first in the period at the end of the silent era and the beginning of sound cinema ('Film Europe')[18] and more recently with the efforts to create a common audio-visual policy for the European Community.

THE FORMATION OF INTELLECTUAL FILM CULTURE IN BRITAIN

British cinema is constructed partly in and by the discourses and practices of economic policy described above. To some extent, as we have seen, these coincide with cultural definitions of British cinema, but there are other cultural definitions which are more or less distinct from economic policy, and which imagine British cinema differently. If, as I have suggested, British cinema is not something which is simply described by academics, journalists, historians, and other cultural commentators, but is in fact the imaginative product of film culture, what is needed is a history of the critical discourses which form this culture, and not merely a history of films, the objects of those discourses. First of all, I want to look at the ways in which intellectual film culture has made sense of British cinema, vaunting and valorizing some films, film-makers, and traditions of film-making rather than others, and how it has responded to the presence of American cinema and distinguished between British and American films.

An intellectual film culture did not really emerge in Britain in a systematic form until the mid-1920s, but from this period there was a certain flowering of intellectual debate about and interest in cinema. This can be seen in the founding of the London Film Society in 1925, and the subsequent development of the Film Society movement. It can be seen too in the publication of specialized intellectual or critical film journals (as opposed to trade papers or fan magazines), which began with *Close Up* in 1927, and in the inauguration of serious film criticism in daily and weekly newspapers and magazines in the mid-1920s. Several books of film theory and history were also published in this period—notably Paul Rotha's *The Film Till Now* (1930); finally, the British Film Institute was founded in 1933,

---

[17] Cf. Steve Neale, 'Art Cinema as Institution', *Screen*, 22/1 (1981), 34.

[18] See Andrew Higson, 'Film-Europa: Dupont und die britische Filmindustrie', in Jürgen Bretschneider (ed.), *Ewald André Dupont: Autor und Regisseur* (Munich, 1992); and '[The] Way West', in Jörg Schöning (ed.), *London Calling* (Munich, 1993).

while a few art cinemas and repertory cinemas opened in London and several other major cities through the 1930s.[19]

The discourses put into circulation by these publications and institutions have more recently been renewed through the publication in the 1960s and 1970s of film histories which either simply reproduced the cultural values, standards, and judgements of earlier writers, or were themselves written by critics and film-makers whose cultural formation and most significant work had been in the earlier period. Another instance of this reproduction of critical discourses is the republication of work itself first published in the 1930s and 1940s.[20]

British film culture in its most serious and intellectual formation has been dominated by a cluster of closely related moral attitudes. These attitudes can be interwoven in different ways, thereby producing different versions of the national cinema, diverse strategies of product differentiation, each with a distinctive relationship to the concepts and practices of established culture, avant-garde and modernist culture, and popular culture.[21]

The first of these determining attitudes is a fear of mass production and what is conceived as a standardized, artistically impoverished, trivial, and escapist mass culture. This distinction between the 'serious' and the 'popular' is manifested particularly in the dismissal of the majority of popular American films as 'a showmanship built on garish spectacle.'[22] Many aspects of commercial British film-making are of course subject to the same types of criticism. This sort of anxiety about 'mass culture' was already apparent in the 1910s, but it was most trenchantly formulated in the discourses which circulated around the documentary movement in the 1930s. The attitude is also consonant with the cultural formation of two other institutions which emerged in this period, the Reithian BBC and the Leavisite construction of English literature and the teaching of English.

---

[19] Jen Samson, 'The Film Society, 1925–39', in Charles Barr (ed.), *All Our Yesterdays: 90 Years of British Cinema* (London, 1986); Rachael Low, *The History of the British Film, 1918–1929* (London, 1971), 15–31; *The Film Till Now* was first published in 1930.

[20] For work by critics and film-makers active in the period about which they are writing, see Ernest Betts, *The Film Business: A History of the British Cinema, 1896–1972* (London, 1973); Basil Wright, *The Long View: A Personal Perspective on World Cinema* (London, 1974); and Charles Oakley, *Where We Came In: The Story of the British Cinematograph Industry* (London, 1964). Elizabeth Sussex, *The Rise and Fall of British Documentary: The Story of the Film Movement Founded by John Grierson* (London, 1975), is a series of interviews with documentarists active in the 1930s and 1940s; Forsyth Hardy (ed.), *Grierson on Documentary* (1st pub. 1946), was republished in 1966 (in London), and again in 1979. Histories which to a great extent reproduce critical judgements established in the middle decades of the century include Roy Armes, *A Critical History of British Cinema* (London, 1978), and George Perry, *The Great British Picture Show* (London, 1974).

[21] I am using the phrase 'established culture' in the sense intended by Raymond Williams in his 'British Film History: New Perspectives', in James Curran and Vincent Porter (eds.), *British Cinema History* (London, 1983).

[22] John Grierson, 'The Course of Realism', in Charles Davy (ed.), *Footnotes to the Film* (London, 1938), 147.

The charges of artistic impoverishment and trivialization tended to recur in later decades, even though the auteurism of new journals like *Sequence* in the late 1940s, and *Movie* from the early 1960s, found much of value in American cinema. The most extreme versions of this attitude see not just American cinema, but the very apparatus of cinema itself as culturally debilitating. This attitude must then be aligned with other attitudes in order to rescue cinema from the cultural abyss.

The second of these attitudes is, predictably, a concern to promote a national cinema which can be described in terms of art, culture, and quality. During the 1910s and into the 1920s, this tended to involve the promotion of a cinema which was parasitic upon the other more established arts, especially theatre and literature. Although heritage films constructed in this way continued to have a certain privileged place in intellectual film culture, the dominant discourse about art in the international arena by the 1920s was modernism, with its concern to establish an autonomous aesthetic realm, a pure art separate from everyday life, each art with its own specific formal tendencies and practices. From the mid-1920s, debates about film as an art-form took place in the context of this modernist sensibility, hence the various versions of pure cinema, defined in terms of a distinct and 'specifically filmic' aesthetic which broke with more established literary and theatrical modes: the essence of the filmic process was assumed to exist variously in the visual, in rhythm, or in montage.[23] Interest was initially focused on the European art cinemas of the 1920s in the USSR, Germany, and France (as well as on certain aspects of the American cinema, notably the comedian comedy of Charlie Chaplin and Buster Keaton, D. W. Griffith's narrational sophistication, and the epic Western). It was in the dissemination of this modernist sensibility that the Film Society and the journal *Close Up* played such an important role.

Indeed, there is something of a paradox here in relation to the culture of Americanism. On the one hand, those interests which are articulated by

---

[23] Harold Weston, *The Art of Photoplay-Writing* (London, 1916), discusses film as an art, but calls it a 'consolidated art' (125), which draws on painting, theatre, the novel, and poetry, but in the end is of more interest as a whole than each of these parts. By 1923 Colden Lore, in *The Modern Photoplay and its Construction* (London, 1923), could talk about film as a distinctive art, with its own aesthetic values, but these are more to do with the emotive powers of the moving image in narrative form, or what he calls pictorial story-telling (13)— but of course intellectual film culture in Britain, as elsewhere, became consolidated around an aesthetic of montage, rather than the power of the image in itself. By 1933 Eric Knight, in 'The Passing of Hollywood', *Cinema Quarterly*, 1 (1933), can confidently write that cinema has its own specific language: 'Progress can only come in both Britain and America, from individuals of courage, men with ability to think independently about the medium, who will learn its own language, and who, while carrying forward the now-forming technique, will have enough maturity to be able to say something worth hearing in the new expressionistic and impressionistic methods' (217). Philip Drummond *et al.*, *Film as Film: Formal Experiment in Film, 1910–1975* (London, 1979), provides a good discussion of the debates about modernism and film in the 1920s.

the heritage film fear the cultural effects of American cinema in Britain; on the other hand, as Peter Wollen has noted, within certain sections of European modernism, 'Americanization stood for true modernity, the liquidation of stifling traditions and shackling life-styles and work-habits.'[24] The traces of this celebration of Americanism are there within British modernism, and can be seen for instance in the pages of *Close Up*, but they are for the most part overwhelmed by the other side of the argument, the fear of American culture. As such, the modernist aspects of British cinema looked more towards continental Europe (which may itself of course have been looking back to America!). In the end, as Alan Lovell has noted, it was the documentary movement which 'captured the interest in film as an art that was developing in Britain in the late 1920s.'[25] More than any other film-makers in Britain in the 1930s, those working within the arena of documentary self-consciously explored intellectual, artistic, and aesthetic ideas and experimentation within this modernist tradition. The postwar development of auteurism began to transform this perspective, by looking once more towards the now redeveloped European art cinemas, and particularly neo-realism, the *nouvelle vague*, and the work of Ingmar Bergman, and by stressing the twin terms of artistic self-expression and psychological realism.

The third moral attitude which characterizes intellectual film culture in Britain is the desire to produce a realist national cinema which can 'reflect' the contemporary social and political realities of Britain as perceived from a social-democratic perspective. This concern was again initially most clearly formulated around the work of the documentarists of the 1930s, and eventually produced a desire for and celebration of a particular representational mode, the contemporary social drama, or melodrama of everyday life. Embodied here is a desire for Englishness—but not the archaic Englishness of the heritage genre or of London's bourgeois society theatre. It is, on the contrary, a desire for a modern representation of England and Englishness, stressing some of the key themes of modernity—the city, industry, social change, a discovery of the under-classes, and so on. The potentially élitist way in which the documentary idea embraced modernism was thus counterbalanced by the rather different way in which it engaged with the cultures of the 'ordinary people' of Britain. This was bound to a social-democratic view of the potential of mass communications systems, the idea that they can be emancipatory forces. There were recurrent calls for an enlargement of the public sphere, a democratization of representation, an extension of the iconography of the social—that is, a democratization of the community of the nation as imagined by the

[24] Peter Wollen, 'Cinema/Americanism/the Robot', *New Formations*, 8 (1989), 7.
[25] Alan Lovell and Jim Hillier, *Studies in Documentary* (London, 1972), 35.

cinema.[26] If this was an effort to 'invite the masses into history,' in Tom Nairn's phrase,[27] it was at the same time very often a top-down look at 'ordinary people', the voyeuristic gaze of one class looking at another, a process of absorbing the working classes into the established national culture.

The fourth concern of intellectual film culture deals with the question of heritage and indigenous cultural tradition. It takes the form of a concern to represent what is imagined to be the national past, its people, its landscape, and its cultural heritage, in a mode of representation which can itself be understood as national, and as traditional. This also involves inserting cinema itself into the national heritage, establishing it as one of the institutions for reproducing the national heritage. An iconography of the national past must be developed, but also a means of displaying it within a primarily narrative mode. The documentary idea is clearly in some ways at odds with the heritage impulse and the realist discourse is reworked in the latter in terms of attention to historical detail, authenticating the representation. A central feature of this impulse is the adaptation of heritage properties, whether novels and plays or buildings and values. The concern for heritage is a concern to reproduce the indigenous, the distinctive, the national; the culture of heritage is assumed to be in the national interest, capable of elevating the general public.

This set of concerns has been substantially challenged by the rather different agenda that has been explored over the last two decades, in a new flowering of intellectual interest in film theory and film history. There is now a split in contemporary intellectual film culture between the dominant discourse of serious film journalism committed to the auteurist concerns of post-war art cinema, and the structuralist and post-structuralist debates of academic film theory and the revisionist and sometimes ethnographic perspectives of the new film history.

There are now numerous writings which offer revised, alternative, and often oppositional perspectives to those that have dominated thinking about British cinema since the late 1920s. One such strand of work attempts to expand our understanding of the political economy of British cinema, going back to primary sources rather than relying on the often journalistic

---

[26] See, for instance, a much-quoted editorial in *World Film News* 1/6 (1936), in which the writer complains that: 'The English film, when it can drag itself away from Plymouth Hoe and Hampton Court and Malplaquet, and when it can forget 1588 and 1815, things to come, and all that, totters only as far as Piccadilly or St James's, or country houses with forty bedrooms, situated in what always looks like Hampshire. Butlers and parlour-maids are necessary evils, but heroes look like thousands a year and heroines like speechday at Roedean. Working people, when presented at all, are only presented as figures of fun by kind permission of Mr Gordon Harker or Mr Sydney Howard.' (4) Jeffrey Richards discusses other examples of this perspective in ch. 14 of *The Age of the Dream Palace* (London, 1984), although he is hardly outside the discourse himself. See also Raymond Williams, 'A Lecture on Realism', *Screen*, 18/1 (1977).

[27] *The Break-Up of Britain*, 340.

glosses of others.[28] Another body of writing deals with the social history of the cinema, characterized by the seriousness with which it treats popular British films, neither simply celebrating popular cinema, as in fan magazines, nor dismissing it wholesale, as in the dominant critical discourses of the middle decades of the century. Instead, such work at its best sets out to delineate the pleasures offered and the ideological work performed by such cinema for its audiences, and to situate film texts in their broader institutional and cultural context. As such, the boundaries of British cinema are being re-drawn and new connections and links are being made. Much of this work nevertheless remains bound to problematic explanatory frameworks which fail to break with the concerns of earlier discourses, particularly with regard to the relationship posited between films and society, and the assumptions made about how films produce meanings and pleasures.[29]

I see this book as a contribution to another body of recent writing which seeks to make strange those ideas about British cinema that have so often been treated as natural and unquestionable within intellectual film culture since the 1930s, a body of work which explores the characteristics of these discourses themselves, and the understanding of British cinema which they have promoted, and which re-evaluates the films which they have held sacred. The authors of such studies have also attempted to rethink previously denigrated bodies of work (both genres and directorial œuvres), drawing on recent developments in textual analysis.[30]

CULTURAL ÉLITISM AND THE FEAR OF DENATIONALIZATION

> A subtle, penetrating, persuasive Americanism is following [the American film]. The entire earth is being unconsciously Americanised by the American movie picture. . . . America is swamping the world.
>
> Boyle Lawrence, writing in *The Morning Post* in 1924.[31]

---

[28] See e.g. Dickinson and Street, *Cinema and State*; and the chapters by Michael Chanan, Simon Hartog, and Margaret Dickinson in Curran and Porter (eds.), *British Cinema History*.

[29] See e.g. Richards, *Dream Palace*; Jeffrey Richards and Tony Aldgate, *Best of British: Cinema and Society 1930–1970* (Oxford, 1983); Charles Barr, *Ealing Studios* (Newton Abbot, 1977); chs. by Tony Aldgate, Sue Aspinall, and Marion Jordan in Curran and Porter (eds.), *British Cinema History*. For some brief comments on this mode of writing, see Andrew Higson and Steve Neale, 'Introduction: Components of the National Film Culture', *Screen*, 26/1 (1985).

[30] See e.g. John Hill, *Sex, Class and Realism: British Cinema 1956–1963* (London, 1986); Ryall, *Alfred Hitchcock*; Andrew Higson, 'Critical Theory and "British Cinema"', *Screen*, 24/4–5 (1983), and '"Britain's Outstanding Contribution to the Film": The Documentary-Realist Tradition', in Barr (ed.), *All Our Yesterdays*; Don MacPherson (ed.), *Traditions of Independence* (London, 1980); Ian Christie (ed.), *Powell, Pressburger and Others* (London, 1978), and *Arrows of Desire: The Films of Michael Powell and Emeric Pressburger* (London, 1985); and Marcia Landy, *British Genres: Cinema and Society, 1930–1960* (Princeton, NJ, 1991).

[31] 'The Industry in Grave Peril; Its Preservation a National Necessity', reproduced in *Motion Picture Studio*, 9 Feb. 1924, 8–9.

Unfortunately, the domination of American films has already Americanised our younger kinema-goers, just as it has disgusted our older generations. It is not a question of our public becoming Americanised. That has already happened, and is an even more serious obstacle in the path of British progress in films than the cramping economic conditions caused by American competition. Our own people actually view the world through American spectacles.

E. A. Baugham, writing in the *Sunday Chronicle*, also in 1924.[32]

The central place of Hollywood films in popular British film culture has of course been a major source of consternation within debates about the possibility of a viable British national cinema since at least the early 1920s. Britain's late- and post-imperialist crisis over national identity is worked out here in terms of 'the potential danger of the Americanization of the world,'[33] the fear of losing an organic national identity and authentic cultural values to a standardized mass culture. The power of cinema is primarily conceived in terms of the effects of films on a mainly working-class audience assumed to be 'the most impressionable sections of the community.'[34] This assumption has of course been a key element of élitist arguments about mass culture and popular culture and has shown some resilience over the years in discussions about British cinema—*vide* Eric Knight's comments in 1933 that 'audience minds begin to grope toward real cinema' only 'vaguely . . . blindly . . . and half-consciously', and Lindsay Anderson's reference in 1957 to cinema's 'massive and impressionable audience.'[35]

There were always more liberal readings of the power of cinema. Harold Weston, for instance, called cinema 'the greatest democratic factor of the twentieth century' in 1916, but by this he understood a top-down democracy rather than a bottom-up one;[36] cinema, he thought, might perform a cultural levelling-up process whereby the masses would become initiated into the realms, practices, and value-systems of high culture:

it is to this newest of arts which is given the power of awakening the people's minds from their apathy towards art in general; it is teaching them aesthetic values by the skilful arranging of light and shade and by the choosing of beautiful spots in which to enact the exterior scenes; it is showing them life in all quarters of the globe and expanding their sense of the beautiful.[37]

[32] 3 Feb. 1924, quoted in 'Fine Start for the Film Weeks', *Motion Picture Studio*, 9 Feb. 1924, 11.
[33] *Kine Weekly*, 31 Jan. 1924, 35.
[34] R. D. Fennelly, representing the Board of Trade, in Board of Trade, *Minutes of Evidence taken before the Departmental Committee on Cinematograph Films*, i (London, 1936), para. 5, p. 1.
[35] 'The Passing of Hollywood', *Cinema Quarterly*, 1 (1933), 216; and 'Get Out and Push', in Tom Maschler (ed.), *Declaration* (London, 1957), 159.
[36] Weston, *Photoplay-Writing*, 126.   [37] Ibid.

The discourse is not unfamiliar. It is there, for instance, in the work of the early Reithian BBC, which described itself as a Temple of Arts and Music,[38] and it feeds into the public service ethos of the documentary movement in the 1930s. But it was really only the other side, the more optimistic side, of the same coin: it was the same 'massive and impressionable audience' that was to be levelled-up and become civilized:

That the Picture Play as a commercial proposition occupies one of the foremost places in the national life of both Great Britain and America is surely a proof that it is no longer to be classed with skating rinks, shooting galleries and other ephemeral pastimes. Perhaps its greatest claim to the serious attention of the thinking populace is its tremendous power to influence the minds of the masses.[39]

On the one hand, there is the thinking populace; on the other, the ephemeral pastimes of the masses; but cinema can become more than ephemeral, indeed, as an art properly handled, it can transform the masses into the thinking populace. This is the function of art.

When the recognition of the ideological power of cinema was linked to the domination of British screens by American films, two powerful lobbies were thrown into some consternation. On the one hand, there were those businessmen and others who believed that 'films are a real aid to the development of Imperial trade; we all know the catch phrase "Trade follows the Film".'[40] The real worry in this context was that American industry had an unfair advertising advantage over its British counterpart.

The second lobby consisted of educationalists, politicians, and other ideologues worried about the potential erosion of British culture at home and in the Empire: the threat of 'denationalization'. In 1923 the President of the British National Film League expressed the concern that 'the nation which today has no films of its own will become inarticulate in a world sense, its aspiration hidden from sight, its culture, its trend of thought overlooked.'[41] Even the Prime Minister, Stanley Baldwin, was impressed in 1925 by 'the enormous power which the film is developing for propaganda purposes, and the danger to which we in this country and our Empire subject ourselves if we allow that method of propaganda to be entirely in the hands of foreign countries.'[42]

It was these concerns which led to the quota regulations, introduced in 1927 to ward off the threat of denationalization: 'The widespread and potent influence of the Cinema makes it of vital importance that there shall be a substantial output of British films which shall not only be of good

---

[38] From the inscription in the foyer of Broadcasting House.
[39] Weston, *Photoplay-Writing*, 13.
[40] The Prince of Wales, reported in *The Times*, 15 Nov. 1923, 10.
[41] Reported in *Bioscope*, 22 Nov. 1923, 41.
[42] Hansard, *Parliamentary Debates* (*Commons*), 29 June 1925, 185, col. 2084.

entertainment value, but shall also be expressive of the character, habits and ideals of our peoples.'[43]

Regardless of such ideals, it has undoubtedly remained the case that the majority of British audiences have consistently supported Hollywood films. As a trade journalist put it in 1925, 'It is hardly too much to say that the ordinary British kinemagoer has been educated actually to prefer an American picture to a native one. . . . They feel that any pictures which are not constructed according to the American conventions fall short of the recognized standard.'[44]

It has long been argued from all shades of opinion that this preference can be accounted for economically, in terms of the limited range of alternatives offered by exhibitors, and the intensive marketing of American films. As we have seen, it is also a commonplace to dismiss—or to worry over— this preference in terms of escapism. More recently, certain strands within intellectual film culture have attempted to analyse the appeals of Hollywood in a more positive way, from the points of view of the audiences that enjoy them rather than the middle-class commentators who do not. Geoffrey Nowell-Smith, for instance, has argued that

The American cinema set out in the first place to be popular in America where it served an extremely diverse and largely immigrant public. What made it popular at home also helped make it popular abroad. The ideology of American cinema has tended to be far more democratic than that of the cinema of other countries. This in part reflects the actual open-ness of American society, but it is above all a rhetorical strategy to convince the audiences of the virtues and pleasures of being American. Translated into the export arena, this meant a projection of America as intensely—if distantly—appealing. When matched against American films of the same period, their British counterparts come across all too often as restrictive and stifling, subservient to middle-class artistic models and to middle- and upper-class values.[45]

Nowell-Smith's re-evaluation of American films in terms of the appeal of apparently democratic aspirations is useful because it displaces the idea that American box-office success in foreign markets is due solely to aggressive economic control, manipulative marketing, and impressionable audiences. It challenges the conventional conservative and radical attacks on American culture by noting, albeit ambivalently, the popular and to some extent even subversive pleasures afforded by Hollywood. But Nowell-Smith's privileging of Hollywood over British cinema also has its problems. To suggest, for instance, that 'British cinema . . . has never been truly popular

[43] Sir Philip Cunliffe-Lister, President of the Board of Trade, and the Minister responsible for the film quota bill, writing in *Bioscope, Special British Film Number*, 18 June 1927, 40.

[44] S. G. Rayment, 'The Story of the Year', *Kinematograph Year Book, 1925*, 12.

[45] 'But do we Need it?', in Martin Auty and Nick Roddick (eds.), *British Cinema Now* (London, 1985), 152.

in Britain' is to ignore the box-office success over the years of numerous British films, stars, and genres.[46]

A strong and popular national cinema must also to some extent be generically rich and resilient, its genres—and its star images—either deeply rooted in the cultural traditions and mythology of the nation, or imaginatively related to the contemporary concerns, pleasures, and anxieties of its audiences. One of the problems in considering British cinema in terms of genre is that American genres are of course central to the viewing experience of British cinema audiences, and several British film genres draw on these American cinematic traditions as much as more indigenous traditions. Even so, the British film industry has produced a number of genres which have a similar indigenous strength to the American Western, gangster, and melodrama genres, despite those arguments that mainstream British cinema has been unable to develop distinctive national cinematic traditions. The consistent critical neglect of these genres has been matched only by the extent to which they have dominated film production in Britain. I will attempt to redress this imbalance in Chapter 4 when I look at *Sing As We Go* as both a star vehicle and a genre film and the part it has played in reproducing ideas of national identity.[47]

WRITING THE ORTHODOX HISTORY OF BRITISH CINEMA

The intellectual film culture of the middle decades of this century has its orthodox history of British cinema. This history identifies a select series of relatively self-contained quality film movements to carry forward the banner of national cinema. This is a familiar feature of debates about the construction of national cinemas outside Hollywood, as can be seen in the relationship between a small group of radical film-makers in the 1920s and understanding of Soviet Russian cinema as a national cinema, or the place of neo-realism in debates about Italian cinema, or the *nouvelle vague* and French cinema. In the case of British cinema, if one movement has pride of place, it has been the documentary movement, but several other movements have been identified and proclaimed as the cultural high-points in an otherwise unimpressive history: Ealing Studios and the quality film movement of the mid-1940s; Free Cinema and the new wave of the late 1950s and early 1960s; and the renaissance of the 1980s. For the most part, some of the work of the 1980s excluded, these are seen as revivals or continuations of the work of the documentary movement, and they tend to be pulled together into one continuous national tradition in conventional

[46] Ibid. 152.
[47] See Landy, *British Genres*, for a recent and impressively wide-ranging study of British cinema in terms of popular genres.

histories of British cinema. Thus a familiar narrative sense of the historical development of British cinema is articulated, a seamless linear chain of causality.

Certain activities prior to the formation of the documentary movement are also retrospectively pulled into this teleology. Thus much is made of the work of Percy Smith and his *Secrets of Nature* series in the 1920s, and certain silent feature films are picked up for their realistic qualities—that is to say, for their similarities to certain of the documentary films of the 1930s. Indeed for some writers, the realism associated with the documentary movement constitutes the only authentic national cultural tradition.[48]

This history is filled out by foregrounding certain feature films which again seem realistic—accounts of the 1930s from this point of view tend to privilege some of Anthony Asquith's and Alfred Hitchcock's films of the 1930s for their attention to the surface details of English provincial life, and other films of the period which deal with social problems such as poverty and unemployment (e.g. *South Riding* (1938), and *The Stars Look Down* (1939)).[49]

Since the history of British film-making has been one of consistent under-capitalization, virtually permanent crisis, and the fragmentation and dispersal of potential, there has been an understandable fear on the part of mainstream critics in facing up to the actual differences and discontinuities which run across British film culture, and a corresponding desire to identify renewed traditions of quality, at the cost of ignoring, repressing, and marginalizing other cinematic practices. One of the problems with this critical-historical identification of an on-going movement of documentary-realist film-making is that most of the conventional historians have seen no problems in writing about the films of the past in the same terms in which contemporary critics wrote about these films at the time of their initial release: 'It is as if that history [of the cinema in Britain] were so self-evident and transparent as not to require a reading or writing.'[50] However, as Michel Foucault has argued in another context, 'we must question those ready-made syntheses, those groupings we normally accept before any examination, those links whose validity is recognised from the outset. . . . The tranquillity with which they are accepted must be disturbed.'[51]

Most discussions of cinematic movements tend to take for granted such

[48] See e.g. David Robinson, 'United Kingdom', in Alan Lovell (ed.), *The Art of the Cinema in Ten European Countries* (Strasburg, 1967), 197–228; Edgar Anstey, 'Development of Film Technique in Britain', in Roger Manvell (ed.), *Experiment in Film* (London, 1949), 234–65. The terms of this discourse can be seen emerging in Rotha, *Film Till Now*; see ch. on 'British Film', 313–22.

[49] See e.g. Ernest Lindgren, 'The Early Feature Film', in Michael Balcon *et al.*, *Twenty Years of British Film, 1925–45* (London, 1947), 13–28; and Wright, *Long View*, 103–7.

[50] Sam Rohdie, 'History and Film', BFI EAS/SEFT xeroxed Seminar Paper, 1973, 2.

[51] *The Archaeology of Knowledge* (London, 1974), 22, 25.

concepts as 'uniqueness', 'originality', and 'coherence'. The term 'move-ment' is conventionally used as a label for films which are seen as depart-ing from the mainstream, and which can be discussed in terms of their difference, their otherness, their self-sufficient and enclosed nature. This uniqueness is defined not only in relation to Hollywood and American cinema, but also to the very idea of genre and standardized, formulaic production. Indeed, the financial inability of small independent producers to indulge in concerted mass production is one of its virtues, at least from the point of view of certain sectors within the intellectual film culture, since it seems to imply a resistance to cultural standardization. The pro-motion of a quality national cinema in Britain in the mid-1940s, for in-stance, involved contrasting the individuality of style and comparative artistic freedom of small independent production units—and later auteurs—with what was seen as 'the rubber stamp of Hollywood entertainment.'[52] As Roger Manvell, one of the most prolific British film writers of the 1940s, wrote,

the emotional atmosphere [of Hollywood films] is nearly always 'dressed' with a certain showmanship. It makes immensely effective cinema, but it seldom lives in the knowledge of the close and personal heart. It turns too easily to sentimentality, to sexual or social heroics. The maturity of American cinema is a technical one. It is immensely at ease with itself because of its huge and assured market, its top-line stars, its effective small part players, its ace directors and its efficient opulent studios. But it lacks the emotional purgation caused by struggle and stricture.[53]

Such utterances seem to pave the way for the celebration of the romantic auteur. And indeed, as the history of most film movements shows, in order to sustain their productive energy, they will tend to fragment into a series of identifiable and bankable auteurs, as happened in Britain in the late 1940s, the mid-1960s, and the 1980s. Thus we are presented with the paradox of individual auteurs whose work is legitimized by mainstream film critics primarily in terms of a discourse of self-expression, yet who are also taken up as representatives of and vehicles for the expression of national culture.[54] Either this, or the movement will concretize into a reproducible genre. In the case of the British documentary-realist tradition, for instance, a genre of shared and repeatable characteristics is first built up, and then transformed and renewed in various ways—although mainstream critics and historians have resisted describing this area of film-making as a genre,

---

[52] Roger Manvell, 'Films of the Quarter', *Sight and Sound*, 15 (1946), 24.
[53] *Film* (London, rev. edn., 1946), 139.
[54] Film-makers have been taken up in this way in recent years by the state, through agencies such as British Screen, Channel 4, and the British Film Institute, and by critics, and other cultural commentators and administrators. Cf. Thomas Elsaesser's discussion of this paradox in relation to West Germany, in *New German Cinema: A History* (London, 1989), esp. 46–8.

since this would be to acknowledge conventionality over against uniqueness, contemporaneity, and immediacy.

Regardless of whether a movement sediments into a genre or fragments into a series of auteurs, if production is to be sustained then audiences, and therefore box-office returns, have to be forthcoming. The recruitment of sufficiently large audiences means, in practice, either moving towards Hollywood and the mainstream, or establishing a separate infrastructure of funding, production, distribution, and exhibition. The documentary movement in the 1930s was founded on just such a separate economic base, funded by state and commercial sponsorship, with films made on minimal budgets. It was not, therefore, dependent on recouping costs from box-office receipts, so the documentary units needed neither to compete with Hollywood in the British market, nor to break into the American market. It was for these reasons, amongst others, that the documentary movement could be taken up so readily in debates about national cinema. This same economic base, however, effectively disbars such film-making from the huge theatrical market, and therefore from developing into a popular cultural form. It is significant, therefore, that attempts to popularize documentary in the late 1930s involved a realignment with the theatrical market and a move to take on some of the narrative forms of the mainstream cinema, a move consolidated during the war years (and virtually reproduced by certain film-makers within the Independent Cinema of the late 1970s and 1980s). I will be looking at this development in more detail in Chapter 5.

3

The Heritage Film, British Cinema, and the National past: Comin' Thro' The Rye

One of the key strategies adopted in the bid to construct a national cinema in Britain has been the exploitation of what we may, following Charles Barr, call the heritage film[1]—that is to say, a genre of film which reinvents and reproduces, and in some cases simply invents, a national heritage for the screen. In the discourse which confirms and celebrates these films, they are constructed as one of the major sites of quality in British cinema. This quality is in part inherited from the already canonic cultural properties adapted for the screen (the novels, stately homes, period costumes, and the like), and in part constructed in the modes of representation adopted for these films.

Heritage films have been produced in Britain since at least the 1910s, and have been central to the revival of British cinema in the 1980s and 1990s; among the most successful British films of the last decade have been *Chariots of Fire* and the Merchant-Ivory adaptations of E. M. Forster novels, notably *A Room With A View* and *Howards End*.[2] Heritage fictions are also an important facet of quality drama on British television, especially in the guise of the classic serial.[3] These up-market English costume dramas (for it is Englishness rather than Britishness which they peddle) share a number of stylistic, thematic, and representational conventions, which suggests that they might usefully be described as a genre. Certainly, they are treated by reviewers and by the industry as distinctive, whether at the stage of planning productions or marketing products—and they tend to be valued as much for their cultural prestige as for any commercial success they might be expected to achieve. Perhaps the term genre is too

[1] See 'Introduction: Amnesia and Schizophrenia', in Charles Barr (ed.), *All Our Yesterdays: 90 Years of British Cinema* (London, 1986), 11–12.

[2] See my discussion of these films in 'Re-presenting the National Past: Nostalgia and Pastiche in the Heritage Film', in Lester Friedman (ed.), *Fires Were Started: British Cinema and Thatcherism* (Minneapolis and London, 1993).

[3] Cf. Paul Kerr, 'Classic Serials: To be Continued . . .', *Screen*, 23/1 (1982).

strong, and these films should be seen as a sub-genre of the historical romance or costume drama—for not all costume dramas are heritage films (they do not all address themselves to the quality end of the market, for instance, or concern themselves unduly with questions of period authenticity). Genre or not, such films constitute a coherent enough body of films for them to be discussed collectively and for better or worse I shall continue to refer to them as a genre.

One central representational strategy of the heritage film is the reproduction of literary texts, artefacts, and landscapes which already have a privileged status within the accepted definition of the national heritage. Another central strategy is the reconstruction of a historical moment which is assumed to be of national significance. Many heritage films are adaptations of novels and plays which already have some sort of classic status. Most of them are set for at least part of the time in the sorts of buildings and landscapes which are now conserved by bodies such as the National Trust and English Heritage, and these settings are generally inhabited by familiar aristocratic English types and the values and lifestyles they bring with them. Those characters are often performed by actors better known for their prestigious theatre work than their film acting, who bring with them all the connotations of that tradition of English acting. The iconography of the genre is completed by the rich *mise-en-scène* of the antique collector, with its tasteful period décor, furniture, and ornaments.

One of the key terms in the discourse which validates these films is authenticity—the desire to establish the adaptation of the heritage property (whether conceived as historical period, novel, play, building, personage, décor, or fashion) as an authentic reproduction of the original. A version of realism is thus at work in the production and consumption of the heritage genre, just as it is in the documentary-realist tradition—except that it is a different version of realism, stressing the value of reproducing what is taken to be a pre-existing historical reality rather than a contemporary reality.

Paradoxically, the two genres most frequently cited in debates about British cinema as a national cinema seem to pull in opposite directions, and to embody different ideological perspectives. Or, if they are not opposed, then the documentary-realist tradition at least tries to modernize and democratize the idea of heritage, by representing the mundane cultural traditions of 'ordinary people', rather than of the canonical, the acclaimed, or the distinctive. This is particularly true of a film like *This Happy Breed*, which I will be discussing in Chapter 5.

One of the champions of the English heritage film in the 1910s and early 1920s was Cecil Hepworth, and I will explore some of the issues at stake in the heritage genre by looking in detail at his literary adaptation, *Comin'*

Thro' The Rye, made in 1923 and released in 1924. This film has a reputation as one of the most accomplished British films of the early 1920s, much praised for its photography of English landscapes and country houses.[4]

Comin' Thro' The Rye was, for the time, a relatively conventional project, from what was already recognizable as a 'typically British school of film-making',[5] and it should be seen as part of a quite self-conscious bid to find an English idiom for film by reference to a perceived heritage. The heritage genre, and this film in particular, are thus part of a deliberate attempt at product differentiation. Consequently, to accuse such films of being primitive, or uncinematic, or too literary, or too theatrical, as many critics have done over the years, is to fail to take into account the particular conditions of this differentiation. Uncinematic may simply mean not like classical Hollywood cinema—but, as this is typically one of the objectives of the heritage film, it is hardly a valid criticism.

Comin' Thro' The Rye is an adaptation of a best-selling Victorian novel by Helen Mathers, a three-decker romantic melodrama first published in 1875 and subsequently reprinted many times over. The book deals with the mid-Victorian gentry class and was addressed to a leisured middle-class readership, but according to Elaine Showalter, in the context of 1870s writing and politics, the novel was relatively sensationalist, not least for its muted feminist protest against the conditions of upper-class women and its reworking of romance conventions.[6] This meant that it was only with some difficulty that the novel could be represented as an unproblematically high cultural text—although Mathers does seem to aspire to some sort of cultural status through her constant references in the novel to classical literature, Shakespeare, and the traditions of the nineteenth-century novel.

By the 1920s, however, the meaning of the book had obviously changed. Not only was it very well known, with new editions still appearing, but it was now no longer a novel about the present but had become a period-piece which had gained a reputation as the 'perfect epitome of a certain type of English life and thought.'[7] More generally, 'Victorian England' had come to signify a charming and respectable national ideal. By selecting this particular novel for adaptation, Hepworth clearly hoped that his film could acquire for itself the literary and ideological quality already invested in the source text and at the same time gain a certain popularity given the wide readership of the book. Hepworth in fact made two versions of the film,

---

[4] See Appendix for credits and plot synopsis for the film.

[5] *Bioscope*, 31 Jan. 1924, 52.

[6] *A Literature Of Their Own: British Women Novelists From Brontë to Lessing* (London, 1978), 153–81.

[7] *Bioscope*, 5 Oct. 1916, 109. There had been 12 edns. of the book by 1887, and new edns. were published in 1915 and 1924. See *British Museum General Catalogue of Printed Books* and *The English Catalogue of Books* (various years).

the first in 1916 with modern-day dress and settings. This was at a time when Hepworth had adopted the policy of 'pay[ing] good money for books or plays that were already successful in the eyes of the public. In other words, cash in on the popularity already secured'.[8]

The Hepworth company already had a reputation for producing tasteful films, well-made by British standards, and often adaptations of well-known novels and plays (including adaptations of Dickens, Shakespeare, and Pinero, and many other currently popular works).[9] To Hepworth, these were 'important and worthwhile pictures', 'lengthy . . . pictures [which] had won great success', 'sterner material among that which is merely entertaining', by comparison with the material produced before the 1910s.[10] Rachael Low notes that films like the 1916 *Comin' Thro' The Rye* were praised for their 'excellent photographic quality, beautiful exteriors, restrained acting and unsentimental stories'. As one reviewer put it, 'Hepworth's productions are always remarkable for their delicacy of touch and the beauty of their countryside settings.'[11] In addition, Hepworth's films were being praised for their Englishness—or rather, these same qualities were understood as essentially English qualities. Thus *Picturegoer* described Hepworth's films as 'representative of English thought, ideals, and character, without any imitation of other countries whatsoever.'[12] The full force of this particular discourse is to be found in the pages of the intensely patriotic *Bioscope*, as in their review of *Drake's Love Story* (1913):

One's first sensation on seeing this very fine production by the Hepworth Company is a feeling of gratification that the splendid chapter of English history which it represents has been immortalised in pictures not by a foreign firm but by a company essentially and entirely English. . . . We must all be ready appreciatively to recognize the laudable efforts of Messrs. Hepworth . . . to establish the art of film manufacture on quite as high and as national a basis in our own, as in other countries.[13]

The 1916 version of *Comin' Thro' The Rye* was equally well received as a supreme example of national cinema:

---

[8] Cecil Hepworth, *Came The Dawn: Memoirs of a Film Pioneer* (London, 1951), 148. As Hepworth's autobiography was published in 1951, it cannot be read as primary evidence. I have tried wherever possible to corroborate Hepworth's recollections with contemporary evidence, but I have also found it useful to draw on the autobiography because it still preserves a certain way of thinking about the cinema, even though it is written well into the sound period.

[9] See e.g. 'F. D.', 'Behind the Scenes, no. 2: Cecil M. Hepworth', *Pictures and Picturegoer*, 17 Mar. 1917, 513; Gertrude M. Allen, 'The Master Mind of the House of Hepworth', *Pictures and Picturegoer*, 20 Sept. 1919, 356; see also Rachael Low, *The History of the British Film, 1914–1918* (London, 1950), *passim*.

[10] *Came The Dawn*, 114, 148, 95.

[11] Low, *British Film 1914–1918*, 83; see also 81; and *Kine Weekly*, 1 Feb. 1924, 40.

[12] Feb. 1924, 15.   [13] *Bioscope*, 27 Feb. 1913, 673.

[The novel] is so essentially English that the task of interpreting it in pictorial form would have been beyond the powers not only of any foreign film producer but also of a great many British ones. In Mr Cecil Hepworth, whose unsurpassed skill in the representation of typically English scenes is well known, Miss Mathers may justly be said to have found an ideal interpreter for her book. . . . In his search for backgrounds, Mr Hepworth seems to have ransacked the country for open-air beauty of the most perfectly and essentially English type. We have never seen a film which embodied more thoroughly the true inner spirit, as well as the outward appearance, of the English countryside. . . . As a great picture-maker, Mr Hepworth has never done a finer or more artistic piece of work.[14]

Hepworth's second version of the film was set in the 1860s, thereby transforming a novel with a contemporary setting into a historical romance with a period setting. Hepworth had, in fact, had some regrets about updating the story for the 1916 version, since clearly part of the appeal of the novel in the 1910s, some forty years after it had first been published, was the way in which it could be read as having preserved in aspic a nostalgically recalled moment in the history of Englishness.[15] The 1923 version is, like the novel, set firmly within the milieu of the gentry and as such can be read as a paean to and a mythologization of a disappearing class and culture and the class system on which it depends. It is a celebration of the traditional upper-class values of honour and propriety (hence the unhappy ending to the film), a reproduction of a moral heritage, 'completed with . . . care and good taste.'[16] It conducts this paean within the discourse of pastoral, employing the photographic conventions of pictorialism—which again lends the film a certain cultural status. The more conservative versions of pastoral relate very closely to the ideological project of the heritage industry. As Terry Morden has noted, 'in Britain, the pastoral has a particular resonance. It lies deep within the national consciousness providing the dominant and enduring image of the British land.'[17]

Looking back, Hepworth himself thought the 1923 version of *Comin' Thro' The Rye* 'my best and most important film'.[18] Contemporary reviewers

[14] *Bioscope*, 5 Oct. 1916, 109. Cf. the review in *Kine Weekly*: 'we are . . . proud to claim the producer of this almost classic work as an Englishman through and through', 5 Oct. 1916, 23–4.
[15] Hepworth recalled that 'many people objected to the introduction of a motor-car in a story that their children had known and loved very many years before such a thing was invented' (*Came the Dawn*, 131), a view which is confirmed by a reviewer in one of the trade papers who 'cannot help remembering that at the time when Helen Mathers wrote *Comin' Thro' The Rye* men did not drive motor cars and women did not smoke cigarettes' (*Kine Weekly*, 5 Oct. 1916, 23).
[16] *Bioscope*, 31 Jan. 1924, 55.
[17] 'The Pastoral and the Pictorial', *Ten : 8*, 12 (1983), 19. Note however that such comments cannot apply across the board to all pastoral representations, since, as Roger Sales, *inter alia*, has argued, there can be radical pastoral too; see *English Literature in History, 1780–1830: Pastoral and Politics* (London, 1983).
[18] *Came The Dawn*, 188.

tended to agree: '*Comin' Thro' The Rye* has excelled [Hepworth's] own high standards'; 'it ranks among his finest achievements. . . . It is the Hepworth school at its very best—and this is praise unstinted.'[19]

The 1923 version of *Comin' Thro' The Rye* was in fact the last film produced by the Hepworth company before it went bankrupt the following year,[20] an economic failure symptomatic of the state of the British film industry in the mid-1920s. While distributors and exhibitors were relatively buoyant from the profits of the American films which they handled, the production sector was in crisis. It was under-capitalized, poorly managed, inadequately resourced, unable to secure sufficiently profitable distribution at home or abroad, and lacked the advantages of vertical integration increasingly enjoyed by the American companies with whom it was competing.

The problems facing the British production industry were not new, but they had reached a crisis—'the British film industry is dying', pronounced *The Morning Post* in early 1924.[21] The build-up had been long-term, and can be traced back to three main causes: the much earlier and much more intense capitalization of the American industry in comparison with the British industry; the much smaller home market in Britain than in America; and the profits that were to be had from involvement in London-based international distribution of American and other films. This third factor encouraged investment in and development of distribution at the expense of production, and the exploitation of American films at the expense of British films.[22] The situation for British producers had been drastically exacerbated by the early 1920s by the blind- and block-booking practices of the major American companies. Although the Hepworth company was one of the more successful British production companies during the 1900s and the 1910s, with its own distribution arm active both at home and in the United States, by the mid-1920s its business methods and the products themselves were out of step with the international standards being set by the American majors. The final straw for Hepworth was a public flotation to raise capital to fund plans for a new studio complex—which, significantly, was already outmoded in its design. The flotation, during a general

---

[19] *Kine Weekly*, 3 Jan. 1924, 81; *Motion Picture Studio*, 17 Nov. 1923, 12.

[20] See e.g. *Bioscope*, 3 July 1924, 30: 'Hepworths have been a pillar of the industry since the earliest days, and their disappearance—should things come to that—will be a serious blow to the prestige of the British film. . . . The fine traditions [Hepworth] established have been a powerful influence for the betterment of the whole industry. With his artistic idealism and his high commercial principles, Mr Hepworth is a man whom the Trade cannot afford to lose'; cf. *Kine Weekly*, 3 July 1924, 66.

[21] Boyle Lawrence, 'The Industry in Grave Peril; Its Preservation a National Necessity', reproduced in *Motion Picture Studio*, 9 Feb. 1924, 8.

[22] See Kristin Thompson, *Exporting Entertainments: America in The World Film Market* (London, 1985). See also Lawrence, 'Industry in Peril', 8–9.

trade depression, was under-subscribed, and Hepworth was eventually forced into bankruptcy.[23]

The trade press and the production sector of the industry were working hard to stave off the impending crisis. The British National Film League had been founded in 1921 with the object of attempting to re-establish British films on an equal footing with American films both in the domestic market and internationally, and 'to raise the standard, improve the quality and promote the general interests of British films.'[24] A campaign of British Film Weeks, with the slogan 'British films for British people', was launched in November 1923.[25] Sentiments were high, with much talk of the power of film, the threat of Americanization, the necessity for cinema to be recognized as a national industry, and so on, with due attention being paid to 'the moral effect of the Weeks, besides the immediate commercial results.'[26] As the *Bioscope* noted, the attendance at the launch party of numerous public figures including the Prince of Wales 'implied that the importance of the industry in general, and home production in particular, is now acknowledged in the most influential circles.'[27] Occasions such as this were, in the long term, paving the way for government intervention to protect the production sector of the British film industry from American cultural imperialism.

One of the films trade-shown during the British Film Weeks was *Comin' Thro' The Rye*. Indeed, Hepworth recalled in his autobiography that the film was specifically prepared for the event. It is obviously significant that for 'such an important occasion' he should have selected a historical adaptation, with all the prestige and conservative bourgeois values that the heritage genre, the historical period, and the literary adaptation could bring to the popular entertainment medium of film.[28] After the screening of his film, Hepworth made a speech in which he predicted that 'the year

[23] See *inter alia* Hepworth, *Came The Dawn*, 180 ff. Commenting on his plans to build new studios, Hepworth wrote: 'I still clung to my archaic idea of using daylight as far as ever possible, [supplemented by] arc-lighting' (ibid. 182). The studios were designed with glass rooves, even though most studios built at this time were fully lit artificially—see Baynham Honri, 'Cecil M. Hepworth—His Studios and Techniques, part 2', *British Journal of Photography*, 22 Jan. 1971, 79.

[24] *Kinematograph Yearbook, 1924* (London, 1924), 139; see also 'British National Film League', a single undated item in the British Film Institute Library subject file, evidently produced by the League itself; H. Rowan Walker, 'British National Film League', *Bioscope*, 3 Jan. 1924, 44; S. G. Rayment, 'The Story of the Year', *Kinematograph Yearbook, 1925* (London, 1925), 5; and Low, *British Film, 1918–1929*, 89–90.

[25] There was a great deal of publicity and comment about the British Film Weeks in both the trade and national press. See e.g. *Bioscope British Films Supplement*, 1. Nov. 1923; *Bioscope*, 22 Nov. 1923, 40–6; 'British Films, Prince of Wales Tribute, Aid to Imperial Trade', *The Times*, 15 Nov. 1923, 10; and 'British Films, a Memorable Repast, a Film-Idealist', in *The Times*, 21 Nov. 1923, 10.

[26] *Bioscope Supplement*, 57.   [27] *Bioscope*, 22 Nov. 1923, 40.

[28] *Came The Dawn*, 189.

of 1923 will go down in history as the year of the renaissance of the British film, and of the sudden dramatic collapse of the American "banana" film', adding that 'a sound moving picture industry is an absolute necessity to the health of any country today. The whole world is being Americanised as a direct result of the fact that the United States possesses the premier moving picture industry.'[29]

Certainly, British films received a great deal of publicity in late 1923 and early 1924, but if there was a renaissance, it was neither accompanied by the collapse of the American film in the British market, nor was it long-lasting. It was precisely the power of the American film industry that forbade any real renaissance of British films, and only a year after the launch of the Film Weeks campaign, November 1924 went down in history as 'Black November' with not a single film in production at any studio in Britain.

Most of the press had gone along with the rhetoric of the Film Weeks, but as the *Manchester Guardian* suggested 'the British film Trade is in a bad way and extremely nervous. The Weeks are a last desperate bid for favour.' The same writer also noted that 'the films of which the Week promoters seem most proud ... have been built entirely around the personality and methods of a specially imported star,'[30] and certainly the most heavily promoted and best-received film was *Woman to Woman*, for which the American star, Betty Compson, was brought over. In its review of 1923, the *Bioscope* noted that 'British pictures during the year were numerous and varied, ranging from big supers (made in the American style with a view to entering the American market) to typically national plays of more modest character but not less artistic merits.'[31]

Hepworth was clearly committed to the latter policy, but a new breed of producers was emerging for whom the policy of competing with Hollywood on its own terms seemed more attractive. Prominent among these were the producers of *Woman to Woman*, Michael Balcon and Victor Saville, who were to become key figures in the British cinema of the next two decades. The American style was in fact becoming increasingly accepted as the international standard, and films which deviated from it were just as likely to be seen as backward rather than as typically national. Hepworth's work is at the very centre of this debate.

The predicaments facing an outmoded operation like Hepworth Pictures trying to survive in the international film industry of the early 1920s are all too evident from the efforts made to secure the future of the company. Hepworth's publicity representative appealed to British exhibitors to show the company's films on the grounds of patriotism and justice and generosity

---

[29] Reported in *Bioscope*, 15 Nov. 1923, 27.
[30] Quoted in *Motion Picture Studio*, 16 Feb. 1924, 8.   [31] 3 Jan. 1924, 47.

towards a pioneer British producer whose 'name and [whose] productions have brought prestige to the industry'.[32] The discourse is in many ways characteristic of certain more conservative strands within the film culture and political culture of the 1920s, expressing a deep anxiety at the erosion of Englishness by American popular culture. The proposed solution takes the form of a moral imperative on the industry: buy British.

What this intervention fails to address is the potential contradiction between ideologies of nationalism, the accumulation of capital, and the development of international markets. More specifically, it fails to address the deep-seated conflict of interests between British producers on the one hand, and on the other hand distributors and exhibitors operating in league with the much more powerful major American companies. The trade press were not slow to point out the inadequacies of the argument, especially from an exhibitor's point of view. An editorial in *Kine Weekly*, for instance, attacked producers like Hepworth for their

lack of vision [and their] narrow insistence on stars, stories and methods which have no value outside a small circle. . . . Grant that a producer of the type of Hepworth considers himself an artiste. Accept the idea that he is trying to find a means of personal expression. But if that attempt at artistry fails, if the expression does not find general acceptance, it is folly to blame the world at large.[33]

The implication is that Hepworth's films were of interest only to a minority; they were in modern terminology art-house films, but still expected to operate within the commercial environment, which was dominated by American standards, methods and products. It was on these grounds of failure to adapt to the conditions of the market-place that Hepworth, and others like him, were criticized:

Our producers—particularly our producers who fail—must face the facts. They have not made the kind of pictures that have been wanted. They have studied their own narrow conception of a public as conceived by them, instead of a broad conception of humanity. They have been too self-satisfied, too insular, too unorganised both in their production and their selling. . . . To ask the exhibitor to book pictures which his judgement and his estimates of box-office potentialities have already caused him to pass by, and to book them because a producing organisation is British instead of because the pictures are worth his while as against what else is in the market, is to appeal to misguided sentiment. And curiously enough, the sentiment is all on one side. For the very firm which is handling Hepworth films [Ideal] has passed its own verdict on British production by ceasing to make films and, instead, making heavy contracts with American producers.[34]

As the 1920s progressed, it became clear that moral appeals to the industry would be insufficient to protect the interests of British producers, and

[32] *Bioscope*, 10 July 1924, 28; see also Low, *British Film, 1918–1929*, 112.
[33] *Kine Weekly*, 10 July 1924, 41.   [34] Ibid.

only the combination of state support and the concentration of ownership and control in the industry as a whole would come anywhere near to offering the sort of protection required. Even then, companies as small as Hepworth Picture Plays would find it difficult to survive for reasons discussed elsewhere, not least since the emerging minority film culture and the development of an art cinema, in which context films like *Comin' Thro' The Rye* might ideally have thrived, were increasingly dominated by European films and a modernist aesthetic very different to Hepworth's.

HEPWORTH AND FILM CULTURE

It is not simply because *Comin' Thro' The Rye* is a heritage film that it has a significant place in the debates about British cinema as a national cinema. It is in many ways the product of a transitional moment for the British film industry, in which one set of filmic and industrial conventions—as adopted by *Comin' Thro' The Rye* and the Hepworth company which produced it—were being superseded by a new set of conventions, those of what is now called classical Hollywood cinema. This was also a period in which debates about the nature of film as an art and about the relations between cinema and national identity were coming to the fore. Indeed, in the press during late 1923 and early 1924, one finds a surprisingly optimistic tone adopted in discussions about the possibilities for British film production. This was despite the parlous state of that sector of the industry, and due in no small part to the propagandizing efforts of the British National Film League. An article in one of the trade papers by a young Iris Barry is typical of this discourse for the way in which it combines issues of art and national identity in relation to cinema:

Art at its source is national. . . . The moment has arrived for the British film industry to take one road or another: to make films using every resource or technique on which it can lay its hands, while remaining in essence British—or to attempt to imitate the films of other countries in spirit as well as in form. . . . And the British producer in considering technique will do well to look, like Janus, two ways—to California certainly, but to Berlin as well. He may look two ways and move in neither, remaining British.[35]

Comin' Thro' The Rye, because it emerged at a time of intense negotiation between different film cultures and different business practices, has had a very ambivalent reception, both at the time, and in subsequent histories. Roy Armes, for instance, in his standard *A Critical History of British*

---

[35] 'A National or International Cinema?', *Bioscope*, 28 Feb. 1924, 29. See also 'Problems of the Industry: E. A. Baugham on British Difficulties', *Motion Picture Studio*, 5 Jan. 1924, 15.

Cinema, sees the two extant Hepworth films of the 1920s, *Comin' Thro' The Rye* and *Mist In The Valley*, as 'retrogressive in so many ways', but notes also that 'Hepworth's approach seemed successful even in 1922 [*sic*]', a view which largely reproduces that of Rachael Low in her *History of the British Film*.[36] The contemporary reception was, in fact, more complicated than this: *Comin' Thro' The Rye* was neither summarily dismissed nor unhesitatingly celebrated. On the one hand, the film was praised for its uniqueness, its Britishness, and on the other hand, it was berated for failing to adhere to the conventions of narrative film-making in continuity style which were being refined in the studios of Hollywood. The reviews in the *Bioscope* and *The Times* can be read as reasonably confident ovations for the film, with *The Times* commenting more generally that 'Mr Cecil Hepworth himself is one of the pioneers of the British film industry, and the work that is put out by the organisation of which he is the head is typical of the best class of British film.'[37]

While this may in fact be damnation by faint praise (there are also several moments of hesitation in *Bioscope*'s review), it is undoubtedly also the sort of praise which Paul Rotha attacked in his influential survey of world cinema, *The Film Till Now*, first published in 1930. Rotha opened his chapter on British films of the 1920s as follows:

The British film is established on a hollow foundation. Perhaps it would be more significant to write that it rests upon a structure of false prestige, supported by the flatulent flapdoodle of newspaper writers and by the indifferent goodwill of the British people . . . The whole morale of the British cinema is extravagantly artificial. It has been built up by favoured criticism and tolerance of attitude. . . . Well-merited castigation would have laid bare, and therefore more easily remedied, the root of the evil. Instead, there have been British Film Weeks and National Film Campaigns which have nourished the cancer in the film industry. As it is, the British film is spoon-fed by deceptive praise and quota regulations, with the unhappy result that it has not yet discovered its nationality.[38]

The journal *Close Up* had been pushing a similar line on British cinema since 1927, and these sorts of critical judgements are almost wholly reproduced in subsequent critical accounts of the period such as the standard histories by Low and Armes.[39] It is therefore not surprising that *Comin' Thro' The Rye*, launched as one of the key films of the British Film Week campaign of 1923, has an ambivalent status in film history. Yet while the

---

[36] Armes (London, 1978), 63; and Low, *British Film, 1918–1929*, *passim*.

[37] 14 Nov. 1923, 19—though a later review was less complimentary; see 28 Jan. 1924, 8. Cf. *Bioscope*, 22 Nov. 1923, 60.

[38] (London, rev. edn., 1977), 313; see also 81–2, on the British Film Weeks.

[39] For *Close Up*, see e.g. Kenneth MacPherson's editorial in the first issue, 'As is', 1 (1927); and Oswell Blakeston—'[t]he disagreeable fact must be faced that Britain lacks film tradition' (18)—'British Solecisms', 2 (1927). Low, *British Film, 1918–1929*; Armes, *British Cinema*.

film is almost certainly the sort of production Rotha would have wanted to see castigated, Hepworth would have been dismayed by the claim that 'the British film . . . has not yet discovered its nationality.' The creation of a national cinema carefully differentiated from the Hollywood film was precisely Hepworth's goal, and he was not in any way of the school that felt that the best way to compete with Hollywood and find a comfortable niche in the market-place was by imitating its films:

It was always in the back of my mind from the very beginning that I was to make English pictures, with all the English countryside for background and with English atmosphere and English idiom throughout. When the Transatlantic films began to get a stranglehold upon the trade over here it came to be generally assumed that the American method and style of production was the reason for their success, and the great majority of producers set about to try to imitate them. The Americans have their own idiom in picture-making just as they have their own accent in speaking. It is not necessarily better than ours and it cannot successfully be copied. We have our own idiom too which they could not copy if they tried. It is our part to develop along the lines which are our heritage, and only in that way can we be true to ourselves and to those qualities which are ours.[40]

These statements are not unusual in the discourse of the period, as the extracts from Iris Barry's 1924 article quoted earlier testify; Barry chastises the British film-maker who makes films which speak 'in an American tone of voice' and specifically mentions Hepworth as a film-maker who has 'remain[ed] in essence British.'[41] Hepworth's comments should then be taken as a cue to reassess *Comin' Thro' The Rye*, which is so often seen as a retarded, even primitive, film by comparison with the prevailing international standards. Even at the time, the more commercially minded reviewers saw it, and other Hepworth pictures of the period, as old-fashioned, and not comprehensively enough addressed to the mass market.[42] Hepworth's recollections suggest, however, that his company was not in any way trying to reproduce or adhere to the conventions being established by the American studios. On the contrary, it was quite self-consciously trying to do something different, to produce a distinctive national cinema. We can, perhaps, be even more precise than this, and argue that Hepworth was deliberately exploiting what would now be called the art cinema end of the market, with all its middle-class pretensions. This view is confirmed by the general tone of the trade press comments on Hepworth's films, by the suggestions in their reviews for exhibitors that this is 'a picture that will interest better class houses', and by the evidence of the limited and

---

[40] *Came The Dawn*, 144; see also 55.
[41] 'A National or International Cinema?', *Bioscope*, 28 Feb. 1924, 29; compare her damning reassessment of *Comin' Thro' The Rye* a couple of years later in *Let's Go To The Movies* (New York, 1972 [1st pub. 1926]), 242–3.
[42] See e.g. the trade reviews cited on pp. 73–83 of this ch.

specialist exhibition that it actually received.[43] Reading the heritage genre in these terms more generally would certainly be a worthwhile and fruitful endeavour.

Hepworth's thinking about cinema at the time of *Comin' Thro' The Rye* was of course the product of the film culture of the 1910s, and the general desire on the part of the industry as a whole to move up-market and establish cinema as a respectable artistic form. Hepworth himself felt in retrospect that he had begun to make 'important and worthwhile pictures' in the years just preceding the First World War, and in the film culture of the 1910s and the early 1920s—prior, that is, to the founding of the Film Society—he was considered an artist of the cinema, 'an artist in the truest sense of the word', 'the poet producer, who can write lyrics with his camera', 'an artiste . . . trying to find a means of individual expression'; and *Comin' Thro' The Rye* was seen as being 'stamped indelibly with the personality of the producer'.[44] Individuality, self-expression, the authorial signature were already being constructed within British film culture as important markers of difference, and, in the film culture of the period, artistry was never far from Englishness. The individual artist is thereby constructed (in Hepworth's case no doubt willingly) as a sort of ambassador of the national culture:

No artist has ever given us with a paint brush more beauteous pictures to gaze upon than some which have flashed (alas! their impression is all too fleeting through the medium of the screen) before our charmed vision during the screening of any one of [Hepworth's] famous productions. . . . [For example] in *Comin' Thro' The Rye* [1916] the incomparable charm of English gardens—of rye-fields, of blossom-burdened trees—vied for supremacy as representatives of English art in its cleanest, grandest form. . . . While the prestige of the English film remains at the status set by the House of Hepworth, then the English film will stand, an undisputed proof of home efficiency.[45]

The problem for Hepworth, for *Comin' Thro' The Rye*—and indeed for subsequent films in the heritage genre—was that 'English art in its cleanest, grandest form' was no longer quite so fashionable. The debate about cinema as an art-form, and prevailing definitions of good film practice, rapidly took off in quite new directions in the mid-1920s, under the influence particularly of German Expressionism and the Soviet montage school, and

---

[43] *Kine Weekly*, 28 Jan. 1924, 8. Note *The Times*, 14 Nov. 1923, 19, had described the film as 'typical of the best class of British film': the recurrent use of the term 'class' in this context is revealing.

[44] Hepworth, *Came The Dawn*, 114; Will-o'-the Wisp, unidentified cutting in BFI Library, 13 Dec. 1919; in a review of *Sheba*, *Bioscope*, 16 Oct. 1919, 67; *Kine Weekly*, 10 July 1924, 41; *Motion Picture Studio*, 17 Nov. 1923, 12.

[45] Gertrude M. Allen, 'The Master Mind of the House of Hepworth', *Pictures and Picturegoer*, 20 Sept. 1919, 356.

under the aegis of the Film Society and *Close Up*, amongst others. Few of the idiosyncrasies of *Comin' Thro' The Rye* are followed up in later British films of the decade aimed at the quality end of the market, and it is no surprise that Rotha, in his survey of British cinema in *The Film Till Now*, can find no place to mention Hepworth's later work: it in no way coincides with his ideas of cinematicity, which had moved away considerably from the more conservative notions of the 1910s as to how film could aspire to the status of art. Rotha, like most of the contributors to *Close Up*, embraced a typically modernist concern to establish a specifically cinematic mode of representation. John Grierson's *Drifters* (1929) was, for Rotha, 'the only film produced in this country that reveals any real evidence of construction, montage of material, or sense of cinema as understood in these pages', although he also singles out the work of Anthony Asquith and Alfred Hitchcock, described in *Close Up* as 'the one man in this country who can think cinema'.[46]

Hepworth certainly did not 'think cinema' in the way that Hitchcock did, and his approach to film as an art involved a much more parasitic strategy *vis-à-vis* the other arts. Numerous efforts had been made throughout the 1910s to establish cinema as an important and worthwhile art by drawing on literature and legitimate theatre, notably by adapting established, familiar literary and dramatic texts—texts, that is, which already had both an audience and a status. Hepworth had been one of the leading figures of this tendency within the British film industry. But with films like *Comin' Thro' The Rye*, it was not only that already established plays and novels were being adapted to the screen. *Comin' Thro' The Rye* also retains stylistic links with the more respectable world and status of legitimate theatre, in contrast to what is, by common consent, the more filmic style of the emergent classical Hollywood film. Thus the acting in some cases is much more heavily mannered and gestural, and the staging much more frontal than in most contemporary American films, with the actors apparently performing to a relatively static camera; the shot is very often in tableau form (long takes, composed in long shot, with strong pictorial values), and there is consequently a relative lack of scene dissection or penetration of space. *Comin' Thro' The Rye* is further parasitic on the status and conventions of other arts in its reworking of certain of the aesthetic and moral principles of pictorialist photography, which by the 1920s was well established as the mainstream photographic art practice.

Hepworth and Hitchcock thus belonged to quite different film cultures. *Comin' Thro' The Rye*'s sprawling narrative, pictorial display and theatricality were a far cry from the accomplished narrative cinema and visual

---

[46] Rotha, *The Film Till Now* (London, 1977 (1st publ. 1930)), 318; Hugh Castle, 'Attitude and Interlude', *Close Up*, 7/3 (1930), 189; see also Barry, *Let's Go, passim*, and Caroline Lejeune, *Cinema* (London, 1931), 8–13.

story-telling of Hitchcock, who much more readily embraced contemporary developments in American and European cinema, and who had a much more populist approach to English culture. He would, no doubt, have done something very different with Mathers's novel had he been so inclined.

Hepworth's approach to cinema was, in fact, already at odds with the more progressive elements in the prevailing debate about film as art. The editor of *The Cinema*, for instance, in a foreword to a 1916 script-writing manual, argued that

The 'picturisation', as it is uncouthly called, of the play or novel . . . hinders the development of the cinema as a separate art, and weds it, unless the subject is handled with notable freedom and license . . . to traditions from which it is trying to shake itself free. . . . [The] smallest but the most important [line of effort in film-production] has been in the construction of the photo-play which owes little or nothing to the drama or literature, but aims at being an embodiment in itself of that newest of all the arts, the art of thinking continuously in pictures, with few or no sub-titles to eke out the exigencies of the story. It is this line of effort which is most closely identified with that great future which, we all believe, is in store for cinematography.[47]

'The art of thinking continuously in pictures': this is not quite yet a theory of montage as would be elaborated through the 1920s, and nor is it something which Hepworth would have had much trouble accepting as a principle. On the other hand, Hepworth's films of the 1910s and early 1920s were heavily reliant on pre-existing written texts. Of course, this was in part a marketing strategy, but one can see that as an aesthetic practice, it did, from one point of view, 'hinder the development of the cinema as a separate art'.

In the same manual, it is stated that 'sub-titles . . . must not be relied upon to interpret action, but should merely assist in carrying the story forward, when the characters refuse to tell the story without them.'[48] Yet, in *Comin' Thro' The Rye*, there are a number of titles which have a symbolic rather than strictly narrative intent, such as the quotations from the traditional song of the same title, which give a sort of poetic intimation of what is to come, rather than indicate that a diegetic character is actually

[47] G. A. Atkinson, 'A Foreword', in Harold Weston, *The Art Of Photoplay-Writing* (London, 1916), 9–10.

[48] Weston, *Photoplay-Writing*, 119. Cf. Low's comparison in *British Film, 1918–1929* of the use of titles in *Comin' Thro' The Rye* (far too many, she feels) with their much more sparing use in *Drifters* (1929); her conclusion: 'the worse the film-maker, the more heavily he relied on titles and the duller the film' (236). Even Hepworth would later comment in his autobiography that: 'Perhaps the greatest menace to the homogeneity of the silent film was the necessity of titles to explain what could not be conveyed pictorially. They should never be used unless it is practically impossible to tell some part of the story without them', *Came The Dawn*, 124.

singing the song; likewise, on a couple of occasions as the action switches back from one scene of action to another, in a moment of parallel editing, Hepworth feels the need to add what are really quite redundant titles— 'Naturally the tragedy makes no lasting impression on those not involved', and 'In Rome meanwhile, the plot is deepening'—which by their presence draw attention to the mechanics of story-telling, and the difficulties which this film has in working fluently with them. Moments such as these suggest that Hepworth was 'trying to think continuously in pictures', yet was still attached to a film practice which relied heavily on inter-titles: once again, the film seems to be caught between different tendencies in the film culture.

THE HERITAGE INDUSTRY AND THE CONSTRUCTION OF THE NATIONAL PAST

In Britain in the 1980s, the idea of heritage was exploited on a massive commercial scale, and inserted itself at the very centre of the construction of the national imagination. But the play on heritage, and the whole process of inventing tradition and conserving particular images and properties of the past in order to represent the nation can be found in many other periods as well. The beginnings of that process of commodifying our relationship with the past on an industrial scale for a mass market can be found in the late nineteenth century, with the development of an organized conservation lobby and the cultural construction and marketing of an idea of the nation embodied in a particular vision of rural England.

To understand the contemporary cultural significance of *Comin' Thro' The Rye* we need to relate it to these broader developments in the formation of the national heritage. Michael Bommes and Patrick Wright have argued that, in producing a national heritage, 'a particular conception of the past [is] produced, privileged, installed and maintained as a public and national "consensus".'[49] Elsewhere, Wright maintains that this national past is 'above all a modern past', 'an imaginary object', which is continually being reimagined, reconceived, reinvented from the perspective of the present, as a response to 'the leading tensions of the contemporary political situation'.[50] The construction of the national heritage—an ideological space as much as anything else—involves not so much the selecting of only certain values from the past, as the transference of present values on to the past as imaginary object.

Wright shows how a significant strand of the British national heritage

---

[49] '"Charms of Residence": The Public and the Past', in Richard Johnson, *et al.* (eds.), *Making Histories: Studies in History-Writing and Politics* (London, 1982), 253.

[50] *On Living In An Old Country: The National Past in Contemporary Britain* (London, 1985), 2, 251.

has been articulated above all in terms of landscape, property, and history, through the activities of the conservation lobby since the late nineteenth century. This lobby has sought to represent particular landscapes as both natural and national, and to render the private property of the upper classes as in the general, public interest, as part of the national imagination. Wright shows in particular how the practice of bodies like the National Trust, founded in 1895, sought to resolve this tension between private property and public interest by promoting the category of national interest, thereby vindicating property relations.[51] The full name of the Trust was initially The National Trust for Places of Historic Interest and Natural Beauty, and it is terms such as these which are used to negotiate this transformation of bourgeois interests, values, and tastes into national culture. The properties, the buildings, and the homes of the bourgeoisie and the aristocracy are re-presented as the national properties which are of most 'historic interest'; their lands, often heavily landscaped, and produced according to specific aesthetic and moral perspectives, are mythologized as places of 'natural beauty'. 'National Heritage', conclude Bommes and Wright, 'is a public articulation or staging of the past . . . [which] appears to involve nothing less than the abolition of all contradiction in the name of a national culture.'[52]

Clearly, although Wright does not broach the subject, cinema is another of the apparatuses by which the dominant representations of the past are reproduced and secured as a cultural presence in twentieth-century Britain. Cinema is one of the means by which the national past is quite literally staged and made generally accessible, as the spectacular object of the public gaze. It is one of the means by which certain types of landscape and property are appropriated as naturally British—for heritage films like *Comin' Thro' The Rye* are replete with stately homes and other ancient buildings and picturesque landscapes (many of them no doubt now National Trust properties); they are further examples of 'how extensively rural and "historical" conceptions of the nation have been elaborated within the changing public spheres of twentieth century Britain.'[53]

These processes need to be related to the strength in British culture of the pastoral tradition, and in particular to the nostalgic, ruralist response to industrialism and modernity described by Martin J. Wiener. Concern and anxiety about the very industrialism that the English bourgeoisie had pioneered, a 'suspicion of material and technological development', became increasingly prevalent in the late Victorian period, expressed in

[51] See ibid. 48 ff.; Bommes and Wright, 'Charms of Residence'; and Martin J. Wiener, *English Culture and the Decline of the Industrial Spirit, 1850–1980* (Cambridge, 1981), 67 ff.

[52] Bommes and Wright, 'Charms of Residence', 253.

[53] Wright, *Old Country*, 68–9.

terms of 'ideals of stability, tranquillity, closeness to the past, and "non-materialism".'[54] In a period which in fact saw the consolidation of urban society, these ideals, Wiener argues, were paradoxically most easily encapsulated in rural, pastoral imagery, the mythology of 'this green and pleasant land': 'this countryside of the mind was everything industrial society was not—ancient, slow-moving, stable, cosy and "spiritual".'[55] This pastoral vision produced a particular conception of Englishness as an ancient inheritance, and England as 'an old country': 'the new national self-image dressed itself in the trappings of an older tradition.'[56]

Alun Howkins has shown in detail how what he calls 'the discovery of Rural England'—the construction of a very specific rural vision of the national landscape and the national character—was achieved in the late nineteenth and early twentieth centuries in art, literature, music, architecture, and garden design.[57] This involved creating a new vision of the nation as England, which was itself reduced to a particular vision of the South Country, the area south of the Thames and the Severn, and East of the Exe, and some other areas topographically and culturally similar, such as the southern Midlands, and even Shropshire. The nation was thus represented as a rural space, but its landscapes were also crucially populated and cultivated, not wild or sublime. It is this rural space, this national landscape, which is reproduced in *Comin' Thro' The Rye*.

Helen Mathers's novel, first published in 1875, can already be seen as a (relatively early) nostalgic, ruralist, and escapist response to the late nineteenth-century conditions of modernity and urbanization. City life, let alone industrial activity, never intrudes upon the consciousness of the novel, and even the business dealings and journeys to the other place of the city by the men of the story are moments of moral ambiguity. One writer, looking back from the time of the First World War, recalled the impact of the novel:

it spoke of England, of the Old Country which is so dear to us all, of a romance which is still as green in our memory as the little rye shoots were green. We all loved Helen. We who lived in the dull towns and great cities, where there are only hot pavements to tread or prim parks to walk in, yearned to walk through the rye even as Helen did.[58]

---

[54] Wiener, *English Culture*, 5, 6.
[55] Ibid.   [56] Ibid. 41.
[57] 'The Discovery of Rural England', in Robert Colls and Philip Dodd (eds.), *Englishness: Politics and Culture, 1880–1920* (London, 1986); see also Peter Brooker and Peter Widdowson, 'A Literature of their Own', ibid.; Alex Potts, ' "Constable Country" between the Wars', in Raphael Samuel (ed.), *Patriotism: The Making and Un-making of British National Identity*, iii. *National Fictions* (London, 1989); and Raymond Williams, *The Country and the City* (London, 1985).
[58] *The Cinema*, quoted in an advertisement in *Bioscope*, 12 Oct. 1916, 191 (I have been unable to trace the original).

This was written on the occasion of the release of Hepworth's first film version, which was just one instance of the increasingly wide circulation of this image of the nation at a time when, as Wiener notes, 'Martial horrors made this rural myth even more appealing than ever. As one writer remarked in 1915, "the soul of England must not be sought in the city but in the countryside".'[59]

One reviewer thought this first film version 'reveals to us the spirit of the true British countryside. It is a perfect pastoral.'[60] This nostalgic pastoralism was even stronger in the 1923 period version of the film, whose *mise-en-scène* locates 'the soul of England' very clearly in the countryside, lending national identity the aura of an ancient construct, continuous and unchanging.

Tom Nairn has argued that 'nationalism . . . is invariably populist. People are what it has to go on', and that 'the mobilizing myth of nationalism is an idea of the People'—but he also argues that there is 'an absence of popular nationalism among the English. There is no coherent, sufficiently democratic myth of Englishness—no sufficiently accessible and popular myth-identity where mass discontents can find a vehicle.'[61]

Nairn suggests that the English mythology is on the contrary dominated by patrician benevolence and popular deference to authority. However, pastoral imagery creates a democratic myth of Englishness in which benevolence and deference are reworked in an ideology of community. Howkins, for instance, shows that 'the ideas of continuity, of community or harmony, and above all a kind of classlessness', were central to the ideal of rural England, producing an image of 'an organic and natural society of ranks, and inequality in an economic and social sense, but one based on trust, obligation and even love', ideas which have been pervasively incorporated by numerous traditions of British films.[62] There is, in other words, a powerful, coherent, and pervasive image of the people in English culture, an image of an organic community which is hierarchically and deferentially organized, as if this were entirely natural. This image of the nation has been a major representational source for British film-making.

What should be clear from the above discussion is the extent to which ideologies of Britishness, of national identity and nationhood, are produced through processes of displacement and condensation: the slippage from the South Country to England, from England to Britain, from urban to rural, from class antagonism to patrician authority, and thence to organic community, and from the interests of one class to the national interest.

---

[59] *English Culture*, 63; Wiener is quoting E. C. Pulbrook, *The English Countryside* (London, 1915), 2.
[60] *Cinema*, quoted in an advertisement in *Bioscope*, 12 Oct. 1916, 191.
[61] *The Break-Up of Britain* (London, 1981), 340, 295, 294.
[62] 'Rural England', 75, 80.

In the 1910s Hepworth was confronted by both the upheavals of the war to end all wars, and the dramatic development of that highly industrialized, aggressively imperialist institution, Hollywood. 'Rural England' seemed increasingly under threat. Hepworth's attempts to produce a national cinema involved turning away from this modernity, drawing on apparently long-standing traditions, films like *Comin' Thro' The Rye* offering themselves as invariant within the continuity of English culture. For Eric Hobsbawm, the poignancy of invented traditions derives precisely from this 'contrast between the constant change and innovation of the modern world and the attempt to structure at least some parts of social life within it as unchanging and invariant.'[63] That structuring is achieved in the heritage film by both drawing on established cultural traditions, and reworking them, reinventing them for the new medium of cinema. Cinema must, in fact, by its very technological nature, imagine the past from the point of view of modernity, it must produce a modern past, very often a past beautiful to the eye of the present-day beholder: the past as an alluring spectacle, both exotic in its difference from the present, and familiar in its authentic reproduction of a traditional iconography.

In *Comin' Thro' The Rye*, we are presented with an alluring image of Victorian England. A particular set of social relations and a class-specific form of social existence which has already passed are reproduced in all their authentic detail as if they had never disappeared, as if they were unchanging, invariant, secure. The diegetic world of the film is imbued with an upstairs–downstairs sense of class relations, and a patriarchal sense of family relations, with a marked division between the public and the private, between what is properly masculine and properly feminine: everyone has their allotted place, the order is clear, relations are unproblematic. These social relations, always potentially antagonistic and exploitative, are presented as natural, even splendid. In so doing, *Comin' Thro' The Rye* seeks to efface history: it attempts both to reconstruct a particular authentic past, and at the same time to posit it as a timeless, unchanging, and unchallenged essence, an Englishness outside the ravages of history and culture.

Except of course that this Englishness, this particular social order, this natural community of the nation, is already crumbling, as it is in so many heritage films, thereby establishing an even more profound sense of nostalgia: nostalgic narratives so often chart a process of moral decline and cultural decay. But there would be no narrative development if these relations were not disturbed, and it is the transgressions of Sylvia, the jealous former lover of the hero, aided and abetted by a maidservant who does not

---

[63] 'Introduction: Inventing Traditions', in Eric Hobsbawm and Terence Ranger (eds.), *The Invention of Tradition* (Cambridge, 1983), 2.

know her place, which enable a drama to proceed. Such transgressions, and the unhappy ending of the narrative, can be seen as presaging the passing away of this particular set of social relations.

Yet if this is the narrative trajectory of the film, the images seem designed to preserve these social relations, to display the wealth and taste of the Victorian gentry, to recapture a lost climactic moment in the history of a class and a gender. The narrative must thus fight against the allure of the image, and as will become clear, for contemporary reviewers at least, it is the image which is the more powerful. The ramifications of this tension between narrative and image become very clear in the transposition of the story from novel to film.

The novel is written in the first person from the point of view of the daughter of a gentleman coming to terms with her position within mid-Victorian patriarchy. The film, on the other hand, rejects all sense of this first person narration and loses the subversive feminine critique of the conditions of patriarchy. As Elaine Showalter has noted, the novel is quite outspoken in its depiction of the heroine's father as sadistic towards and exploitative of his wife and his children, especially the girls.[64] Other men are equally problematic figures, almost without exception; they are either childish, or weak-willed and boring, or pompous and decrepit old fools. In each case, they represent what in her early teenage years the heroine, Helen, sees as the perversity of marriage. Her beloved brother Jack may well be an exception, except that we only know him as a boy, never as an adult man; even the romantic hero, Paul, is inscrutably enigmatic and unable to speak his mind or behave rationally, and his fate is to live with a broken heart until he sacrifices himself on a foreign battle-field. Beyond this critique of men and masculinity is a further critique of the patriarchal conditions faced by women, the physical, cultural, and psychological constrictions of femininity, and especially the marriage market and its commodification of womanhood.

But the film loses the female perspective altogether, and, although a couple of intertitles and a brief scene at the start of the film suggest a mild tyranny in the father, the images generally suggest otherwise: he is genial enough, as are the other men. Likewise, Helen's tomboyish qualities at the start of the film are hardly sufficient to expose the domination of patriarchy; rather the relations of patriarchy are here part of the splendid visual attractions, the period details of the film, especially the full costumes of the women, which in the first volume of the novel are the source of such annoyance to Helen.

This version of the national past, this version of history, in which a critical perspective is displaced by decoration and display, 'an obsessive

---

[64] *Literature*, 175–7.

accumulation of comfortably archival detail', is not in any way confined to the cinema: it is the very substance of the heritage industry and its commodification, idealization, and marketing of the past, 'a perspective in which "the past" is defined entirely as bits and pieces which can be recovered, commodified and circulated in exchange and display.'[65] The difference for cinema of course is that the bits and pieces, the talismanic objects of the past, can circulate only as images. This is not the past itself, but an image of the past, present yet unattainable. This unattainability is intensified in *Comin' Thro' The Rye* by Hepworth's idiosyncratic resistance to the use of close shots; one always feels distanced from the characters, they are never quite recoverable as protagonists contemporary with us, or as objects of easy identification.

This condition of unattainability is also the basis of nostalgia, and a nostalgic relation to the past is the central psychological attitude of both pastoralism and the heritage industry more generally.[66] While the heritage film tries to re-create the past, we know that the past is irrecoverable; the pleasure of re-creation, of plenitude, comes tinged with an overwhelming sense of loss. Nostalgia posits two different times which are opposed to one another, one negative, the other positive: the present, marked by moral disintegration, deterioration, and degeneration, and the longed-for past, marked by purity, truth, and fullness. Nostalgia is then both a narrative of loss, charting an imaginary historical trajectory from stability to instability, and at the same time a narrative of recovery, projecting the subject back into a comfortably closed past. Nostalgia is thus not a spontaneous response to an actual historical moment, but a way of relating to a past imagined from the point of view of the present; it is a response to and a reorganization of contemporary experience.[67] This imagined past is constructed in terms of what the present is felt to lack, it is the imaginary site of plenitude in relation to the experience of loss or lack in the present. Nostalgia thus uses an image of the past to enter into dialogue with the present.[68]

---

[65] Wright, *Old Country*, 252, 74.

[66] See Laurence Lerner, *The Uses of Nostalgia* (London, 1972); Frank Kermode, *English Pastoral Poetry* (London, 1952); Fred Davis, *Yearning For Yesterday: A Sociology of Nostalgia* (New York, 1979); Janice Doane and Devon Hodges, *Nostalgia and Sexual Difference* (New York, 1987); Bryan S. Turner, 'A Note on Nostalgia', *Theory, Culture and Society*, 4 (1987); and Fredric Jameson, 'Post-Modernism, or the Cultural Logic of Late Capitalism', *New Left Review*, 146 (1984).

[67] Cf. Pierre Sorlin, *The Film as History: Re-Staging the Past* (Oxford, 1980), 19, 80.

[68] It should at the very least be registered that other writers have questioned the easy equation of pastoral with conservatism which I have explored in the above pages. The equation seems right as far as the actual texts under discussion are concerned. But it would be wrong to assume that pastoral and nostalgic discourses are always conservative: see e.g. Sales, *Pastoral and Politics*.

PICTORIALISM AND PASTORALISM

In this section, I will begin to analyse in detail some of the ways in which *Comin' Thro' The Rye* might be said to work within what Hepworth called an English idiom, and at the same time how it might as such be seen as producing and celebrating a national heritage. This means of course examining also how it exploits an alternative representational system to that of classical American cinema. I want to explore two areas in particular: the function of the image; and the organization of the narrative and its modes of narration, which obviously in part depend on the function of the image. In this section, I will be concentrating on the function and stylization of the image.

There is an impressive attention to period detail in the film, which has two separate but interrelated functions. First, it was intended to meet the desire for authenticity typical of this sort of quality costume drama, and the film was certainly promoted by the production company in these terms.[69] Secondly, period detail enabled the film to achieve a certain visual splendour, something which again was widely commented on at the time—'as a spectacle . . . this picture will bear comparison with any extravagant foreign productions.'[70] Neither function was lost on reviewers when they had a chance to see the film, and to some extent the discourse is consistent across the trade press, quality national newspapers, and popular fan magazines (although the latter devote far less space to the review of a film which is evidently not seen as of particular interest to its readership). The *Bioscope*, a trade paper, for instance, commented on

the skill with which the Victorian atmosphere has been reproduced, not only in the settings and costumes, but also in the characterisation. . . . Never has the atmosphere of quaintly formal yet graceful and decorative Victorian England been more vividly reproduced on the screen than in this skilful and sympathetic version of Helen Mathers' well-known novel. As an impression of Victorian life and manners, the film is well-nigh perfect.[71]

One gets the impression of a cultural memory being self-consciously refashioned by the film in several reviews:

[69] See e.g. a report, evidently based on a press release, which appeared in various trade papers shortly before the trade show: 'To secure accuracy in the Victorian setting of the story, the leading theatrical and cinema costumiers of London—Nathans, Simmons, Hymons, Gambas, and Clarksons—were ransacked to provide the many correct Victorian costumes necessary, with the result that Hepworths had at their disposal for this film a tremendously large and assorted collection of authentic crinolines and other Victorian costumes. These are worn with great effect throughout the whole of *Comin' Thro' The Rye*', *Bioscope*, 1 Nov. 1923, 72; see also *Kine Weekly*, 8 Nov. 1923, 49.

[70] *Kine Weekly*, 8 Nov. 1923, 49.

[71] 22 Nov. 1923, 62. *The Times* similarly commented on 'the clever way in which the atmosphere of the Victorian era is suggested and maintained', 14 Nov. 1923, 19.

STILL 1. 'Never has the atmosphere of quaintly formal yet graceful and decorative Victorian England been more vividly reproduced on the screen' (*Bioscope*, 1923). Paul Vasher (Shayle Gardner) caught between Helen Adair (Alma Taylor) and Sylvia Fleming (Eileen Dennes) in *Comin' Thro' The Rye*.

STILL 2. 'The settings, both interior and exterior, are a constant delight to the eye, while the costumes have the charm to the modern spectator of quaintness as well as beauty' (*Bioscope*, 1923). Paul and Helen play croquet (*Comin' Thro' The Rye*).

There is a beautiful atmosphere to the well-known story which is largely due to the setting of it in the 'sixties. One is accustomed to regard this period as not very attractive as regards dresses and furniture, but that there is a quaint charm about it is abundantly demonstrated here. Much thought and research have resulted in a convincing portrayal of mid-Victorian days, which extends beyond appearances to manners and sentiments. Indeed, the story is infinitely more credible and acceptable thus dated.[72]

Here are the elements of a familiar discourse: the value placed on the 'sympathetic' adaptation of the 'original' novel; the emphasis placed on setting, costume, and manners; and the appeal of exotic otherness. The historical past becomes mere style, a series of images, achieved by extracting the 'authentic' from its material context. The past is thus transformed into a vivid museum display designed to attract the curious gaze of the spectator: 'The settings, both interior and exterior, are a constant delight to the eye, while the costumes have the charm to the modern spectator of quaintness as well as beauty.'[73]

The popular press begins to deconstruct this discourse—'Victorian England . . . might not have been attractive to live in, but as it is shown on the screen it certainly appears to be so'[74]—but this still acknowledges the spectacular nature of the image. Part of this spectacle is the vision of (a particular version of) Englishness, which is contrasted with the different, more vulgar and garish attractions of American cinema: 'the old world charm of this pleasant picture is so soothing after a spell of transatlantic 'stunt' features.'[75]

Without exception, all the contemporary reviews place great value on the visual qualities of this 'beautiful production'.[76] The *Bioscope* notes 'the brilliant camerawork', and describes Hepworth as 'a producer with a keen feeling for atmosphere and pictorial effect.'[77] *Kine Weekly*, while generally much less favourably inclined towards the film than the obsessively patriotic *Bioscope*, was still of the opinion that 'there is a great deal of merit in this production and, perhaps most of all, in the photography, which is of rare beauty' and adds that 'the exteriors have been chosen most artistically'.[78] The *Motion Picture Studio* found that 'many shots linger in the memory . . . and the photography is peerless.'[79] Hepworth himself later

---

[72] *Motion Picture Studio*, 17 Nov. 1923, 12.

[73] *Bioscope*, 22 Nov. 1923, 63.   [74] *Picture Show*, 9 Feb. 1924, 4.

[75] *Motion Picture Studio*, 26 Jan. 1924, 5. In a fuller review, the same organ had commented: '[the story is] of lovers parted by a vixenish girl, whose passion is only reciprocated when it is comparatively shameless; and this would have been handled by the average American producer with a sordidness and garishness destructive of all the delicate English spirit which here pervades it. Some delightful English scenery is, as ever in Hepworth pictures, a prominent feature of the production. . . . As a fine example of the essentially British picture, conveying native atmosphere in a way which can only be done in this country, the whole production is an interesting, restful and satisfying piece of work,' 17 Nov. 1923, 12.

[76] *Bioscope*, 31 Jan. 1924, 55.   [77] 22 Nov. 1923, 63, 31 Jan. 1924, 52.

[78] Both 22 Nov. 1923, 58.   [79] 17 Nov. 1923, 12.

claimed that 'always . . . I have striven for beauty, for pictorial meaning and effect in every case where it is obtainable. Much of my success, I am sure, is in the aesthetic pleasure conveyed, but not recognized, by the beauty of the scene.'[80]

The terms used here establish the visual conventions of the film as pictorialist, and begin to point to a distinction between pictorialist visual strategies and a more functional or expressive *mise-en-scène*. Although the *Bioscope* suggests that Hepworth has a keen feeling for atmosphere, all the other comments suggest a visual pleasure, a spectacle, which is not apparently integrated into the narrative weave of the film, but which stands out as aesthetically pleasing imagery and camerawork: it is precisely 'pictorial meaning and effect' which is achieved, and not narrative meaning or effect. Exteriors, likewise, are not chosen for their narrative significance, but are chosen 'artistically'.

Pictorialism was a specific photographic practice, an aesthetic movement of the late nineteenth century, which had as its central aim the promotion of photography as a fine art.[81] To achieve this aim, photography was increasingly aligned with painting, constructing it as something much more than a means of mechanical reproduction—constructing it, in fact, as a plastic art, over which the photographer had some considerable control: the spontaneous, the mundane, the mere copy could not be admitted as art within this discourse. The photograph was seen as a means of individual expression, personal vision, a poetic conception, not as an objective scientific document. Pictorialism as art photography was thus conceptualized very much in terms of contemporary aesthetic traditions and values.[82]

Pictorialist photographic practice was popularized through the work of H. P. Robinson (1830–1901), a prominent member of the Royal Photographic Society, well known as both an amateur photographer, and an author of several influential publications. Photography, for Robinson, was 'a means of representing the beautiful':[83]

[80] *Came The Dawn*, 123.
[81] See Morden, 'Pastoral and Pictorial'; Helmut Gernsheim with Alison Gernsheim, *The History of Photography* (London, 1955), esp. 179–82; Alan Trachtenberg (ed.), *Classic Essays on Photography* (New Haven, Conn., 1980); H. P. Robinson, *The Elements of a Pictorial Photograph* (New York, 1973, 1st pub. 1896); Barry Lane (ed.), *Pictorial Photography in Britain, 1900–1920* (London, 1978); and David Bordwell, Janet Staiger, and Kristin Thompson, *The Classical Hollywood Cinema* (London, 1985), 291–3. Note also that other British films of the period were commented on in terms of their use of pictorialist photography; and an article in *Kine Weekly* ('Pictorial Photography', 3 Apr. 1924, 69) summarizes a lecture on the history of the pictorialist tradition in still photography which the reviewer recommends as of great interest to cinematographers.
[82] 'In societies across England, Western Europe and America, pictorialists eschewed the modern and adopted a beaux-arts definition of 'beauty' as formal landscapes, nudes, still lifes, posed and studied compositions. Moreover, it cultivated an archaic look: employing brushwork, engraving tools, dies, soft-focus lenses, it sought the appearance of a hand-made painting or print.' Alan Trachtenberg, 'Introduction', in id. (ed.), *Classic Essays*, p. xi.
[83] *Elements*, 9.

STILL 3. Exteriors are chosen not for their narrative significance, but for their pictorial significance. Colonel Adair

A picture . . . is . . . calculated to give pleasure to the eye of the beholder by the skilful way in which the intention of the producer is expressed by pictorial means, consisting of lines, light, shades, masses, and preferably, but not necessarily, colours. This is the material part of the picture. . . . Beyond . . . is poetry, sentiment story, the literary part of a picture.[84]

The pictorialist landscape photograph, for instance, organizes and displays the landscape as precisely something to be looked at, primarily from the point of view of the outsider, a spectator as opposed to a participant.[85] The immutability and truth of nature were terms central to the pictorialist discourse, but, while 'the study of nature has been recommended as the essential foundation of art', nature itself is not art, it must be pictorially composed.[86] A picture must be interesting, it must aim at truth, but it must also possess spirit: it must not merely imitate. A modicum of individual mannerism was to be encouraged, but above all, the picture must be ordered according to artistic convention: 'harmony of lines and parts, breadth of effect, observation of values.'[87] There is then a tension emerging between truth, personal expression, and artistic convention, which is resolved in favour of the central term: pictorial effect is in the end the product of the photographer working within the conventions of representation upon a sufficiently plastic medium. Robinson's own work, and the work of others which he favoured, is heavily mannered and stylized, both in choice of subject, and in composition, developing, and printing. It is this conventional construction, manipulation, and aestheticization of the image which linked pictorialist photography not only to fine art but also to Hepworth's work on *Comin' Thro' The Rye*.

By the 1890s this pictorialist photography was widely accepted as fine art, and as a practice was institutionalized in the English Linked Ring, and the American Photo-secessionist movements. Later practitioners such as P. H. Emerson (1856–1936) and Alfred Stieglitz (1864–1946) modified the aesthetic in various ways, with Emerson for instance advocating naturalism over against Robinson's academic realism. Emerson, following the dictates of Impressionist painting, also favoured an image that was sharply focused in the centre, but gradually less clearly defined and more softly focused towardss the edges, where Robinson had worked to produce images which were in sharp focus throughout.[88] The underlying sense of the plasticity of the medium does remain, however, along with the desire to produce images which can organize the attention of the spectator. John Taylor has noted that the British pictorialists of the 1910s—that is, in the period immediately prior to the production of *Comin' Thro' The Rye—*

---

[84] Ibid. 13–14.　　[85] See Morden, 'Pastoral and Pictorial', 19.
[86] Robinson, *Elements*, 31.　　[87] Ibid. 40.
[88] See Amy Weinstein Meyers, introductory notes to an essay by Emerson, in Trachtenberg (ed.), *Classic Essays*, 99–100, and ch. 9.

were still operating with an otherwise virtually obsolete, pre-modernist, classical set of compositional rules for capturing the beautiful and the picturesque. Their restraint, decorum, shunning of novelty and innovation, and adherence to convention showed barely any concessions to the French painterly modernisms or the American photographic modernisms.[89]

Cecil Hepworth was operating in a climate when what were now thoroughly conventional aesthetic values of pictorialist photography were very much taken for granted. A popular photography magazine of 1924, for instance, had no difficulty in distinguishing between 'practical snapshot work' and 'elaborately deliberate pictorial photography': pictorial photography, in a non-specialist sense, simply meant quality photography, artistic photography, over against the mere snapshot.[90] There was a family connection too. Hepworth's father, T. C. Hepworth, had published a handbook, *Evening Work for Amateur Photographers* in 1890, as well as for a while in the 1890s editing *Photographic News*, for which Robinson, among others, wrote. Hepworth himself had had some art training,[91] and had been a photographer, as well as contributing to various photographic journals, and writing a primarily technical manual of film-making, *Animated Photography: The ABC of the Cinematograph*, published in 1897.[92] Hepworth also frequently describes images from his films as pictorialist in his autobiography, although he never attempts to define the term, suggesting perhaps that it was so much a part of his common sense that it would never occur to him to do so.

The picturesque photography for *Comin' Thro' The Rye* is, likewise, very much within the pictorialist tradition and, as such, entirely conventional. The *mise-en-scène* of the rye-field in particular encourages the spectator to look at it from a distance as an object of beauty, rather than a narrative space to be inhabited by character and spectator. The recurring shot of the lovers' meeting-place on the edge of the rye-field, and the more emblematic shots prefacing two of the film's three sections, are carefully organized according to the principles laid out by Robinson: the central place of the path, the tree to the left of the picture in middle ground, the play of light across the rye itself, the placing of either characters or a fence in the foreground—all these devices serve to lead the eye of the spectator into the image, to display the field as something to be looked at (see Still 4, and Fig. 1).

Kristin Thompson has discussed the influence of pictorialism on American cinematography in the 1920s, and she concentrates on the attributes of the soft style of filming which came to represent quality cinematography in this period. 'Cinematographers', she notes, 'hoped that by imitating

[89] 'Pictorial Photography in Britain, 1900–1920', in Lane (ed.), *Pictorial Photography*.
[90] 'What to Learn from "the Pictures"', *Snapshots*, July 1924, 139.
[91] See Hepworth, *Came the Dawn*, 178.   [92] London, 1897.

STILL 4. Pastoral England and the picturesque image: the doomed lovers, Paul and Helen, meet on the edge of the rye-field (*Comin' Thro' The Rye*).

Picture divided.   Still unsatisfactory.   Much better.

FIG. 1. An article in *Photograms of the Year*, 1902 reproduces the above diagrams in order to demonstrate to the amateur photographer how to compose 'good' pictures. The shots of the rye field in *Comin' Thro' The Rye* are very similar to the ideal composition above: the trunk of the tree positioned middle ground left, the branches reaching out like an umbrella over middle and right of the image, the pastoral landscape stretching away to the horizon behind, with the path placed centrally to guide the eye.[93]

earlier established styles in the other arts, they could achieve the same public status themselves.'[94] Although there is no direct evidence that Hepworth was influenced by these developments, it would seem clear that a number of the photographic devices and developing and printing practices adopted in *Comin' Thro' The Rye* serve the same purpose—that is, they seek to aestheticize and stylize the image in various ways, with the emphasis being on softness, though not simply in terms of the softness of focus and diffusion of the image that the photographer P. H. Emerson had favoured.

A number of the shots are soft and fairly heavily diffused, with relatively low contrast—notably two shots of Helen praying for the safe return of Paul from Rome, but the extreme softness of these shots is exceptional, having a symbolic function in the context of a film otherwise sharply lit and focused. But there are other images which have a more subdued softness in the background, notably the key shots of the rye-field, particularly those which open the final Harvest section of the film, in which there is a distinct autumnal mistiness over the field. Most of the shots, however, are composed in relatively deep focus, a stylistic strategy closer to the work of Robinson, and one which also enables a clear display of the heritage backgrounds in both interiors and exteriors. However there are two other devices that are used frequently in *Comin' Thro' The Rye* to stylize and soften the image, and the relationship between images: the fade and the vignette.

There is a fade out to black at the end of every shot in *Comin' Thro' The Rye*, and a fade in again at the beginning of the next shot, which device, Hepworth believed, 'created a feeling of smoothness—avoided the

---

[93] Illustrations from H. Snowden Ward, 'The Divine Idea in Composition', *Photograms of the Year*, 1902, 40, and reproduced in Taylor, 'Pictorial Photography', 14.

[94] Bordwell *et al.*, *Classical Hollywood*, 293.

harsh unpleasant "jerk" usually associated with change of scene.'[95] The standard practice for shot transitions at this time was in most cases to cut, with the fade being reserved for those transitions which were intended to imply a time-lapse—in the words of the 1916 script-writing manual quoted from earlier, 'this method of showing your audience that time has elapsed has become a convention, and will be accepted as such by the audience'.[96] Other uses of this device include fading in the opening shot of the film— so that, as the manual put it, 'it is not suddenly jerked upon the scene' (Hepworth's terminology and thinking was evidently not entirely aber- rant).[97] The fade might also be used, at least within British cinema, to imply an entry into a more psychological space, or self-consciously imaginary realm. But even in 1916, it was not considered 'a practical method for opening and closing each scene.'[98]

Hepworth, however, felt that the cut produced an irritating jerk in all circumstances: 'smoothness in a film is important and should be preserved except when for some special effect a "snap" is preferred.'[99] This desire for smoothness is akin to the American cinematographers desire for softness of image, and can be seen as a reworking of pictorialist conventions. As Rachael Whear has noted, 'the technique was appropriate to the soothing, gentle and visually pleasing effects [Hepworth] sought'.[100] It also enables Hepworth to overcome one of the problematic side-effects that troubled American film-makers working in the continuity style and favouring the straight cut between shots, namely the sometimes dramatic changes in contrast and haziness from one shot to the next.[101] The fade used in *Comin' Thro' The Rye* means that one is much less aware of any such discontinuities across shot transitions. Hepworth softens his images in *Comin' Thro' The Rye* in another way as well, through the use of vignettes around almost every image: 'I had found by an early experiment that a soft vignetted edge all round the picture was much more aesthetically pleasing than a hard line and the unrelieved black frame.'[102]

It is in this same paragraph that Hepworth speaks of striving 'for beauty, for pictorial effect', and it does not therefore seem unreasonable to speak of this softening of the image in the same way that Thompson speaks of the soft style of American pictorialist cinematography. Hepworth's bid for smoothness, for a soft image which is gentle on the spectator, is a

---

[95] *Came The Dawn*, 122.

[96] Weston, *Photoplay-Writing*, 31; see also Barry Salt, *Film Style and Technology, History and Analysis* (London, 1983), 195; and Low, *British Film, 1918–1929*, 114.

[97] Weston, *Photoplay-Writing*, 42; see also 41.

[98] Ibid. 42.   [99] *Came The Dawn*, 139.

[100] Film Library Repertory Season programme note on *Comin' Thro' The Rye*, 1951, on BFI Library microfiche for the film.

[101] See Bordwell *et al.*, *Classical Hollywood*, 292–3.

[102] Hepworth, *Came The Dawn*, 123.

deliberate aestheticizing of the image. If we link this to the extremely slow cutting rate of the film, and note that the fade significantly slows down the narrative pace and forswears the dynamic energy of continuity cutting, the foregrounding of the image as image becomes very clear. Admirers of this style found in Hepworth's work a poetic sensibility: 'there is indeed almost a lyric touch in some of these screen pictures, showing dainty white columbine figures gliding, like rose petals blown by the wind, through flower-laden arbours and across mossy lawns.'[103]

Terms such as these establish the link between the style of the images and their heritage qualities, their celebration of a particular version of pastoral; as Terry Morden has pointed out, there is an integral relationship established between pastoral representation and pictorialist photography in the late nineteenth and early twentieth centuries.[104] Pictorialism develops as a way of representing the pastoral, a function which is reproduced in *Comin' Thro' The Rye* and other Hepworth films.

The narrative takes place for the most part in picturesque rural land-scapes, and the country houses that exist therein—notably the appropri-ately named Silverbridge Manor, the home of the Adairs. As landscapes, they are part of the imaginary cultural space of the South Country, that ideal rural version of the national topography.[105] The film also narrativizes the country–city opposition central to pastoralism, particularly in its con-struction of character.

Helen, the youngest Adair daughter and heroine of the film, is closely associated with Nature. In the opening title-shot of the film, the spectator gradually becomes aware that someone is crawling through the ripe rye-field. Eventually, an as yet unidentified Helen grins up at the camera and mouths 'Boo'. She is next seen as a young teenager, playing up a tree with her childhood friend George; later they play in a somewhat wild garden area, with Helen eventually having to hide in some bushes to avoid detec-tion between a quarrelling Paul and Sylvia. Helen as a young girl is rep-resented in these scenes as a joyous innocent child, simple, natural, and pure. It is these very qualities in her both as a girl and as a young woman which appeal to the worldly, experienced, and recently embittered Paul. Her first meeting with Paul is at the end of a path which crosses the

---

[103] *Bioscope*, 22 Nov. 1923, 63.   [104] 'Pastoral and Pictorial'.

[105] The film was shot at Walton-on Thames, site of the Hepworth studios, with further location shots in Cheshire (see Hepworth, *Came The Dawn*, 190), although the drama is not given a specific location in the film itself, which reinforces still further the sense of a gener-alized Englishness based on representations of the 'South Country'. The novel is ostensibly set in Devon, although the reader has to work quite hard to gather this information; it is certainly not a regional novel. Devon is, of course, on the borders of the 'South Country' as defined by Howkins' 'Rural England', but the lack of regional specificity in the narration means that once again, in a general sense, the drama of the novel occupies a space at the heart of 'England'.

rye-field, and she holds a bunch of wild flowers. This place becomes the regular meeting-place of Helen and Paul as lovers, and they return here towards the end of the film to part. This is all very much in the novel's scheme of things too, where Helen, as the story's narrator, constantly describes the flowers and the seasons by which she charts her emotions and her growth as a woman.

Sylvia, the vampish villain of the piece, on the other hand, is first seen in the suburban street in which she lives. As the film progresses, she is mainly filmed indoors—which, within Hepworth's system, has a sort of negative connotation: 'I would never work indoors if I could possibly get into the open air. It was always in the back of my mind . . . that I was to make English pictures, with all the English countryside for background.'[106]

It is almost as if to stay indoors is un-English, unhealthy—and that is precisely Sylvia's problem, at least in terms of moral health. When she does venture outside, she is twice shunned by Helen on 'mossy lawns' and twice rejected by Paul in more wild garden areas. At a horse race, she witnesses the suicidal death of her former lover, Dick Fellows, driven to despair by her actions. It is this suicide which provokes Paul into breaking off his engagement to Sylvia. Finally she goes to Rome—the city—in pursuit of Paul.

Sylvia then is very much a woman of the world, experience to Helen's innocence—but it is a complicated, and morally degenerate existence which she leads. She is the ugly face of progress, the scheming modern woman, to Helen's nostalgic, uncomplicated child-woman, the embodiment of passive moral stability faced with the unfeminine active enterprise of Sylvia. Paul is caught between the pastoralism of Helen, and the tainted, immoral urbanity of Sylvia. It is his absence in Rome, his distance from the charms of Helen and her rye-field, which leads to his moral and romantic downfall. It is perhaps significant that it is not an English city to which he must travel. England, in this representation, remains almost exclusively pastoral, exclusively rural; but it also remains exclusively Protestant, and Paul's downfall is also in part that he leaves the natural landscapes of England for a city of such Catholic artifice, theatricality, and depravity. At the same time, Rome is, of course, the most ancient of cities, so the film even then does not have to bear any intrusions of excessive modernity or industrialization.

The various manifestations of the rye-field in the film add further dimensions to its pastoral representation. The narrative is broken down into three major sections which are each prefaced by an emblematic shot of the rye-field with a superimposed title. The progress of the narrative and the development of the film's various relationships—notably that between Paul and Helen—are charted symbolically through the seasonal situation of the

---

[106] Hepworth, *Came The Dawn*, 144.

rye-field. The first section of the film is entitled 'Seed-time', and does indeed see the sowing of the seeds of romance, but also of intrigue: it establishes the narrative possibilities. 'Summer' sees the ripening of the rye and the flowering of the romance: when Paul is obliged to leave for Rome on business, Helen says, in intertitle, 'The rye will all be harvested by the time you come back, and the field will be as empty as my heart'. The third section is 'Harvest': the various narrative threads are gathered in, the now empty field provides the scene for Paul's return to Helen, but too late, since Sylvia has tricked him into marrying her. Helen's heart is empty.

This pastoralism establishes a natural evolution to the course of love and the narrative as potentially cyclical (there will be another seed-time, another spring). For Helen, the narrative charts both a loss of and an awakening from the bliss of childhood innocence (precisely the quality which had attracted Paul to her in the first place). At the same time the representation establishes this whole way of life as natural, but lost, past, and only to be regained nostalgically (the camera maintains a fairly consistent distance from the characters and their actions; as spectators, we rarely penetrate the narrative space, and must observe from a distance).

The rye-field is primarily a place of leisure and romance for the sons and daughters of the gentry, but there are also two particularly significant shots of agricultural labour. These appear in the emblematic shots which preface each major development in the narrative. Seed-time shows the bare field being hand-sown by a solitary broadcaster in the middle distance. Harvest shows a bucolic labourer—'an old man who looks something like Father Time'[107]—scything the rye by hand, working his way towards the camera. Summer on the other hand needs no human intervention; the rye simply grows, naturally. The men at work are thus effectively part of the natural order, labour is unmechanized, traditional, innocently pre-industrial—almost a solitary communion with nature. The effect is underlined all the more by the separation of these images from the narrative proper in emblematic shots.

Morden argues that it was 'the role and position of the viewer [which] formed the basis for the special relationship that was formed between the pastoral and pictorialism': the viewer is placed as an outsider observing from a distance, an onlooker, a spectator of pastoral England.[108] The landscape becomes an object to be looked at, rather than a place in which one might act. *Comin' Thro' The Rye* initiates a similar spectatorial position. The film's images are predominantly in tableau style with a studied distance between camera/spectator and action or setting, and thus serve to display the English landscape of the rye-field, various gardens and the

[107] Ibid. 190.   [108] 'Pastoral and Pictorial', 20.

country house (and Helen's family home, featured in several scenes, is indeed very impressive as a building, 'a magnificent timbered building which made lovely backgrounds from a dozen different angles'[109]). But it is not only landscapes which are on display: there are also numerous carefully selected and often highly detailed Victorian interior décors and ornaments.[110]

The refusal on so many occasions to penetrate space, and the lingering of shots more than is strictly narratively necessary—and the consequently slow cutting rate—affords the spectator time to look around the image, and produces a *mise-en-scène* in which objects, buildings, and landscapes become heritage fetishes, objects to be looked at, rather than to be used as narrative devices. The attractions of pictorialism—the heritage attractions of the pastoral—are at the same time narrative distractions. This is the *mise-en-scène* of authenticity and of display; it is designed to show off, rather than to tell stories, and, as such, it is narratively excessive.

Morden points to a shift in pictorialist practices in the 1920s and 1930s, as witnessed in magazines like *Country Life*, away from an emphasis on photographs of pastoral landscapes. In its place, *Country Life* begins to concentrate on 'collecting and connoisseurship and other subjects of escape and distraction. The country estate contracted to be represented by its house which was now valued for its architecture, décor, and treasures.'[111] *Comin' Thro' The Rye* seems to be moving in this direction too, its pastoralism tempered by a fascination with and display of Victoriana, a sort of taxonomic *mise-en-scène*. There are thus two types of heritage property on display, the pastoral English landscape, and the collectible Victoriana, the ornamental décor of both interiors and exteriors: 'everything was perfectly in keeping', recalled Hepworth.[112]

The use of mirrors in *Comin' Thro' The Rye* is of some significance here; they are used neither narratively nor to create an illusion of depth within a confined space. Instead, they reflect back the ornaments and furnishings on display. Mirrors thus render even more visible the richness and diversity of the period trappings. At the house party where Helen and Paul are formally introduced to each other, for instance, a large mirror on the wall is positioned to reflect and display otherwise invisible details of chairs and carpets.

Once again, the narrative redundance of Hepworth's *mise-en-scène* is somewhat aberrant. It is undoubtedly the case that within the trade

---

[109] Hepworth, *Came The Dawn*, 190. The building is Moreton Old Hall, Cheshire (see ibid.), now a National Trust property.
[110] See e.g. shots 79–91, which include several interiors during scenes of a house party, a game of croquet, an ornamental formal garden, and a more picturesque landscaped garden.
[111] 'Pastoral and Pictorial', 21.   [112] *Came The Dawn*, 190.

STILL 5. The attractions of heritage England: 'most of the exteriors were taken at Moreton Old Hall in Cheshire, a magnificent timbered building which made lovely backgrounds from a dozen different angles' (Cecil Hepworth, *Came The Dawn*). The young Helen is scolded by her father (*Comin' Thro' The Rye*).

STILL 6. The attractions of heritage England: Victoriana on display. At a house-party, Sylvia (on the stairs) observes Paul and Helen (*Comin' Thro' The Rye*).

discourse of the period, great value was placed on 'pictorial values', but at the same time the standard view was that the story should be paramount. As one contemporary manual put it, a simply furnished set is best because

> there would be less to detract the eye from the action of the play. . . . [If] the action is strong [the audience] will have no time to verify whether the scene is an absolute replica of a room of the kind suggested or not. If the producer goes to the other extreme and crowds his stage, the action will be delayed, for the mind of the audience will be busy in appraising the various articles of furniture in the scene.[113]

It seems reasonable to assume that this distraction away from the action and towards an appraisal of the *mise-en-scène* was not seen as a problem by Hepworth; it is on the contrary an integral part of his aesthetic system. It is not just the setting of the film in the Victorian past, but also its pictorial and pastoral modes of representation and its languid narrative dignity which encourage its spectators to read it as traditional, as part of an apparently invariant tradition of Englishness.

NARRATIVE SOURCES, EXPECTATIONS, AND MOTIVATIONS

To read the contemporary reviews of *Comin' Thro' The Rye* is to gain the impression that it is the visual pleasures of pictorialism and the Victorian heritage which are the film's main attractions. Even the loyal *Bioscope* is more ambivalent about the narrative cohesion and plausibility of the film. Thus although *Comin' Thro' The Rye* is 'a delightful Victorian impression' it also has 'an improbable and rather stilted story'—or at least this is how it would seem if it were not 'invested with real human appeal and dramatic interest by the skill with which it has been told and the distinctive period atmosphere with which it has been surrounded.'[114]

For this reviewer at least, the heritage aspects of the film are able to offset what might otherwise be seen as a problem of narrative motivation and drive—suggesting that different expectations and narrative conventions applied to the emergent heritage film and what we now call classical Hollywood cinema. This is confirmed in a later comment in the *Bioscope*:

> [*Comin' Thro' The Rye*] has the additional attraction of a plot which, though it might well have seemed stilted and unconvincing if brought up to date, is both human and dramatic in the period setting to which it essentially belongs. . . . [Some

---

[113] Weston, *Photoplay-Writing*, 77–8.
[114] 22 Nov. 1923, 60. Compare also the comments of *The Times*, in its first review of the incomplete version of the film that had been trade shown: 'a sentimental drama, which is redeemed from ever becoming wearisome by the clever way in which the atmosphere of the Victorian era is suggested and maintained', 14 Nov. 1923, 19.

of the plot details] are not perhaps very plausible, but they open the way for intensely dramatic situations in which violent passions blaze fiercely beneath the prim Victorian exteriors. It is surprising indeed how thrilling the old story becomes when presented in its true environment.[115]

It is in the Victorian atmosphere that the main appeal of the film lies, however. The authenticity of the period representation—'its true environment'—can thus carry what would in other circumstances appear as narrative problems. There is also a suggestion that we should enjoy the by now somewhat dated Victorian moral values as part of the heritage on display, rather than worry about them as no longer dramatically convincing.

The other main British trade paper of the period, *Kine Weekly*, generally aligned itself much more closely than the *Bioscope* with the standards of American films of the period. As a result, it is much less inclined to overlook what it sees as a lack of narrative motivation, slowness of pace, weak plotting, and inadequate character development, or to pass off such narrative implausibilities as authentic heritage qualities:

The story seems as dead as Queen Anne. It is unreal and unconvincing. The recent tendency of the screen to present films which deal with living, vital themes in a serious way, has taken us very far away from the mincing mannerisms of Victorian days. . . . This production suffers also from mechanical treatment, seen most glaringly in the prolongation of individual scenes beyond their climax . . . [which] makes the film drag very badly at times . . . The picture seems to suffer from over-direction, in the sense that players have been allowed to accentuate types rather than portray characters and contribute to action.[116]

The film was actually reviewed twice by most papers, once during the November 1923 British Film Weeks, when it was shown in an incomplete form, and a second time when the film had been completed and released publicly. The first time round, *The Times* had been admiring, but in its second review it was critical of the added sections in the new version: 'At once improbabilities multiply, the continuity of action vanishes, unnecessary incidents are emphasised, and important ones slurred over.'[117] A number of these points are echoed by the *Bioscope* in its second review, where it mainly confines itself to commenting on the new ending to the film:

The real theme of the film is the love of Helen and Paul. When that is summarily terminated by Sylvia's trickery, the interest of the story also ends and the prolonged agony of the lovers . . . tends to create an anti-climax. . . . The death of Sylvia's little son, though very tenderly and prettily told, is unconvincing in respect of material facts, for it seems improbable that the parents, who were apparently within walking distance of their home, should have heard nothing of their child's mysterious illness.[118]

---

[115] 22 Nov. 1923, 62.   [116] 22 Nov. 1923, 58.   [117] 28 Jan. 1924, 8.
[118] 31 Jan. 1924, 55. The review continues: 'These however are matters of detail which could be amended, if necessary, by cutting and editing. The charm of the film remains

It is worth comparing these comments to the observations of Colden Lore, author of a contemporary British script-writing manual: 'Broadly speaking, the structure of a film story does not differ from that of a novel or a drama. Each must have a central theme, and a plot by which this theme is propounded, *but a film plot must be smoother, more probable* than its cousin of the printed page.'[119] Lore's guidelines for screen-writing are indeed very strong on questions of causality and motivation, and this is one aspect of *Comin' Thro' The Rye* which was less than perfectly handled as far as most reviewers were concerned. In a similar vein, Lore's comments about the requirements of a strong and satisfying sense of narrative closure are heavily underlined, so reinforcing the various criticisms of the ending of *Comin' Thro' The Rye*, in which the compiling of yet more climaxes serves only to produce a sense of anti-climax:

What in a novel or drama merely constitutes the plot, forms practically the whole 'story' of the Photoplay. The plot itself is a chain of circumstances and events arising out of some struggle or clash of interests so contrived that, in a crescendo, after periods of suspense, when the issue is still in doubt, they lead to one big crisis—the climax. *Here the story must end. To prolong it would be to produce an anticlimax.*[120]

Another way of reading the various criticisms of *Comin' Thro' The Rye* is to turn them back on the reviewer. The comments about the stereotyping of characters and narrative coincidence and improbability are thus all familiar characteristics of the criticism of popular melodrama by more high-brow critics. This suggests a number of things: first, it reminds us of the debt which popular cinema owes to nineteenth-century melodrama; secondly, it suggests that Hepworth has failed to pitch his film adequately at a coherent and homogeneous putative audience, since the film falls between the expectations of quality cinema and popular melodrama. There may well be far closer links between these two types of film than is generally acknowledged; there is, for instance, a great deal in common between the psychological realism of post-war European (including British) art cinema and the thematic concerns and modes of representation of popular film melodrama. There was, however, no common agreement that Hepworth had managed to achieve the right blend of ingredients and pleasures in *Comin' Thro' The Rye*. It thus appears too evidently a mix of two genres, the art film and the woman's picture. The two had perhaps not been convincingly enough reconciled, yet the blend in itself has remained

---

unimpaired, and the concluding portion preserves as a whole its sincere and poetical spirit. Incidentally, one may add, Mr Hepworth has had the courage to retain the "unhappy ending"—a decision which is well justified.'

[119] Colden Lore, *The Modern Photoplay, and its Construction* (London, 1923), 27, my emphasis.

[120] Ibid. 29, my emphasis.

a characteristic of the heritage genre—many of BBC Television's classic serials, for instance, can be read as high-class, respectable soap operas.[121]

Part of the problem surely lies in Hepworth's choice of material, and what he has proposed to do with it, for, as we have seen, the novel is indeed popular melodrama, or, in literary terminology, popular romance fiction, addressed primarily to a female readership. Its central protagonist is female; its dominating relationships are between the heroine and her loved ones; its major drama lies in the romance of love thwarted, misunderstood, achieved, and destroyed; and the whole story is told from the insistently feminine perspective of the heroine. The suspense of the narrative is the suspense of 'if only . . .', and the novel is accordingly full of intense emotions, huge coincidences, and the discrepant and often blind points of view of the two main protagonists and the more omniscient but powerless point of view of the reader. All this tends to establish a strong complicity between reader and protagonist. Elaine Showalter discusses the general romance conventions of Mathers's novel in the context of a historically specific tendency in Victorian literature, the series of spectacular best-sellers by women writers of the 1860s and 1870s, such as Mary E. Braddon's *Lady Audley's Secret* and Mrs Henry Wood's *East Lynne* (both published in 1862).[122] This was a very different literature from the women's writing of the previous generation, the work of the Brontës, Mrs Gaskell, and George Eliot; it was a type of sensation fiction whose commerciality and transgressive passions, and especially the fact that it was written by women, shocked both male critics with an allegiance to high culture, and the older generation of women writers and reviewers. Indeed, Mathers wrote the novel in secret, and published it anonymously[123]—this was clearly not a fit book for a woman of her standing to write.

Comin' Thro' The Rye is not, therefore, from this point of view, auspicious material for the production of a quality film addressing a middle-class audience in a traditional English idiom. Yet it does have the advantage of being set in a period which had already been thoroughly mythicized by the heritage impulse. There is a heavily sedimented notion of 'Victorianness' at work in several reviews of the film, for instance, one which is evidently taken for granted in a very unquestioning way by the writers, in phrases such as 'most picturegoers . . . would have liked to see Sylvia punished with a severity befitting her altogether un-Victorian behaviour', and 'the lovers . . . are, quite properly, too Victorian to have the courage of their passion'.[124] We are assumed to have no doubt in our minds as to what constitutes 'Victorian behaviour' here: whatever may have been intended by Mathers, or picked up on by her predominantly female readership,

---

[121] See Kerr, 'Classic serials'.   [122] *Literature*, 153–81.   [123] Ibid. 175.
[124] *Bioscope*, 31 Jan. 1924, 55.

'Victorianness' is now something safe and secure, an unimpeachable image of moral stability which can be looked back on as an authentic and instructive referent, abstracted from its historical context.

In the novel itself, it is precisely the moral sensibility of mid-Victorian patriarchy which is the site of dramatic struggle; a very particular set of cultural tensions and antagonisms are explored in the course of a narrative about learning what it means to become a woman within a very specific class milieu. In the film, however, we are presented with a much more generalized imaginary object, 'Victorianness'. A specifically modern cultural memory of a period and an ideological paradigm is imposed on a text which is the product of that period, whose leading political tensions have been purged, or at least reduced to individual character traits. In the style of this sensation fiction—'a genre in which everything that was not forbidden was compulsory'[125]—'Victorian exteriors' have not as yet been reconstructed in the novel as 'prim', and 'violent passions' do indeed 'blaze fiercely'.[126] A front must certainly be put up for the intolerant father, and on other occasions as well, but it is not a prim front, and there is in *Comin' Thro' The Rye*, as there is in other sensation novels, a running critical commentary, for which one does not have to read between the lines, on how the womenfolk of the gentry class were expected to behave as daughters, wives, and mothers, a commentary which expresses a great deal of anger and frustration. The novel, as such, can be read as attempting to create a space for the emergence of a new woman, even if the heroine does at one point explicitly distance herself from any political version of feminism.

The transgressive qualities of the sensation novel are to some extent contained by the conventional structure of the three-decker novel, as Showalter points out, a process of recuperation which is even more strongly marked in *Comin' Thro' The Rye* than in some of the other novels of the period. This begins to explain how a sensation novel, a transgressive feminist text with a very particular line on mid-Victorian patriarchy, could be reworked as a text which might express the 'charm', 'quaintness' and 'primness' which 'Victorianness' evidently connotes in the early 1920s (these are all terms used in the reviews quoted above).

[E]ven as they recorded their disillusion, their frustration, their anger, indeed, their murderous feelings, the sensationalists could not bring themselves to undertake a radical inquiry into the role of women. . . . Typically, the first volume of a woman's sensation novel is a gripping and sardonic analysis of a woman in conflict with male authority. By the second volume, guilt has set in. In the third volume we see the heroine punished, repentant, and drained of all energy. . . . The very tradition

---

[125] Showalter, *Literature*, 158.
[126] See the *Bioscope* review quoted above, 22 Nov. 1923, 62.

of the domestic novel opposed the heroine's development. It was so widely accepted that marriage would conclude the representation of the fictional heroine, that 'my third volume' became a coy euphemism for this period of women's lives.[127]

The structure of *Comin' Thro' The Rye* is not quite like this, because—and perhaps this is one of its major transgressions—guilt never sets in. Volume one deals with Helen's early teenage years, and her confrontation with various models of masculinity. There is the tyranny of her father, and her idealization of her brother Jack (her friendship with him gradually recedes as their sexual difference is more profoundly culturally demarcated). There is also the potential boredom of her future life if she were to pledge herself for marriage to the sweet but dull and ironically named George Tempest (he is neither adventurous like her brother, nor a passionate, romantic figure). Finally of course there is the enigmatic figure of Paul, her future lover, a figure both carefully eroticized, but also heavily sentimentalized. The conflict with male authority is worked through in various ways: in terms of her relations with her father; in terms of her resistance to the insistent George, who would implicitly in the eyes of her family make the future ideal partner; and in terms of her often forthright commentary on the plight of girls within the society in which she lives.

Volume two, the chronicle of her eighteenth year, far from being an admission of guilt, deals with the 'summer' of her love for Paul and his love for her; it is a fantasy of romance, a fantasy which is conspicuously played out in the absence of her father. Volume three, which ought to be the movement towards the happy ending—the containment, the closure—of marriage, instead does indeed punish Helen for the passion of her romantic fantasy. Sylvia, Paul's former fiancée, successfully plots to win him back by villainous means, and marries him by a trick. When Paul tries to explain to Helen that the marriage is on his part entirely loveless, and implies that they should continue to remain lovers, Helen insists instead on the self-sacrifice of their parting, a form of repentance which drains Helen (and Paul) of all energy. Finding a sort of release in mothering the son of Paul and Sylvia, she is once more struck down by the boy's death in her arms, and eventually the death of Paul.

Showalter suggests that the conventions of the three-decker novel mean that the only proper escape from the tyranny of the father is through marriage. The obvious partner for Helen is George, but the fantasy is of being with the far more exciting Paul. In the end she can have neither.

Mathers could neither abandon the sentimental conventions of the three-decker, nor believe in them. Her solution to this dilemma was perhaps the only one

---

[127] Showalter, *Literature*, 180–1; the ref. is to Thackeray's *The Newcomes*.

possible for a novelist in her circumstances; she concocted a romance for her heroine, but ended it unhappily. Nell [Helen] is left in limbo; we have no right to predict that she will do anything with her life, but at least she is not confined to marriage.[128]

Showalter notes further that the sensation fiction of the 1860s and 1870s broke with 'the code of renunciation and submission that informed earlier [women's] fiction'.[129] But in *Comin' Thro' The Rye* there is still a strong sense of self-sacrifice, which leads, one gathers, to a very serious nervous illness on Helen's part; she does, in other words, submit to the proprieties of marriage, even if it is articulated in terms of her staying away from Paul in his marriage to the evil Sylvia. Herein lies another distance from some of the more sensationalist fiction of the period: while Helen does have a feminist sensibility that may have shocked some of the novel's readers at the time of its initial publication, the more villainous, if not exactly murderous, crimes of passion are displaced on to the figure of the other woman, Sylvia. But even here, there is a feminist critique of male fantasies, since Sylvia is otherwise the perfect woman, immaculately beautiful, admired by everyone that sets eyes on her, always graceful in public, whether in church, on horseback, or on the dance-floor. Helen by contrast is plain-looking (or at least believes herself to be), exuberant rather than graceful, and unable to dance or ride. She is not the accomplished and elegant lady of the etiquette manuals. On the contrary, it is Sylvia who holds this position; and, while Helen knows better, to others it may seem that it is Sylvia who is the abandoned fiancée, and later the neglected wife, and Paul that is at fault. But Mathers shows that beneath this surface, beneath this male fantasy of womanhood, lurks a very nasty character.

A feminist sensibility does still remain, therefore, even if the sensational transgressions of *Comin' Thro' The Rye* are muted by contrast with some of the other novels in the genre, and compromised by the romance conventions of volumes two and three. The sense of a critique of patriarchy has been lost in the transformation from novel to film, as have many of the little details of female deviance, to be replaced by the caresses of the period piece, and the reconstruction of 'Victorianness'. Rather than trying to explore or understand the nuances of women's experience, Hepworth focuses on the externals of their appearance, reducing them to just so much *mise-en-scène*, to authentic period costumes on the bodies of modern stars. Yet it is this very garb which is the source of so much frustration to the young Helen in the novel:

---

[128] Ibid. 176–7. My own reading of the novel is that Helen is actually on her deathbed at the end of the narrative, about to succumb to the same disease which has just killed the child she has been nursing.

[129] Ibid. 162.

By and by I pluck up sufficient spirit to put on the despised female garments that I hate so thoroughly. How cumbrous, and useless, and ridiculous they are! how my gowns, petticoats, crinoline, ribbons, ties, cloaks, hats, bonnets, gloves, tapes, hooks, eyes, buttons, and the hundred and one et ceteras that make up a girl's costume chafe and irritate me![130]

There are marked differences, too, between the ways in which the novel and the film deal with issues of romance and fantasy. Showalter argues that the exploration of feminine fantasies is central to sensation fiction:

These women novelists made a powerful appeal to the female audience by subverting the traditions of feminine fiction to suit their imaginative impulses, by expressing a wide range of suppressed female emotions, and by tapping and satisfying fantasies of protest and escape. . . . The enormous popularity of the women sensationalists reflects the skill with which they articulated the fantasies of their readers, fantasies that they themselves fervently shared.[131]

Hepworth's adaptation however captures little of this feminine fantasy. This is partly because he was evidently trying to create a tasteful period piece as much as a popular melodrama, but partly also because his aesthetic cannot really accommodate a complex and sophisticated narrative development—and it is the passionate energy of the narrative drive which is so important to the expression of fantasy in the novel of *Comin' Thro' The Rye*. Hepworth's primarily distanced tableau narration, likewise, cannot on the whole generate the imaginative qualities and the complicity with the reader which the autobiographical first person narration of the novel achieves.

The structure of the story may be substantially the same in novel and film, but the pacing, and the emotional depth and psychological complexity of the novel are missing from the film. Hepworth's aesthetic does not easily lend itself to the creation of psychological space, as I will demonstrate later in this chapter. The tableau style of narration cannot insert the spectating subject into the narrative space of the film in an identificatory way, but instead leaves the spectator on the outside, looking in from a distance. This is ideal for the display of heritage properties, but not for the development of a powerfully engaging romantic drama.

Steve Neale has argued that one characteristic of the classic film melodrama's potential to move its audience is the distinctive way in which it plays on point of view and its relationship to knowledge.[132] The processing of the drama in many cases involves initially establishing that the full passion of romance cannot be consummated because the characters are unable to see what we as spectators can see only too well. The characters

---

[130] Mathers, *Comin' Thro' The Rye*, 1907 edn., 28.
[131] *Literature*, 158–9.
[132] 'Melodrama and Tears', *Screen*, 27/6 (1986).

thus lack the knowledge which would enable the romance to progress, while the spectator is powerless to intervene ('if only . . .'). The successful movement of the narrative, as Neale points out, often actually requires not simply that the main characters see what they so far have not seen, but that they see each other, that they exchange looks—which also enables the spectator finally to see with the characters. It is this conjunction of looks which in part gives the classical melodrama its emotional power.

It is certainly the case that we see more than the characters in *Comin' Thro' The Rye*: we know that Sylvia is scheming to win back Paul, for instance, but neither Paul nor Helen knows this. There is, furthermore, a relatively knowing play on the desire of each of the two protagonists to see each other when parted by Paul's second visit to Rome. They had last seen each other across the rye-field, as Paul walked away into the distance. Helen later returns to the same spot, and looks across the now empty field, stretching her arms towards where she had last seen Paul, as if to will him back. Paul, meanwhile, recalls that his last view of Helen had been as he looked back across the field to see her being comforted by George, a scene which he subsequently misinterprets. These two empty gazes must be brought back into alignment if the romance is to resume—but Sylvia's intervention makes this impossible. In any case, it is beyond the scope of the film to align the characters' intra-diegetic looks with the look of the spectator, given the virtually relentless use of tableau shots, and relative avoidance of point-of-view shots, or even eyeline matching. Even when Paul and Helen do look at each other, the moment lacks the passion and engagement that a reverse-shot structure might have achieved. The difference from the classical system is underlined by the marked frontality of the acting, so that, rather than looking at each other, they are consigned mainly to looking out at the camera.

The transposition of the narrative from novel to film loses altogether the sense of a critique of patriarchy, or an exploration of the codes and pleasures of romance. In their place is a perspective which idealizes the past. Some of the more downmarket magazines hinted at the problems with this idealization, but in general reviewers seemed much happier with this refashioning of cultural memory, as has already been noted: 'One is accustomed to regard this period as not very attractive as regards dresses and furniture; but that there is a quaint charm about it is abundantly demonstrated here.'[133] The shift from a critique of Victorian clothing in the novel to a celebration of it in the film is, then, part and parcel of the whole transformation of a contemporary romance, albeit one already tinged with nostalgia, into a period piece replete with the paraphernalia of the heritage

---

[133] *Motion Picture Studio*, 17 Nov. 1923, 12; compare this with the more critical view of *Picture Show*—see n. 74, above.

perspective. While the delight in the pastoral vision of the English landscape is evident in both novel and film, there is a new departure in the way
in which the film also fills its images with collectible Victoriana, formal
gardens and the façades of country houses which reek of the past. There
is really only one brief passage in the 510 pages of the novel which gestures towards this heritage sensibility. This particular occasion is very
much in line with the film's perspective on the national past, except that
the reference is to Restoration properties, not Victoriana:

and I look round the room at the dark oak, at the massive sideboard, on which
is carved the date 1690. How small and insignificant that date makes me feel, and
how evanescent a thing life is. For how many generations has not that sideboard
held food and drink? for how many more will it not hold the same? . . . Stately old
houses certainly lessen one's sense of self-importance. It is impossible, in the face
of the stored traditions and memories of many hundred years, not to feel that these
things remain, and we go.[134]

This sense of continuing tradition is not at all typical of the novel, which
is very firmly situated in the present (it is told throughout in the present
tense, for instance). There are otherwise very few descriptions of rooms or
of buildings, or of the décor, furnishings, and ornaments of those buildings, beyond the purely functional descriptions required for narrative
development. This is in marked contrast to the film, where the heritage
elements tend to stall the pace and economy of the narrative, or to lead
the spectator in narratively irrelevant directions. This can be seen particularly in the film's opening sequence. The first shot of the film—on which
the title is superimposed—shows the rye-field (with Helen as a young girl).
The second shot (after the credits) is an emblematic shot of the rye-field
being sown, superimposed with the title 'Seed-time'. Then follows an
intertitle: 'If the spirits of Old Houses have anything to do with the Moulding
of Character it will not be surprising if the occupants of Silverbridge
Manor have some well-marked Peculiarities.'

   The third shot of the film is a long shot of the Manor seen from across
the rye-field. The verbal and visual underlining of the presence and nature
of the house are neither in the novel, nor strictly relevant to the development of the drama in the film—indeed the details of the intertitle are
actually misleading. Their only real function is to display the house as
precisely a heritage property, to instil a particular mode of looking at the
film from the outset.

   Hepworth thus endeavours to use a deviant fiction for a traditional de-
politicized representation of Englishness, but in fact it is the narrative
conventions of the popular romance fiction, more than the feminist voice
of narration, or the absence of a developed heritage perspective, which

---

[134] Mathers, *Comin' Thro' The Rye*, 1907 edn., 221.

seems to constitute his main stumbling-block. Hepworth's aesthetic sensibility does not really seem suited to the passions of the novel; he does not really know how to deal with the narrative conventions of the melodrama—hence the problems he runs into with the critics on this front. What appealed to Hepworth was clearly the genteel framework within which the passions of the melodrama are handled: the class milieu of the setting, but also the language of the novel, for every chapter is prefaced with a quotation from some classical, Shakespearian, or otherwise culturally respectable source, and Helen herself is always demonstrating the breadth of her reading and depth of her learning with further similar quotations. For all intents and purposes, these quotations are narratively redundant (Helen's learning is of no narrative consequence), slowing down the pace of the fiction, in the same way that the pictorialist embellishments and the primarily tableau style of narration in the film retard the narrative.

FILM STYLE AND THE STANDARDS OF AMERICAN CINEMA

The absence of an efficient narrative which can unhesitatingly win the support of the film critics of the period is not simply a problem of having chosen a somewhat anomalous source novel, but is integral to Hepworth's whole film aesthetic. Even within a cinema industry that was much less standardized than its American counterpart, Hepworth's style was highly idiosyncratic. As the *Bioscope* notes, *Comin' Thro' The Rye* is 'an entertainment as effective dramatically as it is unusual in character' and 'bears throughout the imprint of Mr Hepworth's individual style'. The rider that this 'will undoubtedly charm admirers of this typically British school of picture-making' is implicitly an acknowledgement that the style is of limited appeal.[135] It is revealing to compare these sorts of comments to the same trade paper's reference to another British film trade-shown the same week:

Among the modern British stories shown, Graham Cutts' ornate and dramatic version of Michael Morton's *Woman to Woman* takes first place as a polished and elaborate production done in the American style. Apart from its intrinsic qualities as a powerful entertainment, the film proves that British studiocraft is now capable of equalling if not eclipsing the best American work so far as technical finish is concerned.[136]

---

[135] 22 Nov. 1923, 63; 31 Jan. 1924, 52; ibid.

[136] 22 Nov. 1923, 60. Significantly, *Woman to Woman* (which is not available for viewing) was distributed much more quickly and widely than *Comin' Thro' The Rye* (see the entertainments listings in *The Times*, 12 Nov. 1923, 10; and 4 Feb. 1924, 10); it was also distributed in the USA (*Bioscope*, 8 Nov. 1923, 47; *Variety*, 2 Apr. 1924, repr. in *Variety's Film Reviews, 1921–1925*, ii (New York, 1983), no p. nos.). *Comin' Thro' The Rye* was only shown privately in New York a year later when Hepworth hired a hall for the purpose, no American distributor having taken it up (see *Came The Dawn*, 196).

Woman to Woman was the critical success of late 1923 and early 1924—
'in strong drama, *Woman to Woman* . . . is perhaps the outstanding picture of the year'.[137] All the trade papers, the national dailies, and the fan
magazines praised it lavishly, and noted the degree to which it worked
smoothly 'on lines which the Americans have hitherto made their own',[138]
seeing it as 'a challenge to the American producer, accustomed to make
pictures on a similar or greater scale.'[139] The *Bioscope*, quoted above, went
on to note that 'this is a film of exceptional artistic and dramatic interest,
and of outstanding entertainment value . . ., and will fully justify extensive
exploitation.'[140] *Kine Weekly* thought the film 'an outstanding British
achievement and . . . a screen entertainment that is far above the average.
. . . No praise is too high for the artistic direction and the eminently
human way in which Graham Cutts has unfolded the story.'[141]

    Woman to Woman was in many ways a sign of things to come. Although
directed by Cutts, one of the leading directors of the period, a young
Alfred Hitchcock played a large part in the production process, and was
officially credited as assistant director, co-screenwriter, and art director.
His future wife Alma Reville was the editor.[142] The film was, in addition,
co-produced by Victor Saville and Michael Balcon, for whom it was their
first foray into feature film work. These too were names of the future (both
Balcon and Saville worked on *Evergreen* (1934), discussed in the next
chapter). Perhaps the most significant aspect of *Woman to Woman* was
that it was 'produced on lines frankly designed to appeal to America.'[143]
This applied to the technical qualities praised by all the reviewers—*Kine
Weekly*'s comment is typical: the film 'need fear no adverse comparison in
the matter of setting, lighting or photography with the best American
pictures.'[144]

    The film also self-consciously competed with Hollywood on its own
terms through its casting: the American star Betty Compson had been
specially imported for the film. Contemporary reviewers also thought the
narrative construction and mode of narration of the film were in the
American style. The play on which the film was based, 'which had little
intrinsic value as dramatic entertainment', was not adapted with the
aim of preserving some perceived authenticity of the original, but was

[137] P. L. Mannock, 'British Pictures of 1923', *Kine Weekly*, 3 Jan. 1924, 81.
[138] Ibid.   [139] *Motion Picture Studio*, 17 Nov. 1923, 10.
[140] 15 Nov. 1923, 46.
[141] 15 Nov. 1923, 63. Cf. *Motion Picture Studio*, 17 Nov. 1923, 10; and *The Times*, 12
Nov. 1923, 10.
[142] See Donald Spoto, *The Dark Side Of Genius: The Life of Alfred Hitchcock* (London,
1983), 59.
[143] *Motion Picture Studio*, 29 Dec. 1923, 10.
[144] 15 Nov. 1923, 63. Cf. *Motion Picture Studio*, 17 Nov. 1923, 10; *The Times*, 12 Nov.
1923, 10.

STILL 7. The imported American star Betty Compson with Clive Brook in *Woman to Woman*.

'modified for screen purposes—and improved.'[145] The continuity of the film impressed—'the action moves smoothly from the beginning to the end'; 'there is no side-tracking, no involved detail, the [central] theme . . . is kept prominently to the fore.'[146] The balance of spectacle and emotional intimacy and sincerity was favourably commented on, too: 'The producer has given his story beautiful and lavish settings, but never once does he allow these to overshadow or interfere with the action of the plot; they are all part and parcel of the story and are used to lead up to some dramatic climax.'[147]

For once, this was not simply patriotism running riot among the British reviewers, since the reviewer for the American trade paper, *Variety*, made similar comments on the occasion of the film's New York release:

nothing either the British manufacturers or Miss Compson need be ashamed of . . . as a whole it is not any more guilty of the usual sequence of deficiencies than is included in the average features produced and made within our own home territory . . . It's a workmanlike piece of production . . . and rates above some of the vehicles Miss Compson has done on this side . . . After viewing this picture there seems no evident reason for the continual antipathy expressed towards British-made films, as this assuredly must be an example of the better grade of work over there. It is unquestionably equal to a vast majority of the releases viewed in the first run houses over here and vastly superior to those witnessed in our daily change theatres.[148]

Again, technical qualities are praised, with costumes, lavish set design, good photography, and lighting all being singled out for attention. While the reviewer by no means goes overboard about the film, its closeness to American standards enables a warm reception. Another American trade paper suggested this was 'one of the two best English pictures ever shown on the screen',[149] while *Kine Weekly*'s New York correspondent reminded readers that 'we of the States . . . have claimed for many years that our public would accept a British production if thoroughly adapted to our market. *Woman to Woman* is.'[150] Indeed, *Woman to Woman* was one of the few British films of its time to receive American distribution, opening in the United States at the same time as in Britain. It also sold for a good price, and did good business in key cities.[151]

This was in stark contrast to the reception for *Comin' Thro' The Rye*.

---

[145] *Kine Weekly*, 15 Nov. 1923, 63; *Motion Picture Studio*, 17 Nov. 1923, 10.
[146] *Eastern Daily Press*, 5 Feb. 1924, 3; *Kine Weekly*, 15 Nov. 1923, 63.
[147] Ibid. Cf. *Motion Picture Studio*, 17 Nov. 1923, 10.
[148] 2 Apr. 1924, repr. in *Variety's Film Reviews, 1921–1925*, no p. nos.
[149] *Motion Picture News*, quoted in 'Long Shots and Close Ups', *Kine Weekly*, 7 Feb. 1924, 38.
[150] 8 Nov. 1923, 48.
[151] See Frank A. Tilley, 'The Story of the Year', *Kine Yearbook*, 1924, 9; *Bioscope*, 3 Jan. 1924, 47, and 24 Jan. 1924, 30; *Kine Weekly*, 7 Feb. 1924, 38; and *Motion Picture Studio*, 9 Feb. 1924, 7.

The *Variety* review for this film concluded that its differences from the prevailing standards meant that '[a]s far as the American market is concerned it hasn't a chance.'[152] The picture was slated by *Variety* for what were seen as its primitive, antiquated methods:

Comin' Thro' The Rye as a picture is just as much a picture as the average English production was back in 1912 when they were being distributed in this country by Mutual. They haven't advanced a bit. The handling of the story is wretched, the story itself being worse than that; the photography is bad . . . The picture is draggy. It is shot principally in exterior scenes until it gives the impression English must live in their gardens [*sic*]. The photography is what might be termed foggy almost through the picture and the actors walk right up to the camera as in the old days and they make faces at is [*sic*], showing plainly they have too much make-up on.[153]

The aspects of story construction criticized here were the same that the English reviewers worried over, but the criticisms are much closer to those of the *Kine Weekly* rather than the *Bioscope*, since the heritage qualities of a period piece are seen by *Variety* as detrimental rather than mitigating:

the picture is a costume piece laid in the period of the early fifties, which is enough to condemn it in American eyes . . . The story could just as well have been modernized. There was no reason to plant it back in the Victorian days, but for some reason or other the English producer preferred to keep it there.[154]

What I have tried to demonstrate above is that there are in fact very good reasons for the film being a period piece, in terms of its authenticity to the period, and the space it creates for the display of heritage properties, including the (revised) moral properties of the period story itself. But it is evident that the pictorialist cinematography, the pastoral representation, and the heritage qualities of the film are of no interest to the American reviewer. The *New York Times*, less concerned than *Variety* with matters of box-office, and more concerned with film as an art-form, was more optimistic on this count: 'We had hoped for much in this picture—which is a sweet old-fashioned love story—with its beautiful English background.' In the end, though, it is 'an old-fashioned story produced in an old-fashioned way. . . . [A] frayed and clumsy production', particularly disappointing in terms of its theatrical acting. Most of all, the reviewer expresses surprise that 'this production has been highly praised in England —which is strange, for it is hardly comparable with ordinary features produced in this country.'[155] What these American reviews make clear is the vast gap that existed between Hepworth's aspirations and the

---

[152] 31 Dec. 1924, repr. in *Variety's Film Reviews, 1921–1925*, no p. nos. These comments are even more damning if we take into account that *Variety* gives the running time as 80 minutes, implying that the print shown in New York had already been considerably cut.
[153] Ibid.   [154] Ibid.
[155] All quotations from Mordaunt Hall, 'Two Foreign Photoplays', *New York Times*, 21 Dec. 1924, repr. in *New York Times Film Reviews*, i. 1913–31 (New York, 1970), 225.

expectations of the standard American film which dominated the market—and since those aspirations evidently included American distribution, one can but sympathize with *Variety*'s comments that, 'with the English clamouring to get into the American market it seems surprising that they would not educate themselves in the picture producing field and ascertain what is wanted. Certainly this example of production will not sell on this side of the Atlantic.'[156]

Hepworth was evidently well aware of his distance from the increasingly international standards of the Hollywood film, and made little effort to keep abreast of developments in the film world.[157] The most obvious difference between *Comin' Thro' The Rye* and most commercially successful films of the early 1920s is in the pacing and overall structure of the narrative and the degree to which narrative developments are motivated. Both the *Bioscope* and *Kine Weekly* reviewers are concerned that some scenes, and indeed the whole film, are prolonged beyond their climax, and suggest that the film is therefore in need of judicious cutting to improve continuity. Implicit is a desire for a more fast-moving narrative, in keeping with the economy, efficiency, and speed of American films of the period. Certainly, by comparison with an American film such as *Tol'able David* (1921, but not released in Britain until 1923[158]) or *Woman of Paris* (1923, premièred in Britain in 1924[159]), *Comin' Thro' The Rye* has a much looser, less economic, and less well-motivated narrative development.

This is in part a function of the cutting rate, which gives an Average Shot Length (ASL) of about 19 seconds.[160] This is substantially longer than any of the 1920s films for which Barry Salt gives ASLs (although he doesn't give figures for any British films). Salt notes that the slowest cutting rate for the American films of the 1920s which he has analysed is for the films of Rex Ingram, whom he describes as the leading American pictorialist of the period—but even here the ASL is only 7.5 seconds.[161] Salt also notes that European films are generally slower than American films with a much longer ASL: 'when it comes to making zippy movies, the Americans were always in front';[162] but again, the ASLs he gives for 1920s European films are much shorter than that of *Comin' Thro' The Rye*. Salt further suggests that European film-makers during the early 1920s tend to shoot from far back, with a slow cutting rate and without reverse angles.[163]

---

[156] 31 Dec. 1924, repr. in *Variety's Film Reviews, 1921–1925*, no p. nos.

[157] Cf. Hepworth, *Came The Dawn*, 196, 120; see also the comments on his working methods in *Picturegoer*, Feb. 1924, 15, and 'What to Learn from "the Pictures"', 140, 162.

[158] *Kine Yearbook, 1924*, 92.

[159] Entertainments listings, *The Times*, 25 Feb. 1924, 10.

[160] Based on the NFA Viewing Copy, projected at a speed of 18 frames per second, which feels like the right speed.

[161] *Film Style and Technology*, 213.   [162] Ibid. Cf. Weston, *Photoplay-Writing*, 67.

[163] Salt, *Film Style*, 210–11. See also Thomas Elsaesser and Adam Barker, 'Introduction', 306 ff., and Ben Brewster, 'Deep Staging in French Films 1900–1914', both in Thomas Elsaesser with Adam Barker (eds.), *Early Cinema: Space, Frame, Narrative* (London, 1990).

The slow cutting rate of *Comin' Thro' The Rye* is inseparably bound to Hepworth's pervasive use of the tableau shot, with slow fades between each shot, and a preference for reframing (sometimes several times in one shot) rather than scene dissection for following or recentring action. There are occasional edits to closer shots, though nothing closer than a Medium Close Shot (except for letter inserts), and it is in fact only on rare occasions that the scale is greater than waist-up medium shots.

The most common form of scene dissection in *Comin' Thro' The Rye*, where there is any (and in many cases there is not), is to move once into a closer shot (generally a medium shot) on the same frontal axis, around an intertitle; another occasional form of scene dissection is to break up a tableau shot with a letter insert in close up. There are also occasional point-of-view shots and reverse shots, but in general scene dissection is kept to a minimum, and such editing strategies are reserved for quite specific emotionally significant moments within the drama.

As such, *Comin' Thro' The Rye* has a stylistic system almost the opposite of contemporary American films, with their much faster cutting rate and analytical continuity-editing system. Further, where American films are able to work with a relatively shallow staging, given the pace of the montage, much of *Comin' Thro' The Rye* is staged in depth, with often two sites of action as well as a heritage backdrop. This staging in depth is of course only really possible given the long ASL, allowing the spectator time to scan the image. As we have seen, this visual style is part and parcel of a pictorialist cinematography, enabling the display of heritage properties (pastoral landscapes and Victoriana). The longer ASL and the particular narrative rhythm of the film are necessary in order to render the *mise-en-scène* legible, and in order to allow the eye to take in the full richness of the heritage and its visual pleasures. In this respect, *Comin' Thro' The Rye* is closer to contemporary European art cinema than popular American films, and even if it does not have anything like the complex, narratively significant *mise-en-scène* of, say, German Expressionist cinema, the richness of the pictorialist imagery has its own aesthetic and ideological (if not narrative) complexity.

This suggests that there is a contradiction at the heart of most of the trade papers' reviews of *Comin' Thro' The Rye*, since they both celebrate the visual qualities of the film and decry the slowness of the narrative, demanding various cuts. *Kine Weekly*, for instance, complains that 'the treatment is slow and mechanical, it lacks the flesh and blood effect it should have expressed' but adds that 'the photography is really beautiful'.[164] It is, of course, precisely this vulgar carnality, this American virility, that Hepworth is seeking to repress.[165] Hollywood's 'zippy' narrative style,

---

[164] 22 Nov. 1923, 57.
[165] Cf. Weston, *Photoplay-Writing*, 69: 'The American producers seldom err in [underplaying the subjective interest]; their work is too virile, too much alive . . .'

with all the dynamic energy of its tightly directed continuity cutting and
scene dissection, is simply not culturally suited to Hepworth's cinema, the
quality film in an English idiom. As the *Motion Picture Studio* commented:
'The Hepworth method of placid story development seems eminently suited
to the subject; and the dramatic values are at the same time not slurred.'[166]
Even the unhappy ending, with all its moral implications, can be seen as
an integral part of this project, and the whole adds up to a coherent
and consistent stylistic system, fully in accord with the ideology of the
film.[167]

It is debatable whether some of the narrative longeurs criticized in the
trade papers' reviews are strictly necessary even within the representational
project of this film, however. Narrative economy may be secondary to
pictorial richness, but if it thereby sacrifices narrative clarity, it becomes
a problem. This lack of narrative clarity is most glaring at the start of the
plot, which includes several scenes and characters that seem redundant to
the extent that they have very little pay-off or narrative consequence. The
process of establishing that a story is about to unfold is very drawn
out, such that one becomes almost too aware of the mechanics of story-
telling[168]—and, in the contemporary script-writing manual quoted earlier,
Lore recommends that 'all [structurally necessary] incidents must be sufficiently emphasised to impress themselves upon the memory of the spectator,
yet without making, by undue accentuation, the skeleton of the structure
too apparent.'[169]

Part of the problem here is undoubtedly the length and complexity of
the source novel. Clearly the narrative has been drastically compressed for
the film. Yet, in order to do justice to a certain cultural memory of the
novel, Hepworth and his script-writer tried to preserve its overall narrative
scope. For instance, a number of plot-lines are established which are really
unnecessarily complex given their ultimate function within the narrative.
Another script-writing manual recommends that 'one eliminates the essen-
tials from one's story,'[170] while Lore proposes that 'in a Photoplay only the
essential incidents, only those that bring the story forward, are worth
portraying. Mere incident, as such, has no place in the plot. . . . Unless
[incidents] have a distinct contributory place in the story, the photo

---

[166] 17 Nov. 1923, 12.

[167] Note *Bioscope*'s comment that 'Mr Hepworth has had the courage to retain the "unhappy ending"' tends to imply that the happy ending was considered standard for the time
(31 Jan. 1924, 55). Cf. Lore, *Modern Photoplay*, 221: 'Generally speaking . . . the happy
ending is desirable.'

[168] In this respect, at least, it is not dissimilar to the much admired *Tol'able David*, which
also takes an inordinately long time, and several redundant inter-titles, to introduce its main
characters at the start of the film.

[169] Lore, *Modern Photoplay*, 30.

[170] Weston, *Photoplay-Writing*, 49; cf. 41, 115.

playwright must restrain himself.'[171] There are a number of ways in which *Comin' Thro' The Rye* fails to obey these fairly standard narrative conventions. The scenes involving Dick Fellows provide one example. In terms of narrative motivation, what is needed is the knowledge that Paul has broken off his engagement with Sylvia, because of her tainted reputation, which is fairly unequivocally established in an intertitle. Hepworth insists on including several quite long scenes involving Sylvia's lover, Dick (a character who is not even in the novel), and so produces a somewhat uneconomic narrative construction. *Kine Weekly* might well have had these scenes in mind when it noted that characters 'do not contribute sufficiently to the action of the plot.'[172] Script-writing manuals were again adamant about such matters: 'characters should be drawn by, and solely by, the action as it progresses. . . . The unnecessary characters in the plot should be dispensed with; for . . . these characters, which are not of vital necessity to the telling of your plot, will retard it.'[173]

The relationship between Helen and George is also treated very uneconomically. For the sake of narrative motivation and dramatic punch, all that needs to be established is that George and Helen have for some time been close friends; the details are irrelevant. To discard them means effectively discarding most of volume one of the novel, but for the film's purposes this would have been no great loss; the full drama of the romance narrative is not really developed until volumes two and three. The script-writing manuals are again insistent on this point: 'the story must begin just at a point when the struggle [which drives the narrative], that no doubt has been brewing for some time, assumes critical proportions, and be then followed rapidly to its close.'[174]

The same lack of classical narrative efficiency is there also in the several intertitles and shots introducing the other members of Helen's family at the start of the film, which tend to imply that these characters will play a central role in the narrative. While in the novel this may be the case, here in the film it is not: they are really quite marginal figures. Yet even by 1916, script-writers were being encouraged to 'not commence by long scenes describing the character of one individual, however important it may be to the story; but [to] strike right into the heart of his play.'[175] In other words, in a somewhat misplaced attempt to remain faithful to the narrative scope of the novel, a rather inefficient narrative has been produced. Too much has been invested in an effort to present, or show, a

---

[171] *Modern Photoplay*, 64. While it is true that Hepworth films had long been noted for their visual qualities, it is also the case that reviewers had for some time felt that Hepworth's sense of story-construction was inadequate. See e.g. *Bioscope*'s reviews of *Drake's Love Story*, 27 Dec. 1913, 673, and *Sheba*, 16 Oct. 1919, 67.

[172] 22 Nov. 1923, 257.   [173] Weston, *Photoplay-Writing*, 48–9.
[174] Lore, *Modern Photoplay*, 61.   [175] Weston, *Photoplay-Writing*, 47.

ready-made story, rather than to retell it for the screen. This same process could, however, be looked at in a more positive light, for it is as if a certain cultural memory of the novel—and of the social milieu which it depicts—is being documented by the film.[176]

Lore's recommendations are once more precise in this respect: the number of characters in a plot—including those adapted from existing literary works—'should be as few as possible, not only in order to make the plot compact and intimate, but also to minimise the spectator's effort in re-membering who's who.'[177] In strictly narrative terms, the attempt to em-brace such a wide set of characters and incidents in *Comin' Thro' The Rye* seems misplaced given the other shifts that have been made from the novel, in terms of mode of narration, sensibility, and so on. As the reviewer in *The Times* commented, 'the producer had to follow the book closely, but a little alteration of the emphasis on various incidents would have made a great difference.'[178] On the other hand, in terms of the heritage project, the Hepworth style of adaptation seems less misplaced, since it allows for a proliferation of images of country houses, lavish interiors, and cos-tumes—but only at the expense of narrative clarity and easy recognition of characters.

The somewhat sprawling, uneconomic nature of the narrative is thus in part the result of trying to do justice to the narrative scope of a three-decker novel within the quite different structure of the feature film, which probably owes more to the short story than the nineteenth-century novel.[179] In fact the first volume of the novel is itself only weakly narrativized, being quite episodic and impressionistic, and concerned as much with atmos-phere and detail as it is with drama. It is this sensibility which the film reproduces in its own narrative structure and process. Initially relatively episodic in its development, it becomes more action-orientated as the plot develops. But since no clear goal is identified at the outset, there is no clear sense of closure, but the accumulation of endings noted earlier. As early as 1916, British script-writing manuals were arguing against the episodic narrative, calling instead for a strongly goal-directed narrative drive, with tight continuity, cohesion, and economy in the American style: 'Character should be bound to character by force of circumstances, each portion of the theme should bear upon the following portion, and the plot should present itself as a whole, not as a series of incidents insecurely linked together by a number of connecting scenes.'[180]

Hepworth was not however attempting to transform the novel into

---

[176] On the concept of cultural memory in literary adaptation, see John Ellis, 'The Literary Adaptation: An Introduction', *Screen*, 23/1 (1982).

[177] Ibid. 47.   [178] 28 Jan. 1924, 8.

[179] See Gill Davies, 'Teaching about Narrative', *Screen Education*, 29 (1978–9).

[180] Weston, *Photoplay-Writing*, 34; cf. also 48, 52, 54–5; and Lore, *Modern Photoplay*, 29.

conventional screen material in the American style. Hollywood studios tend to exploit a novel for its basic story-line and characterization, cutting out unnecessary details, in order to construct a good drama—which is precisely what the script-writing manuals are recommending. British heritage adaptations like *Comin' Thro' The Rye*, on the other hand, in most cases trade on the prestige of the source novel, and attempt to preserve and reproduce it as an authentic copy. The source novel is as much a part of the heritage on display as the material with which it works, hence the *Bioscope*'s allusions to the joys of seeing the 'old story . . . presented in its true environment.'[181]

In the case of *Comin' Thro' The Rye*, as we have seen, the prestige of the source novel is in fact somewhat more ambivalent than this suggests, and its cultural memory must be carefully negotiated, both to attract an audience and to resist the novel's sensationalist aspects. The novel is thus used for its 1920s connotations of a generalized and mythicized 'Victorianness', not for its more specific mid-Victorian feminist value system. It is in this respect an imaginary object, a reconstructed version of the novel, which is on display in the film, not the original.

MODES OF NARRATION

Comin' Thro' The Rye operates with a different set of narrational strategies from classical Hollywood cinema, one which makes the most of the slow cutting rate and the tableau shots, often staged in depth and occasionally reframed to maintain the centring of significant action. Action for the most part is displayed in long shot or medium shot for the camera as recorder. There are two particular aspects of this narration within the tableau format which are worth commenting on in more detail: the use of the frame-edge to reveal or conceal information in a dramatic manner, and the development of two sites of action within the single frame, staged in depth. Both of these imply a particular mode of perception and spectating, which serves to concentrate the eye on the visible, and to downplay the narrative possibilities of off-screen space (the invisible). This of course relates closely to the pictorialist sensibility of the film and the particular aesthetics of display and to-be-looked-at-ness which this sensibility produces.

The development of two scenes of action within a narrative space staged in depth is, in effect, narration by means of montage within the tableau

[181] 22 Nov. 1923, 63. Cf. Brian MacFarlane, 'A Literary Cinema? British Films and British Novels', in Barr (ed.), *All Our Yesterdays*; and Brian MacFarlane, 'Novel into Film—Transfer and Adaptation: The Processes of Transformation', Ph.D. thesis (University of East Anglia, 1987).

frame, rather than alternation between spaces, or the penetration of space through scene dissection. Thus, while the tableau style is an integral part of Hepworth's particular variant of pictorialism, the image is able to have more than a simply decorative pictorial function: montage within the frame creates a narratively dynamic image.[182]

There are a number of examples of this strategy in the film. Near the beginning of the film, for instance, the unknowingly jilted Dick Fellows returns to the drawing-room of his former lover, Sylvia, apparently to propose marriage to her—only to find another lover, Paul, doing the very same thing. The scene is staged in long shot, with Sylvia furthest from the camera, Dick nearest to it, and Paul in between. Both Paul and Sylvia face the camera, while Dick is in three-quarter profile. Unobserved by Paul, but observed by the spectators and by Dick, Sylvia signals from behind Paul for Dick to refrain from revealing his intentions. The drama and dynamics of the scene depend on the spatial (and emotional) relationships between the three characters, and what is visible and therefore what is known to us—but not to all the characters because of the frontality of the staging. It is also significant that, in a rare moment of inter-shot alternation, we have seen Dick outside the house preparing to return to Sylvia, and also the scene in the drawing room for a second or two before Dick enters, so that we know exactly what is happening.

The organization of such scenes seems, from the point of view of the classical system, static, theatrical, and uneconomic, with little or no cutting, markedly frontal staging, and long takes. It is, however, a perfectly acceptable means of narration within the terms of Hepworth's system of staging in depth in a tableau format. A series of alternating shots would undoubtedly have produced a different sense of suspense, but the tableau style still retains a certain dynamism. The tableau shot staged in depth, with two scenes of action, affords in addition a perfectly coherent means of orientating the spectator in relation both to the characters and the space which they occupy and to the drama which eventually brings them together. Although the camera does not penetrate the narrative space or break it down and analyse it, it is not at the same time a passive camera; the camera and image at the centre of the aesthetic produce and work on a dynamic and dramatic narrative space within the tableau format.

Another scene, which takes place mainly in one long take, employs a number of different strategies for narration, including reframing to centre (new) action, staging in two separate action spaces, and using the frame-edge as a means of concealment. It is near the beginning of the film, before Paul and Helen have met. Paul has told Sylvia that he no longer wants to

---

[182] This way of analysing early films draws on ideas developed by Thomas Elsaesser in a lecture on German Expressionist cinema at the University of East Anglia in 1989.

see her because of Dick's suicide, which she provoked; Helen, unobserved, is hiding in the bushes behind them, 'an unwilling eavesdropper' (as an earlier title has described her). Sylvia, in the foreground, falls to the ground, distraught. As she falls, the camera reframes—rather than cuts—to keep her in the centre of the frame; it then tilts up again to reveal Helen still hiding in the bushes in the background. She creeps out of the bushes and towards the camera, until she is practically standing over Sylvia, who is out of frame (concealed). Helen looks down out of shot at Sylvia, and creeps off, apparently undetected by Sylvia simply because she is concealed out of shot. In an earlier shot in the same scene, Helen fails to notice a hammock until the camera pans to reveal it to us at the same time; that which is concealed, out of frame and off-screen, is apparently not visible to characters until it is visible to us.

This moment of revelation, this entering into the frame, and therefore into the visible, indicates a sudden shock to the emotions, a shock which depends precisely on this play as to what is and is not visible. There is then a rather ambiguous sense of off-screen space. On the one hand, off-screen space is clearly implied: the diegesis would be incomprehensible without it. On the other hand, this strategy of playing on the strictly visible does precisely draw our attention to the confines of the frame itself, rather than to the space off.

There are other ways too in which the *mise-en-scène* of *Comin' Thro' The Rye*, apparently so naïvely primitive and irredeemably pictorial, can be seen to have important narrational functions. There is, as we know, a fairly sophisticated naturalistic construction of character through landscape and *mise-en-scène*. The progress of the narrative, and the development of personal relationships, as noted earlier, is charted in part symbolically through the seasonal situation of the rye-field, a point which is underlined by occasional intertitles, and by the fact that the two main lovers, Paul and Helen, meet on numerous occasions at the same spot in the rye-field, initially by coincidence, and later by arrangement. The frequent return to the same romantically imbued spot in the rye-field, and to the same camera set-ups showing virtually identical character placements and movements, builds up important narrational and visual rhymes and echoes, which underline the emotional significance of each visit to the field. On the occasion of their first meeting, Paul walks down the path towards Helen and the camera. When he leaves her for his second, fateful visit to Rome, he repeats the movement in reverse, within the same shot set-up.

After Sylvia has initiated her plot to win back Paul, Helen returns on two occasions to the spot in the rye-field, seen in the same camera set-ups, to attempt to commune with the absent Paul, to attempt to recapture the emotions of her earlier visits. The visual rhyming of the shots invests them with the same emotions for the spectator, a nostalgic sense of romantic loss. Later, Paul joins her in the field, having hurried back from Rome. They part sorrowfully, having established that he has been tricked into marrying Sylvia. Helen is left alone in the familiar spot, and falls to the ground, quite disconsolate. It is a moment of profound loss, which is conveyed as much by the *mise-en-scène*, and its echoes of previous scenes, as it is by the actions of the characters.

The initial impression gained from viewing *Comin' Thro' The Rye* is that Hepworth can have had no interest in the debates about editing which became so vital and energizing during and after the 1920s. Even in his autobiography, published in 1951, he can still be found vigorously defending the use of fades between shots or the use of a tableau shot rather than scene dissection.[183] He also argues vehemently against the use of reverse-field cutting, for instance, evidently with little regard for the psychological involvement of the spectator which such editing enables.[184] On closer investigation, however, it becomes clear that Hepworth does not altogether eschew the classical system of narration through the juxtaposition and alternation of shots in *Comin' Thro' The Rye*. The narrational possibilities of cross-cutting between two sets of characters and spaces, both within a scene, and between scenes, are exploited at various times, and this in itself is a marked diversion from the novel's narrational strategies, since the first person narration of the novel effectively disbars this sort of play with time and space. When one reads Hepworth's statement that 'smoothness in a film is important and should be preserved except when for some special effect a "snap" is preferable' in the context of the sentences which surround it, one can see it as an argument for using more conventional (classical) editing strategies for certain effects, but for the main part working with tableaux and fades to black.[185] A close analysis of *Comin' Thro' The Rye* reveals that some of the more standard (classical) forms of scene dissection and means of psychologizing narrative space are indeed used in the film; these include point-of-view shots and other forms of eyeline matching; medium close shots; alternation, including reverse shots, and so on. These devices are, however, reserved for particularly poignant narrative moments of high emotional drama—the classical system after all is a much more intensely psychological narrative system, more identificatory and engaging for the spectator.

This occasional use of scene dissection should not be seen as merely inconsistent, but as a deliberate mode of stylistic differentiation designed to push home a point.[186] The shorter average shot length at such moments produces a much faster pace and rhythm to the film than in the usual slow tableau style; that is to say, the occasional moments of relatively elaborate

---

[183] *Came The Dawn*, 139.   [184] Ibid. Cf. 136.   [185] Ibid. 139.
[186] This way of analysing apparently aberrant films produced once the classical style was, for all intents and purposes, in place, was suggested to me by a lecture on D. W. Griffith's feature films by Mike Allen, at the University of East Anglia, Norwich, in October 1989.

scene dissection in various ways formally convey to the spectator some of the agitation felt by characters within the diegesis.

Four narrative sequences in particular employ far more scene dissection than the rest of the film, and the effect is to render them more dramatically significant. Each sequence is also more emotionally engaging than those which surround it because of the use of shots and editing structures that imply character psychology. The subjective state of the characters involved is thus constructed more through montage than through acting.

The first sequence deals with the machinations surrounding the character of Dick Fellows, and so effectively sets the main narrative in motion. The sequence opens with Sylvia talking to a friend. She looks off-screen and there is a fade to the reverse shot, matching Sylvia's eyeline to reveal the approach of Dick. Later in the scene, Paul arrives, and there is a series of reverse shots cutting between Dick and Sylvia and the approaching Paul. When Dick eventually leaves, he walks out of one shot and is picked up continuing the same movement and still in medium shot in the next shot.

This scene is thus in part constructed in classical continuity style, with eyelines, actions, and directions matched from shot to shot—except that there is a fade to black between each shot, almost defeating the flow of the continuity, and certainly slowing the scene down considerably. There are, in addition, at least two shot transitions in the scene which do not attempt to preserve continuity at all—the fades in these cases clearly being intended to imply temporal ellipsis, when in the rest of the scene they imply temporal continuity.

After a slightly longer fade, the next scene shows Paul and Sylvia in her drawing-room, with Paul proposing marriage. This scene is intercut with two shots of Dick outside, also resolving to go back to Sylvia and propose marriage. Eventually, all three are again in the same space and shot. The sequence as a whole thus reveals an important system of alternation and scene dissection, with several shots significantly shorter than the ASL for the film, and a much faster cutting rate for the sequence overall.

Two scenes later, we rejoin these same characters the next day at a horse race in which Dick is riding. Again, the scene is built around shot alternations, fading between shots of Paul, Sylvia, and Dick's parents in the grandstand watching the race, and shots of the race itself, including Dick's fatal fall. The cutting rate is again much faster than the film's average, although there is also an idiosyncratic divergence from classical continuity, in that the eyelines are completely mismatched (Barry Salt argues that European film-makers in this period were generally not matching eyelines as consistently as American film-makers[187]).

A second sequence working with more or less classical conventions deals

---

[187] *Film Style*, 210–11.

with the occasion of Paul and Helen's second meeting in the rye-field, on his return from his first business trip to Rome. This sequence is of course central to the initiation and development of their romance, which is the core of the narrative. The drama is initially built up through alternation, including a point-of-view shot, indicating perhaps the emotional disturbance, nervous agitation, and general psychological intensity of this scene for Paul and Helen.

A third sequence, to some extent rhyming with the second sequence, shows Paul's farewell to Helen in the rye-field when leaving for Rome the second time—the trip which enables Sylvia to come between Paul and Helen, and thus precipitate the climactic unhappy ending. When Paul walks off along the path through the rye, he leaves a disconsolate Helen in the foreground. There is a fade to George, her childhood sweetheart, in a contiguous space to the right of Helen, looking off-screen at her. However, rather than cutting to his point of view, we return to the previous shot of Helen on the edge of the field, with Paul in the far distance, and George joining her in the shot. Another fade takes us to a medium shot of Paul, who turns round to the camera, and looks off beyond it, and we gather from his expression that he sees George and Helen together. After an initial moment of hesitation, he apparently thinks nothing of it—but again, there is no cut to his point of view, and the sequence ends here. Editing thus reveals the two spaces either side of the central tableau of Helen and the rye-field, but there is a refusal to complete the sequence in the classical manner by showing the reverse shots from these contiguous spaces—that is, a refusal to include point-of-view shots from the positions of the two men. The significance of this strategy only becomes clear in the fourth sequence to be discussed.

This fourth sequence deals with the discovery and repercussions of a false announcement placed in *The Times* by Sylvia, implying that George and Helen have married. This is probably the most drama-laden sequence of the film, sealing the fates of all involved, and there are various stylistic aspects which should be noted. There are, for instance, several unusually close shots of individuals in the sequence as a whole. Probably more significant, however, is the scene which explains the 'missing' point-of-view shot from the earlier scene when Paul had turned to see Helen and George together as he left for Rome. Paul, now in Rome, has received a letter forged by Sylvia, enclosing the false announcement of a marriage between Helen and George. A first shot shows him reading the letter and newspaper, the next is an insert of the announcement, and the third returns to Paul reading and reacting. There is a fade to a heavily masked vignette shot of George and Helen hugging in the rye-field. The shot is a subjective flashback, the only one in the film, and perfectly matched as a reverse-angle point-of-view shot from his perspective looking back across the field at the couple. This dramatic break with Hepworth's usual style in this film thus clearly establishes a deep, subjectively felt, emotional poignancy to the moment, and fully justifies the refusal to grant the point-of-view shot in the earlier sequence.

The tenor of the sequence is continued in the next scene. Sylvia has arrived in Paul's hotel room suddenly and unannounced, to find him holding a gun to his mouth. She tries to comfort him, but—somewhat confused—he decides to go to a bar. The next shot shows him sitting at a table in the bar, in medium close shot; he looks off-screen. There is fade to a couple 'making love' at the next table; then another fade and we return to Paul, still looking off-screen. He turns and eventually stares out past the camera, evidently resolving to go off and 'make love' to Sylvia. Although to a viewer used to classical continuity, this trio of shots is difficult to read because of the length of the shot transitions via fades to black, this is again a point-of-view set-up, once more establishing the narrative importance of such shots to Hepworth. Here, the point-of-view set-up is used to establish character psychology, to construct a psychological space, at a moment which is rendered significant precisely through this system of shot alternation.

These various psychologizing forms of scene construction are, however, exceptions rather than the rule within *Comin' Thro' The Rye*. They certainly have their effect, but as a whole, the film seems emotionally barren by comparison with contemporary American films. It lacks the prevailing international conventions of psychological realism, and of course some of the major criticisms of the film on its release were to do with the weakness of the construction of character and the reliance on stereotyping. Although there are some medium close shots, eyeline matches, reverse shots, and glance-object shot structures—key devices in establishing character in classical cinema—these are not used regularly, and for the main part, as we have seen, the shots remain in tableau form. We are thus not able to penetrate consistently into a psychological space through scene dissection: an observational stance prevails over an identificatory engagement with characters.

This is reinforced by the occasional highly gestural theatrical acting in the film. On the one hand, a tableau style almost demands semaphoric acting; on the other hand, it is evident from contemporary reviews that by 1923 such acting is too recognizable as acting: 'the tendency of players to overact . . . induces an artificiality which eventually becomes an irritation.'[188] It is uneconomic, therefore lacking in naturalism. The external signs of emotional states are too evident, too familiar as signs, and are no longer easily read for meaning—although in the case of the *Bioscope*, the implication is again that these melodramatics can be excused by the archival

---

[188] *Kine Weekly*, 22 Nov. 1923, 58.

nature of the film; the performers are felt to 'enter thoroughly into the spirit of both the story and the period.'[189]

Given that the modes of narration adopted by Hepworth in this film are seen by many as primitive, it is revealing to look at the marked narrational differences between the film and the novel from which it is adapted. One way of describing the use of tableau shots and the minimal extent to which space is psychologized through montage or point of view is as a narration from outside the narrative space (except at those key moments identified). It is, as such, a narration which is able to observe the heritage on display within those tableaux, and which depends upon an objective visibility rather than a subjective point of view.

The novel on the other hand is narrated in the first person from the point of view of the heroine, Helen—that is, from very much within the narrative space. In the film, we travel with Paul, Sylvia, and George to Rome, for instance, but in the novel we only know what happens there from what Paul reports on his return to Helen. The novel is much broader in its temporal scope, covering the ten years or so from Helen aged 13 to the broken young woman of her early twenties. The whole novel is written, somewhat idiosyncratically, in the present tense, despite this time-span, thus emphasizing further still the experience of the resolutely first person narration. The novel codes the narrative voice very much as experiential and autobiographical, whereas the film codes the narrative voice as distanced and observational. The novel seems much more concerned to explore the nature of female identity within upper-class Victorian patriarchy, within an intensely romantic (even if revisionist) mode. The film, on the other hand, is concerned as much with displaying the heritage qualities of the setting and its inhabitants as it is with the narrative of melodrama.

CONCLUSIONS

Hepworth's film aesthetic is, in effect, camera-based, as befits someone for whom the technology itself held such a fascination. It is primarily an aesthetic of the shot and the image: hence the preponderance of the tableau and the pictorialist details. It is thus in marked contrast to the aesthetic which came to dominate intellectual film culture from the late 1920s, which understood the production of filmic meaning and pleasure to be generated primarily through montage, the combination of one shot with another. It is not surprising then that later critics and historians, from Rotha to Armes, can find little enthusiasm for Hepworth's films subsequent to his pioneer days. It is significant too that the documentary idea was very

[189] 22 Nov. 1923, 58.

much formulated around the aesthetic of montage, and that the documentary-realist tradition came to dominate the debates about British cinema as a national cinema.

In *Comin' Thro' The Rye*, the implication is so often that the tableau shots and the frontality of the staging simply illustrate a pre-existing story, however much the film may actually diverge from the story and its narration in the novel. But the films favoured by a Rotha or a Grierson create their meanings through montage; the film explicitly tells the story, it writes it through the shots.

Hepworth's aesthetic owes something in this respect to the narrational and other representational strategies of what Noël Burch has called the Primitive Mode of Representation of early cinema, and what Tom Gunning has called the Cinema of Attractions.[190] The classical film is concerned with an intensely identificatory, engaging mode of story-telling, in which the narrational form works to integrate the spectating subject into the narrative space. The cinema of attractions, and later films such as *Comin' Thro' The Rye*, on the other hand, are more concerned with showing. For *Comin' Thro' The Rye*, this means in part a pictorial *mise-en-scène* which puts the décor, the sets, the props, and the costumes on display; but it also means that the story, the drama itself, becomes another of the attractions on display. Rather than the camera engaging with the story and integrating the spectator into the narrative space through scene dissection, use of close-ups, eyeline matching, and so on, the camera for the main part stands back and observes the characters and their actions from, as it were, a respectful distance. It is, as I have suggested, as if the pre-given story is being observed by the camera (and by the audience) as it unfolds before it like a stage play.

Gunning links the attractions of early cinema to certain traditions of avant-garde and modernist film-making. Thus, he notes the stress in the writing of Fernand Léger and others on the radical possibilities of cinema as a 'harnessing of visibility'[191]—and as I have noted, there is a sense in which Hepworth's use of the frame-edge and general pictorialist style implies a similar aesthetic of visibility. At the same time, unlike Léger, Hepworth was not averse to drawing on theatrical or literary conventions, or 'imitating the movements of nature' in order to produce a quality film.[192]

---

[190] Noël Burch, *Correction Please, or How We Got Into Pictures* (London, 1979); 'Film's Institutional Mode of Representation and the Soviet Response', *October*, 11 (1979); 'Porter or Ambivalence', *Screen*, 19/4 (1978–9); 'A Primitive Mode of Representation?', in Elsaesser with Barker (eds.), *Early Cinema*; and Tom Gunning, 'The Cinema of Attractions: Early Film, its Spectator, and the Avant-Garde', ibid.; and 'Building an Ending: Vitagraph Films and the Cinema of Narrative Integration', a paper for the festival of Vitagraph screenings at Pordenone, autumn 1987.

[191] 'Cinema of Attractions', 56.

[192] Fernand Léger, 'A Critical Essay on the Plastic Qualities of Abel Gance's Film *The Wheel*', in *Functions of Painting*, Edward Fry (ed.) (New York, 1973), quoted in 'Cinema of Attractions'.

It would be wrong to see *Comin' Thro' The Rye* as entirely or even as primarily constructed according to the principles of the cinema of attractions. The Hepworth of 1923 could never have accepted Méliès's declaration that 'the scenario . . . has no importance, since I use it merely as a pretext for the "stage effects", the "tricks", or for a nicely arranged tableau.'[193] But *Comin' Thro' The Rye* can all the same be seen in part as providing Hepworth with the scope to string out a narrative in front of (and, indeed, inside) various heritage attractions. And the pictorialist composition, framing, and manipulation of the image, along with the content of the image, were indeed all intended to produce a nicely arranged tableau. *Comin' Thro' The Rye* is either torn between two impulses, to display the heritage (the exhibitionism of the cinema of attractions) or to tell the story (the voyeurism of classical narrative cinema); or the two impulses are the same—the story is on display as part of the heritage, as one of the attractions.

Comin' Thro' The Rye is also, of course, not characterized by the recurring look at the camera by the actors, which Gunning sees as another feature of the cinema of attractions. The title-shot of the film does have Helen crawling towards the camera through the rye-field, and miming 'Boo!' direct to camera, however; as such, if we are familiar with the conventions of most feature-length narrative cinema of the period, the shot is somewhat disconcerting. It could be suggested that this shot does not really count, since it has a marginal relationship to the narrative space, preceding as it does the opening of the story proper. But then there are other shots which have a similar marginal relationship to the narrative space, notably the three emblematic shots which preface each section of the film. Such shots can in fact be seen as attractions in the quite specific way that Gunning defines the term. The fact that they are also the shots which are the most rigorously pastoral suggests that the pastoralism of *Comin' Thro' The Rye* can also usefully be understood as one of the attractions of the film, only weakly integrated into the romance narrative proper.

There is then a rather radical sense in which *Comin' Thro' The Rye* can be understood as constructed out of a series of relatively autonomous attractions. This sense of autonomy is reinforced by the lack of classical continuity across the shots and sequences of the film (the slow pacing of the narrative, the use of the fade between shots, the tableau shot itself . . .). But in the end, the narrative must surely hold the spectator in place.

It would be inappropriate, then, to see *Comin' Thro' The Rye* solely in terms of the cinema of attractions, however fruitful Gunning's argument may be. For, as we have seen, the visual story-telling, the narrative rhythm

---

[193] Georges Méliès, 'Importance du scénario', in Georges Sadoul, *Georges Méliès* (Paris, 1961), 118; quoted in Gunning, 'Cinema of Attractions', 64 (Gunning's translation).

and continuity, and the construction of meaning through montage which Kuleshov, Pudovkin, and their contemporaries so admired in the American cinema of the 1910s and early 1920s, are not entirely absent in *Comin' Thro' The Rye*.[194] The difference is rather that these strategies are not aesthetically central, and that there are heavy traces of the cinema of attractions.

The difference of Hepworth's cinema was explicitly taken as a national characteristic by Iris Barry, in the article referred to at the start of this chapter. She argued that

Probably British films will always tend to be what the best popular British novels have been: developments of character, or the capturing of local or historical atmosphere, while the American film will increasingly develop pure action (in which they are supreme because they understand suspense). . .[195]

This seems to me remarkably perceptive, and this distance from a purely action-oriented cinema is something that I shall be exploring in relation to later British films from other genres in subsequent chapters, in terms of the stress on character and atmosphere in and the narrative episodicism of *Sing As We Go* (1934) and films within the documentary-realist tradition. The episodic narrative is already seen as problematic in the context of the prevailing international standards in Weston's 1916 script-writing manual, even though it is not yet an account of what we would now recognize as an entirely classical method and still finds detailed scene dissection unusual. But it may be that the episodic narrative can be seen as a marker of difference for British cinema as a national cinema over against these very standards, set by the foreign powers of American cinema.

Hepworth's thinking about cinema also in various ways prefigures the aesthetic of André Bazin, whose work was so influential on a later generation of art cinema directors, and who also argued carefully against the traditions of montage.[196] Much of what Hepworth says in his autobiography can be understood as an elaboration of the aesthetic centrality of the image: the emphasis on framing, and on the centring of significant action within the frame; on the disposition and gesturing of actors; and on the integrity of the individual shot or scene, for instance. This question of maintaining the integrity of the pro-filmic scene is particularly interesting.

---

[194] See e.g. Ron Levaco (ed. and trans.), *Kuleshov on Film: Writings of Lev Kuleshov* (Berkeley, Calif., 1974); V. I. Pudovkin, *Film Technique* (London, 1933); and Sergei Eisenstein, 'Dickens, Griffith and the Film Today', in *Film Form* (New York, 1949).

[195] 'A National or International Cinema', 29. Cf. her later dismissal of *Comin' Thro' The Rye*, in *Let's Go To The Pictures*, 242–3.

[196] See André Bazin, *What Is Cinema?*, i and ii, essays sel. and trans. by Hugh Gray (London, 1967 and 1972); *Jean Renoir* (New York, 1973); and *Orson Welles: A Critical View* (London, 1978). Note that, although Hepworth's films, including *Comin' Thro' The Rye*, were made some time before Bazin was writing, Hepworth was in fact writing his autobiography around about the same time that Bazin's work was being published in France.

Hepworth suggests at one point, for instance, that, in shooting a heated conversation between two figures, 'even [in sound films] I would rather, for the sake of smoothness, keep them both in view in one longer shot and allow the expressions of both faces to be studied together.'[197] Later, he discusses the shooting of a scene of a dog rounding up sheep: 'this called, I felt, for one long scene [i.e. shot] rather than a number of short ones, for that would not be convincing since the effect could be so easily faked.'[198] For Hepworth, the power of montage is evidently far less interesting or meaningful than maintaining the integrity of space, time, and performance in the pro-filmic event; and as we have seen, Hepworth clearly often staged these events in deep space in such a way as to be narratively meaningful.

Space in *Comin' Thro' The Rye* thus has two important functions. Its first function is as narrative space; this may appear to be a neutral space in which the narrative can simply unfold, observed by the camera; but it is also a space which is at times organized to be narrationally meaningful. It is, in this sense, not a neutral narrative space, but an active narrative space, even a psychological space.

The second function of space in *Comin' Thro' The Rye* is as heritage space, an exhibitionist use of the frame, of framing, and of that which is framed. Heritage space displays objects, dresses, buildings, and so on, as signs of an authentic national past, and calls for an observational, but also an admiring and confirming gaze. Once again, there are two ways of understanding this heritage space, one as an apparently more neutral space, the other with a more active relationship to that which occupies the space. Heritage space is apparently neutral in the same way that the heritage genre is so often a genre of adaptation: the historical period in question— here, the Victorian—is apparently simply illustrated, its authentic signs put on display for the discerning viewer. Adaptation is never in fact a neutral process, however: it is a transformative process. Likewise, it is not so much that the historical period is simply illustrated, rather it is that an imaginary past is constructed at the level of representation. The framing of the heritage space proposes that it is a neutral framing, but in fact it needs to be understood as one which plays an active role in generating the spectacle of the past, which is in this way a modern past. The past, in this system, is not so much a specific place or time, as the imaginative construct of a specific mode of representation, a specific set of production values, a series of familiar signs: it invites its spectator to engage with these images (and sounds) as authentic and desirable, as a solid referent for the national historical imagination.

---

[197] *Came The Dawn*, 139.
[198] Ibid. 151. Low records that the shot ran for 7 minutes (*British Film, 1918–1929*, 116).

This contrast and tension between the neutral and the active is synonymous with the relationship between camera distance and camera engagement. What Charles Barr has described as 'Hepworth's extreme reluctance to interfere with the spatial coordinates of characters and spectators' needs to be contrasted with an, if not equal, at least significant number of occasions when the camera does penetrate space, psychologize it, and reorientate the spectator to it.[199] This ties in with Barr's particularly fruitful suggestion that, while this apparently cold, distanced, observational stance in Hepworth may in some ways be typical of much of British cinema, it is only half the story—except that Barr cannot see the other half of the story with respect to Hepworth.[200]

The documentary-realist tradition can also be seen in terms of this tension between distance and engagement, as I will demonstrate in Chapter 5. The classic documentaries of the 1930s seek to construct a public, observational gaze at their subjects, one which prefers the distanced group shot to the subjective penetration of space; but the closer the documentary idea becomes involved with the narrative feature film, the more it has also to construct the private, interior gaze of psychologically complex individuals, to take on board the practice and the implications of the point-of-view shot.[201]

Barr extends this argument to suggest that all of British cinema can be understood in terms of this public–private tension: 'It as though a social world were distinguished from an imaginative world, with different rules governing them.'[202] In *Comin' Thro' The Rye*, it is this combination of the social world—the display of the national past, the exploration of heritage space—with the imaginative world of the popular melodrama—the delimitation and psychologization of narrative space—which creates the distinctiveness of the text. Except of course that the social world—here, the national past—is itself an imaginary object.

Another way of thinking about this relationship between heritage space and narrative space is in terms of the distinction that Noël Burch has made between the experience of narrative, and what he calls the diegetic effect. Drawing on the work of Christian Metz, Burch defines diegesis as the complete spatio-temporal world implied by a representation.[203] A strongly narrativized film will have a diegetic effect which exceeds those spatial and temporal instances strictly required for the narrative to make sense; but

---

[199] 'Introduction', *All Our Yesterdays*, 23.   [200] Ibid. 24.

[201] Cf. Andrew Higson, ' "Britain's Outstanding Contribution to the Film": The Documentary-Realist Tradition', in Barr (ed.), *All Our Yesterdays*.

[202] 'Introduction', *All Our Yesterdays*, 24.

[203] See Noël Burch, 'Narrative/Diegesis: Thresholds, Limits', *Screen*, 23/2 (1982); and Christian Metz, *Film Language* (New York, 1974), esp. 3–15, 98.

the narrative process, the process of centring the spectator's attention, attempts to regulate and restrict the production of the diegetic effect, to limit it to that which is needed. In this sense, diegesis is synonymous with narrative space.

But with *Comin' Thro' The Rye*, in addition to the attractions of the romantic melodrama, there are also the attractions of the heritage on display (the framing and the framed, the heritage space). The comments of contemporary reviewers, as well as the existence of the 1916 modern-dress version of *Comin' Thro' The Rye*, suggest that the period setting is not necessary for the playing out of the tragic romance: the period setting, as spectacle (the spectacle of locations, interiors, décor, and costume), exceeds that which is narratively necessary. What is produced is the diegesis of history, or at least of 'Victorianness'; what is imposed upon the imagination of the spectator is the exotic spectacle of the national past, the English heritage. The tension of *Comin' Thro' The Rye* is then also the tension between, not simply spectacle and narrative, but diegesis and narrative, as two relatively distinct ways of organizing the perspective of the spectator in relation to the film.

What I have tried to do in this chapter is to shift away from those readings of *Comin' Thro' The Rye* which regard it as retarded and theatrical, and to move towards explaining what are aberrations within the classical film system as in fact constitutive of an almost perfectly coherent and consistent alternative system. Hepworth implies that this is a system which speaks in an English idiom, and which enables the production of important and worthwhile pictures, which might raise the standard and improve the quality of British cinema as a whole. As a system, it is a coherent enough means of orientating the spectator in relation to the hermeneutics of the film, whether the hermeneutics of the narrative or the heritage. Each aspect of this admittedly idiosyncratic system works quite adequately in conjunction with each other aspect of the film to achieve this orientation.

Comin' Thro' The Rye should thus be seen as a historically specific response to the increasing domination of British cinema by American films and American standards. This specificity consists of the particular place the film has within a directorial œuvre and a generic tradition, and the promotion which it was given as part of an industry-wide effort to improve the interests of the British production sector. Its place within a rapidly changing film culture is also of course historically specific: as an attempt to produce a tasteful quality film for a middle-class audience, it is a precursor to later versions of art cinema and the heritage film; but in the context of the emergent intellectual film culture, it is of little interest— hence its ambivalent reception. As will become evident in the chapters which follow, *Comin' Thro' The Rye* also shares certain features with popular music-hall comedies like *Sing As We Go* and films from the documentary-realist tradition (the subjects of the next two chapters), such that the film, for all its idiosyncrasies, may be seen as constitutive of a national style.

4

Economic Competition and Product Differentiation—Popular Cinema and the British Film Industry in the Mid-1930s: Sing As We Go and Evergreen

INTRODUCTION: TWO FILMS OF 1934

For twenty five years the American film trade has monopolised the entertainment of the world. The American film has gone everywhere, and influenced fashion, trade and thought in every country. 'Motion pictures' have been synonymous with 'American motion pictures', and we have been perfectly prepared to accept the American idea without questioning as the inevitable material of screen entertainment.

C. A. Lejeune, film critic for the *Observer*, 1933.[1]

Because of the established and irrefutable superiority of the American product, and the business technique created around that product, it is understandable how and why the Hollywood impress has made itself felt wherever the motion picture finds an outlet.

Maurice Kann, editor of the American trade paper, *Motion Picture Daily*, 1938.[2]

Sing As We Go and *Evergreen*, both produced in 1934, can in many ways be seen as pivotal films for that particular moment in British cinema history. *Sing As We Go* was the product of an independent; *Evergreen* was made at the studios of one of the majors. They were both musical comedies, and they were both major box-office successes in Britain. Significantly, *Evergreen* also did very well in the United States, thereby underlining one of the major differences between the two films: one is specifically designed for export to the prime American market, while the other is (quite knowingly) inexportable. The two films can thus be seen as representatives of the two relatively distinct production policies outlined earlier: the larger company takes the route of direct competition with Hollywood, tackling it on its own terms, and in its own territories; the smaller outfit

---

[1] 'Films of the Quarter', *Sight and Sound*, 2/5 (1933), 21.
[2] 'Hollywood and Britain—Three Thousand Miles Apart', in Charles Davy (ed.), *Footnotes to the Film* (London, 1938), 185.

explores the possibilities of product differentiation and market specialization. Thus the policies involve both economic and cultural criteria, and need to be understood as strategies adopted by different sectors of the rapidly expanding British film industry in a bid to create a national popular cinema that could compete successfully with, or at least coexist profitably alongside, the films of the American majors. A detailed analysis of the production, distribution, and exhibition contexts of the two films, combined with a consideration of their respective styles and thematic concerns, will enable a more thorough appraisal of these two strategies.[3]

The two films clearly share a great deal: as with the vast majority of commercial films, they both bid for a share of the market by playing on already well-established star-images, and by working with easily recognizable generic conventions. It is the differences between the two films, however, and not the similarities, that are most telling for the purposes of this case-study. *Sing As We Go* was produced by Associated Talking Pictures (ATP), one of the larger and more successful independent production companies of the period. Along with the other films produced by ATP in the mid-1930s, it was intended for the domestic and Empire markets. *Evergreen* was made at the Shepherd's Bush Studios of the altogether much larger and better resourced Gaumont-British (G-B), one of the two British vertically integrated corporations established in the wake of the quota regulations of 1927 (ATP, by contrast, had only a small and in 1934 embryonic distribution arm, and no tied cinemas). In the mid-1930s, G-B were making films with what they hoped would be the necessary production values to enable them to succeed in the American market as well as the domestic and Empire markets. *Evergreen* was made at perhaps the highpoint of this optimistic, internationalist phase in G-B's history—by the end of 1936, their ambitious production programme and their bid for a sizeable share of the American market was in tatters.

The two films thus involve different economies of scale and cultural aspirations, and are aimed at different, if overlapping, markets. They also relate very differently to the dominant formal paradigm of classical Hollywood cinema, and draw on relatively distinct, class-specific, and to some extent indigenous popular cultural traditions for their respective form and shape, their brands of comedy and song, and their modes of performance and address; in other words, they appeal to their audiences in often markedly different ways. Both films seek to establish themselves as popular cultural artefacts, but they also aspire to the status of quality productions. They both, for instance, make occasional nods towards European art cinema and the intellectual film culture of the period: *Sing As We Go* has

---

[3] See Appendix for plot synopses and credits for the two films. This chapter began life as a paper for the conference on Popular European Cinema, Warwick University, Sept. 1989.

several montage sequences derivative of the Soviet avant-garde; and *Evergreen* has a production number which appears to be a pastiche of *Metropolis*. *Sing As We Go* also trades on the cultural status of J. B. Priestley, who was commissioned to write the screenplay, while *Evergreen* tries to achieve the professional standards of the quality Hollywood film.

Both films are star vehicles for the biggest British female stars of the 1930s, Gracie Fields and Jessie Matthews, who had both made their names on the stage as popular musical performers before entering films.[4] They come from very different national cultural traditions with different cultural statuses and different class-specific national audiences, however. *Sing As We Go* uses a loose episodic narrative to provide a framework for the songs and broad comedy that Fields was known for in the mainly working-class and lower-middle-class entertainment forms of variety and music-hall. *Evergreen*, on the other hand, showcases the persona of Matthews, forged in the more respectable, middle-class musical-comedy/revue of London's West End, a tradition more easily accommodated by the narrative form of the classical film than the short 'turns' of the variety act ever could be. For where the classical film works with an extended, causally developed, goal-seeking narrative form, music-hall of course depended on a series of short, relatively self-contained novelties, acts, or turns, primarily comic and/or musical—and it is this latter shape as much as the former that organizes the viewing experience of *Sing As We Go*.

Andy Medhurst has suggested that Gracie Fields's films of this period raise 'the central problematic of the 1930s variety star film—how to accommodate such performers within existing genres.'[5] As he notes, these films and those of other British variety performers in this period 'were never particularly trying to be seamless narrative texts; they were unashamed vehicles for the talents of their stars',[6] and *Sing As We Go* is indeed little more than a narrative excuse for a collage of songs, comic gags, and visual spectacle. Like *Comin' Thro' The Rye*, it works very much within the conventions of the cinema of attractions, even though the two films deal with such different subject-matter and class milieux, and on the face of it bid for such different cultural statuses. The attractions of *Sing*

---

[4] Various contemporary polls and surveys provide evidence of their popularity; see e.g. *The Bernstein Questionnaires* (audience polls carried out in 1928, 1932, 1934, 1937, and 1946–7, in the Granada chain of cinemas; the results of these questionnaires are available at the British Film Institute Library, London); *Film Weekly*, 5 Apr. 1935, 11; *World Film News*, 1/11, Feb. 1937, 29; *Kine Weekly*, 14 Jan. 1937, 40*a*, 13 Jan. 1938, 49, and 12 Jan. 1939, 61; and the comments of respondents to a Mass Observation survey in March 1938 cited in Jeffrey Richards and Dorothy Sheridan (eds.), *Mass Observation at the Movies* (London, 1987), 63, 73, 79, 84, 93, 107 (Matthews), and 41, 49, 59, 73, 83, 109 (Fields).

[5] 'Music Hall and British Cinema', in Charles Barr (ed.), *All Our Yesterdays: 90 Years of British Cinema* (London, 1986), 174.

[6] Ibid. 175.

STILLS 8 and 9. Publicity photos of Britain's two biggest film stars of the 1930s, Gracie Fields (*left*) and Jessie Matthews (*right*).

As We Go are only loosely integrated into an episodic narrative with an under-motivated causality. Although this anti-classicism is partly the result of the film's construction around Fields's stage persona, it also owes something to the fact that the film was directed by Basil Dean, one of the country's leading theatre producers, and very much a man of the theatre, whose self-confessed aim was to transfer quality plays to the screen.[7] Although *Sing As We Go* was actually made from an original screenplay, the frontality of the staging, and the lack of scene dissection or reverse-field camera placements give away Dean's theatre background. On the other hand, there are several montage sequences in the film which are full of optical effects and rapid juxtapositions which are much more specifically cinematic in feel.

Evergreen came out of a very different production context. It was directed by Victor Saville, a consummate industry professional who had been in the film business since the 1910s, producing his first feature film in 1923, the well-received *Woman to Woman*, discussed briefly in the previous chapter. The co-producer of that film was Michael Balcon, who, by 1934, was Head of Production at G-B. As a director, Saville had a well-developed classical style, and was very popular with audiences of the mid-1930s.[8] It is also worth noting that, by the late 1930s, Saville was working very successfully at MGM, whereas Dean had returned full-time to the theatre world. *Evergreen* is a relatively lavish, big-budget musical, with several ostentatiously big production numbers ('the production is on a lavish scale hitherto rare in British musicals', commented *Film Weekly*).[9] It is a polished studio film, which quite successfully emulates contemporary Hollywood musicals in terms of subject-matter and theme, energy, staging, and art direction. In a verdict very similar to one delivered by the same trade paper on *Woman to Woman* a decade earlier, *Variety* described it as 'the first musical from across the sea that comes this close to competing successfully with the best efforts of Hollywood.'[10] It has all the narrative integration, linearity, and fluidity of the classical film, a modernist, specifically cinematic (as opposed to theatrical) play with time, and a classical construction of cinematic space as greater, and more spectacular, than theatrical space, despite its origins in a successful West End show. This was not an adaptation in the Dean or Hepworth mould, attempting

---

[7] Thorold Dickinson, the film's editor, later recalled Dean as 'a theatre man, he made canned plays.' David Badder and Bob Baker, 'Thorold Dickinson', an interview in *Film Dope*, 11 (1977), 5.

[8] See *The Bernstein Questionnaires* for 1934 and 1937; and Cyril Rollins and Robert Wareing, *Victor Saville* (National Film Archive booklet, n.d.).

[9] 7 Sept. 1934, 36.

[10] 15 Jan. 1935, repr. in *Variety's Film Reviews, 1934–1937*, v (New York, 1983), no p. nos. American reviews of *Woman to Woman* are discussed in ch. 3, above.

above all else to be faithful to the source text, but one that began from a well-constructed, cinematic screenplay in the Hollywood mould, with new songs, routines, and production numbers being added.[11] In other words, the style and form are conceived in international terms.

The two films are different not only in terms of the cultural background of the two stars or the form of the films but also in terms of their subject-matter and sensibility. Fields's adventures in *Sing As We Go* are framed by a plot concerning unemployment and the depression in the Lancashire cotton industry, although most of the film is set in the popular working-class holiday resort of Blackpool, thereby dealing as much with working-class leisure as it does with work or its absence. The attempt to represent a specific regional locality, reinforced by the pervasiveness of regional and class-specific accents, also lends the film a marked resonance in terms of debates about national cinema. *Evergreen*, on the other hand, constructs a completely different world of work and leisure in the high-class showbusiness world of London's West End, with some wonderfully lux-urious settings, and a few aristocrats thrown in for good measure. But although this setting and milieu is just as specific and circumscribed as that of *Sing As We Go* (or indeed of *Comin' Thro' The Rye*), it is not in any way a local or peripheral culture, in terms of the dominant nationalist ideologies. On the contrary, it aspires to a certain universality—which was of course precisely the intention of the producers, with their eyes firmly on the American market.

These differences in milieu and sensibility can be seen as characteristic of most of the films of the two stars, as both Jeffrey Richards and William K. Everson have argued. Richards, for instance, suggests, in what is perhaps a rather too easy, but certainly persuasive socio-historical analysis, that 'while Gracie maintained her popularity by being the people's heroine with her roots in the community, Jessie gained hers by becoming the embodiment of an essentially individualist middle-class success ethic.'[12] For many in the 1930s, Fields was evidently something of a national institu-tion. The critic Caroline Lejeune, for instance, reckoned she was 'as much a part of English life as tea and football pools, our green-hedged fields and the Nelson column.'[13] At the same time, the more up-market commenta-tors like Lejeune had problems with what they saw as the escapism of Fields's films: 'we have an industrial north that is bigger than Gracie Fields

---

[11] See Michael Balcon, *A Lifetime in Films* (London, 1969), 87.

[12] *The Age of the Dream Palace* (London, 1984), 224; cf. the exhibitors' survey reported in *World Film News*, Feb. 1937, 6–7; and William K. Everson, 'Jessie Matthews', *Films In Review*, 26/10 (1975).

[13] Quoted, but with no source given, in Joan Moules, *Our Gracie: The Life of Dame Gracie Fields* (London, 1983), 61.

running round a Blackpool fun fair,' argued Lejeune,[14] while one of her colleagues suggested that

If we could only see her in a real piece of life, full of strong emotion and of humour that has a human basis, she would be tremendous. Gracie is the most real person that we have met. She can give us the films of the people which have been so conspicuously absent from the British schedules, and which have been the foundation of the great film industry in America. She has never ceased to be one of the people, and as one of the people she could make us laugh and cry.[15]

This is a very interesting commentary. While it celebrates Fields as the authentic representative of the people, it also tries to distance itself from popular culture, calling for realism rather than comedy, and by implication for a responsible cinema rather than the irresponsibilities of mere entertainment. It is a discourse which eventually finds itself more at home with the types of films discussed in the next chapter than with popular comedy —but it is significant all the same that the discourse can be invoked with Fields in mind, thereby establishing important links with the documentary-realist tradition.

In fact, Fields did eventually appear in some straight roles in her Hollywood films in the early 1940s for Twentieth Century Fox, but at the time of *Sing As We Go*, a move to Hollywood was almost unthinkable, given the national specificities and therefore audience appeal of the films she was then making. *Sing As We Go* does supersede her earlier films at ATP as far as the quality of the screenplay and the production values of the film are concerned, but it has not yet developed into an attempt to contain Fields's persona and cultural energy within the parameters of a more classically constructed narrative film, as was the case with her later films at ATP and Fox.

In the rest of this chapter I will explore these various issues in more detail and assess the implications of the strategies which the two films represent for the question of national cinema in Britain. I will begin by outlining something of the general state of British cinema, the film industry, and the relationships between genre and popular culture in the mid-1930s. Within this broad context, I will look more closely at the industrial strategies of ATP and G-B, and in particular their organization as companies, the policy statements of their main executives, and the various ways in which those policies were put into practice. The cultural practices

---

[14] In a review of *Jew Süss*, *Observer*, 7 Oct. 1935 (this and most subsequent references to film reviews from daily and weekly British newspapers and magazines, excluding specialist publications such as the trade press, have been drawn from cuttings kept on microfiche at the British Film Institute Library, London; these cuttings do not provide page numbers).

[15] Eric L. Wigham, 'You Fans—Why not Give Gracie a Chance', *Manchester Evening News*; quoted, with no further details given, in Moules, *Our Gracie*, 59.

of ATP and G-B enabled them to mobilize production values in their films which were designed to appeal to the expectations of different sectors of the national and international audience. In this context, I will look at the question of star-image, but also the differential distribution of particular visual, aural, and narrative attractions across the two films. This will involve examining the aesthetic form of the two films in some detail, and especially the relationship that each has to the international standards of classical Hollywood cinema.

THE BRITISH FILM INDUSTRY AND ITS GENRES IN THE MID-1930S

One of the most important conditions of British cinema in the mid-1930s was the fact of state intervention in the form of the protectionist quota, introduced in 1927 to regulate the percentage—but, significantly, not the quality—of British films in circulation. A second important condition was the relatively recent transition to sound films, which had required huge capital expenditure. A third condition was the effects of the world-wide economic depression. Where the introduction of the quota had provided an artificial safety-net, particularly for small production companies, the effect of the latter two conditions had been to some extent to reverse this tendency, rendering film production both too expensive and too risky for the smallest ventures. These same conditions had enabled the strongest players in the field—the two British vertically integrated combines—to consolidate their position even further. A fourth set of conditions to take into account were those that prevailed in the United States. The American majors had had to take on board new financial arrangements as a result of their own transition to sound and the expansion of the exhibition sector in the 1920s. Coupled with the effects of the depression, this meant that, while the American companies did not really lose any significant ground in Britain in this period, neither were they able further to monopolize the distribution market.

Cinema-going in Britain in 1934 was a hugely popular and inexpensive form of entertainment, with the highest measured per capita attendance in the world.[16] American films still dominated the popular imagination and

---

[16] About 18.5 m. admissions per week, 80 per cent of them paying 1 shilling or less, for a population of about 45.5 m. See Simon Rowson, 'A Statistical Survey of the Cinema Industry in Great Britain in 1934', *Journal of the Royal Statistical Society*, 99/1 (1936); and H. E. Browning and A. A. Sorrell, 'Cinemas and Cinema-Going in Great Britain', *Journal of the Royal Statistical Society*, 117/2 (1954); see also Tony Aldgate, 'Comedy, Class and Containment: The British Domestic Cinema of the 1930s', in James Curran and Vincent Porter (eds.), *British Cinema History* (London, 1983); *The Bernstein Questionnaire* of 1934; and Rowson's memorandum to the Moyne Committee, in Board of Trade, *Minutes of Evidence taken before the Departmental Committee on Cinematograph Films*, ii (London, 1936), paras. 11–13, p. 110.

accounted for about three-quarters of the films shown during the year, but the remaining quarter for British films represented a significant advance over the previous decade's figures and was about 10 per cent above the quota of British films which the law required to be exhibited.[17] Although a proportion of this 10 per cent would have been 'quota quickies', the trade generally felt that the worst excesses of low-budget production designed to exploit the quota laws were behind them and that British film production was generally in good health.[18] In addition, the total number of British feature films registered was substantially up.[19]

It is very difficult to obtain accurate box-office figures for individual films in this period, and one must rely on various more or less partial surveys of popularity, and the occasional indication in passing of the box-office success of individual films. John Maxwell, head of ABPC, the other major, was reported in 1935 as claiming that only about ten films a year grossed £100,000 in the UK, and of these, six were generally American.[20] From 1937 *Kine Weekly* published an annual break-down of the previous year's box-office successes. The first survey—of 1936—is fairly general, based on an analysis of the returns of eight circuits, including ABC and G-B's houses, but it does tend to confirm the general picture. Of the top twelve money-makers, only three were British. One of them was René Clair's *The Ghost Goes West* (1935), another the Gracie Fields vehicle, ATP's *Queen of Hearts* (1936), and the third was G-B's Hitchcock thriller *Secret Agent* (1936). Two Jessie Matthews films were runners-up, *First a Girl* (1935) and *It's Love Again* (1936).[21]

BIP (re-named ABPC in 1933) and G-B, the two companies that had built up vertically integrated operations in the wake of the 1927 Quota Act, were by this time well established, although, in the light of events later in the decade, G-B were clearly over-extending themselves. Most of the 'quota quickie' companies set up to exploit the quota regulations had been weeded out, and the traumas of converting the industry to sound had been weathered. Alexander Korda's British-made *The Private Life of Henry*

---

[17] See Rowson, 'Statistical Survey'; F. D. Klingender and Stuart Legg, *Money Behind The Screens* (London, 1937), 13; and *Kinematograph Yearbook, 1935* (London, 1935), 12.

[18] An editorial of a special *British Film Supplement* in the popular magazine, *Picturegoer*, for instance, claimed that exhibitors 'no longer apologise to their patrons for the home product' (5 May 1934, 3). While this was partly no doubt an attempt precisely to raise the profile of British films with domestic audiences, the sentiment is expressed more generally in trade papers of the period. 'Quota quickies' were cheaply and quickly made films designed to get round the quota regulations; of course they also did the already poor reputation of British films a great deal of harm.

[19] See Margaret Dickinson and Sarah Street, *Cinema and State: The Film Industry and the British Government* (London, 1985), 64; Rowson, 'Statistical Survey'; Klingender and Legg, *Money*, 13.

[20] *Kine Weekly*, 5 Sept. 1935, 19.

[21] 'Relative Popularity of the Year's 12 Best, by Public Viewer no. 1', *Kine Weekly*, 14 Jan. 1937, 40*a*.

8th (1933) had been a huge success at the American box-office at the end of the previous year with a prestigious run at New York's Radio City Music Hall, enabling it to become the biggest grossing British film in America to date. Korda had, in the words of the critic Caroline Lejeune, 'done more than any other producer in the country to put British films on the map of the world',[22] and the *Kine Yearbook* review of 1933 claimed that *The Private Life of Henry 8th* 'has been given such a reception wherever it has been seen—from Leicester Square to Hollywood—that the words "British production" have acquired a new and highly complimentary significance.'[23]

Other British films from Herbert Wilcox, Korda, and G-B among others had also been successful at the box-office in the USA prior to 1934.[24] The success of these films, but particularly of *The Private Life of Henry 8th*, encouraged many others—including G-B—to ignore the unique conditions that enabled this breakthrough and themselves bid, at great expense, for a place in the American market. The American distributors were unlikely in general to relax their hold on the American market and allow competitors to come in to the field. However, certain prevailing circumstances meant that there were temporary spaces for new product from other than the usual sources in the early 1930s. The financial implications of the Wall Street Crash, coming on top of the transition to sound, had required the American studios to cut back on production, at a time when exhibitors had introduced the double bill in a bid to win back audiences. Hence there was a temporary shortage of American films, and one of the majors, United Artists, looked to Britain to fill up the schedule. *The Private Life of Henry 8th* was thus the first film to be financed and distributed by United Artists for London Films, under much more favourable financial arrangements than previous Anglo-American deals.[25]

As Kristin Thompson has pointed out, the Depression also meant a general decline in American economic exports, including film exports, from 1929 to 1934.[26] This implies that the lower number of American films and the higher number of British films in the British market in this period may have had as much to do with the effects of the American Depression and the temporary respite in American market control as with the quota regulations

[22] *British Film Supplement*, in *Picturegoer*, 5 May 1934, 4.

[23] S. G. Rayment, 'Lessons for 1934 in the Story of 1933', *Kinematograph Yearbook, 1934*, (London, 1934), 11.

[24] See e.g. Herbert Wilcox, 'The Best is Yet to Come', *British Film Supplement*, in *Picturegoer*, 5 May 1934, 14.

[25] See Simon Hartog, 'State Protection of a Beleaguered Industry', in Curran and Porter (eds.), *British Cinema History*, 67; Kann, 'Hollywood and Britain', 191–2; Dickinson and Street, *Cinema and State*, 76–7.

[26] *Exporting Entertainment: America in the World Film Market, 1907–34* (London, 1985), 166–7.

or the rationalization and increasing vertical integration of the industry. Together, these factors enabled the British production industry to re-establish itself after the disasters of the mid-1920s, and there was a boom in production from 1933 to 1936. Against this have to be offset the rising costs of production, the particular sources and methods of funding the boom through City insurance companies, and the fact that by 1934 the Hollywood film industry was recovering from the effects of the Depression. This suggests in retrospect that the rapid expansion of the British film industry in the first half of the 1930s was over-ambitious, leading to the collapse of the production sector in the years between 1936 and 1938.

The major British exhibitors were, in any case, less optimistic about the qualities and box-office potential of the British film, and were still expressing anxiety over the quota regulations.[27] But the situation prevailing in 1934 generated increasing self-confidence on the part of the production sector of the industry and encouraged much speculation and debate in the trade papers and the press about the revival of not just a film industry, but a national cinema in Britain. There was, however, no consensus as to how this national cinema could best be reproduced. ATP, of course, was of the view that films should be thoroughly British, and that producers should concern themselves only with exploiting those corners of the protected national market and the Dominions that had not already been systematically colonized by Hollywood. In defending this policy in 1938, Basil Dean at the same time attacked the other more internationalist policy adopted by G-B, amongst others:

The film that seeks to become international must first be convincingly national. Deep in the life of every nation lies the inexhaustible material with which that nation's films should be written and acted. With each nation's film activity strong and resurgent in its own right we can march confidently upon the road to the future. When that day of real advance comes, let us hope we shall have turned our backs for ever upon a condition of overgrown and domineering internationalism that sooner or later must die of its own redundancy.[28]

By the time that these conservatively nationalist comments had appeared in print, with their intimations of the timelessness and invariance of authentic culture, G-B and most of their competitors had indeed drawn back from the policy of internationalism. In the mid-1930s, however, they had argued that it was essential for producers seeking a higher profit margin to establish links with American distributors, imitate Hollywood films, and operate in the international arena, especially the American market. Many

---

[27] See, for instance, the series of questions asked on behalf of the Cinema Exhibitors Association in the House of Commons on this matter in June 1935, Hansard, *Parliamentary Papers*, 17 June 1935, p. 303, col. 14. Also of course the debate around the Moyne Committee report, and the run-up to the renewal of quota regulations in 1938.
[28] 'The Future of the Stage and Screen', in Charles Davy (ed.), *Footnotes*, 183–4.

trade commentators concurred with the *Kine Yearbook's* review of the year in America in 1935 when it suggested that 'right now the English production has a much better than ever chance of scoring a popular success in America.'[29] As Michael Balcon, head of production at G-B, explained to the readers of the *Evening News* in 1936,

Until recently . . . the market for British films has been strictly limited. Things are better now, but the popularity of British films is still largely centred in the home country; and that is a problem we British producers have always to bear in mind. We can get back quite a good proportion of our outlay from the cinemas of Great Britain and the Empire; but if we spend really considerable sums of money on a production and wish to get that back 'with plenty to spare' (as of course we do!) we must look further afield for larger returns on our outlay.[30]

The unabashed way in which the profit motive is here stated reveals the extent to which it is economic gain which motivates cultural practice within a large corporation like G-B. But only a year later, severe financial loss had given the 'problem' which Balcon cites a different complexion. By this time, even *Kine Weekly* had changed its tune: 'Few now can deny that the panacea for our Industry's ills lies in economy, and concentration on our home markets.'[31] The assault that G-B had launched on the American market was perhaps doomed to long-term failure. In effect, as a strategy, it involved the paradoxical situation of competing with the American majors as producers, yet attempting to collaborate with them as distributors and exhibitors in both the British and American markets. Either way, the argument was that films must be first and foremost good entertainment if they were to do well at the box-office. The exhibitor Sidney Bernstein, for instance, argued that 'I have always been anxious to show British films, but . . . as a showman bearing the responsibility of entertaining the public I know that patriotism is not enough.'[32]

Even though *Sing As We Go* and *Evergreen* are the results of different policies, they both succeeded in entertaining British audiences—but they did so according to relatively distinct ideas of what constitutes good entertainment—bearing in mind of course that they are both genre films and star vehicles. But there was no avoiding the fact that 'good entertainment' in the international market invariably meant 'in the Hollywood style' and therefore *Evergreen*, not *Sing As We Go*. Although to some extent these policies could and did coexist in the British film industry of the mid-1930s, there is also a certain conflict of interests at stake. Tighter quota regulations

---

[29] Tom Kennedy, 'The Year in America', *Kine Yearbook*, 1935, 19.
[30] 'Putting the Real Britain on the Screen', 1 Oct. 1936, 11.
[31] 'R. H. B.', 'After Ten Years—The Lessons of the Quota Act', editorial in *Kine Weekly*, 14 Jan. 1937, 4.
[32] 'You, the Public, have the Last Word', *British Film Supplement*, in *Picturegoer*, 5 May 1934, 10.

as to the number of foreign, and especially American films that could be screened in Britain were, for instance, much more strongly favoured by those pursuing the domestic policy, and there was some disagreement between Dean and the representatives of G-B during the negotiations over the renewal of the Cinematograph Act in 1937.[33]

The success of *Evergreen* and *Sing As We Go* was in part due to their generic nature, and the genres inhabited by the two films were among the most prolific and popular genres in Britain in the mid-1930s. In terms of the number of films produced, the key genres are melodrama, comedy, musicals, and drama (especially crime and spy thrillers)[34]—although a full account of the period would have to take into account the various historical costume pictures and Empire epics as well. As in Hollywood, musicals were often adaptations of successful stage plays (*Evergreen* comes into this category), but there was also a broad range of musical types, or subgenres, drawing variously on music-hall, variety, revue, and musical-comedy. Jessie Matthews was just one of several established stage stars who went on to develop careers in films—others included Jack Buchanan and Matthews's husband Sonnie Hale. Likewise, Gracie Fields was not the only music-hall star of the 1930s to appear in films designed to exploit their star-images and performance styles. This type of film-making was, as Tom Ryall suggests, one of the more vigorous if critically shunned cinematic strands of the period, 'rooted firmly in British popular culture' and 'crystalliz[ing] into a distinctive category of British film production in the 1930s.'[35]

The idea of a specifically British musical genre, distinct from the American musical, is implicit in an article early in 1934 in *Kine Weekly*. The article noted the current cycle of musicals on release and in production, and expressed concern that British producers should not try to 'imitate' spectacular Hollywood musicals like *Footlight Parade* (1933). 'A musical cycle is also in full swing in this country but it is more of an effort to combine narrative with music than to put over big spectacular routines.'[36] These are interesting comments in the light of the critical reception for *Evergreen* later in the same year, since the film was generally felt to work successfully with Hollywood's musical conventions.

The development of the comedy genre in Britain in this period was seen at the time as an even more nationally specific generic variation. Sidney Bernstein argued in *Picturegoer*'s *British Film Supplement* that comedy was the only British genre that did consistently well at the box-office:

---

[33] See Rachael Low, *Film-making in 1930s Britain* (London, 1985), 40–2.
[34] See Linda Wood, *British Films, 1927–1939* (London, 1986), 115–16; and Tom Ryall, *Alfred Hitchcock and the British Cinema* (London, 1986), 71–2.
[35] *Alfred Hitchcock*, 83, 74; see also Medhurst, 'Music Hall'.
[36] *Kine Weekly*, 26 July 1934, 37.

Comedy pictures like *Turkey Time, Jack Ahoy, Aunt Sally*, and even Gracie Fields epics have made Hollywood reflect and consider and have definitely kept from the American companies millions in revenue that would have accrued to them from their own productions. . . . It is in the realm of comedy that British films achieve their greatest success.[37]

American comedies, on the other hand, were he felt too much 'designed to appeal to the youth of their big cities'.[38] Bernstein adds that it is only in the comedy genre that the British film industry can claim to have major stars in the likes of Ralph Lynn, Tom Walls, Jack Hulbert, Cicely Courtneidge, and Gracie Fields. In a similar vein, a trade review of an earlier Gracie Fields film suggested that 'the picture is *essentially English* in its fun,'[39] while the *Film Lovers Annual* of 1933–4 noted that such performers

present a type of comedy which is *essentially English* and appeals strongly to the English mentality. . . . [The] appeal [of American comedies] is not, I venture to think, nearly so strong. . . . How many American stars nowadays can prove so powerful a magnet to the box-office as our own Jack Hulbert or Cicely Courtneidge? I am not saying their productions reach the same level of technical excellence as some of their foreign rivals, but I do believe they are giving you, the public, what it wants.[40]

The wise-cracking American comedy evidently did not go down well in most British cinemas. In an article noting the popularity of Jack Buchanan in Britain, *Variety* suggested that

the natives . . . have much less liking for sophisticated smartness than is generally realised. Further, the recent tendency in American films to relegate straight comedy in favor of non-stop wise-cracking by featured players finds little favor in the English, who are at heart lovers of essentially simple films.[41]

The comedy of performers from the music-halls like Gracie Fields had required the development of sound in order to enable its incorporation into films, and it is the strength of the comedy genre at this time which adds fuel to the argument that it was as much the transition to sound as the introduction of quota regulations which enabled the British film revival of the early and mid-1930s. The other side of this, however, was the

---

[37] *British Film Supplement*, in *Picturegoer*, 5 May 1934, 10–11.

[38] Ibid. 11. See also a US Dept. of Commerce Report of 1931 commenting on the state of the film market in Britain: 'The farces were among the most successful of British pictures, while most of the American were relatively unsuccessful. . . . Farce is a form of humor more appreciated on its native heath than elsewhere.' Motion Picture Division of the Bureau of Foreign and Domestic Commerce, 'European Motion Picture Industry', 1931, 8, quoted in Dickinson and Street, *Cinema and State*, 45–6.

[39] In a review of *Love, Life and Laughter, Kine Weekly*, 15 Mar. 1934, 37; my italics.

[40] London, 7–8; my italics.

[41] 'British Mades Best B.O. at Home', 3 Jan. 1933, 13.

reception given to British comedy in the USA. The *New York Times* was well within the American critical mainstream when it commented in early 1935, in a review of *Evergreen*, that 'British humor . . . is still pretty deadly according to any up-to-date standards. . . . English comedians have a habit of displaying the comic understatement of a keystone cop.'[42]

It would have been this lack of understatement amongst other things which rendered a film like *Sing As We Go* virtually inexportable, certainly as far as the American distributors were concerned, but also evidently from the point of view of British distributors. When Michael Balcon was outlining G-B's policy of producing films for both domestic and American distribution, he made it clear that they would not be distributing comedies to the United States, since 'there is still some difference of opinion between the two countries as to what is funny and what is not.'[43]

ASSOCIATED TALKING PICTURES

ATP was the forerunner of the renamed Ealing Studios, taken over by the ubiquitous Michael Balcon in 1929. It was established in 1929 by Basil Dean, best known as a West End theatre impresario, who saw in the talkies the possibility of producing 'quality' films adapted from respectable middle-brow plays and novels, a policy which he carried out with little success throughout the 1930s. ATP was one of several independent pro- duction companies set up at about this time, but one of the very few to survive the severe financial problems of the period, although they were themselves in financial difficulties throughout the 1930s.[44] In January 1930 it was announced that ATP had struck a deal with the American major RKO, who would provide production finance and distribution, with the companies operating under the name of Associated Radio Pictures. Dean saw himself producing his quality productions for both the British and American markets under this arrangement, but RKO had other plans, insisting on a roster of low-budget 'quickies' (such as the first Fields film). In 1932, when Dean realized that RKO were interested in ATP produc- tions only as a cheap means of fulfilling the British quota, the deal was ended. There was one distinct area of benefit for ATP, however, since part of the deal had involved bringing over up-to-date American equipment as well as some personnel, including the cameraman Bob Martin, who later worked on *Sing As We Go*, and J. Walter Ruben, who directed another of ATP's 1934 productions, *Java Head*.

[42] 11 Jan. 1935, 29.
[43] From an interview in *Film Weekly*, 18 Jan. 1936, 8.
[44] See Sue Harper, 'A Note on Basil Dean, Sir Robert Vansittart and British Historical Films of the 1930s', *Historical Journal of Film, Radio and Television*, 9 (1989), 193.

Between the end of the RKO deal, and the relaunch of ATP in late 1933, the company was a very modest outfit, but other developments were underway. The involvement of the Courtauld family enabled the company to rebuild the studio at Ealing, which was opened in 1932. The studio initially had a very modest floor capacity, capable of accommodating only one production at a time, thus restricting output to about four films per year. According to a contemporary account, the studio was 'finely planned' and 'looks almost impossibly modern.'[45] Two further sound stages were opened in late 1934. ATP also launched their own distribution company, ABFD, in 1933, in a bid to achieve suitable distribution for their films while at the same time retaining independence, deemed important after the abortive RKO experience. They also planned to derive income from the distribution of other independent films, initially with little success. At the same time, ATP adopted a new and less ambitious policy, forsaking the American market altogether. In explaining the new policy, Dean prefaced his remarks with the proud but defensive statement that 'the ARP Studios (shortly to be re-named the ATP Studios) are, and always have been an entirely British project, financed entirely by British capital.' He went on to say that 'the world economic crisis has told against the chances of the successful working-out of [the] Anglo-American scheme. It has therefore been decided to re-orientate our policy. Our business will in future be built entirely upon British lines, with an eye mainly to the British Empire market.'[46]

Dean justified the policy by arguing that 'before one can achieve a sound internationalism, one's pictures must stand upon a broad basis of national reputation.' A key aspect of this self-consciously nationalistic policy was to put 'quality before quantity',[47] and Dean's preferred way of achieving quality was to maintain close links with the more culturally respectable worlds of theatre and literature, pushing through adaptations of culturally respectable plays and novels, so echoing Hepworth's policy of a decade or so earlier. ATP films produced in this way included Galsworthy's *Escape!* (1930) and *Loyalties* (1934), *Three Men In A Boat* (1933), *Lorna Doone* (1934), C. L. Anthony's *Autumn Crocus* (1934), and a Mozart bio-pic, *Whom The Gods Love* (1936). *Lorna Doone* and *Midshipman Easy* (1935) also fall into the fairly widespread category in the 1930s of historical films, made with the intention of bringing to the screen significant moments from national history.[48] By all accounts these films were never box-office successes

---

[45] Clarence Winchester (ed.), *The World Film Encyclopedia* (London, 1933), 386; see also 'Basil Dean's Great Plans for ABFD', *Kine Weekly*, 11 Jan. 1934, 10d; and Cyril Rollins and Robert Wareing, 'Basil Dean', unpublished TS, with corrections by Basil Dean, in the Basil Dean Special Collection at the British Film Institute Library, 4.

[46] Quoted in 'New British Renting Unit', *Kine Weekly*, 2 Mar. 1933, 5.

[47] Both quotations from an interview in *Kine Weekly*, 11 Jan. 1934, 10d.

[48] On Dean's historical films, see Harper, 'Note on Basil Dean'.

and overall lost a substantial amount of money, subsequently leading to Dean's resignation from the company in September 1938.[49]

Dean's involvement with the theatre in the 1930s was never simply restricted to making film adaptations of plays, and he himself continued to work in theatre throughout the decade, despite his involvement with ATP, producing three to four West End plays each year. In his policy statement of 1933, for instance, he had noted that 'Regarding my own work as a producer, I have no intention of severing my connection with the legitimate theatre ... and it will be part of the company's policy to exploit such stage successes as I may be fortunate enough to secure from the film point of view where suitable.'[50]

Indeed, for a short time, ATP were formally associated with the Cambridge Theatre in London. The plan—a failed venture—was to transfer to the screen any successful plays, with the original author doing the screenplay and the actors from the theatre production appearing in the film version.[51] The production of these quality pictures and the links with theatre were inspired by a missionary zeal to educate British film audiences away from Hollywood's mass culture, a zeal which parallels the work of the BBC under Sir John Reith at the time.[52] As a policy, it was not much admired by others in the trade, or by those concerned with promoting popular cinema to the mass audience. An editorial in the popular magazine, *Film Weekly*, was particularly scathing:

[Dean] is years behind the times in his outlook. He obviously regards the stage as the principal source of screen material and Hollywood as the natural enemy of British producers. Both ideas have gone out of fashion because they have been proved fundamentally wrong. . . . Nor will the production of plays necessarily lead to the production of good films. Dramatists must be encouraged to write direct for the screen, not to write for the stage and then adapt their plays into films. Mr Dean seems to be theatre-minded first and film-minded afterwards.[53]

It was not this policy of tying film to theatre which kept ATP afloat. The fortunes of the company in fact depended primarily on the hugely successful films of perhaps the two biggest British stars of the 1930s, Fields, first signed in 1931 and subsequently making seven films for ATP—'our mainstay in the first days of our independence ... saving our financial

---

[49] Balcon, for instance, recalled that, 'Much to the credit of Basil Dean and Reg Baker, all the films with Gracie Fields and George Formby were commercially successful, but, alas, the other films made at the studio lost overall a substantial amount of money', *Lifetime*, 118–19.

[50] Quoted in 'New British Renting Unit', *Kine Weekly*, 2 Mar. 1933, 5.

[51] See Basil Dean, *Mind's Eye* (London, 1973), *passim.*; Rollins and Wareing, 'Basil Dean', 9; Harper, 'Note on Basil Dean'; and Basil Dean, 'Finding and Keeping Britain's Stars', in *British Film Supplement*, in *Picturegoer*, 5 May 1934, 12.

[52] See Harper, 'Note on Basil Dean', 191–2.

[53] 'Basil Dean: Brainwave', 16 Feb. 1934, 3.

bacon'[54]—and George Formby, signed in 1934. Both were northerners from working-class backgrounds, and both were already major figures on the music-hall circuits. Their films were unhesitatingly designed as star vehicles, to exploit the talents and images already familiar from their variety acts. After the success of Fields's early films (*Kine Weekly* had described her in 1933 as 'England's premier entertainer'[55]), she was able to command enormous fees by any standards for her film work, which inevitably put up the cost of production dramatically. She signed a contract in August 1933 giving her £22,000–25,000 per picture, which was only the first of the several highly lucrative contracts she negotiated with ATP, reputedly making her the highest paid British star of the time. To put this in perspective, it is worth noting that her first film, *Sally In Our Alley*, released just two years earlier, had been completed for less than £25,000, with the leads, including Fields, being paid a total of only £1,171.[56]

Despite the apparent profligacy of Fields's salary, and the somewhat uncommercial nature of Dean's emphasis on literary and theatrical properties, policy statements issued by ATP in the mid-1930s show a healthy concern for the streamlined efficiency of successful commercial production. From 1934 ATP's schedule was organized around the production of no more than a few carefully and extensively planned pictures per year, each built around 'outstanding British personalities'.[57] They also adopted the practice of working in semi-autonomous production units, some four years after the major Hollywood studios had done so. The practice was justified both in Hollywood and at ATP in terms of the conjunction of good management practices and the quality of creative personal expression: 'the directors [of ATP] believe . . . in the policy of encouraging stars, young directors and all technicians to stamp their own individuality upon the pictures.'[58] However the practice was justified, there was no doubting that economy rather than extravagance was the order of the day:

The company was utterly opposed to the cheap quota picture . . . [but] did not hold with the view that the entertainment value of a picture could be computed in terms of the money spent on it. . . . By unceasing vigilance, quality could be made commercially profitable. ATP would always set quality before quantity, and confine itself to making a limited number only of the highest grade films each year.[59]

[54] Dean, *Mind's Eye*, 203, 204.
[55] In a review of *This Week of Grace*, 3 Aug. 1933, 14.
[56] See Item 3 of Basil Dean Special Collection, BFI Library.
[57] Dean, Chairman's speech to the Associated Talking Pictures AGM, 20 Dec. 1935, in Basil Dean Special Collection; also reported in *Today's Cinema*, 21 Dec. 1935, 4.
[58] Ibid. On the organization of production in the Hollywood studios, see Janet Staiger, 'The Producer-Unit System', in David Bordwell, Janet Staiger, and Kristin Thompson, *The Classical Hollywood Cinema: Film Style and Mode of Production* (London, 1985), 320–2.
[59] Dean, speech to AGM, 1935.

The products were to be commercially profitable, but it would be a culturally respectable profit without guilt: economy may have been in order, but this was no factory for mass production. As the *Motion Picture Herald* commented in 1931, 'good pictures are created, not manufactured.'[60]

Dean had earlier proposed that 'our business will in future be built entirely upon British lines',[61] but ATP was in fact employing American-trained personnel in key positions, and using business practices very similar to those prevailing in the American film industry. The standards of Hollywood were such that even those policies which were formulated most self-consciously as different from Hollywood were bound to involve the use of at least some American methods.

Sing As We Go was obviously an early prototype of this mode of production, being billed in advance in the trade papers as one of the 'super-features' to be made by ATP in 1934.[62] 'Super-feature' was a term generally reserved for the epics of the film industry and could carry with it a sense not only of the expensiveness of Fields herself but also of cultural prestige. ATP were evidently taking all steps possible to distinguish their films from the cheap formula quota pictures.

Both *Sing As We Go* and *Evergreen* were in fact relatively expensive productions, each costing £60,000–65,000, which was somewhere between the average cost of a programme picture and that of a super-feature like Korda's *The Private Life of Henry 8th* (£93,000), *Catherine The Great* (1934, £128,000), and *The Scarlet Pimpernel* (1934, £144,000), or another of G-B's 1934 films, *Jew Süss* (£100,000). The average cost of a British picture was estimated in late 1935 to be around £30,000.[63] But *Sing As We Go* does not look like an expensive film—its production values

[60] Florabel Muir, 'Hollywood Considers the Unit', 15 Aug. 1931, 12, quoted in Staiger, 'Producer-Unit', 320.

[61] Quoted in 'New British Renting Unit', *Kine Weekly*, 2 Mar. 1933, 5.

[62] See e.g. *Kine Weekly*, 4 Jan. 1934, 25; 11 Jan. 1934, 23; and 26 Apr. 1934, 23.

[63] The costs of the Korda films are given by Dickinson and Street, *Cinema and State*, 86; the *Jew Süss* figure is given in Low, *Film-Making*, 142. See also Reginald Crow, 'Film Showing', 457–8, and Mackenzie Winter, 'Men and Money behind Moving Pictures', 461–6, both in Winchester (ed.), *Film Encyclopedia*. The estimation as to the average cost of British films is given in the *Sunday Dispatch*, 3 Nov. 1935, quoted in Wood (ed.), *British Films*, 40. Simon Rowson estimated that the 50 to 60 films made each year without any designs on the export market, and excluding 'quota quickies', cost between £15,000 and £20,000 (memorandum to Moyne Committee, para. 23, p. 112). It is difficult to be entirely accurate about these figures, and certainly I have come across no firm figure for *Evergreen*, simply various indications that it cost about £60,000: see *National Film Theatre Booklet*, Dec–Jan 1972–3: 'A big budget for a British film at the time—around £60,000' (36); and Low, *Film-Making*: 'At £60,000 was an expensive production for a British studio' (137). With *Sing As We Go*, it is possible to be somewhat more accurate, since the budgets for ATP films are held at the BFI Library, and *Sing As We Go* is given at £64,917/1s/9d! (Item 3, in Basil Dean Special Collection). However, Dean proudly notes in his autobiography that he was able to bring the film in £1,500 under budget, so the final figure may be slightly less (*Mind's Eye*, 206).

seem more suited to a low-budget feature. It certainly does not look as expensive as *Evergreen*, which is so evidently lavish in sets, costumes, size of cast, and production numbers. The main reason that *Sing As We Go* did cost so much was of course Fields's salary, which made up about half the budget.[64]

Cost is one thing, but quality another—and these films seem so far removed from Dean's idea of quality productions. Dean constantly reiterated the view that 'the company was utterly opposed to the cheap quota picture',[65] although he recognized later that the Fields and Formby films amounted to 'successful factory-farming'.[66] Even so, Dean explains in his autobiography that he was upset by the critics' complaints about the 'poverty' of the Fields films which they saw as 'mere vehicles', and, in order to combat this perceived poverty, Dean hired the services of respected populist writers like J. B. Priestley and Walter Greenwood.

Priestley wrote the original script for *Sing As We Go* and his name was used as a marketing point, at least to showmen through the trade papers. One of the big successes of 1933 had been Gaumont-British's *The Good Companions*, adapted from the already successful novel and play by Priestley. A full-page advertisement in *Kine Weekly* announcing *Sing As We Go* stressed only the presence of Fields, the title of the film, and 'an entirely original screen story by J. B. Priestley, author of *The Good Companions*.'[67] The involvement of Priestley, given his literary and theatrical reputation, was also a way of garnering intellectual acclaim. Priestley was in many ways a sensible choice given Dean's aspirations, since he could bring with him not only his solid cultural respectability and his refined narrative sense, but also his class and regional background. Moreover, he had only recently completed *English Journey*, his 'rambling but truthful account of what one man saw and heard and felt and thought during a journey through England during the Autumn of the year 1933', which included a description of the diverse pleasures and attractions of Blackpool, the setting for *Sing As We Go*.[68]

Sing As We Go can therefore be seen as the beginning of Dean's efforts to refine the Fields star-image and tailor her appeal more to the tastes of

---

[64] It is entered in the accounts as £30,000. After 1933 the Fields films, with budgets ranging from £59,000 to £89,000, were always substantially more expensive than the rest of ATP's films, which tended to be in the £25–35,000 bracket. *Sing As We Go* was in fact one of four films made by ATP in 1934, and one of the others was a Fields picture too, *Love, Life and Laughter*, budgeted at £59,000. The other two films of that year were *Lorna Doone* (£33,000) and *Java Head* (£29,000). All figures taken from original budgets in Item 3 of Basil Dean Special Collection, BFI Library.

[65] *Today's Cinema*, 21 Dec. 1935, 4.

[66] *Mind's Eye*, 237.

[67] 10 May 1934, 35. By coincidence, *The Good Companions* was directed by Saville and had Matthews in one of the starring roles.

[68] London, 1934. The quotation is from the title-page of the book.

middle-class audiences and the demands of classical narrative film form.
The success of this film led to Priestley writing the screenplay for Fields's
next film, *Look Up and Laugh* (1935), while Greenwood was brought in
for Formby's first ATP film, *No Limit* (1935). For Dean, these films could
also be seen as culturally respectable high-quality products because of their
social themes. He encouraged his writers to produce something more than
'commonplace' stories, and develop 'serious' social themes and 'realistic'
settings.[69] He later wrote of *Sing As We Go* that 'Jack [Priestley] used the
current depression in the Lancashire cotton industry as the framework of
his story—solid enough to support its broad humours without loss of
credibility. . . . This was a great advance on the fabrications of Gracie's
previous films.'[70]

It is difficult, however, to accept that the story, as laid out in the finished
film, is really as 'solid' as Dean implies. The theme of the depression really
only tops and tails the diverse attractions of Fields's picaresque exploits;
it is a means of getting into and out of the carnivalesque location of
Blackpool, a location which hardly speaks the language of depression. The
social theme is, as Dean suggests, a framing device, but it is hardly a solid
force for narrative integration, a point I shall return to later in this chapter.

GAUMONT-BRITISH

. . . international films are what good directors make.

Alexander Korda, 1933[71]

The story of Gaumont-British is very different from that of ATP. In 1933,
already one of the most powerful British film combines, they reorganized
their corporate and financial management, and their distribution and production structure. The corporation now controlled two studios, more than
300 cinemas, a film printing laboratory, a national distribution company,
and 14,000 employees. One aspect of the reorganization was the adoption
of a policy of producing pictures for world consumption, 'pictures with
[an] international outlook', as G-B chief Mark Ostrer put it.[72] A substantial proportion of their annual production budget was earmarked for making

---

[69] On *Look Up and Laugh*, Dean commented that 'once again we had broad comedy
based upon a serious theme', *Mind's Eye*, 207; and on *Queen of Hearts*, he wrote 'as
for the story, well, once again, we appeared to have slipped back into the commonplace', ibid. 208. Harper, 'Note on Basil Dean', shows that a concern for realism was
a feature of Dean's historical films too.

[70] *Mind's Eye*, pp. 204–5.

[71] In an interview with Stephen Watts, 'Alexander Korda and the International Film',
Cinema Quarterly, 2 (1933), 13.

[72] Quoted in *Today's Cinema*, 31 Dec. 1935, 1.

high-cost prestige films designed to have an impact in the American market—*Evergreen* being one of these films. In the early 1930s, they had concentrated on European markets and the production of multiple versions of their films in different languages (notably German);[73] as they expanded, they sought bigger markets, inevitably looking towards the United States, which according to G-B's C. M. Woolf 'represents 60% of the gross of any picture'.[74] Deals with the Hollywood majors were not new to G-B, which had sold a significant block of shares to Fox in 1929, thereby generating much concern within the trade as to the potential loss of control of major interests in the British film industry to an American company. This concern was renewed in 1936, when negotiations between G-B and Loew's (MGM) were revealed in the press.

G-B had control of two studios, the Gaumont-British studio itself at Shepherd's Bush, and the studio of the G-B subsidiary, Gainsborough Pictures, at Islington. Michael Balcon was head of production at both studios from 1931, but overall policy was dictated by the Board of Directors of G-B. Both studios were, by British standards at least, modern, efficient, and streamlined outfits, with seven floors in all (compared to ATP's three by late 1934). The Gainsborough studios had been completely rebuilt and modernized after a fire in 1930 (ironically its design over two storeys caused many problems for the organization of production). The Shepherd's Bush studios were described in 1933 by *The World Film Encyclopedia* as 'the finest studio in Great Britain . . . huge . . . [with] all the paraphernalia of the last word in modern film studios.'[75] But this was a popular British publication, and its judgement stands in stark contrast to that of an American trade journalist reviewing British production facilities. By comparison with the major Hollywood studios, the physical organization and layout of Shepherd's Bush seemed to him out-dated, inefficient, and 'more of a handicap than a help',[76] a view confirmed to some extent by Balcon's recollections in his autobiography about the initial inadequacies of the studio and the difficulties of scheduling films there.[77] The differences between G-B's facilities and those of the bigger Hollywood studios were the sort of details which ensured that G-B faced a long uphill struggle in attempting to make films on a par with the American companies and to gain a similar share of the international market.

The output of Shepherd's Bush and Gainsborough between them was between fourteen and twenty-three films per year for the period 1931 to

[73] See Andrew Higson, '[The] Way West', in Jörg Schöning (ed.), *London Calling* (Munich, 1993).
[74] Reported in *Kine Weekly*, 2 Aug. 1934, 5.
[75] Winchester (ed.), *Film Encyclopedia*, 392. See also 'Gaumont-British great studios', *Kine Weekly*, 11 Jan. 1934, 113.
[76] Kann, 'Hollywood and Britain', 192. [77] *Lifetime*, 58, 61–2.

1936 (ATP produced three to five films per year for the same period), with the Shepherd's Bush studios turning out sixteen films in 1934, and Gainsborough seven.[78] In his autobiography, Balcon noted that the Jessie Matthews vehicles were one of G-B's six most important production categories,[79] but he also recalled that 'on the whole our films in those years were not as good as they should have been, and they were costing more than they should have.'[80] The trade press at the time was more optimistic. *Kine Weekly*, for instance, noted in early 1934 that G-B films had a reputation for doing good business and for

making the public and the exhibitor 'British-picture minded' . . . The past year has abundantly demonstrated the fact that the home product has won an established place. This position has been attained in the teeth of fierce opposition and by quality of production. Patriotism or nationalism does not influence the picturegoer in his or her preference for entertainment . . . British pictures have won a place by merit and not by virtue of their nationality.[81]

The concept of quality here is clearly one in which Hollywood sets the standards, and where national specificity is of no value. In justifying the new 'internationalist' production policy to the Gainsborough shareholders in late 1933, Woolf argued that 'in the long run, the production of 'quality films' is more economical and more profitable than making cheap and hasty products; for only with films of world standard in technique and entertainment can the company hold its own in the world market.'[82] This is as neat a statement as any of the thinking behind the more internationalist of the two production strategies adopted by the British film industry. The concept of quality is very different from ATP's. If many of G-B's films were, like ATP's, adapted from plays or novels, it was not as adaptations particularly that they were to be valued, riding on the back of source material which might carry with it a certain cultural prestige (except perhaps in the case of some of the historical epics). On the contrary, quality for G-B tended to mean well-made films, or at least films which looked well-made and had a certain international appeal, according to the standards of the best of the Hollywood studios' output of the period. Within the film culture of the period, this was a more specifically cinematic and a more populist concept of quality than that operated by Dean at ATP, but it also implied a belief that high cost necessarily meant high quality, and that Hollywood necessarily meant good cinema: 'we must pursue a production

---

[78] By way of comparison, the figures for feature films released by the American majors in 1934 were as follows: Columbia, 43; Fox, 52; MGM, 43; Paramount, 55; United Artists, 20; Universal, 44; Warner Bros, 58; see Jack Alicoate (ed.), *Film Daily Yearbook, 1935* (New York, 1935), 369.

[79] *Lifetime*, 62–3.   [80] Ibid. 95.

[81] 11 Jan. 1934, 89. Cf. Low, *Film-Making*, 142.

[82] Reported in *Kine Weekly*, 7 Dec. 1933, 5.

policy ever less and less parochial and more and more international in appeal.'[83] It was assumptions such as these which proved in the long run to be the main stumbling-blocks in G-B's bid for international success.

In an unprecedented bid to consolidate their position in the United States, G-B set up their own booking agency in New York in 1934, with plans to release G-B films in thirty-two American cities, promising 'to spend as much money on the exploitation of our pictures as American producers spend on their product.'[84] According to *Kine Weekly*, this was 'one of the most important developments in the history of British Productions.'[85] G-B arranged for Fox to handle the actual physical distribution of their films and secured attention-grabbing openings for a number of their biggest productions at the prestigious Radio City Music Hall and the Roxy, both in New York. As part of this strategy, *Evergreen* began a successful and critically acclaimed run at the Music Hall in January 1935, some four months after it had opened in London. According to David Quinlan, it was the biggest British box-office success in the USA since *The Private Life of Henry 8th* a year earlier.[86] However, *Variety* reported that *Evergreen* was 'quite a disappointment at the Music Hall' and that box-office business was 'lachrymal, . . . sinking house to under $55,000'.[87] Even so, G-B continued to exploit Matthews's star image for the export market, and her next film, *First a Girl* (1935), opened for a week at the Roxy in January 1935 some three months ahead of its London première, while *It's Love Again* (1936) opened at the Roxy the following May. Outside New York, however, bookings for G-B films were never impressive, and distribution costs were very high.[88] *Variety*'s review of 1934 noted that

An important sidelight of '34 was the first genuine threat of the foreign film market in the U.S. This came in the decision of Gaumont-British to set up shop in this country, convinced that the pictures it was turning out in England merited such a move. Today this side of the big foam is becoming conscious of the ability of Britain to make marketable films for American audiences. London Films, with its *Henry the VIII* drew immediate attention and this picture supplied most of the impetus.[89]

A year later, the same paper reported that, as in 1934, thirty-three British films were distributed in the United States in 1935, with some improvement in overall takings.[90] But it is clear that such competition would not

---

[83] Balcon, *World Film News*, 1/3, June 1936, 6.
[84] C. M. Woolf, quoted in *Kine Weekly*, 2 Aug. 1934, 5.
[85] Ibid.
[86] David Quinlan, 'The Thirties—Star of the Decade: Jessie Matthews', in *British Sound Films—The Studio Years, 1928–1959* (London, 1984), 26. Quinlan offers no evidence for his claim and I have been unable to confirm or deny it.
[87] 15 Jan. 1935, 9, and 22 Jan. 1935, 9.
[88] See 'British Film's Conquest of America', *Film Weekly*, 2 May 1936, 26–7.
[89] 1 Jan. 1935, 3.   [90] 1 Jan. 1936, 54.

be allowed to become a real threat—and Variety saw the G-B move in
1934 as no more than a sidelight on the year, while the figures on 1935
are derived from a general article on all foreign films in the American
market. Evidently, British films counted as foreign-language films, high-
risk ventures marginal to the distribution system. The ultimate, and very
costly, failure of G-B's venture in the American market was, according to
G-B director Mark Ostrer, 'not due to any lack of merit, but to the fact
that we are not accorded playing time in the most important situations,
these being almost exclusively controlled by American producing interests.'[91] The G-B move may initially have appeared to Variety as a genuine
threat, but the American majors clearly went out of their way to protect
their existing collective interests and contain the threat as far as was possible.

Another strand to G-B's 'internationalist' policy was to buy the services
of American writers, producers, directors, and stars—the latter to be used
as selling-points for G-B films in the United States and other markets
(including Britain) dominated by Hollywood: 'Our ultimate aim: . . . to
produce pictures with the greatest possible appeal to the greatest possible
audiences in all parts of the world.'[92]

This strategy can be seen at work in the make-up of Evergreen's production team: Saville himself had been to Hollywood a few years earlier to
gain experience directing an early sound film (as in fact had Basil Dean),[93]
and Rodgers and Hart, the American song-writing team, had written the
songs for the original London stage show, with additional material for the
film by another American, Harry Woods. The cameraman, Glen
MacWilliams, was also American, as was choreographer Buddy Bradley
(although he too had worked on the original show). Saville had even tried
to cast as the male lead an enthusiastic Fred Astaire, who had already
made his mark in Flying Down To Rio (1933), and was at the time
appearing on stage in London in The Gay Divorcee.[94] Similar measures
designed to tailor the Matthews musicals to the needs of the export market
were constantly being taken: in It's Love Again, she was paired with
American star Robert Young, while Gangway was mostly set in New
York, with Matthews playing a female reporter involved with gangsters.[95]

Inevitably, this policy of hiring American stars and other personnel forced
G-B on to the defensive and they had to work hard to convince certain
sectors of the trade and the film culture that they were still making British
films. On the introduction of the policy, Woolf had insisted that 'Although

[91] Quoted in Kine Weekly, 11 Apr. 1937, 8.
[92] Balcon, World Film News, 1/3, June 1936, 6.
[93] Rollins and Wareing, 'Victor Saville', 3, and eid., 'Basil Dean', 4.
[94] See Jessie Matthews, Over My Shoulder (London, 1974), 137, and Michael Thornton,
Jessie Matthews: A Biography (London, 1974), 110–11.
[95] Cf. William K. Everson, 'Jessie Matthews', Films in Review, 26/10 (1975), 592.

our pictures will be made for the world market, it is our intention to make them as strongly British in sentiment as they are today. At the same time we shall go out to compete with America for the services of the best directors and artistes.'[96] Balcon justified the policy in similar terms: 'There is no British style. Or if there is, it is a bad one. We aim to make our pictures technically as good as the best that America can produce—though we shall of course approach our subject from the British viewpoint. But that is not a question of style; it is a matter of feeling.'[97] Attempting to explain the G-B position in more detail later in the same year, Balcon set out to answer

the question of why British producers have neglected the home country and the Empire in the past in choosing subjects to film. We have not been exactly blind to the attractions of the English scene or the Empire story as film fare. But we have had to tread carefully in the paths of international film markets. . . . We have been fully aware of the fact that American producers have for years been punching American ideas, habits, merchandise, and morals into English cinema audiences by means of about four million feet of film a year. We know that the Empire, and Canada especially, is much more familiar with the American scene through the cinema than it is with British scenery and ideas. But don't forget that we have been building up our industry during the past five years or so. Sometimes it has been hard enough to make our films presentable in markets used to the high technical perfection of the Hollywood film. We haven't felt much like experimenting with subjects that might not have suited the tastes of people overseas. But now I think that we can say that we have got things on the move. America is finding that our films can be quite attractive.[98]

It is interesting that in this more detailed statement, the idea of a distinctively British sentiment or feeling—a justification often used in defence of national cinema—has been dropped. The argument is now clearly against any form of product differentiation or market specialization, and clearly for trying to play Hollywood at its own game, and even in its own (massive) back-yard. Films must appeal to an imagination already colonized by American cinema; the threat of denationalization is to be met not with a reaffirmation of English or British culture (the terms are interchangeable here), but with an attempt to exploit that colonized imagination even further.

Balcon was not, as far as one can ascertain, completely at ease with this policy, which went against both statements that he had made about production policy in the 1920s, and the strategies that he adopted at Ealing in the 1940s (the latter no doubt partly in response to the ultimate failure of G-B's internationalism). Certainly, even during his time at G-B, Balcon

---

[96] Quoted in *Kine Weekly*, 2 Aug. 1934, 5.
[97] In an interview in *Film Weekly*, 18 Jan. 1936, 8.
[98] 'Putting the Real Britain on the Screen', *Evening News*, 1 Oct. 1936, 11.

had reserved a place for other types of films too, notably Robert Flaherty's realist epic *Man of Aran*, made for G-B and released in 1934, the same year as *Evergreen* and *Jew Süss*. In his autobiography, Balcon comments on what in retrospect seemed the 'mistaken policy' of hiring American stars. His experience at G-B, he noted in a much-quoted remark, 'helped to confirm my growing conviction that a film, to be international, must be thoroughly national in the first instance.'[99] It is worth noting the similarity between this comment and one quoted earlier from Basil Dean in 1934: 'before one can achieve a sound internationalism, one's pictures must stand upon a broad basis of national reputation.'[100] In other words, when Balcon moved to Ealing and took over control from Basil Dean, he adopted an already well-established policy, even down to the rhetoric of its justification.

Balcon in fact left G-B for MGM-British in December 1936, by which time G-B had abandoned their efforts in the American market and cut back their production schedule considerably. As noted earlier, the failure of the policy was attributed to 'the resistance not of the American public . . . but of powerful interests in the American industry.'[101] By this stage, the general admiration for G-B and its policies had severely dwindled. In 1937, the whole of the production sector of the industry—and not just G-B's expansionist strategy—was in crisis, lending an unexpected poignancy to the deliberations of the Moyne Committee about how best to improve the 1927 Quota Act, which was now up for renewal. An editorial in *Kine Weekly*—once a keen supporter of G-B's internationalism—indicates something of the new climate of opinion. The author tabulates various reasons for the failure of the production sector and offers some thoughts on the way forward:

First is the crazy and persistent delusion that it is possible to break into the American market by the purchase of American stars. In the main, the result of this policy has been additional cost without any commensurate increase in the selling value of the production concerned. . . . All we have done so far in our attempt to break down the American monopoly is to provide some Hollywood throwouts with their winter's keep. . . . Few can now deny that the panacea for our industry's ills lies in economy and in concentration on our home markets. . . . The material for good, solid, popular product is ready to our hand, and only waiting to be woven into screen entertainment full of the drama and comedy of real life. We

[99] *Lifetime*, 88, 61. Cf. the rather more modest and less internationalist policy statement made by Balcon in *Bioscope*, 18 June 1927, 46; on the other hand, note that even his first film as a producer, *Woman to Woman* (1923, discussed in the previous chapter), had featured an American star brought over in a bid to secure international appeal for the film. On Balcon's differences with the G-B management in the mid-1930s, see also Geoff Brown, 'A Knight and his Castle', in Jane Fluegel (ed.), *Michael Balcon: The Pursuit of British Cinema* (New York, 1984), 19.

[100] Quoted in *Kine Weekly*, 11 Jan. 1934, 10d.

[101] Isidore Ostrer, quoted in *Today's Cinema*, 22 Jan. 1937, 10.

have enough national characteristics of our own without slavishly imitating those mannerisms which we have (mistakenly) supposed would ensure an entry into the American market.[102]

Balcon himself seemed to have done his reputation as a producer no harm, and he was generally held in high esteem during the 1930s, as his appointment as Head of Production at MGM-British would suggest: 'No man has been more identified with the revival of British films and no man has been directly responsible for the making of more good ones.'[103] The move to MGM was of course short-lived, and the shifting climate of opinion on the fortunes of the British film industry, especially its production sector, in effect paved the way for Balcon's subsequent move to the much more modest and economic set-up at Ealing Studios.

As a corporate strategy, G-B's efforts in the mid-1930s seem to have all the hallmarks of a potentially successful, well-directed economic attempt to establish a national film industry capable of operating in the international market-place. It was an ambitious effort by the industry to put its own house in order, building on the strong economic base that a vertically integrated corporation provided, competing directly with the international market-leaders by emulating their product, seeking to gain a foothold in their own home market, and engaging in aggressive promotion of its own fare. But by comparison with Rank, who made a similar assault on the American market in the mid-1940s, it lacked their greater economic power, their level of capitalization, and their market control. In other words, it had a less monopolistic hold over the domestic industry than Rank, and so was less attractive to American distributors working in Britain, who might then have developed reciprocal arrangements for G-B in the United States. As it was, G-B never pulled off any substantial deals with the major American distributors, and it was forced to resort to setting up its own American distribution agency. The shift from attempted collusion to attempted competition at the level of distribution would not help matters, however, since it was not in the interests of the Motion Picture Producers and Distributors Association as a whole, or any of the individual majors, to open up any of their chains of theatres to foreign competitors. The long-term success of the American film industry was due in no small way to the tightness with which the industry was integrated both horizontally and vertically and the degree of co-operation between the majors. There really was no room for competitors, except perhaps under the freak short-term conditions which enabled *The Private Life of Henry 8th* to make a mark; and there was no incentive for the American majors to make room.[104]

---

[102] R. H. B., 'After Ten Years—The Lessons of the Quota Act', *Kine Weekly*, 14 Jan. 1937, 4.

[103] P. L. Mannock, 'Leo gets Micky', *Picturegoer Weekly*, 2 Jan. 1937, 10.

[104] Cf. T. H. Guback, *The International Film Industry* (Bloomington, Ind., 1969).

The situation was succinctly summarized by Korda and his colleagues in mid-1936:

American producing companies can spend £200,000 on a picture and recover the cost and a reasonable profit in their own country and can then afford to sell the picture in the British market for a sum which would not yield to a British company a profit on a picture costing a quarter of that amount. On the other hand, it has not yet been possible for British pictures to earn any substantial revenue in America.[105]

A combination of factors thus mitigated against G-B's efforts: first of all, the size of the home market available to American films, enabling a high profit margin to be reached by such films; and secondly, the tight control of that market by the vertically integrated American majors, who would invite films made outside their own studios into this market only on their own terms. As the Moyne Committee noted, these factors created 'enormous advantages [for] the American film industry, which enable it to enter on a scale of production with which the British industry has found it impossible to compete.'[106]

The problem was primarily economic, but cultural matters must still be attended to: the short-term gains which G-B were able to make were due not only to their relative economic power, but also to the types of films that they were making, and the production values with which they were invested. I will now explore these essentially cultural matters in more detail.

JESSIE MATTHEWS: STAR-IMAGE AND THE STAR SYSTEM

The huge commercial potential of the star system was something generally appreciated within the British film industry, and many agreed with Sidney Bernstein's assessment that 'the failure to develop British film stars is an important factor which prevents our pictures achieving maximum success at the box-office.'[107] There was much discussion in the trade and popular press as to how Britain could actually build up stars on the same scale as Hollywood. The Gaumont-British strategy involved importing American stars—though not all of them were in the top rank. Popular support for this policy was important, and G-B evidently had a friend in the fan magazine *Film Weekly*, which worked hard throughout the mid-1930s to promote G-B's interests. An editorial in 1935 argued that

You cannot 'build up' a star to any extent unless you have the power to ensure the widest possible exhibition of her pictures throughout the world, and particu-

---

[105] Memorandum to the Moyne Committee, in Board of Trade, *Minutes of Evidence taken before the Departmental Committee on Cinematograph Films*, i, para. 7, p. 36; cf. Simon Rowson, memorandum to the Moyne Committee, para. 23, p. 112.

[106] Moyne Committee, *Cinematograph Films Act, 1927: Report of a Committee Appointed by the Board of Trade* (London, 1936), Cmd. 5320, para. 19, p. 9.

[107] *British Film Supplement*, in *Picturegoer*, 5 May 1934, 10.

larly through Britain and America. Hollywood has the power and uses it super-latively well. Britain lacks it, and cannot acquire it except by producing pictures of international appeal—which, to the American film trade, primarily means pictures with international stars. Hence the need for 'ready-made stars' in this country. We cannot sell our own future stars—or their pictures—to America without those Hollywood 'names' for which our producers are now bidding. That is why *Film Weekly* supports the importation of Hollywood talent.[108]

The logic of the argument seems impeccable, but, as a leading American trade journalist later commented, this sort of policy was

understandable perhaps as a temporary measure until producing in Britain finds firmer ground, [but it] has no lasting value. Recognising that for success in the international market—which means selling to America—personalities are essential, Great Britain will have to find another answer. That answer is the development of her own stars. Not merely stars acceptable to the British public, but stars of proven drawing-power in the United States. . . . [This] will mean experimenting constantly with new faces, surrounding them with the most expert production ingredients, and finding stories with a flavour of appeal to American audiences.[109]

Both Dean and Balcon were clearly fully aware of the importance of stars for a profitable and successful production programme. The question of finding stars of international appeal did not accord with ATP's production policy in the mid-1930s, and Dean was evidently happy to continue work-ing with the (anyway huge) domestic appeal of Fields, and to provide support by signing up other similar personalities such as Formby. Balcon on the other hand was faced precisely with the problems that the quota-tion above identifies. With his longer experience in the industry and greater knowledge of Hollywood studio production and publicity methods, Balcon also had a more professional and economic approach to star-building and the exploitation of a star-image. This was more than evident in the case of Jessie Matthews, 'one of [G-B's] biggest star successes'[110]—as she herself recalls, 'G-B . . . poured their resources into my screen image'.[111]

Matthews had already had a highly successful career on the stage, even though she was still only 27 when she made *Evergreen*. She came to G-B in 1932, against Balcon's wishes, to make *There Goes The Bride*, but after seeing the rushes, Balcon signed her up and pushed her into two more films before *There Goes The Bride* was even released. When it was re-leased, as Balcon noted in his autobiography, '[Matthews] performance was unmistakably first class and a star was born. She was hailed by the critics, given a long-term contract with G-B, and made a series of musical films exploiting her many talents.'[112]

---

[108] 23 Aug. 1935, 3.   [109] Kann, 'Hollywood and Britain', 197.
[110] Balcon, *Lifetime*, 63.   [111] Matthews, *Over My Shoulder*, 140.
[112] *Lifetime*, 64. It is ironic, to say the least, that the man who so carefully built up Matthews's star-image should describe the process in terms of the mythology of 'a star is born'.

Beginning with this picture, her films at G-B were 'specially written or acquired as vehicles for her' and central to G-B's production schedule.[113] Exploiting this particular category of film was initially considered something of a gamble since it was felt that Hollywood had cornered the market in the production of sophisticated musicals: 'we knew we were challenging fate (and Hollywood!) with *Evergreen*.'[114] The success of *Evergreen* obviously put paid to such doubts, even though its New York box-office was not spectacular, and encouraged G-B to mine as intensively as possible what appeared to be an immensely rich vein. G-B evidently worked hard to protect their star commodity with suitable contracts and to build up and exploit Matthews's star-image and potential, not only through press and publicity, but also through the way in which they designed her vehicles.[115] Her films traded on both a consistent narrative image—several of her key roles played on impersonation, role-playing, and mistaken identity—and a spectacular body image, in effect an eroticization of this narrative image.[116] Matthews recalled in particular the way in which cinematographer Glen MacWilliams altered her make-up and the lighting of her face for *Waltzes from Vienna* (1934), the film she made with Hitchcock prior to *Evergreen*, thereby establishing an element of the *mise-en-scène* that was crucial to the appeal of her subsequent pictures. Saville's role as director was of paramount importance too, renewing Matthews's and G-B's confidence in her own abilities, and establishing the right production ingredients around her.[117]

As Jeffrey Richards has pointed out, the key element of her star-image is the paradoxical figure of 'innocent sexuality', and certain terms recur obsessively in contemporary (and indeed subsequent) celebrations of her image.[118] For the reviewers of the mid-1930s, she was both 'the essence of graceful charm', and at the same time full of 'impudence'; she had a 'childlike beauty', with 'elfin qualities of charm and sweetness'; 'her pert little face photographs irresistibly', and she had 'irresistible vitality . . . transparent honesty . . . [and] extreme grace of movement'.[119] There is, no doubt, a certain Englishness about this celebration of the child-woman by comparison with the somewhat brasher sexuality of some of the major

---

[113] Ibid. 65; see also 86.   [114] Ibid. 87.

[115] See Matthews, *Over My Shoulder*, 142–3; *Daily Mail*, 27 Oct. 1933; Thornton, *Jessie Matthews*, passim.

[116] Thornton, *Jessie Matthews*, 128, reports that, after some moral concern in the US and in Britain about 'scanty attire' in *First A Girl*, Saville said to Balcon, 'Hell, Mick, we've got to sell that body.' Thornton gives no source, but even if the story is invented, it accurately summarizes what G-B actually did.

[117] See ibid. 109–10; and Everson, 'Jessie Matthews', 587–8, 580.

[118] *Dream Palace*, 207.

[119] *Film Weekly*, 7 Sept. 1934, 36; *News Chronicle*, 20 Oct. 1932; *Daily Mail*, no further details given, quoted in Thornton, *Jessie Matthews*, 90; *Daily Express*, quoted ibid. 84; *Observer*, 30 Oct. 1932; *Daily Mail*, 26 Oct. 1932.

STILL 10. 'The essence of graceful charm' (*Film Weekly*, 1934), 'her pert little face photographs beautifully' (*Observer*, 1932). Jessie Matthews in period costume for the Edwardian music-hall sequence in *Evergreen*.

female Hollywood stars of the period, but it is simply a more paternalist variation of the patriarchal fetishizing of the female body, and not in itself uncommon in American cinema (as the star-images of Ruby Keeler, or indeed, in later decades, Marilyn Monroe, attest).[120] Significantly, it is left to Caroline Lejeune, one of the few female reviewers of the period, to offer a rather less voyeuristic and prurient assessment of Matthews's qualities when she writes that 'her movement and poise . . . is enchanting; she has found just how to get the maximum effect with the minimum appearance of effort.'[121] Indeed, this comment might serve as a summary of the qualities required of any movie actor to operate successfully in the classical narrative film.

G-B built up a strong and fairly regular production unit for the ten key films in which Jessie Matthews had starring roles between 1933 and 1939— seven of which were musicals. Victor Saville directed Matthews's five critically and commercially most successful films. He was, alongside Hitchcock, G-B's most accomplished director—'a top-notch director', the *Sunday Times* called him in 1935,[122] while Balcon noted with pride that 'a few years ago, such directors as Victor Saville, Walter Forde and others were comparatively unknown to the film world. Now their names on a picture's "credit titles" make Hollywood itself sit up and take notice.'[123]

Matthews's husband Sonnie Hale, who had already co-starred in four films, took over from Saville to direct another three, all musicals. Glen MacWilliams photographed seven of the films, Alfred Junge art-directed at least six, and various other figures cropped up in the credits fairly regularly. As Richards has noted, 'the result of the labours of this team was a product that was glamorously international in appeal.'[124] The publicity for *Evergreen* itself stressed above all the star profile of Matthews, 'this new wonder star . . . Princess Personality herself', but also urged showmen (exhibitors) to exploit the spectacle and lavishness of the film, which G-B had deemed to have the right production ingredients for an international appeal.[125]

Variety described Matthews as 'the most sensational discovery in years',[126] and in its review of *Evergreen*, the *New York Times* celebrated this 'joyous

---

[120] Although Marie Dressler and Shirley Temple were the major female American stars of the early and mid-1930s, it makes sense to compare Matthews, with her star-image so heavily sexualized, to American stars of the period whose images were similarly sexualized, such as Jean Harlow.

[121] *Observer*, 10 June 1934.

[122] 10 Nov. 1935, in a review of *First A Girl*.

[123] 'Youth Must Carry on the Fight for Supremacy', *British Film Supplement, Picturegoer*, 5 May 1934, 7.

[124] *Dream Palace*, 216.

[125] See the Press Book for *Evergreen*, held at the BFI Library.

[126] Quoted in Quinlan, 'The Thirties', 26 (no further details given; I have been unable to trace the original).

and captivating nymph, . . . the feminine counterpart of Fred Astaire. If Hollywood has the welfare of its customers at heart, it will immediately team her with Mr Astaire in what should certainly be the perfect partnership.'[127] In fact, various Hollywood studios did attempt to sign Matthews, particularly after the relative success of *Evergreen* in the USA, and although the bids came to nothing for various reasons, the interest shown was significant.[128] *Picturegoer* described Matthews as 'our most important feminine star' and 'Britain's only world film star' in 1937, and went on to note (perhaps rather late, in view of the impending crisis in the British film industry) that

Jessie Matthews is the only English screen actress who, without having a Hollywood campaign devoted to her, has a name which is news in the United States and is strong enough to carry a picture. She is in fact one of the single biggest assets we have in the fight to secure a proper place for British films in the international market.[129]

Although she clearly was a major star and was acclaimed by British and American critics in all her major films, there is also evidence from comments in *Variety*'s reviews of *First a Girl* and *It's Love Again* that Matthews was not yet universally accepted as a box-office certainty in the United States.[130] In other words, as the New York box-office takings for *Evergreen* also suggest, G-B's policy of exploiting Matthews's star-image in films which surrounded her with Hollywood-style production values was not entirely paying off.

EVERGREEN AND CLASSICAL CINEMA

Whatever reservations there may have been about her selling-power in the United States, there is no doubt that both British and American critics were impressed by Matthews in *Evergreen*. Their praise for the film did not stop there, however, but applied more generally to the overall lavishness

---

[127] 11 Jan. 1935, 29.

[128] See Brown, 'A Knight and his Castle', 22; *Daily Mail*, 27 Oct. 1933; Matthews, *Over My Shoulder*, 142; *Evening News*, 25 Mar. 1935; Thornton, *Jessie Matthews*, 115, 121, 127; and Everson, 'Jessie Matthews', 585.

[129] 'An Open Letter to Jessie Matthews', editorial, 16 Jan. 1937, 5. The view was confirmed by Jeffrey Bernard, General Manager of G-B, in an article in *Kine Weekly* on 'Selling Films in the United States': 'The popularity of some of the British stars is astonishing. For example, Jessie Matthews, who has already been acclaimed by both exhibitors and the public, as one of the most attractive offerings in the world' (14 Jan. 1937, 37).

[130] 'British-made picture has Jessie Matthews at her best, and where her name can carry it's due for nice business. Where she is not known, or where they didn't care for *First A Girl*, she'll be a draw on her next trip,' *Variety*, 20 May 1936, repr. in *Variety's Film Reviews, 1934–1937*, v (New York, 1983), no p. nos.

of the production, the authenticity of the period detail for the Edwardian scenes, and the modernist spectacle of the art deco sets for the contemporary scenes. *Kine Weekly* thought the film 'capital popular entertainment. A potential box-office success',[131] which was 'smoothly adapted,' with 'lavish and artistic treatment': 'the money lavished on the production, which includes tuneful and scintillating dance ensembles, enables it to compare with the best.'[132] Not all the newspaper and magazine reviews were as glowing as those in the trade press, but this didn't deter the film-going public from making it a box-office success. Most reviewers found something of value in the film, particularly Matthews's performance, and even the newly established British Film Institute magazine, *Monthly Film Bulletin*, uncertain about such popular melodrama, conceded that 'the technique of this production, its presentation, everywhere rises above the material it is handling.'[133]

The most interesting comments in the American press are those which concern the extent to which the film is able to compare with contemporary Hollywood musicals. The *New York Times* thought this was 'the most pleasurable musical comedy yet offered us by the ambitious British screen industry' and picked out the 'suave and expert technical arrangement, . . . its . . . superb songs . . . [and] the presence of Jessie Matthews'.[134] *Variety*'s reviewers were in broad agreement—'an intelligent and munificent bid to compete with recent Hollywood musical talkies . . . [which] succeeded to a greater degree than anything of the kind [yet] essayed in an English studio. . . . A strong contender for American recognition.'[135] The reviewer for the *New York Times* added that 'toward the end, the film goes in for several extravaganza numbers in the blazing Hollywood style, executing them tastefully and well.' *Variety* was more critical of these dance routines, however: 'Both attempts fall short because of lack of ingenuity from a photographic standpoint, but are interesting in pointing to the fact that London is cognizant of what is needed.'[136]

Clearly fully cognizant of what was needed to make a mark in the international arena, Saville and his co-workers had produced a thoroughly classical narrative film in *Evergreen*. It has a wonderfully Oedipal plot.

---

[131] 26 Apr. 1934, 26.   [132] Ibid. 43.   [133] 1/4 (1934), 29.
[134] 11 Jan. 1935, 29.
[135] 8 May 1934; see also a second review on 15 Jan. 1935.
[136] 15 Jan. 1935, repr. in *Variety's Film Reviews, 1934–1937*, no p. nos. Subsequent Saville–Matthews films were also admired by American reviewers, as witness *Variety*'s review of *It's Love Again*: 'Picture rates as the outstander (excluding such specials as *Henry 8th*) to come from the other side for production values, imaginativeness, lighting and staging. It can hold its own with the average Hollywood musical without resorting to the standard Hollywood plot . . . London is catching up rapidly. . . . The production is handsomely staged, offers some novelty ideas and is more understandable than most British comedies are to the American mind,' 20 May 1936, on the occasion of the New York première, repr. ibid., no p. nos.

STILL 11. 'A boy's best friend is his mother': the young lovers (Jessie Matthews and Barry Mackay) playing mother and son on stage, with Leslie Benn (Sonnie Hale) (*Evergreen*).

Jessie Matthews initially plays Harriet Green, a famous music-hall star, who is retiring from the stage to marry the Marquis of Staines. When a former lover for whom she had borne a child that no one knows about returns and threatens to blackmail her, she is forced to disappear without telling her intended husband. The action is then picked up some thirty years later when Matthews reappears as the daughter, Harriet Hawkes, who is herself a performer. A young publicity agent, Tommy Thompson, and one of her mother's former collaborators involve her in an elaborate publicity stunt in which she is required to impersonate her mother returning in a new show as if she has not aged. The show is a great success, and the press and audience seem convinced by the stunt, especially when the now aged Marquis of Staines turns up and apparently (mis)recognizes the daughter as the woman he was once to marry. He also seems to think that Tommy, who is by now quite fond of Harriet, is the illegitimate child mentioned in a letter many years previously. The Marquis apparently falls in love with 'Harriet Green' once more and proposes marriage to her once again. Meanwhile, the two young lovers are forced to go around as mother and son, to perform in a second new show called 'Harriet Gilbert and Son' (in which the first number is billed as showing that 'a boy's best friend is his mother'), and even to live in the same house, a gift from the Marquis.

Finally, all is resolved on the romantic front when the Marquis reveals that he had seen through the stunt from the first, and offers no obstacle to the consummation of Tommy's and Harriet's relationship—that is, 'father' steps down to allow 'son' to become the lover of 'mother'. In a complicated intensification of this Oedipal structure, the blackmailer also reappears, obviously possessing information which threatens the status of the new 'Harriet Hawkes'. In order to restore an acceptable social equilibrium, the 'son' must also challenge the authority of this second 'father' in order to win the hand of his 'mother'. This too is successfully completed, thus enabling the formation of the required and expected couple of the classical narrative film.

The plot is unfolded in a smooth and linear fashion, with an almost effortless continuity. Unlike the more 'primitive' *Sing As We Go*, point of view and the construction of space are also handled in classical fashion, with gazes off-screen being used to construct a coherent sense of space. There is generally a much more classical sense of editing, with more reaction shots and cutaways, more close-ups, more reverse-field cutting for dialogue scenes, and so on. The editing and the sets are also efficiently subordinated to the demands of the narrative and its narration. As some of the contemporary reviewers noted, one of the features of the film is the extent to which the spectacle of the production numbers and other song-and-dance routines is tightly integrated into the narrative, rather than simply accumulating into a series of turns or novelties: *Kine Weekly* noted that 'extravagant dance numbers are smoothly dove-tailed into the development',[137] while the *New York Times* thought the film 'especially skilful in its attempt to interrupt the tale at any given moment so that Miss Matthews may dash into a song and dance.'[138] Even those moments where the film attempts a Busby Berkeley-style production—where the theatrical space of the show is superseded by a purely cinematic construction of space—are well-enough integrated to prevent the spectacle seeming gratuitous or out of place.

Evergreen takes on board the iconographic, thematic, discursive, and structural conventions of contemporary Warner Bros. backstage musicals. Numerous familiar scenes are there: the chorus-line auditions and rehearsals, the back-stage goings-on of the showmen attempting to raise adequate finance, the big production numbers, and so on. All the key character types are there too: the matinée idol, the chorus girl who becomes a great star, central protagonists who are performers, and who therefore have the necessary motivation and expertise to perform song-and-dance routines off-stage. There is also the requisite light comedy, and the ever-present narrative problem of forming the right couples. Several of the production numbers recall some of the set-pieces from *Golddiggers of 1933* (1933)—as does the brief reference to the lack of jobs, especially for chorus girls, in the early 1930s. As in *Footlight Parade* (1933), there are references to the ongoing competition between musical theatre and the talkies. The finale is clearly influenced by Busby Berkeley's choreography, with its moving rings of scantily-clad chorus girls—although, as *Variety* noted, it lacks Berkeley's use of the overhead camera, and so loses much of its visual impact.

Contemporary American musicals like Warner Bros.' *42nd Street* (1933), *Golddiggers of 1933* and *Footlight Parade* are also much harder hitting, gutsier, and sexier, with a more compelling sense of energy, vitality, and movement—although there is no denying that Matthews herself stands up very well, and some of the numbers and routines do have the joyous exuberance of contemporary American musicals. If the American films are brash where *Evergreen* is at times effete, they are in that respect similar to *Sing As We Go*, which has its own generically unique brand of gusto and energy. British films were in general perceived as slow by comparison with contemporary American films, and 'the characteristic leisureliness with which most British films unfolded' was a problem in relation to the American market, and indeed in relation to American competition in the British market.[139] Balcon, for instance, wrote in 1937 that:

---

[137] 26 Apr. 1934, 43.   [138] 11 Jan. 1935, 29.

[139] W. H. Mooring, 'British Film's Conquest of America', *Film Weekly*, 2 May 1936, discussing films of 1934.

STILL 12. Sonnie Hale with the Warner Bros.-style chorus-line in a musical rehearsal sequence (*Evergreen*).

STILL 13. The sub-Busby Berkeley finale. Sonnie Hale, Jessie Matthews, and Barry Mackay are in the centre (*Evergreen*).

The consensus of opinion amongst both the trade and the public is that, generally speaking, the tempo of the British picture is very noticeably slower than that of the American product.... As a rough estimate, I put the tempo of British pictures about half-way between German ones and American ones. Three or four years ago our pictures were very much slower than they are now: every year marks an appreciable acceleration: one of the most vitally important tasks facing us in British production is to accelerate this process until our tempo matches that of Hollywood.[140]

Once again, there is little evidence here of Balcon attempting to differentiate G-B's product from Hollywood's fare or to build a distinctive national cinema from indigenous cultural traditions, rather than the traditions of classical American cinema. An American trade journalist confirmed Balcon's view, seeing the slower tempo of British films as an affliction— deviance from the international standards established by the Hollywood studios could only be so understood from that hegemonic viewpoint. And if British films were to be commercially successful exports, that is the viewpoint that must indeed be adopted. National specificity was perceived as a symptom of insularity and élitism, it would seem; it was valid only for a more discerning audience:

[A] common complaint about British films is lack of pace, which does indeed afflict many of them. Actually, this slackness is not always present, and to the more discerning American filmgoer this is quickly apparent. But films are not made for the intelligent few. To succeed they have to be of mass appeal, and to the masses they must therefore be acceptable. About the average Hollywood output there is an unmistakable breeziness and speed, both part of the American mentality. They are as much an indispensable part of the attraction as the settings or the players who perform in them.[141]

The pacing of the narrative was clearly one element on which British companies had to work if they wanted their films to do well in the export market. With regard to *Evergreen*, it is the scenes which are designed precisely to motivate the narrative momentum which are the most problematic. The opening Edwardian sequence (and the later rendition of Edwardian-style songs) slows the tempo right down and is unnecessarily long given the amount of narrative information that must be conveyed. At other times, the film has all the briskness that would be expected of an American musical of the period, particularly when the narrative focus of the film shifts from the mother to the daughter. Thus, once the initial

---

[140] *Kine Weekly*, 14 Jan. 1937, 31.

[141] Kann, 'Hollywood and Britain', 300–1. When *First A Girl* was released in New York in 1935, *Variety* commented that 'one of the film's prime defects is the lethargic tempo . . . the retarded movement,' 8 Jan. 1935, repr. in *Variety's Film Reviews, 1934– 1937*, no p. nos. On the release of *It's Love Again*, the same paper felt that 'a clip of about 10 minutes would have smartened it considerably, and more could be ripped out to the quickening of the tempo,' 20 May 1936, repr. ibid., no p. nos.

machinations of the plot have been successfully processed, first establishing
the star-image of Harriet Green and the mystery of her private life, and
then setting in motion her daughter's impersonation of her, the plot is
organized much more centrally around the complicated romance between
Harriet Hawkes/Green and Tommy Thompson.

With this shift in narrative focus, the film moves closer to the more
sophisticated art deco world of Astaire and Rogers musicals (although
only *Flying Down To Rio* (1933) could have been seen before production
on *Evergreen* had started).[142] The emphasis is on the couple more than the
ensemble, the melodrama is played as light comedy more reminiscent of
Astaire than of, say, Cagney in *Footlight Parade*, and the range of
motivations enabling characters to break into a song-and-dance routine
shifts significantly, taking on more securely the conventions of what has
been called the integrated musical.[143] Thus at one point, the motivation of
putting on a show and the use of a stage or rehearsal space for dancing
are abandoned. In their place, the desire to express an excess of emotion
motivates a solo dance by Matthews in which the dance space is appropriated from the huge, highly-polished living-room floor of the couple's art
deco house.[144] The dancing here is also different, much more graceful than
the hurly-burly of the show numbers with big chorus-lines.

In this dance in particular, Matthews achieves a level of eroticism rare
in British cinema. However, by comparing *Evergreen* with *Top Hat* (1935),
another nearly contemporaneous film, one can see that, where in *Top Hat*
romance is achieved and expressed through the harmoniously dancing
couple, in *Evergreen* sexual desire is constantly thwarted and repressed. In
the dance sequence just referred to, Matthews is forced to dance on her
own in order to express her feelings. She also dances alone for much of
the final dance-number of the film. Although the climactic finale at last
brings the couple together and consummates the love affair, the single shot
of a chaste kiss and clasped hands which celebrates their unity is very
brief—and coy in its metaphorical intent.

The film also tries to balance both the cultural respectability of a virtu-
ous Edwardian sexuality, and the requirement that the classical film enables
a more prurient, voyeuristic (male, heterosexual) gaze at the female body
by the spectator. Thus, in the opening sequence of Harriet Green's farewell
performance set in a respectable Edwardian music-hall, the audience in the

---

[142] *Flying Down to Rio* was trade shown in Britain on 20 Feb. 1934, but not released until
Aug. 1934; *The Gay Divorcee* was not trade shown until 3 Dec. 1934, nor released
until Apr. 1935.

[143] See e.g. John Mueller, 'Fred Astaire and the Integrated Musical', *Cinema Journal*,
24/1 (1984).

[144] Cf. Jane Feuer on the myth of spontaneity in 'The Self-Reflexive Musical and the Myth
of Entertainment', in Rick Altman (ed.), *Genre: The Musical* (London, 1981); and Jane
Feuer, *The Hollywood Musical* (London, 1982).

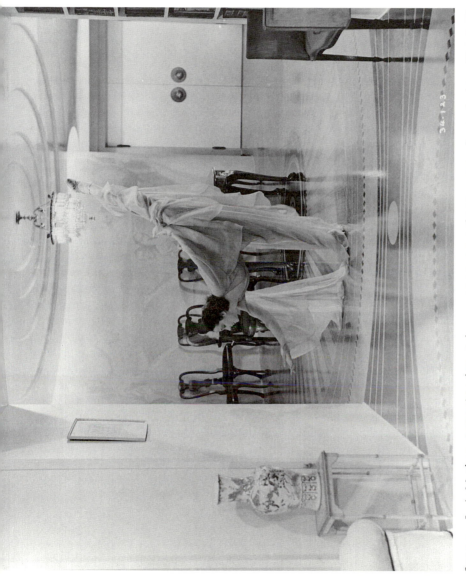

STILL 14. Jessie Matthews appropriates her art-deco apartment as a performance space for a solo dance (*Evergreen*).

music-hall are offered only images of Harriet Green in full-length Edwardian gowns; the spectators in the cinema, on the other hand, are able to
witness Jessie Matthews stripping down to her underwear back-stage to
change costume. The scene is narratively redundant, gratuitous, but as an
image it provides the spectacle of the female body that is expected of the
classical film and suggests also that the film is overall going to be a bit
more risqué than a high-class Edwardian music-hall show.

This tension between the Edwardian and the modern (for 1934) is exploited on several occasions in the film. When Matthews is playing the
daughter impersonating the mother, she is supposed to appear to be about
sixty years old to her theatre audiences; yet the costumes in which she
performs suggest something else altogether: the disjunction is precisely that
of the chaste and the prurient. The scene of back-stage undressing in the
Edwardian music-hall is recalled in a much later scene which, in a sense,
completes the exchange of sexualized looks that is only partially established in the first scene. The later scene is crucial, since it is the point at
which Harriet Hawkes, the daughter, reveals to her audience at the theatre
that she has been impersonating her mother Harriet Green. In the middle
of a big production number, Harriet unexpectedly pushes the other dancers
out of the way, moves to the front of the stage, strips down to her underwear, flings off her wig and proceeds to perform an exuberant tap dance
to confused jeers from the audience who feel they have been cheated. In
the earlier scene, only the cinema audience had witnessed the striptease,
but this time, the theatre audience are able to see it too. Once more, it is
the paradox of innocence and eroticism that is constructed as one of the
central appeals of Matthews's star-image, playing on both a certain English middle-class respectability and a more modern, international version
of the woman as image.

Evergreen, then, draws on the conventions of the contemporary Hollywood musical, and the classical film's particular articulation of sexual
difference and the eroticization of the gaze. It also works with the conventions of the melodrama, again handling them with ease and confidence,
and two key scenes in particular exhibit a very powerful melodramatic
effect in their *mise-en-scène* and use of sound. The first scene involves
Matthews as the real Harriet Green, who must mysteriously disappear
from her friends. At the end of the long opening sequence, Harriet rides
off alone in a horse-drawn carriage through the empty night streets of
London. She passes the Tivoli, where she has been performing, and hears
strains of her best-known song being sung by her friends still revelling
inside, unaware of her plight. She watches the lights being turned off outside
the theatre, effectively extinguishing her own existence, and she slowly
removes her engagement ring. It is a very nostalgic moment, invoking a
powerful sense of loss. The film plays on the difference between what she,

STILLS 15 and 16. The female body on display: Jessie Matthews stripped down to her underwear to end the masquerade in the modern-day sequence of *Evergreen* (below); and a publicity still for the same film (right), the original caption for which read: 'SYLPHS OF THE SOUND STAGE. This LADDER OF LEGS belongs to the sparkling array of beautiful showgirls marshalled by Director Victor Saville to appear in the many spectacular numbers in the new talkie version of the C. B. Cochran success *Evergreen*.'

and what the spectators of the film, know and can see, and what the Marquis and her other friends know and can see. Her gaze out of the carriage cannot be met by theirs, the sense of longing it embodies cannot be overcome until her daughter returns to take her place at the end of the film.[145]

The second scene rhymes with and recalls the first, and it is only at this point that Matthews's unreciprocated look can be returned by her lover and her audience. The scene begins in a court room where Harriet Hawkes is being tried for fraud and the impersonation of her own mother. The defence's case is that there is no fraud; Matthews as the daughter can offer the same pleasures to her audience as her mother had provided thirty years earlier. To prove this, a phonograph of the mother singing the song heard in the first scene is played in court, and the daughter joins the recording of her now dead mother in a duet, eventually drowning out her mother's voice by her own magnificence, charming both the judge and the audience in the gallery. From a close-up of Matthews's face bathed in light, the camera pans along the beam of light to reveal its source as a court-room window. This dissolves to a spotlight in a theatre, and the camera pans back down the beam of light to reveal Matthews still singing the same song, but now on-stage, at the start of the big finale. In this reprise of the earlier scene, the sense of loss engendered by the absence of the mother is triggered by the faint recording of her voice, but Matthews as the daughter performs with such brilliance that we are presented with an experience of plenitude. The court-room scene at the same time finally gives a legal seal of approval to the impersonation and its pleasures. This ultimately removes all obstacles to the consummation of Harriet's and Tommy's relationship, which is given to us in the final shot of the film.

The result of G-B's internationalist policy, its push for ever greater profits, its bid to appeal to domestic and foreign audiences attuned to the pleasures and ideologies of American cinema, is then to produce a film which works very successfully within the conventions of that cinema. There are minor deviations from the standard—the pacing of the narrative and the handling of desire, for instance—but, for G-B, these were not to be celebrated as the positive signs of national difference, exclusive badges of uniqueness to be worn proudly by a national cinema that regretfully had to work with foreign traditions in order to build up audiences. On the contrary, these were precisely deviations to be ironed out: difference was not the name of the game.

SING AS WE GO, PERFORMANCE AND THE CINEMA OF ATTRACTIONS

If *Evergreen* self-consciously emulates classical Hollywood cinema, *Sing As We Go* opts for a very different cultural stance, one that can be seen as

---

[145] See Steve Neale, 'Melodrama and Tears', Screen, 27/6 (1986).

nationalist to *Evergreen*'s internationalism. One of the most remarkable aspects of *Sing As We Go* is the flimsiness of its narrative, in contrast to the strength of individual moments within it. Even the most classical cinema is marked by a tension between narration and description, narrative and spectacle, movement and stasis, voyeurism and exhibitionism: that indeed is central to the pleasures of such cinema. Although the narrative system struggles to fix the meaning of an image, there is always more than the narrative can hold in place. As Stephen Heath puts it, 'narrative never exhausts the image. . . . Narrative can never contain the whole film which permanently exceeds its fictions.'[146] The potential redundancy of the image, this 'something more', is not, however, wasted by Hollywood. While *mise-en-scène* is predominantly organized in the interests of clinching narrative significance, it is also developed as something fascinating in itself, a source of visual pleasure, a spectacle. In certain genres—and particularly performative genres like the musical and the comedy—the tensions are intensified. This is particularly the case with *Sing As We Go*; here, one needs to ask not whether the narrative is suspended for musical and comic inserts, but whether narrative structure or narrational function can in any way be seen as the guiding principles in the mapping out of the diegesis, or the central motivations for the diverse attractions of the film.

There are in effect three story-lines in *Sing As We Go*. First, there is the story of the closure of Greybeck Mill, the attempts to involve Sir William Upton and his artificial silk process in an effort to reopen the mill, and the final scenes of its actual reopening. Grace (Gracie Fields) is established as one of the mill-workers, a member of a tight-knit community, but a special member, an acknowledged ring-leader. A second story-line deals with the picaresque adventures of Grace travelling to and seeking gainful employment in Blackpool, 'that most native of English pleasure grounds'.[147] The third story-line is a love-triangle romance involving Grace, her boss, the upper-class Hugh (who has no idea of Grace's affection for him), and Phyllis, a conventionally pretty young Londoner with a 'refined' accent, who is befriended by Grace, but who also falls in love with Hugh. The triangle is resolved in favour of the conventionally pretty Phyllis, rather than the less glamorous Grace/Gracie Fields,[148] pairing off with the

[146] 'Film and System: Terms of Analysis', *Screen*, 16/1 (1975), 10; see also pt. 2 of the article in 16/2 (1975); Roland Barthes, 'The Third Meaning', in *Image-Music-Text*, essays sel. and trans. by Stephen Heath (London, 1977); Kristin Thompson, 'The Concept of Cinematic Excess', *Ciné-tracts*, 1/2 (1977); Jan Mukarovsky, 'The Esthetics of Language', in Paul L. Garvin (ed. and trans.), *A Prague School Reader on Esthetics, Literary Structure and Style* (Washington, DC, 1964); and Laura Mulvey, 'Visual Pleasure and Narrative Cinema', *Screen*, 16/3 (1975).

[147] C. A. Lejeune, in a review of *Sing As We Go*, *Observer*, 16 Sept. 1934.

[148] Because of the weakness with which Gracie Fields's role is narrativized, I have at times referred to the role as 'Grace/Gracie Fields', by which I intend to imply that narrative role and the performative presence of the star attraction are virtually indistinguishable. Where I intend to refer strictly to the narrative character, I use the term 'Grace', and where I refer strictly to the performer, I use the term 'Gracie Fields' (or 'Fields').

conventionally handsome male lead.

Structurally, each of these narratives is classically developed in terms of moving in a linear fashion from an initial equilibrium, through a phase of disequilibrium, to a final, new, goal-fulfilling equilibrium. But these story-lines are never fully fleshed out in the way the above description might imply: the plots are skeletal and overall the narrative development, although linear, is highly episodic, with new possibilities and openings constantly being explored. Causality and motivation are weak, and potentially serious narrative points—such as Grace's love for Hugh—are underdeveloped and thereby rendered inconsequential. The main attractions of the film are the scrapes which Grace gets involved in, on the way to and in Blackpool, and the various turns she performs as a result. The first narrative line is only occasionally inserted into this more carnivalesque space, where it struggles to remind us of the background and the motivation for Fields's presence in Blackpool, to give the semblance of narrative cinema, to attempt to order and regulate the pleasures of the film.

There are certain ways in which *Sing As We Go* adopts a classical stance in its narrative movement, its diegetic effect, and in the processing of its songs.[149] The motivations for the shift into songs, for instance, aspire to *Evergreen*'s classicism. Thus Grace/Gracie Fields is required by narrative circumstances to put on some sort of show for all but one of her songs. On the one occasion when there is little or no sense of putting on a show, the myth of spontaneity is at work again as Grace is moved by an excess of emotion to sing a romantic love-song having 'just lost the only chap I ever loved'. The romantic love-song also has some narrative relevance in its sentiments, as does another song performed by Grace when she inadvertently finds herself in front of an audience at the Tower Ballroom in Blackpool. The audience are expecting to see the 'beautiful' winners of a bathing beauties contest; instead they are confronted with the less conventionally beautiful Grace/Gracie Fields, who anyway is looking extremely bedraggled. Grace sings 'Little Bottom Drawer', a song about being a spinster, which also sums up the way in which things seem to be progressing for her narratively.

These songs are rather different from the conventions of *Evergreen* and contemporaneous Hollywood musicals in terms of iconography and performance. There are no song-and-dance routines, no big production numbers—although the Tower Ballroom performance could be read as a parody of the big production number, and the montage of romantic scenes which follows the love-song could be read as a sort of alternative version of the big number. In place of such conventional Hollywood routines, we have

---

[149] See Noël Burch, 'Narrative/Diegesis: Thresholds, Limits', *Screen*, 23/2 (1982), on the concept of the diegetic effect.

community singing led by Grace/Gracie Fields—a form of singing which potentially embraces the cinema audience as part of the community, also singing along.

In general, motivation is handled in a much more cavalier and therefore by comparison more 'primitive' fashion than in *Evergreen*. For instance, Grace's excessively emotional state may motivate the initial singing of the love-song—but the emotional intensity of the scene is completely undercut by the re-emergence of one of the film's running gags, Stanley Holloway as a comic policeman. By huge coincidence (his every appearance is by huge coincidence!), he is drunk, in uniform, and below Grace's window as she sings. He picks up the song in comic fashion, but it is then returned to Grace. The intensity of feeling conveyed by the song subsequently finds a visual expression in the quite brilliant montage sequence which follows on from the song: a series of images reprise various minor and major romances recalling characters from each little episode of the film.

But the sequence does not stop there. There is a brief return to Grace as she completes the song (which continues as background music) and turns to look soulfully out of the window. With minimal motivation, there is a wipe to a shot which begins another montage sequence. In a way which looks forward to the Humphrey Jennings of *Listen to Britain* (1942),[150] this second sequence offers an impression of Blackpool at the end of another day, but also at the end of this particular visit, and this particular narrative. It thus prepares the way for the movement into the equally impressive closing scenes. The sequence starts off classically enough, but then shifts into the realm of an impressionist visual imagination, a collective diegetic fantasy, the formation not of one couple, but of many couples, who are themselves situated in a wider locality. It also involves a radical switch in point of view, from the individual within the diegesis (the performance of the song) to the omniscient camera-narrator and cinema audience (the montage sequence). The continuity maintained by the aural track effaces the shift, but the shift is there all the same, and quite exhilarating in the sudden, under-motivated leap it makes from a protagonist-centred linear narrative, to the realms of montage cinema and the more pluralist perspective on the diegesis which this affords.

Tom Gunning has argued that 'the cinema of attraction does not disappear with the dominance of narrative, but rather goes underground, both into certain avant-garde practices and as a component of narrative films, more evident in some genres (e.g. the musical) than in others.'[151] *Sing As We Go* is an impressive instance of the emergence of the cinema of

---

[150] Discussed in the next ch.

[151] 'The Cinema of Attraction: Early Film, its Spectator and the Avant-Garde', in Thomas Elsaesser with Adam Barker (eds.), *Early Cinema: Space, Frame, Narrative* (London, 1990), 57.

attractions within the field of narrative cinema. Indeed, it makes more sense to see *Sing As We Go* not as a narrative film in which music and comic gags feature as interruptions or inserts, but as a film which is organized around its various attractions, which include the relatively avant-garde practice of montage. The attractions are the point of the film, not its flaws: the pleasures of this film are less the drama of narrative integration, and more the attractions of potential disintegration.[152] The narrative is merely an excuse for a carnival, a licence for the transgressions of the cinema of attractions.[153] Once the licence has been granted, so to speak, the film can proceed according to its own desires. Like the tradition of carnival which Mikhail Bakhtin has described, this film celebrates its own 'temporary liberation from the prevailing truth and established order' of classical cinema; it suspends the hierarchical rules, norms, and prohibitions of the classical film.[154] Narrative cinema has in this instance been carnivalized; what we see is the reverse side of narrative cinema, the life of the narrative film turned inside out.[155] Inevitably, for the reviewer attuned to the conventions of classical cinema, the film was thoroughly deviant, its plot a 'tenuous and disjointed affair that serves (only just) to hold the picture together.'[156]

Within this tradition of popular pleasures, the attraction exhausts its own appeal, rather than motivating a narrative shift through space and time. The visit to the circus in *Sing As We Go* seems quite gratuitous, for instance. Grace is looking for Phyllis, who has found her way to the circus; two shots of Phyllis watching the circus acts are inserted, but the location itself is of no narrative consequence. Grace does find Phyllis there, but there are many more shots of the acts and the location than are narratively necessary; this redundance then transforms them into an overt spectacle, the pleasure of which is intensified by seeing Grace floundering about in the sea-lion pool: the narrative insists on its existence, but the pleasures of the scene lie in the gags themselves.

There are several other sequences made up of entirely self-contained gags, with no narrative pay-off. This is probably most marked in the scene in Uncle Murgatroyd's house near the start of the film, which involves a series of jokes about clocks, tripe, boozing, and the castrating effects of middle-aged asexual women. The scene undoubtedly establishes certain

---

[152] Cf. Donald Crafton, 'Pie and Chase: Gag, Spectacle and Narrative in Slapstick Comedy', in Eileen Bowser (ed.), *The Slapstick Symposium* (Brussels, 1988), on the function of gags in slapstick comedy.

[153] Cf. the quotation from Méliès used in the previous chapter: 'As for the scenario, . . . [it] has no importance, since I use it merely as a pretext for the "stage effects", the "tricks", or for a nicely arranged tableau.' Quoted by Gunning, 'Cinema of Attractions', 57.

[154] *Rabelais and His World* (Cambridge, Mass., 1968), 10.

[155] Cf. Bakhtin, *Problems of Dostoyevsky's Poetics* (Manchester, 1984), 122.

[156] *Film Weekly*, 26 Oct. 1934, 36.

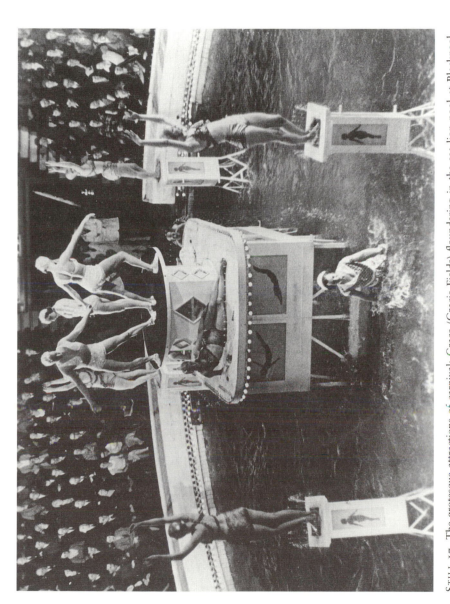

STILL 17. The grotesque attractions of carnival: Grace (Gracie Fields) floundering in the sea-lion pool at Blackpool Circus in *Sing As We Go*.

character traits and provides the initial motivation for Grace's visit to Blackpool, but for the most part it is an excuse for a bit of comic business. There is little sense in which the meanings and pleasures of the sequence are dependent on the shots which precede and follow it; rather, like the other gags in the film, it is meaningful only in itself, as a gag. Gags may develop into, or provide the space for further gags, but those gags do not necessarily have any bearing on the narrative elements of the film. This sense of parallel developments—the causality of narrative, but also the accretion of gags—can be seen particularly in the case of the running gag involving Holloway's comic policeman: Grace asks him the way on first arriving in Blackpool; disguised as a fortune-teller, she reads his fortune; she is chased by him at the Pleasure Beach and at the Tower Ballroom, where he later watches her singing; he drunkenly takes up her love-song; and he delivers her a message as she is about to depart from Blackpool. The policeman is thus a pawn in the narrative: his every intervention is either of no narrative consequence (asking the way in Blackpool), or could have been handled without his presence (delivering the message); but in terms of comedy, his presence is a great attraction: that, of course, is his function.

In a more obvious way than in most musicals, the narrative is precisely a vehicle for a comic singing star, who is 'its impetus and reason for existence',[157] and the gaps in the development of the narrative are bridged by the presence of Fields herself. It is her performance and charisma which hold the film together, not the principles of narrative continuity. In this film, moreover, Fields has a performative theatrical presence, rather than a more conventionally classical screen presence; the spectacle of Fields, her star-image, is not in this case resolutely integrated into a narrative flow which can barely contain her down-to-earth gusto. *Kine Weekly*'s comments on Fields's previous film, *Love, Life and Laughter* (1934), seem just as pertinent here:

the construction of the entertainment is a trifle lacking in firm unity, but its weaknesses in this department are brilliantly offset by the genius, versatility and amazing showmanship of Gracie Fields. . . . The genius of the star . . . by the sheer force of her personality, forms a human and fascinating connecting link between the film's many widely entertaining departments.[158]

Sing As We Go is, then, performance-orientated, rather than action-orientated—and what actions there are should be appreciated for their performance, rather than for their psychological realism or their function within a causal chain. Indeed, Basil Dean evidently quite consciously adopted a strategy for foregrounding performance in Fields's films at this time: 'in

---

[157] Ibid.   [158] 15 Mar. 1934, 37.

leaving [Fields's] personality to its own devices, untrammelled by technical niceties, I was prompted by my theatre experience.'[159]

There is then something of a tension between Grace, the narrative character, and Gracie Fields, the attraction. The tension is true of all stars, but in Fields's case (and especially in this film), it seems to be accentuated. Her performance style, developed in and for the variety stage, neither eschews direct address nor seeks the subtleties of naturalism at all costs. It would perhaps be more appropriate to describe her as a diegetic character rather than a narrative character, given the weakness with which she is integrated into a tightly circumscribed narrative trajectory. She clearly does inhabit a relatively autonomous imaginative world, but it is not a world (a diegesis) where space and time are rigorously organized by narrative requirements. Grace/Gracie Fields's role in that space is to perform, to entertain, but not necessarily to trigger the next causal shift in the narrative. She can inhabit this diegetic world performatively, but she is not necessarily required to move through it narratively.

The delineation of space, and of the characters who occupy it, constantly exceeds that which is strictly narratively necessary. In a strongly narrative cinema, the diegesis—the implied world of the fiction—is made linear. In the absence of that strong narrative control, that which is visible of the diegesis is multiplied: we are witness to elements of that diegesis which narratively need be no more than implied. Those elements become the space for another performance act, another gag, or another song. Thus, the performance of the gag with no narrative function does not halt the diegesis, or leave it—it simply uses it differently.[160]

The film is, then, a musical, but one whose roots are firmly in the tradition of the music-hall and variety. Scenes and sequences are relatively self-contained and the over-riding impression of the film is of one act or turn or novelty after another: 'It is all very inconsequent, but rich and lively slapstick.'[161] The film thus has the format of variety's mixed bills, with the narrative merely providing the space for the playing out of a series of acts: the songs and the comic business, of course, but also the attractions of Blackpool.

It is these popular pleasures which make the film. Like carnival, it is a radically hybrid, exuberant, and excessive mix of pleasures: a series of more or less ritualized spectacles, and comic, often parodic, gags and songs, stressing regional customs and accents, and often mocking figures of authority. While Dean may have aspired to uplift the appeal of a Fields film, he could not at the same time entirely resist the fascination of the popular

---

[159] *Mind's Eye*, 210.

[160] I cannot therefore agree with Crafton, 'Pie and Chase', who suggests that the performance of a gag halts the diegesis (see e.g. 51).

[161] *Sunday Express*, 16 Sept. 1934.

culture which she represented, a culture which resists the disciplines and regulations of bourgeois sentiment.[162]

Space in *Sing As We Go* is used primarily as performance space, as the diegesis of carnival, and not as narrative space. But space also functions as spectacle in its own right. The diegesis of carnival is also the carnivalesque diegesis, the realm of visual pleasures which transgress the boundaries of the narrative and its requirements, which resist its containments. That is to say, Dean tends to use locations as an often fairly gratuitous spectacle, another attraction, sometimes only weakly integrated into the plot or into the narrative space of his films: their excessiveness is the extent to which, as locations, they supersede any purely narrative function.

'Blackpool and Gracie are the principal characters' commented one critic; another suggested that Blackpool was the 'scintillating, substantial pivot' of the film.[163] Certainly, the attractions of Blackpool are pivotal to the narrative, but it is perhaps more the lengths to which Dean goes to include yet another attraction that renders Blackpool scintillating. This is true not only of the spaces which are on show, but also of the perspective from which they are seen: there are several panoramic shots of crowds on the front at Blackpool, at the Pleasure Beach, and so on, and on another occasion the camera is fixed to the roller-coaster on which Hugh and Phyllis take a ride. Blackpool, then, is the heart of the film. The film leads into Blackpool, but, like a holiday, the journey returns home in the end— triumphantly, in this case, as if the duty and authenticity of labour were more desirable than the transitory pleasures of the holiday resort. The Pleasure Beach itself is literally the centre of the film—it takes us just over half an hour to get there, and when we leave, there are another thirty minutes of the film left: the film seems circular, rather than linear.

The choice of this location is obviously crucial to the pleasures of the film. Blackpool is first of all of course a hugely popular working-class holiday site, 'a pleasure resort for the crowd.'[164] But at the level of representation, Blackpool—and the Pleasure Beach as a heightening of that experience—means more than just a resort. For Priestley in his *English Journey* (1933), it is 'the great roaring spangled beast':[165] not just a place, but a metaphor for a certain regime of pleasure, 'cheerfully vulgar . . . terrifying . . . crazy . . . [full of] fantastic idiocies.'[166] In one telling passage,

---

[162] Cf. the terms in which Bakhtin discusses the popular pleasures of carnival (see the 'Introduction' to *Rabelais*; and *Dostoyevsky's Poetics*, 122–37); also Peter Stallybrass and Allon White, *The Politics and Poetics of Transgression* (London, 1986), for the way in which they take up Bakhtin's categories, and in particular their argument that carnival did not disappear, but rather reappeared in a variety of carnivalized cultural forms and practices.

[163] *Film Weekly*, 26 Oct. 1934, 36; *Kine Weekly*, 13 Sept. 1934, 29.

[164] J. B. Priestley, *English Journey* (London, 1934), 265.

[165] Ibid. 263.   [166] Ibid. 263–6.

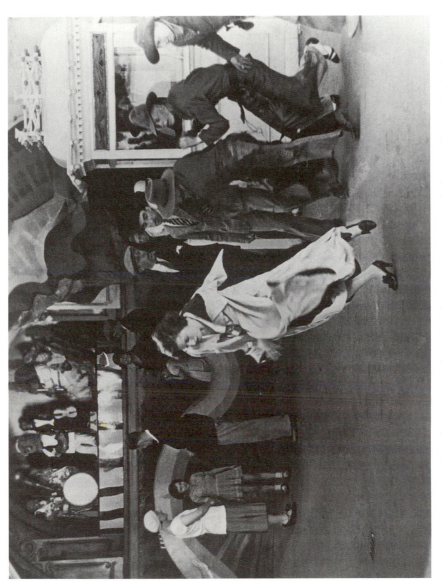

STILL 18. All the fun of the fair: a group of stage cowboys pursue Grace at Blackpool's Pleasure Beach (*Sing As We Go*).

Priestley describes Blackpool out of season, when 'the three piers had done with frivolity for this year and were now engaged in their proper stern task of holding up against the dark raging sea.'[167] As so often in discussions of modern British culture, there is here the contrast between the frivolous and the 'proper stern task', between the popular and the serious, between the gratuitous and the utilitarian. The pleasures of Blackpool are profoundly non-utilitarian—they are, on the contrary, vulgar, grotesque, transitory, irresponsible, often organized around bodily sensations.[168] What really stands out is the perverse diversity of these pleasures. Like the music-hall stage, a variety of attractions compete for attention and refuse attempts to present a smooth, integrated, streamlined form. It is precisely this sense of variety which fascinates Priestley:

> this huge mad place, with its miles and miles of promenades, its three piers, its gigantic dance-halls, its variety shows, its switch-backs and helter-skelters, its array of wine bars and oyster saloons and cheap restaurants and tea houses and shops piled high and glittering with trash; its army of pierrots, bandsmen, clowns, fortune-tellers, auctioneers, dancing partners, animal trainers, itinerant singers, hawkers; its seventy special trains a day, its hundreds and hundreds of thousands of trippers .[169]

Blackpool can be all of this because it is a holiday resort. It is the site for and the sign of the licensed transgressions of the very audiences to whom *Sing As We Go* is addressed: 'In his one week of 'freedom' in the year the worker . . . comes here to escape, to get out of the rut of time and money and limited leisure of life in his home town.'[170] Blackpool carnivalizes time and possibility for the visitor; in the film, it is as place, space, and spectacle that it is carnivalesque. Of course, it is all highly ritualized, highly structured—but within that structure, something else, something other than the routine, is possible. Blackpool provides the space for that something else, it functions as the variety stage of this particular series of music-hall acts as film. It is a performance space which already brings the connotations of variety and of popular pleasures and transgressions to the film.[171]

One can even see *Sing As We Go*'s various montage sequences as acts, turns, or novelties. The sequence which depicts Grace's journey from Greybeck to Blackpool is perhaps the clearest example of montage as an attraction. Narratively, all that is required of the sequence is that it

---

[167] Ibid. 264.
[168] Cf. Tony Bennett, 'A Thousand and one Troubles', *Formations of Pleasure* (London, 1983); and 'Hegemony, Ideology, Pleasure: Blackpool', in Tony Bennett, Colin Mercer, and Janet Woollacott (eds.), *Popular Culture and Social Relations* (Milton Keynes, 1986).
[169] *English Journey*, 265–6; cf. Tom Harrisson, 'The Fifty-Second Week: Impressions of Blackpool', *Geographical Magazine*, 6 (1938), 387.
[170] Ibid. 392.   [171] Cf. Bennett, 'A Thousand and one Troubles'.

establish that Grace has travelled to and arrived at Blackpool, perhaps for reasons of realism confirming that, owing to lack of money, she has cycled there. But the sequence as presented in the film vastly exceeds this minimal narrative function. In addition to various visual and verbal gags, and a raucous instrumental version of the title-song, the sequence functions almost like a showreel of montage effects, a self-conscious display of special effects: overt graphic discontinuities within and between shots, shaped wipes, split screen and reverse-printed superimpositions, and other avant-garde optical effects reminiscent of Vertov's *The Man With A Movie Camera* (1929, USSR).

The editing strategies generally used in this film tend to differentiate it from more classical texts. Scenes tend to be frontally composed, in theatrical style—Fields for instance, often stands frontally (facing the camera) even when addressing someone off left or right. There is relatively little scene dissection, relatively little reverse-field composition or use of over-the-shoulder shots—although there is some cross-cutting between different sites of action within a scene for dramatic effect.

There are also several instances of non-continuity editing: the montage sequences, of course, but then classical Hollywood also has its montage sequences; but there are also various ostentatious shot transitions (shaped wipes, an iris out from a crystal ball, and so on). There is a chase sequence that has been visibly jump-cut to create a greater sense of pace. There are some moments of faulty continuity, too, such as an inexplicable break in continuity in the middle of the scene at the music publisher's. A more interesting example of this sort of aberrance, because of its perverse unreadability, comes in a scene at Uncle Murgatroyd's house near the beginning of the film. Grace says goodbye to a young lad, in long shot; the theme tune is briefly heard being whistled, but without evident diegetic motivation; there is an unmotivated dissolve to Grace in medium shot gazing directly at camera, followed by another dissolve to Hugh, her boss, in medium shot on the phone at the factory, and a final dissolve back to Grace. It is extremely difficult to read the sequence at all (is Grace daydreaming about Hugh?) because of the lack of motivation for the shot transitions, and the lack of evident continuity across them. On other occasions in the film, there are a number of fairly long-held shots, which neither convey very much narratively nor are very interesting in themselves as images; in a number of cases, they are reaction shots of Grace, who does not actually seem to register any reaction, as if her mere presence in the frame was sufficient attraction.

Sing As We Go's mode of address also deviates from more classical representations in various ways. This is partly because the film draws on theatrical models: hence the frontality of the staging in various scenes, but also some excessively loud dialogue, as if pitched to the back of the auditorium. More notable perhaps is the occasional use of direct address to camera which betrays the music-hall origins of the film. In the closing shots of the film, for instance, Grace marches with a crowd of workers into the newly reopened factory. Initially, they are all singing the title-song, but Grace/Gracie Fields detaches herself from the group, turns to camera, and concludes the song for 'us'.

Does this mean that in these moments of direct address, the character of Grace is, as it were, severed from the diegesis and the illusion of a self-enclosed fictional world is dashed? I would argue not, since by this move and by various others—such as the visibility of diegetic audiences of one sort or another within the frame—the text implies a live, theatrical audience, which can itself then be understood as part of the diegesis of the film. The address to camera thus comes across not as an address to the actual audience in the cinema at the moment of exhibition, but to an implied live audience, who can feel the presence of the performer. The implied live audience, and the space which it occupies, is thus part of—strictly, I suppose, an extension of—the performance space of the film. This feeling of liveness inevitably establishes a certain complicity with the actual cinema audience. Significantly Fields, by her own account, hated making films and much preferred working the halls because of the direct contact with an audience which that allowed. However much her early films at ATP tried to reproduce that contact, they could not in the end sufficiently compensate for its actual absence.[172]

The attractions of liveness are the attractions of a pre-eminently exhibitionist cinema, one which acknowledges its visibility. The theatrical presence of the performers, the look at the camera and so on, are all elements of self-display. This mode of address is one which revolves around the act of showing, not the process of story-telling and the suspense of the voyeuristic. It delights in the gag in and for itself, and for the skill of its performance for an audience whose presence is not denied.

The non-classical form of *Sing As We Go* was evidently not a problem in box-office terms, and *Kine Weekly* had no hesitation in recommending the film as 'marvellous entertainment. A box-office certainty', noting of the narrative construction simply that 'the action . . . follows clever cameo sketches, linked together by a neat story.' The reviewer goes on to suggest that the film is

unquestionably Gracie Fields's best . . . [She] has a great part . . . The supporting characters are brilliantly drawn . . . and the photography superb . . . Sentiment is not lacking, and the effective manner in which it punctuates the humour is a striking tribute to the competency and showmanship of Basil Dean's direction.[173]

---

[172] See Gracie Fields, *Sing As We Go* (London, 1960), e.g. 193; also Moules, *Our Gracie*, 53.
[173] 13 Sept. 1934, 15.

It is no surprise that the serious reviewers in the so-called quality national newspapers, catering for a primarily middle-class readership, were less convinced by the qualities of the film, which was culturally somewhat removed from their idea of good cinema. Thus *The Times* argued that despite her commercial success, Gracie Fields 'has yet to make a good film', but it did concede that since

the story of *Sing As We Go* was written by Mr J. B. Priestley and it is directed by Mr Basil Dean, [there is] evidence that a real effort has been made to provide her with a vehicle worthy of her talent. She is no longer expected to carry the whole weight of the production on her shoulders.[174]

However, the *Daily Telegraph* reviewer felt this was still too evidently a Gracie Fields vehicle, and somewhat repetitious at that: 'It is all very jolly and riotous—and after half an hour or so, rather tiring, because "plus ca change, plus c'est la même chose" . . . Little more than a series of "turns" for the star comedienne, necessarily all on somewhat similar lines.'[175]

The names of Priestley and Dean (given his theatre work) clearly connote quality for such reviewers, but they feel that they have been let down, since the film 'finally emerged as a "vehicle" for the talents of the irrepressible Miss Fields',[176] and while they can concede that she is good at what she does, and undoubtedly commands huge respect at the box-office ('the admirers of Gracie Fields will find her at the full blast of her vivacious comic genius'[177]), it still does not make the film one that they would feel happy recommending to their own readers. There are clearly two audiences for the cinema being delineated here: the general public, who generate a great deal of income for the trade, and who are satisfied by the likes of Fields, and a more discerning audience, who demand something more culturally sophisticated and intellectually stimulating. As Dean recalled, press notices for ATP's Fields films 'were usually critical since I made no concessions either to the current conventions in story-telling or technique.'[178]

ATP attempted with each subsequent film to hone the attractions of Fields more and more into something that could work within the confines

---

[174] 17 Sept. 1934.

[175] 17 Sept. 1934. Cf. the *Observer*, which suggested that the film was not worthy of the talents of its 'eminent writer' (16 Sept. 1934) and the *Sunday Express*, which dismissed the film as 'a grand bit of work from Gracie and an astonishingly feeble story from J. B. Priestley' (16 Sept. 1934). The relatively up-market fan magazine, *Film Weekly*, was caught somewhere between the quality press and the popular and trade press: 'One would have expected a better plot from an author of Priestley's reputation, than the tenuous and disjointed affair that serves (only just) to hold the picture together. But, if the outline of his story is weak, he has at least given Miss Fields a perfect setting and a variety of funny situations' (26 Oct. 1934, 36).

[176] *Observer*, 16 Sept. 1934.   [177] *Daily Telegraph*, 17 Sept. 1934.

[178] *Mind's Eye*, 206.

of the classical film narrative and attain a certain cultural respectability. This meant containing the performance for the narrative, rigorously developing the character as narratively functional, and resisting the dysfunctional aspects of carnivalesque performance. The strategy certainly paid off with the quality critics, whose reviews improved steadily as the films moved closer to classical standards.

Queen of Hearts (1936), to take just one example, was directed by Monty Banks rather than Dean, and is certainly, in classical terms, a much slicker film, with better timing, and a much stronger, more extended narrative with several relatively rounded characters. One has much less sense of it being constructed out of a series of turns—Fields's performance is now used up narratively, and there are none of the montage sequences of *Sing As We Go*.[179] It also owes more to Hollywood for its generic characteristics, since it is a backstage musical with two big production numbers and a chorus-line in the lavish show with which the film climaxes. Direct address is reworked as address to an actual diegetic audience, rather than an implied one—that is, as interlocution within a carefully linearized narrative space. *Queen of Hearts* is also a rags-to-riches fantasy, a wish-fulfilment of social mobility—'oh, its all been a wonderful dream', says the Fields character at one point. The sense of wish-fulfilment and of social mobility in *Sing As We Go* is much more muted, of course: the film, the characters, the audience, are out for a good time, they live for the present, not for the telos of closure, the fulfilment which the classical narrative seeks to provide. And indeed, the charge of the ending comes as much from the performance of the song and its visual rendering as it does from a sense of satisfying narrative exhaustion.

DESIRE, THE FEMININE, AND IDENTIFICATION IN *SING AS WE GO*

Thomas Elsaesser has suggested that 'there is a central energy at the heart of the Hollywood film which seeks to live itself out as completely as possible.' He illustrates this by looking briefly at the 'two major genres of the American cinema (the Western and the Gangster film)': 'There is always a central dynamic drive—the pursuit, the trek, the quest, the boundless desire to arrive, to get to the top, to get rich, to make it—always the same graph of maximum energetic investment.'[180]

---

[179] *The Times* commented on *Queen of Hearts* that 'that gawky, carefree schoolgirl of the screen has suddenly grown up . . . the humour is more controlled and there are moments when Miss Fields ceases to be just a talented comedienne and becomes an actress,' 9 Mar. 1936; cf. *Film Weekly*: 'this time it is Gracie the film actress not Gracie the variety artist, who holds the screen' (7 Mar. 1936, 4).

[180] 'Vincente Minnelli', in Christine Gledhill (ed.), *Home Is Where The Heart Is: Studies in Melodrama and the Woman's Film* (London, 1987), 219.

This 'boundless desire to arrive' is also almost invariably eroticized in pursuit of the formation of the ideal romantic couple in the classical film. In *Sing As We Go*, however, there is a certain dissipation of this narrative energy and pace; the highly episodic nature of the film means that it lacks the sort of drive described by Elsaesser. This is hardly experienced as a lack, however, since the format of the film, a veritable montage of attractions, provides its own energy and vitality, with the action moving rapidly from place to place, song to song, gag to gag, according to a principle of contiguity rather than causality. It is the variety of actions and the mode in which they are combined at the level of editing which provides the experience of a fast snappy pace, not the rigorous and relentless development of one line of action to its logical conclusion.

Sing As We Go necessarily produces a rather distinctive articulation of desire and of sexual difference given this difference in narrative form. The formation of the couple in classical cinema figures as a key motivation for narrative integration, but in *Sing As We Go* the communal and the collective have as strong a role in narrative integration and closure as the formation of the erotic couple. As we have seen, the point at which Grace acknowledges that she has lost 'the only chap I ever loved' is marked by the performance of an intensely romantic song and a sort of 'diegetic fantasy' of wish-fulfilment in the montage sequence which follows: all but one of the possible, actual, and imagined romances within the film are reprised. The film thus signals its movement towards closure by showing the formation of many couples rather than one, in which each couple is a unit within the larger community. The one potential romance which is not able to be reprised is Grace's love for Hugh, but in the next sequence of the film, Grace's potential frustration is swept aside by the revelation that Hugh, who has just left Blackpool with Phyllis, has appointed her as Welfare Officer at the newly reopened factory. The maternal role which she was seen to have in relation to the rest of the workers at the start of the film is thus made official, and she can once more be absorbed into, but at the same time stand out from, the crowd of ordinary people with whom she marches back into the factory. In this affirmation of the collective, Grace herself is revitalized, but as a mother-figure. Narrative closure then is not the formation of the couple, but the (re-)formation of the collective: initially as a community of other couples, and finally as a community of workers.

Accents, customs, and location mark this as a regionally specific community, but it also functions as a microcosm of the national community. Several of the marching workers are waving Union Jacks, and, in the final shot of the film, a Union Jack is superimposed onto the screen, filling the whole frame. The figure of the mother is at the centre of this community, and at the centre of the frame, binding the community together by attending

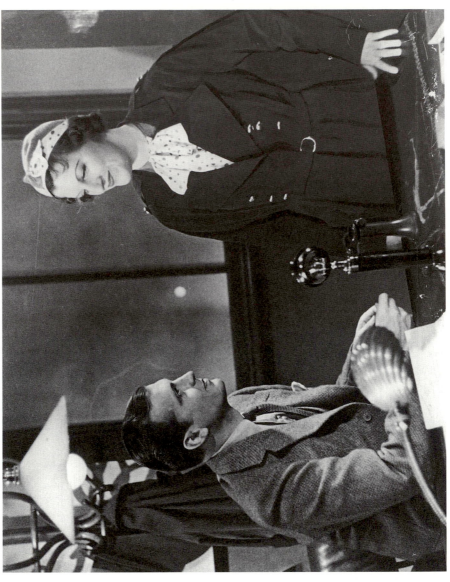

STILL 19. An exchange of looks which cannot be consummated: Hugh, the factory manager (John Loder) and

to its welfare, by entertaining it—and by denying her own desires. This same articulation of the mother as the symbolic centre of the national community resurfaces in several war-time feature films dealing with the home front and national security.

Hollywood's relentless and sexualized drive towards individual wish-fulfilment and narrative closure can perhaps be seen as culturally specific. British films like *Sing As We Go* and *Comin' Thro' The Rye* which seek to be self-consciously national films, very often seem to deal with sexual repression, or a resigned sense of loss, rather than with the pleasures of wish-fulfilment. That sense of loss is often replaced, however, by the sense of plenitude which comes from seeing the emasculated individual being absorbed once more into the security of the community, as in *Sing As We Go*, but also again in several war-time features in the documentary-realist tradition.[181]

Matthews's mode of performance in *Evergreen* produces a certain eroticism, and her clothes and her position within the *mise-en-scène* invite a voyeuristic gaze from the spectator, so reproducing a classical ('American') articulation of desire. Fields's performance in *Sing As We Go* and her deliberate deglamorization within the *mise-en-scène* stands in marked contrast to this, suggesting instead a sense of frustration and asexuality. This enables the film to resist a cross-class romantic liaison—it is the upper-middle-class Phyllis who wins Hugh's heart, not the working-class Grace. It also enables the possibility of same-sex friendship rather than rivalry, since Grace's lack of conventional glamour offers no threat to Phyllis. Indeed Grace takes on a maternal role in relation to her, protecting her, for instance, from a lounge lizard who has got her drunk, and putting Hugh off the scent at the cost of dashing her own romantic hopes. Can the film be seen as potentially progressive in creating a space for pleasure for the unglamorous mother-figure, the ordinary woman? Or is this achieved simply at the cost of other pleasures being placed out of bounds? Fields's 'grotesque' body does serve to celebrate her ordinariness, her deviance from the ideal; on the other hand, it also strengthens the appeal of the ideal—it is the grotesque body which is in the end the object of fun.

Grace first meets Phyllis when they are both queuing up to enter for Blackpool's Bonniest Bathing Belles competition. She looks Phyllis up and down, and decides that she is no longer going to bother to enter: 'if you're going in for it, I'm not gonna waste my time.' 'Oh, I don't know', replies

---

[181] Cf. Raymond Durgnat's remark that 'though it is often said that British films avoid erotic themes, many of them deal very movingly with its frustration, or tepidity, or absence' (*Eros In The Cinema* (London, 1966), 68; quoted in Charles Barr, 'Introduction: Amnesia and Schizophrenia', in id. (ed.), *All Our Yesterdays*, 25). Also Barr's comments about some of the later Ealing films: 'desire, the intensity of feeling . . . is habitually damped down into a more muted and resigned sense of loss' (*Ealing Studios* (Newton Abbot, 1977), 17).

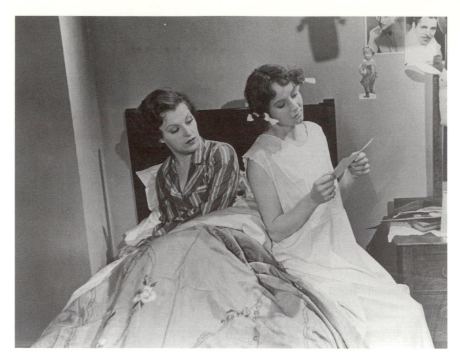

STILL 20. The unglamorous star, the ordinary person: Grace is unimpressed by her fellow maid's pin-ups of Hollywood stars (*Sing As We Go*).

STILL 21. The ideal couple: both middle-class, both southerners, both glamorous: Hugh and Phyllis (Dorothy Hyson) (*Sing As We Go*).

Phyllis. 'I do', retorts Grace. The film, then, plays on the spectacle of the female body. Has Grace/Gracie Fields simply internalized patriarchal standards, and accepted her lot, or can she actually be seen as challenging those standards? At the simplest level, the film seems to reduce women to just another seaside novelty, another spectacle, another attraction of the film. This is really the function of the beauty contest itself: an endless parade of young women in swimming costumes. As Murgatroyd says to Ezekiah, 'Let's have an eyeful of young women.' But Grace's response to this, when she sees them ogling at the contest, is to call out 'Mind your eyes don't drop out!'

In another scene already described, a crowd at the Tower Ballroom are waiting expectantly to see the three contest winners appear before them on the stage. By various mix-ups back-stage, an extremely bedraggled and dramatically deglamorized Grace is revealed instead. To appease the jeering crowd, she sings 'Little Bottom Drawer', about the experience of 'years and years of being a lonely spinster on the shelf.' The scene can be read as a celebration of the ordinary, and a parody of patriarchal convention, and thereby of the conventions of the classical narrative film and its particular regime of visual pleasures. The spectacle of the female body is, however, still one of the attractions of the film, and it should not be overlooked that Phyllis tells Hugh not to be such an old grandmother, after he has tried to stop her 'making a show of yourself'. The implication is that Phyllis is entering the competition not to invite the male gaze and impress the male spectator, but for her own pleasure.

Sing As We Go does then seem to operate with a somewhat contradictory system of looking in relation to sexual difference: in part a classical system, but one that is troubled both by Grace/Gracie Fields's deglamorization and parody of that classical system, and by Phyllis's self-satisfying, guilt-free exhibitionism. What then happens to the processes of identification within this system? In answering this question, it is necessary to take into account the tension between the mode of address of live performance and the mode of address of classical narration.

There is, on the one hand, an invitation to identify with Grace as integrated narrative protagonist. On the other hand, there is the play on liveness, on the presence of an audience, and on the imaginative boundaries of performance space, as opposed to narrative space, which is set in motion by the use of direct address, above all else. In these instances, the invitation is to identify with the position of a theatrical audience being addressed live by the performers—that is, not to see with the characters, but to look at them precisely as a spectator, separate from them. Thus, the absence of point-of-view shots and the tendency of Fields to address the spectator directly, as another person, mean that identification is not easily constructed on an individual-to-individual basis, despite the fact that Fields is so eminently the centre of attention in the film. This is exacerbated by Fields's unusually frontal performance, which can be seen as a strategy for displaying the central attraction of the film at all costs, underlining her visibility, stressing her performative qualities rather than her narrative characterization. Further, we might suggest that her deliberate deglamorization and deidealization—her extraordinary ordinariness—renders her as very different from the ideal glamorous figures of identification of the classical film. Rather than the spectator becoming as one with the Fields character for the duration of the film, Fields becomes one of us.

CONCLUSIONS

Sing As We Go gains its strength from the tension between the linear forces of narrative (the forces that contain), and the non-linear pleasures of the gag, the song, the spectacle, the attraction (the forces which disrupt). But in so far as the film belongs to a performative genre rather than a strictly narrative genre, the transgressions from the classical model are licensed, for the excess and the tension are part of the conventions and expectations of the genre and constitutive of its central pleasures. Even so, the experience of transgression—licensed or not—can be exhilarating.

Is this exhilaration in part an acknowledgement of the degree to which *Sing As We Go* differs from classical Hollywood cinema? Not entirely, because, as Peter Kramer has argued, classical Hollywood cinema always operated according to a double standard.[182] Alongside the tight, economic narrative feature film, the studios were also producing cartoons, comedy shorts, serials, and so on—and also, of course, very weakly narrativized, and thereby classically aberrant, feature films: musicals like *Flying Down To Rio* (1933), or comedies like the early Marx Brothers films, with their live performance conventions and carnivalesque anarchy.

Structurally, *Flying Down To Rio* is very similar to *Sing As We Go*. Instead of a journey to the playground of Blackpool, we have a trip to the exotic pleasure space of Rio to unleash all sorts of libidinal fantasies, bodily pleasures, and gratuitous spectacles. It is in effect a very classy variety show, with a proliferation of protagonists, songs, bands, and dance routines. It seeks to satisfy the desire for tourist spectacle too, with a montage of post-card images of Rio, which are tilted and wiped, giving the impression of shuffling through a pile of snapshots. Spectacular visual pleasure is also provided in the optical effects of the orchid song and the

---

[182] 'The Double Standard of Classical Hollywood Cinema', paper presented at Society for Cinema Studies Conference, Bozeman, Montana, USA, 29 June–3 July 1988.

dancing on the aeroplanes. All of this is presented on the flimsiest of narrative motivations, as in *Sing As We Go*.

American films like *Flying Down To Rio* are generically licensed spaces for the intrusion of non-classical devices. Direct address is possible under certain circumstances, such as the chorus which sings to camera in one of the songs from *Forty-Second Street* (1933). *Flying Down To Rio*, as noted, uses various special optical devices, including shaped wipes, while *Forty-Second Street* has various overhead shots for the Busby Berkeley sequences, as well as a prismatic montage of dancing legs reminiscent of the French avant-gardes of the 1920s. These films are in many ways the American equivalent of *Sing As We Go*, but the sensibility, the setting, and the milieu of *Sing As We Go* insist upon its difference from Hollywood, just as strongly as *Evergreen* insists that it has become Hollywood.

Both *Sing As We Go* and *Evergreen* aspire to the position of a national cinema, but by different economic and cultural routes. They adopt different modes of address in order to appeal to the desires and expectations of different, if overlapping, sectors of the far from homogeneous national audience, as well as relating differently to the various international audiences. *Evergreen* is the product of an industrial strategy which necessarily identifies a national audience as synonymous with a mass audience; it seeks to win that mass audience by adopting an international style—although on closer inspection, it turns out to be inflected slightly differently from American films working with that style. *Evergreen*'s formal and thematic details are, in the end, perhaps of less interest—because of their relative familiarity—than the industrial strategy and cultural practice which the film represents. As a film, it does not do much in the way of imagining a national community, nor does it particularly seek to invoke a distinctively national cultural tradition. Indeed, its project might be seen as the effacement of such difference, rather than its celebration. And where differences were apparent—as to the American press—they were to be read as flaws within the strategy. Internationalism might involve aspiring to certain standards, certain qualities, but, whatever the rhetoric of the policy-makers and the public relations experts, those standards were not particularly to be measured in national terms.

Sing As We Go, on the other hand, is one of many such British films of the period which work self-consciously with cultural traditions, reference-points, and performers which are nationally specific, and in many cases regionally specific. There are numerous other films which feature comic variety artists like Fields, or which exhibit the same brand of comedy or the same version of the musical. The development of this genre of British films is heavily dependent on a media experience and spectacle which pre-exists the cinema—notably music-hall (and, subsequently, radio and television). This type of film-making, addressed to a primarily national audience, and drawing on modes of entertainment and star-images established in other media, is not unique to Britain, and several other European film industries have used the same strategy in an effort to establish a national popular cinema—or at least to produce a type of film which is popular enough to be able to generate sufficient profits in the domestic market alone. The cultural specificity of such films renders them virtually inexportable, and indeed few of the British examples of this sort of work had any international circulation, certainly not within the American market—even though they were the generic mainstays of British cinema in the 1930s and later decades.[183]

It is perhaps the case that an indigenous national cinema commanding mass audiences, as opposed to an art cinema, or a popular cinema with international aspirations, exists only in the form of such critically despised genre films, which rely so heavily on pre-cinematic star-images and modes of entertainment. Such films are certainly among the few examples within the European film industries and cultures of well-established generic conventions and star-images not particularly dependent on Hollywood.

Sing As We Go needs to be understood in this context. The particular way in which it displays its attractions should be seen as an attempt to incorporate the experience and the cultural repertoire of music-hall and its audiences. The star-image of 'Our Gracie', forged in the music-halls, was, of course, one of those attractions. It is foregrounded in the film by casting Fields in a role which gives her the diegetic name of Grace, a strategy used with several other comic performers whose popularity precedes their entry into films. *Evergreen* was also of course based on a theatrical entertainment. It was a remake of a successful West End show, and starred Matthews and Sonnie Hale, both successful revue artists, but the film is hardly sold on the strength of these theatrical reputations. *Evergreen* also shuns the theatrical performative mode of broad gesture and playing to the camera. Indeed, as it is a back-stage musical about a theatrical performer, it is able to play heavily on the relationships and differences between theatre and cinema. It offers its audiences a reproduction of the theatrical experience, complete with diegetic audiences, but it also suggests, like so many contemporaneous Hollywood musicals, that the cinema experience is more impressive than that of the theatre. Cinema, in this move, does not denigrate theatre, as it does television in the 1950s. It celebrates the experience of theatre, so attempting to attract its aficionados, but at the same time it appropriates the experience, transforming it into a celebration of the better cinematic experience. This is particularly evident in the show sequences when the space of the proscenium-arched theatre is superseded by what is

[183] See Jean-Pierre Jeancolas, 'The Inexportable: The Case of French Cinema and Radio in the 1950s', in Richard Dyer and Ginette Vincendeau (eds.), *Popular European Cinema* (London, 1992).

in effect an infinitely extendable stage, a purely cinematic construction of space, where the space of the musical number becomes larger than the space of the narrative.[184]

Sing As We Go also on occasions constructs a purely cinematic space. The montage sequence which follows on from the performance of the love-song, for instance, visually updates the film's various romances, including the romance of Blackpool itself, in a fashion that only the cinema could achieve. Where this purely cinematic construction of space is an imaginative extension of an actual stage in *Evergreen*, in *Sing As We Go* the imagination of montage replaces the need for a stage altogether.

The strategies being used in these two films can thus be seen as symptomatic of the film industry's attempts to achieve a state of media supremacy, in a period characterized by competition between different media and entertainment forms for mass, and thereby national (and potentially international) audiences.[185] Both films work to absorb or incorporate other already existing media and entertainment forms, and to appropriate and accumulate their audiences, in so far as they are different from the already constituted cinema audience, itself of course never a homogeneous and singular entity. *Sing As We Go*, for instance, attempts to reproduce the participatory community audience of pre-cinematic modes of entertainment such as music-hall, the pleasures on offer at Blackpool, and more generally the tradition of carnival. Bakhtin has argued that

Carnival does not know footlights, in the sense that it does not acknowledge any distinction between actors and spectators. Footlights would destroy a carnival, as the absence of footlights would destroy a theatrical performance. Carnival is not a spectacle seen by the people: they live in it, and everyone participates because its very idea embraces the people.[186]

Part of Fields's attraction, more than with most theatrical performances, was that she could metaphorically cross the footlights and embrace the people. *Sing As We Go* tries to reproduce this experience of the collectively participating audience both within the diegesis and at the point of exhibition (through the repetition of songs, for instance); at the same time, the film seeks to assimilate this experience with the rather different spectatorial experience of the classical film. Thus *Sing As We Go* tries to overcome the fact that the technology of film replaces the living encounter of audience and performer with the impersonality and lack of presence of the projected celluloid image. It tries to reproduce cinematically the performative

---

[184] See Alan Williams, 'The Musical Film and Recorded Popular Music', in Altman (ed.), *Genre*; and Low, *Film-Making*, 137.

[185] See Dudley Andrew, 'Family Diversions: French Popular Cinema and the Music Hall', in Dyer and Vincendeau (eds.), *Popular European Cinema*.

[186] *Rabelais*, 7; see also *Dostoyevsky's Poetics*, 122.

spontaneity and variety of music-hall, and the contact and complicity with an audience.

One of the early script-writing manuals quoted from in the previous chapter suggests that 'Whereas in a drama it is desirable to make the spectator emotionally more or less a participant in the story as it unfolds itself, in a comedy he should be the witness only—the spectator in the strict sense of the word.'[187] That is certainly one aspect of the spectator–text relationship here: *Sing As We Go* does not seek to efface the experience of spectating in the way that the classical narrative film does. But I would argue that the sense of participation, rather than simply spectating, is not lost either; on the contrary it is self-consciously acknowledged in the film's textual strategies.

Sing As We Go is, then, addressed to an audience familiar with the conventions of both music-hall and cinema. It is also addressed to a mass audience on a national basis. It does more than this, however, in that it also constructs an image of the nation as a coherent, knowable, and self-sufficient community—which, moreover, includes the film's audiences. As Tony Aldgate and others have argued, the film can be read as a highly optimistic text, performing a consensual and conservative nationalizing function.[188] Priestley's script for the film situates the plot in the context of economic depression and unemployment, which is documented in the opening montage sequence of the film. But for Priestley, this was evidently not enough: cinema must in the end be an uplifting experience.

[I am not] in favour of a policy of giving us great slabs of English working class life, miles of celluloid showing us factories and engineering shops, folks sitting down to endless meat teas, and a dreary round of housework, machine-minding, football matches and whist drives. . . . [The film] needs a bit of glamour, an increased tempo, a touch of the fantastic, people who are more vivid than the ordinary run of folk.[189]

The fantasy of *Sing As We Go* is not only the play-time of Blackpool, but also the consensual solution it offers to the Depression. The film promotes as strong an image of inter-class solidarity—that is, a potentially national solidarity—as it does of intra-class solidarity. While a cross-class romance may be forbidden, it is by just such a cross-class co-operation between the worker, Grace, the boss, Hugh, and Sir William Upton, that Greybeck Mill

[187] Colden Lore, *The Modern Photoplay and its Construction* (London, 1923), 216.
[188] See Aldgate, 'Comedy and Containment'; Richards, *Dream Palace*. Cf. Tony Bennett and James Donald, 'Postscript to Block 2', in *The Historical Development of Popular Culture in Britain*, Open University Popular Culture Course Booklet, U203, Block 2, Units 7 and 8; and Marcia Landy, *British Genres: Cinema and Society, 1930–1960* (Princeton, NJ, 1991), 337–41.
[189] *World Film News*, 1/8 (1936), 3.

can be reopened. The sentiments and the fantasy of collectivity are of course exercised in various ways, perhaps most powerfully in the closing sequence of the film, in which Grace is reunited with the people of her particular class and locality. The conjunction of the words of the song— 'sing as we go'—the interpellation of the audience in the cinema through the direct address to camera, and the presence of the numerous Union Jacks, produces a powerful sense of the nation as a secure, all-embracing but at the same time close-knit community, a functioning consensus.[190]

This image of the nation is achieved narratively; indeed it emerges at the moment of narrative closure, a closure which this hegemony makes possible. Therein lies a problem, since I have argued that the central pleasures and guiding principles of the film as a whole are not concerned with narrativity. The carnivalesque qualities of the film, its celebration of popular but vulgar cultural forms, its delight in the gag and the gratuitous moment, all run against the pressures of narrative closure. The closure of the film in fact sees narrative pleasures once more in competition with the pleasures of performance. Such exhibitionist moments, along with the vulgar attractions of Blackpool, the transgressions of holiday-time, and even the very character of Grace/Gracie Fields, constitute the 'too much' which exceeds a consensual view of national life. Hugh, Phyllis, and Sir William may all visit the playground of the working class, but their bourgeois values are no match for the values of the Pleasure Beach or the bodily pleasures of Blackpool's Bonniest Bathing Belles competition—indeed they are seen to enjoy this regime of pleasure.

The carnivalesque—the temporarily irresponsible and commanding pleasures of those without authority—is, from this point of view, at the centre of *Sing As We Go*. Of the three plot-lines which attempt to impose some structure on the film, the least tightly structured is that of Grace's picaresque adventures. Significantly, the other two plot-lines both have bourgeois characters as key protagonists (Hugh and Sir William), and are both much more serious attempts to frame and regulate the carnivalesque: the bourgeois form of narrative seeks to contain the irresponsible forces of popular pleasure. But carnival is always a licensed transgression, 'a permissable rupture of hegemony',[191] a legitimate letting off of steam, rather than a permanent and irreconcilable disruption; it is a means of controlling excess energy. Narrative containment, the force of narrative closure, is from this perspective inevitable—and the closure in the end

---

[190] This is a variation of 'the myth of the audience' that Jane Feuer has identified at work in the classical Hollywood musical, enabling *Sing As We Go*, like so many other musicals, to perform an integrating function and to produce a utopian community. See Feuer, 'Self-Reflexive Musical'.

[191] Terry Eagleton, *Walter Benjamin, or Towards a Revolutionary Criticism* (London, 1981), 148. See also Stallybrass and White, *Politics and Poetics*, 12–16.

restores the social and economic status quo, even if Grace has to be elevated
to (incorporated into) the realms of personnel management. Carnival here
is generic rather then necessarily subversive.

The figure of Grace/Gracie Fields is also much more ambivalent than
simply irresponsible; there is again a tension between Gracie Fields the
attraction and Grace the narrative character. As Grace, she is the symbol
of the worker who refuses to be beaten, and the mother-figure who keeps
other people's irresponsibilities in check. Depression and unemployment
do not injure her personal dignity or her pride in her local culture; she
survives without too many problems, and the mills are eventually reopened
by her intervention. As Gracie Fields, she is one of the people, an adven-
turer, but also a clown and a fool. She has a running feud with a policeman; she is abused by a male customer at the boarding house where she
temporarily works—but gets her own back by pouring a bowl of rhubarb
over his head; she masquerades as a human spider in a freak show; she
mockingly impersonates a fortune-teller; she appears bedraggled before a
crowd expecting to see bathing beauties, and so on. If at times she appears
ridiculous, she also has the power to ridicule others, to cock a snook at
authority. In Priestley's description, she takes 'an impish delight in mocking whatever is thought to be affected and pretentious.'[192]

To confuse matters, Priestley the script-writer ensures that in *Sing As
We Go*, Grace/Gracie Fields also parodies the affectations and the vulgari-
ties of Blackpool itself. The film thus both indulges in the popular pleasures of working-class culture but at the same time worries over them,
debunking the remnants of more traditional vulgar forms such as the
fairground and the circus and ridiculing what it sees as the seriality, repeti-
tiveness, and grotesqueness of modern mass culture. Thus the seriality of
the bathing beauties, who all look the same from a distance, is matched
only by the grotesque rendering of the male spectator's voyeurism, while
her stint as song-plugger underlines the endless, repetitive performance of
a single song, and so on. What remains unique is the figure of Grace/
Gracie Fields herself: in each case, it is the vitality, the spontaneity, and the
authenticity of Grace/Gracie Fields's performance which rides above the
mass phenomenon or the vulgar fairground attraction being parodied.

The combined talents of Priestley and Dean conspire to create a Gracie
Fields film which is of better quality and more respectable than the vulgar
origins of her reputation—yet which must continue to celebrate those
origins and reproduce the established star-image in order to guarantee a
commercially viable audience. It is this contradiction which produces the
schizophrenic nature of the film, both inviting its audiences to participate
in the popular pleasures of the carnival tradition, and evincing the horrified

---

[192] *English Journey*, 253.

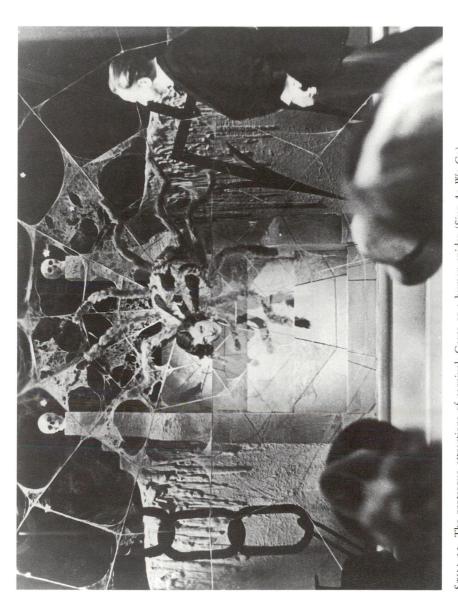

STILL 22. The grotesque attractions of carnival: Grace as a human spider (*Sing As We Go*).

fascination of the bourgeois spectator gazing from a distance at this other scene of mass culture and the 'huge seething mass of humanity.'[193]

Sir William and Hugh, the film's most bourgeois characters, both visit Blackpool and what another character refers to as the 'dark Pleasure Beach'—and so see at first hand the mass/popular culture in full flow. In both cases, although they evidently enjoy themselves, there is a strong sense of slumming. 'I'll take a stroll through the Pleasure Beach—haven't seen one of these things for years', says Sir William to his chauffeur on arriving at its entrance. It is something strange, something 'other', through which he can wander, bemused. Of course, Sir William and Hugh are no match for the attractions of Blackpool and the music-hall culture and they are rapidly absorbed into this other scene. On the other hand, the relatively minimal penetration of space by the camera produces a gaze which maintains a safe distance for the potentially bourgeois spectator, who can observe the crowd and their antics from the safety and security of the cinema seat.

The distanced gaze of the camera in *Sing As We Go* may be read as equivalent to the distanced gaze of the bourgeois spectator watching the carnival from a safe place. As Peter Stallybrass and Allon White have commented, 'at the fair the subordinate classes become the object of a gaze constituting itself as respectable and superior by substituting observation for participation.'[194] They go on to argue that 'that moment in which the subject is made the outsider to the crowd, an onlooker, compensating for exclusion through the deployment of the discriminating gaze, is at the very root of bourgeois sensibility.'[195]

This same gaze and the same sensibility and attitude are central to the documentary-realist tradition, the subject of the next chapter. Here, it splits the viewing position of the film between an invitation to embrace the pleasures of Blackpool, and an exhortation to remain aloof from such ephemeral enjoyments. It is this latter attitude towards the vulgar fun of Blackpool and of the music-hall which the production of the film as a quality product seems to want to encourage. Film can offer more than these sites, it is implied; it can introduce us to superior cultural forms and practices—this is how a film like *Sing As We Go* can exist alongside ATP's other productions which seem on the surface to aspire to something quite different.

This reading of the film is entirely in keeping with Priestley's own reading of Blackpool. It may be 'the great roaring spangled beast', but it is a beast which instils in him a certain anxiety; it may be 'a pleasure resort for the crowd', but the crowd also instils in him a certain anxiety.[196]

[193] Harrisson, 'Fifty-Second Week', 387.   [194] *Politics and Poetics*, 42.
[195] Ibid. 187.   [196] *English Journey*, 263, 265.

Blackpool, he suggests, 'is a complete and essential product of industrial democracy. If you do not like industrial democracy, you will not like Blackpool.'[197] Priestley, at the very least, is undecided about whether he likes it or not—or rather, to be precise, he is nostalgic for a Blackpool which in his opinion no longer exists:

it is not as good as it was . . . it lacks something of its old genuine gaiety. Its amusements are becoming too mechanised and Americanised. . . . The entertainers are more calculating, their shows more standardised, and the audiences more passive. It has developed a pitiful sophistication—machine-made and not really English— that is much worse than the old cheerful vulgarity. . . . [The] less intelligent and enterprising, are, I feel, fit patrons of the new Blackpool, which knows what to do with the passive and listless, but [they] would not have been quite up to the energetic old Blackpool, crowded with vital beings who burst out of their factories for the annual spree as if the boilers had exploded and blown them out. . . . Blackpool . . . was the Mecca of a vulgar but alert and virile democracy.[198]

The film can be read as a critique precisely of Priestley's new, Americanized Blackpool. The cultural democracy has been tainted, 'it is a bit too cheap. . . . Too much of it is simply a trumpery imitation of something not very good even in the original.'[199] (This critique of American popular culture is also there in the film. The appeal of Hollywood is represented here by a maid at the guest-house where Grace briefly works, who takes photographs of American film stars to bed with her—an imaginary infatuation in an age of mechanical reproduction which Grace dismisses with disdain.)

The other side of this critique of mass culture is the nostalgic celebration of the supposedly authentic working-class culture which is presumed to have preceded it. Hence the hesitations within the text of *Sing As We Go*, where Blackpool wavers between being a real place, a site of virile, democratic working-class pleasures, and being a metaphor for a tainted mass culture. The film purports to call back into existence—in fact, to invent— the authentic working-class communities of 'old England', knowable communities, in contrast to the anonymity and garishness of mass culture. There is, then, a touch of heritage nostalgia in this film, and a touch of pastoral too. Pastoral is not necessarily a question of subject-matter, but is an attitude, a perspective on social relations—in this case, the relations of urban society.[200] The performance space of *Sing As We Go*'s carnival thus constitutes an urban pastoral, where the heritage space of *Comin'*

---

[197] Ibid. 266.   [198] Ibid. 267–8.

[199] *English Journey*, 402. Harrisson is equally anxious, feeling that 'this wonderland . . . is the price England pays for industrialism', 'Fifty-Second Week', 392.

[200] See William Empson, *Some Versions of Pastoral* (London, 1968), esp. his argument about 'the pastoral process of putting the complex into the simple' (22).

Thro' the Rye produces a more classical rural pastoral. Here, the urban pastoral imagines the complexities of the nation in the simplified form of a small, self-contained, and organic urban community, in which the classes and the sexes know their places and coexist harmoniously. It is this community which once more inhabits Greybeck and its mills at the end of the film—a microcosm of the national community, unified around the figure of the mother, 'consensus personified'.[201]

Sing As We Go is very much a pivotal film, caught in the interplay between a variety of competing cultural practices. Raymond Williams's distinction between dominant, residual, and emergent cultural forms may be useful in considering this interplay.[202] The dominant film practice in the 1930s is clearly the international standard of classical Hollywood cinema. In *Sing As We Go*, however, we can also see the residue of earlier cultural forms and practices. As Williams argues, 'certain meanings, experiences, and values which cannot be expressed or substantially verified in terms of the dominant culture, are nevertheless lived and practised on the basis of the residue—cultural as well as social—of some previous social and cultural institution or formation'.[203] The music-hall elements, the cinema of attractions, the regional references, have not been entirely incorporated by the dominant film culture and persist precisely as a residue of earlier and less culturally respectable practices, representing 'areas of human experience, aspiration and achievement which the dominant culture neglects, undervalues, opposes, represses, or even cannot recognise.'[204]

Interwoven with the processes of classical narration and the eruptions of the highly localized version of the cinema of attractions in *Sing As We Go* are instances of montage which echo the new, potentially democratic and avant-garde cultural practice of documentary and its discourse of realism, which is, in Williams's terms, the emergent. Documentary, as I will demonstrate in the next chapter, emerges as a film form which, amongst other things, seeks to represent the working class audio-visually as a complex collective formation with its own milieu, values, and aspirations. Documentary, of course, is valorized in terms of a discourse of realism. This discourse also emerges in contemporary reviews of *Sing As We Go*: several critics foreground the attempt to represent, authentically, a specific region of England. *Kine Weekly*, for instance, was impressed by what it saw as 'an amusing, human and interesting mass study of north country character. . . . The opening scenes, employed to establish plot, give an authentic

[201] This is the title of the chapter on Gracie Fields in Richards, *Dream Palace*. Note that the particular procedures being discussed here may also be understood as a means of constructing a consensual image specifically of 'the northern working class', and assigning them a place within the national formation.

[202] *Marxism and Literature* (Oxford, 1977), 121 ff.

[203] Ibid. 122.   [204] Ibid. 123–4.

indication of the state of affairs in the industrial north, and shed illuminating light on the poverty of its family life.'[205]

It is interesting to note here that reviewers read the regional specificities of *Sing As We Go* quite differently from the equally specific southern rural locations of *Comin' Thro' The Rye*. The pastoral of *Comin' Thro' The Rye* is invariably read in terms of an essential Englishness. *Sing As We Go*, however, is felt to describe only a corner of England, despite the various ways in which the film promotes the metaphor of local community as national community. The urban pastoral of the industrial north does not yet have the easy national identity which critics perceive in war-time films which work with similar (though generally less northern) versions of urban pastoral.

The Times, for instance, described *Sing As We Go* as 'a sincere effort to make a film which should truly represent an aspect of English life.' The reviewer agreed that 'a great deal of trouble has been taken in providing the authentic background of Blackpool' but felt that, in the end, 'it is not really successful.'[206] The comments are typical of the more up-market reviewers, for whom the main problem was that *Sing As We Go* was a star vehicle, above all else, which compromised its attempt to represent northern working-class culture realistically. 'At the cost of being repetitious', wrote C. A. Lejeune, 'I suggest that there is still unemployment, there is still ship-building, and there is still farming [and] we have an industrial north that is bigger than Gracie Fields running around a Blackpool funfair.'[207]

Having fun, indulging in the pleasures of carnival, are seen as inappropriate responses to the hard realities of life:

Blackpool and Bolton are there in truth, but there through the eyes of the studio and not through the intimacy of the English journey. In these days of social unhappiness you cannot scratch the surface of an economic problem for the benefit of a gifted comedienne, nor can you employ comic effect to issues which are conditioning the very existence of countless persons. If this is to be the way of putting England on the screen, then stay in your studios, producers, and leave England to documentary.[208]

In fact, *Sing As We Go* does share something with British documentaries of the period, even if the film did not go far enough in producing a realist national cinema for the serious critics. John Grierson, leading spokesman for the documentary movement, actually cites the Gracie Fields films as some of the more realistic British films of the 1930s, adding that 'the English music hall . . . is in the direct line of observation . . . [but] we have

---

[205] 13 Sept. 1934, 29.   [206] 17 Sept. 1934.
[207] In a review of *Jew Süss*, *Observer*, 7 Oct. 1934.
[208] Paul Rotha, 'Films of the Quarter', *Sight and Sound*, 3 (1934), 117.

too many . . . cosmopolites of the world's cities, to whom Lancashire is only Gracie Fields's hundred-thousand a year and the men of the Clyde are not even a whisper in consciousness.'[209] Among the characteristics which many documentary films share with *Sing As We Go* are the self-conscious location shooting and use of non-professional actors, at least for crowd scenes; the emphasis on the working-class, and on the collective as much as the individual; and the distance which the camera keeps, for the most part, and the frontality of the staging—together representing a refusal of the individualized, psychologized point of view of classical narrative cinema.

Another formal feature which plays an important part in both *Sing As We Go* and documentary films of the period is the use of montage. The montage sequence tends to function as a summary passage in classical cinema,[210] but in *Sing As We Go* it does more than this; indeed, it might be said to do the opposite, on occasions, opening up the diegesis beyond its narrative requirements, instead of condensing it or closing it down. The opening sequence of the film, for instance, is classical enough as a summary and condensation of place, locality, and situation, and there is an impressive economy of narration through the juxtaposition of sounds and images. There is also however an added charge of authenticity through seeing such patently real location shots of industrial activity, which are hardly typical characteristics of British feature films of the period. The montage sequence which details Grace's journey to Blackpool also exceeds a purely narrative function, in its exhibition of numerous verbal and visual gags and special effects. The sequence also celebrates the energy, vitality, and above all modernity of communication itself, in a way that was to become typical of contemporaneous British documentary film-making.[211] The montage of romances after the love-song also echoes the way in which montage in documentary films works to construct a public rather than a private sensibility: the privacy of Grace's emotional situation is placed in the wider context of the romance of the community at large, and indeed the general situation of Blackpool as it closes down for the night.

Sing As We Go bids for both cultural respectability and popular acclaim and seeks to do so not only by constructing a sense of both the national and the local, but also by working with a complex mix of dominant, residual, and emergent cultural traditions. The film is, like carnival, a

[209] 'The Course of Realism', in Davy (ed.), *Footnotes*, 158.

[210] See David Bordwell, *Narration In The Fiction Film* (London, 1985), 160. Contemporary examples include sequences establishing the rise to power of the gang-leader or a particular form of weaponry and attack, as in *Scarface* (1932); and the establishing of place, as in the opening sequence of *42nd Street* (1933).

[211] Grace travels by bike, but the sequence also has shots of trains and buses in urgent transit, a point which provoked *The Times* to comment that Dean 'has shown once again his penchant for sending trains and omnibuses diagonally across his screen in the best modernistic style' (17 Sept. 1934).

complex hybrid of voices, forms, and cultures, both high and low, respect-able and vulgar. This is evident particularly in the bizarre combination of the semi-documentary and the star-vehicle musical organized around a single extraordinary individual. The film is thus characterized by a series of fascinating oppositions: work vs. pleasure; community vs. the indi-vidual; extended narrative vs. self-contained novelty; continuity vs. mon-tage, and so on. It is a very similar set of tensions to those typifying the documentary-realist tradition which I will be exploring in the next chapter.

5

The Documentary Idea and the Melodrama of Everyday Life— The Public, the Private and the National Family: Millions Like Us *and* This Happy Breed

INTRODUCTION: THE DOCUMENTARY IDEA AND THE PUBLIC SPHERE

> I liked the notion that, in making films of man in his modern environment, one would be articulating the corporate character of that environment and finding again, after a long period of sloppy romanticism and the person in private, an aesthetic of the person in public.
>
> John Grierson[1]

> Documentary films are being used more and more to interpret and dramatize the life of a nation, not only to itself but to other nations.
>
> Paul Rotha[2]

It is well known that, under John Grierson's guidance, an official Film Unit was established in 1929 at the Empire Marketing Board (EMB), which specialized in the production and distribution of what came to be known as documentary films. This unit moved to the General Post Office (GPO) in 1933 with Sir Stephen Tallents, the civil servant whose expertise in public relations had done so much to enable the work of the Film Unit. These units developed a system of state sponsorship for their film-making activities, supplemented by commissions from corporate industry, a framework

---

[1] Quoted in Forsyth Hardy, 'The British Documentary film', in Michael Balcon, *et al.*, *Twenty Years of British Film* (London, 1947), 47 (no source given). Various parts of this chapter have appeared previously in the following publications: 'Addressing the Nation: Five Films', in Geoff Hurd (ed.), *National Fictions: World War Two in British Films and Television* (London, 1984); ' "Britain's Outstanding Contribution to the Film": The Documentary-Realist Tradition', in Charles Barr (ed.), *All Our Yesterdays: 90 Years of British Cinema* (London, 1986); and 'Re-constructing the Nation: *This Happy Breed*, 1944', in *Film Criticism*, 16/1–2 (1991–2), and Wheeler Winston Dixon (ed.), *Re-viewing British Cinema 1900–1992: Essays and Interviews* (New York, 1994).

[2] From the dust-jacket of *Documentary Film* (London, rev. and enlarged 3rd edn., 1952); all subsequent quotations from this book are taken from the material written for the 1st edn., pub. in 1936, unless stated otherwise; this material was not revised for the 3rd edn., except for the addition of new footnotes.

which enabled a number of other independent documentary film production companies to be established from the mid-1930s.

An article in *The Times* in 1932 suggested that, in the work of the EMB Film Unit, there existed 'a possibility . . . of freeing British films from a slavish competition with American methods and of establishing for them a character of their own.'[3] In the first edition of his influential survey, *Documentary Film*, published in 1936, Paul Rotha—by this time himself a documentary film-maker—described such work as 'this country's most important contribution to cinema as a whole',[4] a view which rapidly became commonplace within at least certain sectors of the intellectual film culture. Thus by 1938, *The Times* confirmed its early hopes: 'The film of fact . . . is . . . the distinctively British contribution to the art of the moving pictures. English producers of fiction films can scarcely do more than show America that they have mastered a technique that was first developed at Hollywood.'[5]

A decade later, Forsyth Hardy opened his account of the development of British documentary with the observation that 'there is no novelty today in the claim that documentary is the distinctively British contribution to cinema.'[6] Such views of course stand in marked contrast to the critical debate of the late 1920s, when critics like Rotha and the various contributors to the journal *Close Up* complained that British cinema had neither produced anything of any note nor developed an indigenous tradition of film-making. Grierson, the leading spokesperson for British documentary, also felt that there was nothing distinctive about British cinema at this stage: 'we have not yet evolved a style.'[7] By contrast, *The Times* article of 1932 quoted above remarked of the EMB documentary films that 'here—in the use of portraiture, the rhythm of cross-cutting, the remarkable fluidity of movement from scene to scene—is British film-work with a style as strongly marked and as individual as the Russian.'[8]

---

[3] 'Films of Substance', *The Times*, 2 Apr. 1932, 8; the article is unsigned, but Paul Swann attributes it to Grierson, though offers no evidence for the attribution; it seems most unlikely, given the lavish praise that is heaped on Grierson himself in the article (see *The British Documentary Film Movement* (Cambridge, 1989), 47 and n. 74).

[4] *Documentary Film*, 96.

[5] 'Films for New York', 8 Dec. 1938, 18; cf. Paul Rotha, submission on behalf of Associated Realist Film Producers to the Moyne Committee, Annex III, Board of Trade, *Minutes of Evidence taken before the Departmental Committee on Cinematograph Films*, i (London, 1936), 70; the influential survey, *The Factual Film*, opened with the statement that 'the documentary is Britain's outstanding contribution to the film' (The Arts Enquiry, London, 1947, 1); cf. David Robinson, 'United Kingdom', in Alan Lovell (ed.), *Art of the Cinema in Ten European Countries* (Strasburg, 1967), 197.

[6] 'British Documentary', 45.

[7] *Artwork*, Autumn 1931, repr. in Forsyth Hardy (ed.), *Grierson on Documentary* (London, 1979 [1st pub. 1946]), 30. Cf. Grierson's assessment of British cinema at the end of the decade, 'The Course of Realism', in Charles Davy (ed.), *Footnotes to the Film* (London, 1938), 157–8.

[8] 'Films of Substance'.

To claim that documentary was Britain's outstanding contribution to cinema was deliberately to disregard the appeals of popular cinema and commercial narrative film-making, a view that was not entirely acceptable within the intellectual film culture of the middle years of the century. Thus Dilys Powell, the *Sunday Times* film critic, writing in 1946, could not allow that documentary on its own constituted a national cinema: 'ultimately it is on the quality of its entertainment films that the prestige of a national cinema must rest . . . : however marked the element of imagination in a documentary film, it is to the essentially creative work that we turn for the full judgement of value.'[9]

The presence of the documentary movement in the 1930s was therefore not enough for Powell, who felt that there was still no 'school of British cinema' in this period: 'The national characteristics of the British, whether good or bad, had not been infused into a national cinema.'[10] The influence of documentary and the experience of war, however, 'set the English film on the path in which masterpieces may be created [and] established precisely what was lacking in the English cinema before 1940, a traditional English style.'[11]

This was certainly the prevailing opinion within the intellectual film culture of the period. Some two decades later, the tradition was well and truly established, such that one critic could claim that 'through the first seven decades, every sustained period of success of the British film has seemed to be based in a realist approach to contemporary life.'[12] Realism is thus equated first of all with documentary, then with the most impressive, valuable, and significant tradition in the history of British feature films. Given the extent to which this view has become the orthodox version of British cinema's achievements as a national cinema, no study of the question of national cinema in this country would really be complete without some exploration of the films valorized in such claims. It is to this which I turn in this chapter.

I will initially establish certain parameters within which films in this tradition operate, looking first at the relationship between the documentary idea and the concept of the public sphere, and then at the way in which that idea was perceived both as a realist practice and as a key strategy in the development of a national cinema. Following a general survey of the field of documentary in the 1930s and early 1940s, focusing in particular on the initial development of the story-documentary, I will look at two feature films from the mid-war period which emanated from

[9] 'Films since 1939', in Arnold L. Haskell *et al.*, *Since 1939* (London, 1948), 75 (first pub. as a pamphlet in 1946).

[10] Ibid. 65. On the other hand, it was widely believed within the intellectual film culture that 'British entertainment films are at their best when they approach a documentary style' (Charles Davy, 'Post-script: The Film Marches On', in Davy (ed.), *Footnotes*, 320–1).

[11] Powell, 'Films since 1939', 75–6.   [12] Robinson, 'United Kingdom', 197.

the commercial sector of the industry, but which were influenced in various ways by documentary.[13] In the discourse of the period, 'it was in these documentary-feature war films that the renaissance of our cinema first took permanent form.'[14] I will concentrate initially on *Millions Like Us* (1943), a film felt by many contemporary commentators to be 'essentially British in character' and 'instrumental in creating the national style',[15] and then compare it with the equally well-received *This Happy Breed* (1944). In these films, as in earlier story documentaries, the nation is represented metaphorically as a small, self-contained, tight-knit community, a unity-in-diversity, but one which is structured like a family. This image of the nation is achieved through a particular set of narrational procedures including episodic montage construction, and an organization of looks which inter-mixes what I call the public gaze of the documentary with the private gaze of individual narrative protagonists. Finally, I will look more cursorily at the way in which this mode rapidly became conventionalized and sedimented in the mid-1940s into a genre of mainstream commercial film-making, with its own rules and regulations, to some extent severed from the broader political questions raised within the documentary sector in the 1930s. The chapter, like the previous two, is therefore a case-study in product differentiation, since the films in question are primarily about contemporary Britain, were made for domestic consumption in the first place, and were self-consciously set against the classical Hollywood cinema.

Of course, there are already numerous accounts of both the documentary movement itself and the subsequent feature films and television programmes which in one way or another draw on (or depend on) the rhetoric of documentary film-making of the 1930s. Much of this accounting has been done by surviving members of the documentary movement—'largely as anecdote', as Annette Kuhn has observed—while more critical analysis of the movement has until recently only been undertaken very partially, particularly in relation to the question of national cinema.[16] There are now

---

[13] The distinction proposed here between a commercial sector and a documentary sector of the film industry is not entirely adequate, since some documentaries were exploited commercially, especially during the Second World War; however, for want of a better distinction, I will persevere with this one.

[14] Roger Manvell, 'The British Feature Film from 1940 to 1945', in Balcon *et al.*, *Twenty Years*, 82.

[15] Catherine de la Roche, 'Britain's Film Directors, No. 1. Frank Launder and Sidney Gilliat', *Our Time*, Dec. 1946, 101.

[16] '"Independent" Film-Making and the State in the 1930s', *Edinburgh '77 Magazine*, 2 (1977), 44. 'Anecdotal' accounts and/or memoirs of the documentary movement include: Elizabeth Sussex, *The Rise and Fall of British Documentary* (London, 1975); Eva Orbanz *et al.*, *Journey to a Legend and Back: The British Realistic Film* (Berlin, 1977); Paul Rotha, *Documentary Diary* (London, 1973); Harry Watt, *Don't Look At The Camera* (London, 1974); James Beveridge, *John Grierson, Film Master* (New York, 1978); Basil Wright, *The Long View: A Personal Perspective on World Cinema* (London, 1974), 107–15. Classic and more or less contemporary accounts include: Hardy (ed.), *Grierson on Documentary*; Rotha, *Documentary Film*; Roger Manvell, *Film*

a couple of more extensive revisionist studies of the politics and organization of the British documentary film movement, drawing on primary research materials not previously used.[17] Theoretically rigorous and detailed analyses of the films produced by the movement, focusing on the formal devices and strategies which they use, and the perspectives which they develop, are still few and far between, however.[18] This is also true of the later films which might be said to have been influenced by the work of the documentarists in the 1930s.[19] Even so, there is no doubt that many aspects of the documentary film movement and the development of British cinema during the Second World War have been more thoroughly researched than have the periods and developments dealt with in the previous two chapters.

Peter Wyeth and Don MacPherson have argued that 'this tradition . . . has set the very terms in which film-making is thought about in Britain'.[20] To that extent, the dominant discourse about documentary film in Britain is not inaccessible—but the central operational terms of this discourse and the cinema which it supports have still not been thoroughly examined. In particular, there has not been any adequate examination of the ways in

(London, rev. and enlarged edn., 1946); Hardy, 'British Documentary'; and The Arts Enquiry. For more recent critical analyses, see Alan Lovell and Jim Hillier, *Studies in Documentary* (London, 1972); Kuhn, ' "Independent" film-making'; Don MacPherson (ed.), *Traditions of Independence: British Cinema in the 1930s* (London, 1980); Rachael Low, *The History of the British Film, 1929–1939: Documentary and Educational Films of the 1930s* (London, 1979); Stuart Hood, 'John Grierson and the Documentary Film Movement', in James Curran and Vincent Porter (eds.), *British Cinema History* (London, 1983); Dai Vaughan, *Portrait of an Invisible Man: The Working Life of Stewart McAllister, Film Editor* (London, 1983); Erik Barnouw, *Documentary: A History of the Non-Fiction Film* (New York, 1974); Andrew Tudor, *Theories of Film* (London, 1974); Paul Marris (ed.), *Paul Rotha* (London, 1982); Andrew Higson, 'Britain's Outstanding Contribution'; Robert Colls and Philip Dodd, 'Representing the Nation—British Documentary Film, 1930–1945', *Screen*, 26/1 (1985); Paul Swann, 'John Grierson and the GPO Film Unit, 1933–1939', *Historical Journal of Film, Radio and Television*, 3/1 (1983); id., 'The Selling of the Empire: The EMB Film Unit', *Studies in Visual Communication*, 9/3 (1983); and John Caughie, 'Broadcasting and Cinema, 1. Converging Histories', in Barr (ed.), *All Our Yesterdays*.

[17] Paul Swann, *British Documentary Movement*; and Ian Aitken, *Film and Reform: John Grierson and the Documentary Film Movement* (London, 1990). Low, *British Film, 1929–1939*, is also fairly comprehensive, but she has not gone to the unpublished records which Swann and Aitken researched.

[18] See e.g. Annette Kuhn, '*Desert Victory* and the People's War', and John Ellis, 'Victory of the Voice', both in *Screen*, 22/2 (1981); Malcolm Smith, 'Narrative and Ideology in *Listen To Britain*', in Jeremy Hawthorn (ed.), *Narrative from Malory to Motion Pictures* (London, 1985); David Pearson, 'Speaking for the Common Man', in Marris (ed.), *Paul Rotha*.

[19] See e.g. Charles Barr, *Ealing Studios* (London, 1977); John Ellis, 'Made in Ealing', *Screen*, 16/1 (1977); Andrew Higson, 'Addressing the Nation: Five Films', in Hurd (ed.), *National Fictions*, and 'Space, Place, Spectacle', *Screen*, 25/4–5 (1984); John Hill, *Sex, Class and Realism: British Cinema 1956–64* (London, 1986); and Antonia Lant, *Blackout: Re-inventing Women for Wartime British Cinema* (Princeton, NJ, 1991).

[20] 'The Third Front', *Sight and Sound*, 47/3 (1978), 143.

which films within the documentary-realist tradition seek to articulate a sense of the public and the national in relation to the personal and the individual. This aspect will be one of the central concerns of the present chapter. I do not intend to say anything particularly original about the organization of the documentary film movement or about the course of the British film industry during the war period—although I will need to say something about these matters in order to prepare the ground for the analyses of the films which follow. I will also be working deliberately with some of the better known and more accessible manifestations of the contemporary discourse about British documentary film practice—and using as examples the films most frequently cited within that discourse—in order to produce a clear picture of the dominant form of the documentary idea in circulation in the late 1930s and early 1940s.

The documentary idea and the documentary movement were the products of the cultural and political debates of the late 1920s and 1930s, and developments in film were only one strand in a much broader field of social-democratic cultural practice. During the 1930s, social documentation was exploited in radio, painting, theatre, journalistic and literary writing, photojournalism and photography, social anthropology (e.g. Mass Observation), and so on—such that Grierson could argue that 'the documentary idea was not basically a film idea at all . . . The medium happened to be the most convenient and most exciting available to us,' and 'the documentary film movement might, in principle, have been a movement in documentary writing, or documentary radio, or documentary painting.'[21]

Social documentation as a mode of cultural practice was by no means

---

[21] 'The Documentary Idea: 1942', in Hardy (ed.), *Grierson on Documentary*, 113 and 'The Story of the Documentary Film', *The Fortnightly*, Aug. 1939, 121–2. On radio, see Paddy Scannell, '"The Stuff of Radio": Developments in Radio Features and Documentaries before the War', in John Corner (ed.), *Documentary and the Mass Media* (London, 1986); on painting, see Lynda Morris and Robert Radford, *The Story of the Artists International Association, 1933–1953* (Oxford, 1983); on photojournalism, see Stuart Hall, 'The Social Eye of Picture Post', *Working Papers in Cultural Studies*, 2 (1972); on photography, see *Humphrey Spender—Worktown—Photographs of Bolton and Blackpool, Taken for Mass Observation, 1937/38*, exhibition catalogue, Gardner Centre Gallery, University of Sussex, Brighton, 1977, and David Mellor, 'Patterns of Naturalism: Hoppé to Hardy', in *The Real Thing: An Anthology of British Photographs, 1840–1950*, exhibition catalogue, Arts Council of Great Britain, 1975; Jon Clark *et al.* (eds.), *Culture and Crisis in Britain in the Thirties* (London, 1979) has material on literature and theatre; Frank Gloversmith (ed.), *Class, Culture and Social Change, A New View of the 1930s* (Brighton, 1980), has material on literature, art, and Mass Observation; for further discussions of Mass Observation, see Tom Jeffery, *Mass Observation: A Short History*, Occasional Papers no. 55, Centre for Contemporary Cultural Studies, University of Birmingham, 1978; David Chaney and Michael Pickering, 'Democracy and Communication: Mass Observation, 1937–1943', *Journal of Communication*, 36/1 (1986); on literature and documentary, see also Chris Pawling, 'George Orwell and the Documentary in the Thirties', *Literature and History*, 4 (1976); see also Aitken, *Film and Reform*, 175 ff.

new and the aesthetic and ideological perspectives of the documentary movement need to be related back to the writing of the 'social explorers' of 'Darkest England' in the late nineteenth and early twentieth centuries.[22] There is another ancestry to the documentary movement which needs to be noted, however: the development of official public relations activity, corporate advertising, and state propaganda policy in Britain.[23] Thus the development of the Empire Marketing Board and the establishment of a Film Unit there are closely related to those cultural and political debates about the actual and potential social and educational role of cinema in helping to forge and reproduce national and imperial unity discussed in Chapter 2.

Public relations and social documentation are not always and necessarily the same thing, but in this case they do have in common the desire to develop film as a tool in the ideological enterprise of producing a public sphere of communication, a public field of meaning, where the term 'public' implies something held in common, something without contestation, in the general interest. Conceived in social-democratic terms, documentary practice establishes a relatively neutral information flow from state to citizen, educating, informing, and instructing the electorate of a new enfranchisement, propagandizing about the relationship between the social welfare of the citizens and the work of the state's major institutions, reproducing the idea of 'the state as benevolent mediator of a mass political democracy'.[24]

Grierson would have agreed with critics such as Jürgen Habermas that the capitalist-controlled mass media work against the principle of the public sphere as a space in which rational and critical discussion of issues of general interest can take place between informed citizens. The rules of the market-place and private interest in the flow of ideas and information hold sway over public interest, such that the public sphere is no longer simply a site for the circulation of information, but one in which information— and access to it—is managed and regulated in the interests of the most powerful social groups.[25]

---

[22] Colls and Dodd 'Representing the Nation', 22–3; cf. Peter Keating (ed.), *Into Unknown England, 1866–1913: Selections from the Social Explorers* (London, 1976); Philip Dodd, 'Englishness and the National Culture', in Robert Colls and Philip Dodd (eds.), *Englishness: Culture and Politics, 1880–1920* (London, 1986); Peter Brooker and Peter Widdowson, 'A Literature for England', esp. 141–58, ibid.; Raymond Williams, *The Country and the City* (London, 1985).

[23] See Swann, 'Grierson and GPO Film Unit', and id. *British Documentary Movement*; and Aitken, *Film and Reform*, esp. 90 ff., and 150 ff.

[24] Kuhn, '"Independent" Film-Making', 45.

[25] On the debate about Habermas's concept of the public sphere and its relation to the media, see Jürgen Habermas, *The Structural Transformation of the Public Sphere: An Inquiry into a Category of Bourgeois Society* (Cambridge, 1989); Peter Hohendahl, 'Jürgen Habermas: "The Public Sphere" (1964)', and Jürgen Habermas, 'The Public

For Grierson and his colleagues, however, the development of a documentary cinema apparently independent of the capitalist media was a means of maintaining, renewing, and extending the principles of the bourgeois public sphere. For them, the documentary movement was a means of informing the public by putting ideas and information into mass circulation. Grierson himself clearly saw the documentary as having a democratic function in expanding the public sphere:

The basic force behind [the documentary units] was social not aesthetic. . . . We were, I confess, sociologists, a little worried about the way the world was going. . . . The world had become very complex—and civic comprehension difficult. We were conscious of the abstraction of life under the new metropolitan skies. We saw that poverty of community life went hand in hand with the lack of civic comprehension. And of one thing we were pretty sure—that the old stiff-backed educational system was not doing very much to help towards comprehension. Nor particularly was the new myth-making machinery of the star-struck cinema. But if we were jealous of this myth-making influence and made film the instrument of our door-step drama, it was partly by accident. We were interested in all instruments which would crystallize sentiments in a muddled world and create a will toward civic participation.[26]

Within this context, documentary cinema was appropriated as the ideal social-democratic means of mass communication, documentation, and education, the ideal means of 'bridging the gap between the citizen and his community'.[27] Ernest Barker argued in the late 1920s that we 'cannot see a nation. It has many members, divided by an infinity of differences; and the unity of its character must be a matter rather of faith than of sight.'[28] The Griersonian project can in part be understood as a response to this situation, an attempt to render visible and knowable that which is invisible,

Sphere: An Encyclopedia Article (1964)', both in *New German Critique*, 1/3 (1974); John Keane, *Public Life and Late Capitalism: Towards a Socialist Theory of Democracy* (Cambridge, 1984); Michael Bommes and Patrick Wright, '"Charms of Residence": The Public and the Past', in Richard Johnson *et al.* (eds.), *Making Histories: Studies in History-Writing and Politics* (London, 1982); Alexander Kluge, 'On Film and the Public Sphere', and Miriam Hansen, 'Co-operative Auteur Cinema and Oppositional Public Sphere: Alexander Kluge's Contribution to *Germany in Autumn*', both in *New German Critique*, 24–5 (1981–2); in Britain, the concept of the public sphere has been taken up most interestingly by the media sociologists associated with the journal *Media, Culture and Society*, mainly in relation to broadcasting: see e.g. Paddy Scannell, 'Public Service Broadcasting and Modern Public Life', *Media, Culture and Society*, 11/2 (1989) and 'The Media and the Public Sphere', in Peter Golding *et al.* (eds.), *Communicating Politics* (Leicester, 1986); from a slightly different point of view, see David Chaney, 'Public Opinion and Social Change: The Social Rhetoric of Documentary and the Concept of News', in E. Katz and T. Szecsko, *Mass Media and Social Change* (London, 1981).

[26] 'Documentary Film', 122.   [27] Ibid. 123.
[28] Ernest Barker, *National Character and the Factors in its Formation* (London, 2nd edn. 1928 [1st pub. 1927]), 5.

those manifold relations which constitute the national community. Thus, what appealed to the documentarists about the Soviet montage films of the late 1920s was 'their emphasis not on the personal life but on the mass life, their continuous attempt to dramatize the relation of a man to his community.'[29] From this perspective, documentary practice potentially binds together the individual subjects of a nation through a system of mass communications, reproducing the nation as a rational communicative community. It gives the nation a public, social image, a means for moving beyond the blind faith of patriotism by dramatizing that 'community in anonymity which is the hallmark of modern nations'.[30]

For Grierson and Rotha, the task of documentary—'the public service which it is the duty of cinema to perform'—is the 'teaching of citizenship', and the transformation of the spectator into 'a thinking, reasoning and questioning member of the community', 'not merely . . . a passive voter but . . . an active member of the State': 'The Documentary Film, quite simply, aims to bring about an awareness in every person of their place in everyday life and of the responsibilities of good citizenship implied by that membership.'[31]

There are a number of problems with these arguments about the role of documentary cinema in servicing a democratic public sphere—problems which I will be exploring in my discussions of some of the films which draw on these arguments. First, while wider access to ideas and information may have an emancipatory, democratizing effect, the form in which those ideas are presented—in this case, documentary film—may actually discourage the individual from participating in rational discussion by situating the discussion in the text itself, such that the individual is once more outside the public sphere, a mere passive, if enlightened, spectator of it. Second, confronted with the new mass public with its potentially diverse, multiple, and contradictory interests, any attempt to impose a concept of the general interest, or the public interest, or the national interest, is

---

[29] Grierson, *New Clarion*, 11 June 1932, collected in Forsyth Hardy (ed.), *Grierson on the Movies* (London, 1981), 39.

[30] Benedict Anderson, *Imagined Communities: Reflections on the Origins and Spread of Nationalism* (London, 1983), 40; see also Colin Mercer, 'That's Entertainment: The Resilience of Popular Forms', in Tony Bennett, Colin Mercer, Janet Woollacott (eds.), *Popular Culture and Social Relations* (Milton Keynes, 1986), 181.

[31] Paul Rotha, 'A Survey of Recent Film Literature in Britain', *The Year's Work in the Film, 1949* (London, 1950), 79; Grierson, 'Documentary Film', 123; Rotha, Foreword to 1st edn. of *Documentary Film*, 27; ibid. 48; and Rotha, submission to the Moyne Committee, Annex II, 'Definition of a Documentary Film'. Cf. the following comments in an official report on the Ministry of Information's non-theatrical distribution work during the early part of the war, repr. as 'Celluloid Circus', in *Documentary News Letter*, 2/9 (1941): 'The MoI's "Celluloid Circus", as it is affectionately known in the Ministry's Film Division, is creating again the market-place discussion; the public forum is returning to village and town alike with a new orator—film, to lead a lively, well-informed discussion of the country's war-time problems' (170).

necessarily the site of ideological struggle: all social interests manifestly do not have an equal voice, consensus must be negotiated or acquiescence imposed. Third, underlying many of these claims about the role of documentary is the idea of the benevolent state acting as impartial patron of the documentary movement. Terms such as 'public education', 'public comprehension', and 'good citizenship' which recur across the documentary discourse indicate the extent to which the documentary idea was precisely an effort to produce and regulate an official public sphere, an attempt to discipline public life. In Grierson's words, 'it was, from the beginning, an adventure in public observation', involving, as Rotha put it, 'presenting one half of the populace to the other'.[32] The public must be educated, they must comprehend the values of citizenship, but they must also be observed, surveyed, analysed, categorized—that is, they must be policed.[33] Hence the number of key documentaries of the 1930s which focus on the work and the living conditions of the lower classes.[34] Observation and surveillance, of course, imply a point of view, and the point of view of the documentarist was situated for the most part outside the public milieu which was being documented in these films. Grierson, for instance, spoke of 'an unknown England beyond the West End', and of his desire to 'travel dangerously into the jungles of Middlesborough and the Clyde':[35] the documentarist was thus separated both physically and morally from the object of investigation; he (and sometimes she) did not know the jungles beyond the West End because they were not his habitat but the habitat of the dangerous classes, 'the great unwashed'—and it was

---

[32] 'Documentary Film', 121; and Rotha, *Documentary Film*, 115.

[33] Cf. Keating's descriptions of the Unknown England mode of writing of the late nineteenth century; the writers were invariably upper-middle or upper class and for the most part saw their task as the gathering of information in order to promote the cause of social reform and to influence the public conscience: 'Out of this concern there develops a distinctive branch of modern literature in which a representative of one class consciously sets out to explore, analyse and report upon the life of another class lower on the social scale than his own.' ('Introduction', in Keating (ed.), *Unknown England*, 13); as a cultural practice this earlier form of social documentation was carried out in the belief that 'the only way to heal the division [between the classes] is for the governing class to know about the governed' (ibid. 30). Cf. also Peter Stallybrass and Allon White, *The Politics and Poetics of Transgression* (London, 1986); and Dick Hebdige, *Hiding in the Light* (London, 1988), 21–2.

[34] e.g., among the better known films, *Industrial Britain*, *Housing Problems*, *Enough To Eat*, and *North Sea*.

[35] *Spectator*, 14 May 1932, quoted in Jeffrey Richards, *The Age of the Dream Palace: Cinema and Society in Britain, 1930–1939* (London, 1984), 245; and *Artwork*, autumn 1931, collected in Hardy (ed.), *Grierson on Documentary*, 32. Cf. Keating's writers of the late nineteenth century who cast themselves as explorers of the unknown (see Keating, 'Introduction', *Unknown England*); William Booth, for instance, entitled one of his books *In Darkest England and the Way Out* (1890), while George Sims, in his *How The Poor Live* (1883) 'record[s] the result of a journey into a region which lies at our own doors—into a dark continent that is within easy walking distance of the General Post Office' (in Keating (ed.), *Unknown England*, 65).

precisely the otherness of this 'general public' which threatened, which was dangerous.

Documentary, in the end, constituted an attitude: 'documentary is not this or that type of film, but simply a method of approach to public information.'[36] But it was, as I have tried to suggest, an attitude not just to public information but to the public too, and one which tried to hold together profoundly contradictory tendencies. It is the same attitude as that of the bourgeois onlooker gazing at the carnival of *Sing As We Go*.

REALISM AND NATIONAL CINEMA

> Experience has shown that it is usually the short film of the documentary kind, and not the popularly conceived feature film, that presents the most authentic picture of our national life. Of necessity, the feature film must bear the burden of highly paid actors and expensive settings to secure its appeal; whereas the modest short film, making do with things and people as they really are, comes nearer to a direct statement of how we live than do the films of fiction.
>
> *The Times*, 1938.[37]

The attitude of the documentary movement implies at one level a radical challenge to the dominant form of cinema in the 1930s. The cinema of spectacle—founded of course on the pleasurable economies of American cinema, 'the streamlined showmanship of Hollywood'[38]—encouraged cinema-going as a routine habit, an utterly familiar social practice, underpinned by the idea of going out to be entertained, to be uplifted from everyday reality into a world of wish-fulfilment, a world of 'dreams stuffed with ersatz romance'.[39] The documentary idea constructed a quite different social function for cinema, one which posited cinema as a means of communication and analysis, not a medium of entertainment which simply circulated spectacular cultural commodities within the international marketplace: 'The purpose of the documentary film is to get away from the theatrical tradition, with its purely entertainment appeal, and to find in the wider fields of actuality an appeal which will be more educative, more intellectual, more aesthetic and therefore more durable.'[40]

---

[36] Basil Wright, 'Documentary Today', *Penguin Film Review*, 2 (1947), 37; see also Hardy (ed.), *Grierson on Documentary*, 113; and Basil Wright, *The Use of the Film* (London, 1948), 38. Cf. also Keating's characterization of the Unknown England writing of the late nineteenth century as embodying 'a frame of mind, . . . a way of looking', with a shared set of values (Preface, in Keating (ed.), *Unknown England*, 9).

[37] 'Films of Great Britain', 1 Nov. 1938, 12.   [38] Manvell, *Film*, 136.

[39] Roger Manvell, 'The Quarter's Films', *Sight and Sound*, 15 (1946), 97.

[40] Harold Nicholson, *Daily Telegraph*, 31 Jan. 1936, quoted in Rotha, submission to Moyne Committee, i, 70.

We have here then two competing professional ideologies, two competing justifications for cinematic practice: the commercial film industry's ideology of showmanship, and the documentary movement's ideology of public service. Critics derided the former as an American phenomenon, against which 'the documentary film was . . . an essentially British development . . . [whose] characteristic was this idea of social use.'[41] Within the documentary movement, then, cinema was proposed as an apparatus which could be self-consciously used to construct a national imaginary. Grierson, for instance, argued to the Moyne Committee of 1936 that

The shorts field has already in its documentary section demonstrated how different aspects of the national life can be described and brought alive. Large films must rely so much on the play, and the story film is so unrelated to reality, that if the ordinary working [people] and traditions of the national life are to be presented, one must look mainly to the shorts field for their presentation.[42]

The documentary movement in the 1930s was thus at the forefront of attempts to establish an authentic, indigenous national cinema in response to the dominance of Hollywood's irresponsible cinema of spectacle and escapism. Hollywood was the embodiment of an encroaching mass culture, against which must be erected, in this case, a responsible and artistically respectable cinema—and, as we have already seen in Chapter 2, it was the documentary movement which 'captured the interest in film as an art that was developing in Britain in the later 1920s'.[43] The documentary film units became the site for the most systematic explorations of and experiments with intellectual and artistic ideas. Central among these ideas were questions of montage, influenced by the film-maker theorists of the Soviet cinema, 'this new rhetorical cinema [which is] the most complete approximation to our ideas'.[44] Rotha had argued in *The Film Till Now* that the poverty of British cinema was directly related to the absence of both a school of avant-garde film in Britain and a 'school of thought for the

---

[41] Grierson, 'Documentary Film', 123. Ironically, as Grierson himself was well aware, the development of the EMB and subsequently the public relations work of the GPO owed a great deal to American PR and advertising techniques, including the widespread use of modernist art devices, and the philosophy of writers such as Walter Lippman; see Swann, *British Documentary Movement*, esp. 4.

[42] In Board of Trade, *Minutes of Evidence . . . Committee on Cinematograph Films*, ii, 134.

[43] Lovell and Hillier, *Studies in Documentary*, 35. It is probably easiest to appreciate this today by looking at the experimental colour animation work which Len Lye did for the GPO Film Unit—e.g. *Rainbow Dance* and *Trade Tattoo* (both 1937).

[44] C. A. Lejeune, *Cinema* (London, 1931), 168. See also Rotha's discussion of sound and image montage in *Documentary Film*, which is clearly heavily influenced by the writings of Pudovkin and Eisenstein: e.g. 'nothing photographed, or recorded on to celluloid, has meaning until it comes to the cutting-bench; . . . the primary task of film creation lies in the . . . editing' (79).

furtherance of filmic theory, such as is found in other countries.'[45] In later editions, Rotha argued that the documentary movement had filled this gap,[46] while his *Documentary Film*, published in 1936, was intended 'to replace the theoretical discussions in *The Film Till Now*', since he now believed that 'the documentary method may well be described as the birth of creative cinema.'[47]

At the heart of the documentary idea is a powerful differentiation between the 'realism' of the documentary and the 'escapism' of mass entertainment. The realist cinema, a serious, committed, engaged cinema, became the key moral standard in the call for an indigenous national cinema.[48] Claims for realism are invariably multivalent, and certainly there are a number of conflicting assumptions underlying the claims for the realism of the documentaries of the 1930s and the feature films that have been seen as influenced by them, or as otherwise close to them. One point of departure is the fact that cinema was felt by many within the intellectual film culture to be an intrinsically realist medium. Roger Manvell, for instance, in his widely read *Film*, first published by Pelican in 1944, argued that cinema 'is an art based on the realistic approach to the material of life.'[49] But within that philosophy, some films are more realistic than others, and it must then be asked: What is it that makes a film realistic? What is it that creates the impression of realism?

The term realism as discussed in relation to documentary suggests a set of aesthetic principles of verisimilitude and motivation common to almost all claims to realism. In so far as these principles are codified across a range of texts, one of the most pervasive claims for realism is bound up with those textual strategies which serve to efface the marks of codification, transforming representation into presentation: 'the real is not articulated; it is.'[50] The various partial discourses of a text, whether a narrative text

[45] Paul Rotha, *The Film Till Now* (London, 1967 [1st pub. 1930]), 314; cf. Grierson: 'theory is important, experiment is important' ('The Documentary Producer', *Cinema Quarterly*, 2 (1933), 8).

[46] See n. 1, p. 314, added for later editions. Cf. Lejeune's description of the work of the documentarists as 'the British avant-garde' (*Observer*, 21 Aug. 1932, quoted in Rotha, *Documentary Diary*, 35); and J. B. Priestley, *Rain Upon Godshill* (London, 1941), 80–81. Such views rapidly became the orthodoxy, to the extent that, in Roger Manvell's 1949 collection, *Experiment in Film* (London, 1949), the chapter on the development of avant-garde and experimental film in Britain is by the documentarist Edgar Anstey and deals almost exclusively with documentary and other 'realist' film-making ('Development of Film Technique in Britain'); see also Basil Wright, 'Realist Review', *Sight and Sound*, 10 (1941).

[47] Foreword to 1st edn. of *Documentary Film*, 25; ibid. 71.

[48] The term 'realism' became virtually synonymous with documentary in the 1930s; *vide* two important organizations of the period, *Realist* Film Unit and Associated *Realist* Film Producers.

[49] *Film*, 47.

[50] Colin MacCabe, 'Realism and the Cinema: Notes on some Brechtian Theses', *Screen*, 15/2 (1974), 12; compare the following comments in a review of the documentary *Our*

or not, tend to be hierarchically ordered in relation to a meta-discourse which is thereby able to present itself as the position of truth, shifting attention away from the production of representation to the content of the represented.

This 'classic realism' has never been enough for either the documentary idea or British intellectual film culture more generally, however, and there have always been other, more clearly argued, claims for the realism of the British documentary-related tradition as different from Hollywood's 'melodramatic fantasies'. At the very least, the realism vs. escapism distinction in British intellectual film culture suggests a nuancing or even transgression of the strategies used by classical Hollywood to achieve verisimilitude and motivation. This transgression produces a certain freshness which seems realistic to contemporary reviewers and film historians, and has been most noticeable in relation to questions of theme and iconography: each successive realist movement in British cinema and television has been celebrated for both its commitment to the exploration of contemporary social problems, and its working out of those problems in relation to landscapes and characters which are deemed realistic for their seeming non-conventionality.

One of the most consistent criticisms of the commercial cinema from within the documentary movement during the 1930s—and it has been echoed in numerous subsequent statements—was that it failed to provide any positive representations of working-class people.[51] Films within the documentary-realist tradition, by contrast, have consistently been proclaimed as politically progressive because they extend the conventional social

School, in *Documentary News Letter*, March 1941, 47: 'The revolutionary step of including a shot of the unit shooting a scene seems to me to strike a wrong note. If one aims at bringing reality to the screen, any reminder of the technical processes by which this is achieved can only destroy that reality for the audience.' My discussion of realism draws in addition on the following: Roman Jakobson, 'On Realism in Art', in Ladislav Matejka and Krystyna Pomorska (eds.), *Readings in Russian Poetics* (Ann Arbor, Mich., 1978); Paul Willemen, 'On Realism in the Cinema', in John Ellis (ed.), *Screen Reader 1* (London, 1977); Raymond Williams, 'A Lecture on Realism', *Screen*, 18/1 (1977), and *The Country and the City*; John Barrell, *The Dark Side of the Landscape: The Rural Poor in English Painting, 1730–1840* (Cambridge, 1980); Roland Barthes, 'The Realistic Effect', *Film Reader*, 3 (1978); Gérard Genette, 'Verisimilitude and Motivation', xeroxed typescript in University of Kent Library, trans. of 'Vraisemblance et motivation', *Figures II* (Paris, 1969); John Ellis, *Visible Fictions* (London, 1982), 6–10; John Hill, 'Ideology, Economy and the British Cinema', in Michèle Barratt, *et al.* (eds.), *Ideology and Cultural Production* (London, 1979), and *Sex, Class and Realism*; Manual Alvarado, 'The Documentary Enterprise: Realism and Convention', in Elizabeth Cowie (ed.), *BFI Production Board Catalogue, 1977–78*, (London, 1978); and Higson, 'Space, Place, Spectacle'. See also the discussion of realism by Grierson and Rotha in, respectively, Hardy (ed.), *Grierson on Documentary*, and *Documentary Film*.

[51] See e.g. Paul Rotha, 'Films and the Labour Party', address delivered at a Special Labour Party Conference on Film Propaganda, Edinburgh, 3 Oct. 1936, reproduced in Marris (ed.), *Paul Rotha*, 49; and *Documentary Film*, 56.

discourse and deal positively with working people, within an iconography of authentic sounds and images. The authenticity of place and character, for instance, is achieved by breaking some of the studio conventions of classical cinema—shooting on location in actual British landscapes, using unknown, or unglamorous, or non-professional, or untrained performers, and so on. This surface realism involves fetishizing certain iconographic details into a spectacle of the real, as distinct from its narrativization or incorporation into a rational communicative framework.

An authentic iconography is not in itself enough, however, and invariably there is a second claim for the realism of documentary-related films, as distinct from the Hollywood tradition. This we can name moral realism, in that it involves a moral commitment to a particular set of social problems and solutions and to a particular social formation. What is important is the attitude itself, the moral obligation of cinema, 'its responsibility in showing the broader movements of history to the world'.[52] Inevitably, moral realism is to a degree bound up with the claim for surface realism, involving an iconographic commitment to the representation of 'ordinary people'; but it also involves a particular construction of the social in terms of universal human values—for Manvell, the hallmark of the best British films of the war period was 'the sincerity with which human values are handled, and the authenticity of situation and environment in which these values are involved.'[53]

The concern for factual accuracy is thus gathered up in the desire for moral truth, focused on the figure in the landscape. The most successful narrative films in the documentary-realist tradition reveal a concern for personal relations and human values which invest the landscapes of the diegesis with a greater sense of moral urgency and a more compelling sense of human sympathy, while the real historical details of these landscapes legitimate and authenticate the moral universe. It is an implicit acknowledgement that narrative film is precisely fiction and must therefore be made as credible and plausible as possible by rooting the drama in history. This is of course really only an intensification of the realist strategies of classical Hollywood, which can be used to make plausible an entirely imaginary world.

The realism of the documentary film was conceived from the outset as 'something more than a prosaic description',[54] however, despite the strength of the sociological, propagandist strand in the movement with its rhetoric

---

[52] Manvell, *Film*, 81. On the moral aspect of this realist discourse, see also Annette Kuhn, 'British Documentary in the Thirties and "Independence": Re-contextualising a Film Movement', in MacPherson (ed.), *Traditions of Independence*, 26.

[53] 'The British Feature Film from 1940 to 1945', in Balcon, *et al.*, *Twenty Years*, 84; see also John Ellis's discussion of these issues in 'Art, Culture, Quality: Terms for a Cinema in the '40s and '70s', *Screen*, 19/3 (1978).

[54] Rotha, submission to the Moyne Committee, 'Definition of a Documentary Film', 69.

of social responsibility, education, and instruction—hence Grierson's definition of documentary as 'the creative treatment of actuality'.[55] There was always an undertow running against the most ardently voiced educative-sociologistic tendency within the movement which sought to acknowledge and foreground the aesthetic work of the text. This we may call poetic realism: it involves a more perfect conjunction of surface realism and moral realism, a conjunction which transcends ordinariness, which makes the ordinary strange, even beautiful—but, above all, which has emotional depth and integrity. Writing about the various documentary-influenced feature films of the mid-1940s, Roger Manvell, for instance, suggested that 'the use of the word realistic to describe the new British cinema is not enough. There is always a poetic quality about the emotional treatment in these films. Accuracy in the presentation of events and situations is not enough: there must also be understanding and humanity.'[56]

The artistic, the creative, and the poetic, had been installed right at the outset as key aspects of the documentary idea, even if Grierson was, in the end, proud that 'an adventure in the arts [had come] to assume the respectability of a public service.'[57] It was this quality—especially in feature films—which was most admired within the broader intellectual film culture of the 1940s. In a sense, poetic realism constitutes the happy balance between the various conflicting and competing ideas and impulses which make up the documentary idea as a whole. It holds all excesses in check: the responsibility of realism blocks off the path to self-indulgent aestheticism or cloying sentimentality, while the poetic sensibility tempers both the objective coldness of the document, and the tendency towards establishing action as the ultimate logic of narrative movement and energy. It attempts, above all, to hold together the irreconcilable discourses of artistic endeavour and public service.

The strand of poetic realism in intellectual film culture and the documentary idea thus allows a (guarded) inscription of the artist in filmic discourse: the poetic film is a film of personal vision which foregrounds the work of the director. The romantic tendency is, however, held in check by the continuing demand for moral commitment, but there inevitably remains

---

[55] The earliest use of this phrase by Grierson that I have come across is in 'The Documentary Producer', 8; numerous accounts of documentary ascribe a slightly different phrase to Grierson: 'the creative *interpretation* of actuality'; I have not been able to find a published instance of Grierson using this phrase, however, even if there are many uses of it by other writers; see e.g. Wright, *Use of Film*, 40.

[56] *Film*, 135. On the question of poetic discourse, see the work of formalists and linguistic structuralists such as Roman Jakobson (e.g. 'Concluding Statement: Linguistics and Poetics', in T. A. Sebeok (ed.), *Style in Language* (Cambridge, Mass., 1960)) and Jan Mukarovsky (e.g. 'Standard Language and Poetic Language', in Paul L. Garvin (ed. and trans.), *A Prague School Reader on Esthetics, Literary Structure and Style* (Washington, DC, 1964)). Note that Aitken links Grierson's ideas quite explicitly to this formalist concept of poetic discourse (*Film and Reform*, 115–17).

[57] 'Documentary Film', 123.

a tension here between the sociological and the aesthetic, the moral and the poetic.

The poetic discourse in effect transformed public observation into the fascinated gaze, which could render exotic and romanticize the object of documentation into a thing of aesthetic beauty, conceived in familiar terms. Grierson, as ever, outlined the possibilities in 1932: 'realist documentary, with its streets and cities and slums and markets and exchanges and factories, has given itself the job of making poetry where no poet has gone before it.'[58]

Edgar Anstey, himself a documentarist, recalled how Robert Flaherty had 'turned the forbidding expanses of the Black Country into some of the loveliest landscape scenes that have ever been photographed' in *Industrial Britain* (1933); the beauty, for Anstey, lay in the pictorialist qualities of the image 'with black chimneys where convention demanded trees and sunlight reflecting from wet rooves instead of from sylvan lakes.'[59] Manvell rightly called this 'industrial romanticism', and himself delighted in the urban pastoral of 'man against the black-blue sky, factories against the rolling clouds, the countryside of Britain'.[60] 'The flash and swirl of machines', he suggested, 'the lovely photogenic qualities of sunset over the pitshaft, the smoky shapes and grey perspectives of industrial Britain lent themselves to the cine-eye and to montage.'[61]

MONTAGE AND THE PUBLIC GAZE

> In matters such as technical slickness, finished performance, modern atmosphere, and popular appeal, no other mass of film production begins to compare with the Hollywood product. These factors in combination give a 'last word' air to the most humble and incidental prop. . . . It would be useless to attempt to compete with American production in the matter of massed incidental publicity.
>
> John Grierson, 1930.[62]

The documentary idea sought to articulate a public sphere of responsible social activity, a field of ideas and issues assumed to be in the general

---

[58] 'Documentary (2): Symphonies', *Cinema Quarterly*, 1 (1933), 137, also in Hardy (ed.), *Grierson on Documentary*, 41.

[59] 'The Regional Life of Britain as Seen through British Films', in Roger Manvell (ed.), *The Year's Work in the Film, 1950* (London, 1951), 45.

[60] *Film*, 100.

[61] This passage appears only in the 1st edn. (1944) of *Film* (85), and appears to have been dropped for the 2nd edn. For a more critical view of this sort of romanticism from within the circle of the documentarists, see Rotha, *Documentary Film*, 153; and Priestley, *Rain upon Godshill*, 81–3. I have discussed the question of romanticism in the British realist tradition at greater length in 'Space, Place, Spectacle'.

[62] 'Film Propaganda', memorandum to the Inter-Departmental Committee on Trade Advertisement and Propaganda, July 1930, PRO BT61/40/1 D.O.T. E12251B, paper no. 14, quoted in Swann, *British Documentary Movement*, 126.

interest. This was constructed in contradistinction to the foregrounding of individual desire and wish-fulfilment in the classical narrative film, which was assumed to deal only with personal conflicts of an essentially emotional nature. Rotha, for instance, felt that 'the private passions and petulances [of human beings] are of little interest' to the documentary filmmaker, who was more concerned with developing 'a method of communication and propaganda to project not just personal opinions but arguments for a world of common interests.'[63] Grierson, too, could see no need for fantasy, 'nor the dribblings of personal sentiment or personal story'; he argued that 'the individual life is no longer capable of cross-sectioning society . . . its particular belly-aches are of no consequence in a world which complex and impersonal forces command', concluding that 'the individual as a self-sufficient dramatic figure is outmoded' since it is unable to 'reveal the essentially co-operative or mass nature of society'.[64] What was more important for him was the development of new forms of cultural practice like the documentary film: 'We have all been abstracting our arts away from the personal, trying to articulate this wider world of duties and loyalties in which education and invention and democracy have made us citizens.'[65]

For Grierson, this meant 'abandon[ing] the story form, and seek[ing], like the modern exponent of poetry and painting and prose, a matter and method more satisfactory to the mind and spirit of the time.'[66] By the late 1930s, however, several of Grierson's colleagues felt that documentary must temper its modernism, re-engage with the story form, and embrace at least some aspects of commercial narrative cinema, in order to reach anything like a national popular audience. Indeed, the conjunction of a liberal humanist morality and a social-democratic politics also insisted that British documentary-realism should mark out a space within the public sphere for the expression of the private, the personal, the emotional, and the individual, which meant, in effect, drawing on the resources of narrative cinema. The history of the realist tradition in British cinema, and the development in particular of the melodrama of everyday life, becomes the history of the changing conceptualization of the relation between the public and the private, the political and the personal, the state and the citizen. This developing relation involves different mobilizations of the devices and strategies of documentary and narrative fiction, and especially the modes of looking associated with each type of cinema.

[63] *Documentary Film*, 123, 70.
[64] *Clarion*, Aug. 1930, repr. in Hardy (ed.), *Grierson on Documentary*, 23; 'Documentary (1)', *Cinema Quarterly*, 1 (1932), 72, also in Hardy (ed.), *Grierson on Documentary*, 39; and ibid.; see also Aitken's discussion of Grierson's antagonism to an aesthetic of personal relations, *Film and Reform*, 189 ff.
[65] *Clarion*, Aug. 1930, repr. in Hardy (ed.), *Grierson on Documentary*, 23.
[66] Ibid. 39; see also Aitken's discussion of Grierson's interest in European modernism, *Film and Reform*, 113–14.

Documentary and fiction films construct two relatively distinct systems of looking which bind the spectator into the ideological work of the text in different ways. The tradition of continuity editing within classical narrative cinema develops in part to establish the relations in space between individual protagonists; the visual devices of eyeline matching, the point-of-view shot, and other forms of reverse-field cutting which are employed to this end tend to individuate the look and invest it with emotions in a way appropriate for the representation of private and personal conflicts and aspirations. Furthermore, the experience of the look of the camera at the pro-filmic event and the look of the spectator at the screen are virtually lost in the experience of watching the story unfold, which tends to draw the spectator into the organization of looks within the diegesis, rather than the look of the spectator at the screen. Such drama depends upon the full diegetic effect, the containment of the gaze within the self-enclosed world of the fiction played out for us on the screen.

Montage editing in documentaries of the 1930s developed as a way of producing a broad overview of 'universalized' social processes and people, on the other hand, producing a quite different system of looks, and a different relationship of the spectator to the figures on the screen, eschewing psychological realism. It is typically a distanced, observational look, an apparently objective public gaze in which, to put it crudely, the camera no longer looks from the position of diegetic figures, from within the place and the morals which they inhabit. This look no longer calls upon the facility of reverse-field cutting, or the inter-view of individuals, and is thus relatively distinct from the narrative system of point of view and the identification of the look with the dramatis personae. As John Caughie has suggested in relation to televisual discourse, 'the figures of the drama exchange and reverse looks, the figures of the documentary are looked at and look on.'[67] The public gaze of the documentary is thus the visual enactment of the moral and physical separation of the documentarist from his or her object of investigation. The developing form of the 'realist' tradition in British cinema as an articulation of the public and the private is, then, dependent on the different ways in which these two systems of looking are combined in the films. This is never simply an aesthetic matter, since it also depends on the changing valorization of the institutions of documentary and narrative film-making within the mainstream of British film culture.

The mixing of techniques derived from both 1930s documentary film-making and from classical narrative cinema is also a combination of narrational forms. Classical cinema provides a primarily linear narrative:

[67] 'Progressive Television and Documentary Drama', *Screen*, 21/3 (1980), 30; see also Hall, 'Social Eye', and Bill Nichols, 'Documentary Theory and Practice', *Screen*, 17/4 (1976–7).

a tightly economic narrative organization of time, action, spectatorial involvement, and identification. The documentary provides the principle of
constructing texts out of a montage of fragments. This montage construction is dependent on a much broader diegesis, a more metonymically
extensive organization of space and time, with its attendant impression of
greater realism. Together, these forms produce characteristically episodic,
multiple, parallel narratives. This strategy will then tend to open up the
realms of the narratable—in particular, montage construction is able more
easily to represent community, public life, the social.[68]

Montage has the ability to deal with the multiple, to establish connections and relations, and make visible systems of interdependence across a
broad social fabric, which is so vital. 'Montage is a theory of relationships', argues the German film-maker Alexander Kluge, but 'mere documentation cuts off relations: nothing exists objectively without the emotions,
actions and desires, that is, without the eyes and senses of the people
involved.'[69] Film-makers of the 1930s and early 1940s found themselves
reaching towards classical narrative strategies, and the attendant system of
individualized looks, for very similar reasons.

The closer British documentary-influenced film-making moves towards
the economic and formal systems of mainstream commercial cinema, and
the more conventionally it is formalized as a genre, the more easily it has
been able to capture the popular imagination, and something akin to a
national audience—despite the fact that the documentary mode of address
was presented as more democratic and more capable of articulating a sense
of the public or the social. The democratization of cinema which the
documentary movement sought to achieve was stalled, however, by its
anxiety about popular cultural forms and practices, and, in particular, the
forms of American cinema; documentary might have aspired to the status
of a democratic mode of communication, but it also aspired to the status
of high culture, a serious, socially responsible, and artistically respectable
cultural practice. It was thus caught once more between appealing to a
national popular audience and appealing to a bourgeois audience. The
period of the mid-1940s was crucial in this respect because there was an
effort to use the documentary idea in a national popular context, primarily
by interrelating with narrative practices. This then raises important questions
about the relationship between narrative form and the possibility of building a popular audience, and indeed about the political implications of this
sort of populist communication strategy in general.

---

[68] Cf. the German film-maker and critic Alexander Kluge: 'Telling stories, this is precisely
my conception of narrative cinema; and what else is the history of a country but the
vastest narrative surface of all? Not one story, but many stories. . . . This means montage' ('Public Sphere', 206).

[69] Ibid.

Of all the types of documentary developed within Britain in the 1930s, it was the story-documentary which became the most significant represen-tational form in this respect. Working with a loose narrative framework and a more or less classical dramatic structure, the story-documentary sets out to dramatize abstract ideas, social processes, or situations by focusing on the experiences of groups of people or individuals of the type whom it is assumed might well be involved in such situations, but who are, in this case, playing a role under the guidance of a director. This type of docu-mentary therefore involved advance scripting, including the scripting of dialogue. Protagonists were required to act according to preconceived directions—although such performers were not usually professional actors, and were often the people who would actually be involved 'in real life' in the task being represented.[70] An imagined if verisimilitudinous geography had to be created through editing, the building of sets, and the selection of locations. Characters needed to be more thoroughly individuated, and there had to be more synchronized dialogue and less direct address or voice-over commentary, in an effort to create a fuller diegetic effect. 'If, by severe standards, this was fiction' as one contemporary commentator put it, 'then it was a fiction with the realism uppermost—an adventure was reconstituted, as nearly as could be imagined, to the real event.'[71]

Documentary sets out to produce a new image of the 'national commu-nity' as a complex network of social groups through the devices of mon-tage and the public gaze. The image can be seen as relatively progressive, in that it tentatively articulates 'the nation' and 'ordinary people' as the same, rather than seeing the nation only in terms of the upper classes, as in the heritage film. The 'ordinary people' are inserted into an already formed bourgeois public sphere, however. This sphere is extended, demo-cratized even, to the extent that a new public enters it, but the relations which exist between different social groups are hardly altered. Indeed, for the state, the function of official documentary is to win the consent of this new public for the existing order.[72]

The documentarists themselves clearly felt that they were doing some-thing new, something progressive. Rotha, for instance, argued that the

---

[70] Cf. the following comments in a *Documentary News Letter* editorial, 'The Man on the Screen', 1/5 (1940), 3: 'In *North Sea*, fishermen were asked to interpret a story involving emotional experiences which they had not themselves had, but which were closely related to the circumstances of their daily work and which grew naturally out of it.'

[71] William Whitebait (George Stonier), discussing *San Demetrio, London, New Statesman*, 9 Dec. 1944 (this and most subsequent references to film reviews in daily and weekly British newspapers and magazines, excluding specialist publications such as the trade press, are drawn from cuttings held on microfiche at the British Film Institute Library, London; no page numbers are given on the cuttings).

[72] Cf. Sir Stephen Tallents, *Post Office Publicity* (London, 1935), 6, quoted in Swann, 'Grierson and GPO Film Unit', 21.

films of the EMB unit in the early 1930s 'represented the first attempt to portray the working class of Britain as a human, vital factor in present day existence', and that 'the documentary method of expression must be the voice of the people speaking from the homes and factories and fields of the people.'[73] Anstey claimed in retrospect that *Housing Problems* (1935), a film about slum clearance and rehousing schemes, 'wasn't our film', it was the slum-dwellers' film, and his role as co-director was simply to document.[74] Another commentator looking back on the documentary-realist tradition felt that, in these films, 'the working class is given a language and a means of expression and that under the constraints of capitalistic production relations.'[75] The views are familiar enough by now, having been repeated so often. But if we take the last comment, we can see that such a view constructs the working class initially as mute, and subsequently as the passive beneficiaries of generous patrons. They are subjects who must be civilized, who must be educated and incorporated into democratic citizenship, who must be humanized; they are not yet of the public sphere.

There is no denying that such films do extend the boundaries of permissible discourse, the boundaries of the representable, and that in this extension, working-class figures are indeed often placed at the centre of the diegesis—though rarely as active subjects. The system of looking constructed for this cinema, however, suggests a very different reading, since in many ways it situates the spectator as a bourgeois outsider, looking in on this other class as spectacle. From this perspective, the working class are effectively captured—held in place, tamed—as the objects of a benignly authoritative gaze, the gaze which surveys and categorizes, from a distance. The gaze is not purely observational and analytical, it is also the fascinated gaze; as Peter Stallybrass and Allon White have commented of Christopher Mayhew, 'his attempt at social analysis is inseparable from his scopophilia.'[76] The gaze is superior, but it is also voyeuristic. It wants to render the other class visible and therefore known, but it also wants to keep it at a safe distance. This point of view can solicit the admiration of the spectator as the workers and their workplaces are aestheticized into heroic things of beauty (for example, the bodies of the miners in *Coalface*, or the sublime industrial city seen from above in *Saturday Night and Sunday Morning*);[77] it can also solicit the sympathy of the spectator, as the working-class figure is so evidently the victim of circumstances. This image

---

[73] *Documentary Film*, 97, 113.
[74] In interview with Sussex, *Rise and Fall*, 62.
[75] Klaus Wildenhahn, 'Approaches to the Legend', in Orbanz (ed.), *Journey to a Legend*, 12.
[76] *Politics and Poetics*, 130, but see the whole of ch. 3; cf. Keating, 'Introduction', *Unknown England*.
[77] See Colls and Dodd, 'Representing the Nation', on *Coalface*, 24–5; and Higson, 'Space, Place, Spectacle', on *Saturday Night and Sunday Morning*.

of the heroic labourer as a part of the natural scheme of things—as a figure
in the landscape—of course has a long history in the pastoral tradition of
representation.[78]

Some of the documentarists, especially those who moved into the area
of the story-documentary, were aware of the difficulties of this point of
view. Pat Jackson, for instance, felt that

The early school of documentary was divorced from people. It showed people in
a problem, but you never got to know them, and you never felt that they were
talking to each other. You never heard how they felt and thought and spoke to
each other, relaxed. You were looking from a high point of view at them. You
were inclined to look at, instead of being with and part of.[79]

One class is constructed in the image or from the point of view of another:
the ideal trajectory (though not always the most realistic) is the transformation of the worker from a victim into a 'dignified human being' with
an assigned role in the social system. That, for Harry Watt, was the credo
of the documentary movement: 'we set out to dramatise reality and give
a dignity in films to the everyday person and the everyday event.'[80] Dig-
nifying the ordinary person meant seeing them in terms of apparently
universal human values—rather than, say, as class types. But those universal values are of course historically specific bourgeois values, the values of
the bourgeois ego.

DOCUMENTARY FILM PRACTICES IN THE 1930S AND EARLY 1940S

Having explored some of the general principles of the documentary idea
and some of the forms with which it works, in this section I will look in
more detail at some of the better-known documentary films of the 1930s
and early 1940s and the iconography and textual devices employed therein.

Manvell suggests that 'the realist's urge [is] to see life steadily, to see it
whole, to analyse society and the functions of mankind.'[81] The documentary
film achieves this by instituting a public gaze at public processes—routine

---

[78] Cf. the comments of the literary critic William Empson on Grierson's film *Drifters*,
    Some Versions of Pastoral (London, 1968 [1st pub. 1935]), 8; also John Barrell's work
    on the representation of the rural poor in 18th-cent. pastoral painting, *Dark Side of
    Landscape*, and Ginette Vincendeau's discussion of French populist films of the 1930s,
    'Community, Nostalgia and the Spectacle of Masculinity', *Screen*, 26/6 (1985), 20.

[79] In interview with Sussex, *Rise and Fall*, 76.

[80] From an undated National Film Theatre programme note by Harry Watt, repr. in
    Screen, 13/2 (1972), 47.

[81] *Film*, rev. edn., 80. The phrase 'to see life steadily, to see it whole' is an implicit
    reference to Matthew Arnold and E. M. Forster. See E. M. Forster, *Howards End*
    (Harmondsworth, 1989 [1st pub. 1910]), 67, 165, 264, 314, and the ed.'s n. on 348.
    I am indebted to Andrzej Gasiorek for this information.

operations whose scope is normally too great for the mere individual to perceive: 'it is the job of documentary films to illuminate these mechanical and repetitive processes.'[82] Rather than dealing with the desires of an individual protagonist, which, crudely speaking, might be seen as the work of the classic narrative film, the documentary tends to deal with the work of a particular public institution or activity which can be broadly perceived as social. *Night Mail* (1936), for instance, deals with one aspect of the work of the GPO—the overnight mail train from London to Scotland; *Industrial Britain* (1933) deals with the idea of work, and specifically industrial labour as a continuance of the age-old traditions of craftsmanship; and *Western Approaches* (1944), a war-time story-documentary about the work of the Merchant Navy, 'sketched in the whole organization and operation of the Atlantic convoys—so that each character in this drama becomes representative of the thousands who have taken part in the greater drama behind it.'[83]

In order for individual characters to become representatives of a nation rather than of a specific class or other restricted social group, labour is taken out of the context of exploitative economic relations and reimagined in a generalized pastoral vision of humanity. *Drifters* (1929) thus becomes a film about 'the ardour and bravery of common labour', 'the unconscious beauty of physical labour in the face of work done for a livelihood.'[84] This heroic figure of the working man (and sometimes woman)—in effect, the noble savage—re-emerges time and again in documentary discourse, whether as the industrial craftsmen of *Industrial Britain*, the coalminers of *Coalface* (1935), or the fishermen of *North Sea* (1938).

Many of the documentaries of the period focus on poverty as a social problem; thus *Housing Problems* (1935) looks at the problems of slum-dwellers, while *Enough to Eat* (1936) deals with poor nutrition. The spectator is addressed as a citizen who has a role to play in solving the social problems presented in the films; the ideal spectator of *Enough to Eat* is thus a citizen who recognizes that it is his or her duty to eat better, and to encourage others to eat better, as much as someone who recognizes that it is the duty of the state to provide the material means for better nutrition.

If the spectator is invited to recognize him or herself as a rational and responsible subject, a member of the general public rather than of a particular class, race, or sex, so public institutions are represented in these films as benevolent, even charitable bodies which stand above sectional interests in order to help alleviate social problems. Thus, *Housing Problems*, sponsored by a commercial gas organization, becomes a film celebrating

---

[82] *Documentary News Letter*, 2/8 (1941), 147.
[83] *Monthly Film Bulletin*, 11/132 (1944), 140–1.
[84] Grierson, 'The Course of Realism', 150; and Rotha, *Documentary Film*, 97.

the role of British gas companies in aiding slum clearances and the construction of new housing equipped with modern gas appliances. It is a characteristic slippage from private interest (increased sales of consumer items) to public interest (slum clearance). At the same time, by depoliticizing social problems, the working class can be presented as the victims of social circumstance—and whether as heroes or victims, they elicit a gaze which is both sympathetic yet fascinated.

It is the gaze of one class at another, even if it masquerades as the public gaze, the apparently neutral, observational gaze of the rational and responsible citizen. The implications of this gaze can be seen in *Housing Problems*, where the relation of the spectator to the film is clearly regulated by the upper-middle-class male voice-over which introduces and takes us through the film. The middle-class professional, the expert, thus intervenes between the spectator and the diegesis, keeping us at a distance from, and guiding our view of the slum-dwellers, the working-class victims of the film. In so doing, it sanctions a public gaze at these victims, rather than addressing the spectator as involved in and empathetically identifying with their emotional states.

This voice-over also situates the various other discourses of the film—notably the discourses of the working-class interviewees—and regulates their meanings in relation to each other. It is a voice which can elaborate, which can move beyond the experience of any particular individual, which can make comparisons and construct relations, whereas the anecdotes of the interviewees—comparable to the music-hall turns of *Sing As We Go*—are restricted, able to draw on personal experience and private drama, but unable to provide an overview.

This organizing voice-over finds its visual equivalent in the high-angle shots of the slums from above. These shots attempt to convey an overview of the slums in general, rather than the restricted view of any single slum-dweller—and to this extent, the position of the shots renders the point of view outside the capacity of those dwellers.[85] The voice-over and these overseeing shots also situate the spectator at a point from which all the varyingly private discourses of the interviewees are intelligible. In other words the means by which one idea or activity is related to another, and the means by which one sector of society communicates with another, are constructed as natural, as above the particular power relations which structure a social formation, and as outside the control or jurisdiction of any individual citizen.

Housing Problems cannot be simply written off for the way in which it places the spectator in relation to the working-class protagonists in the

---

[85] Cf. my discussion of similar shots—and a similar perspective—in the British new wave films of the late 1950s and early 1960s, in 'Space, Place, Spectacle'.

film through this hierarchical arrangement of discourses, however. There is still an incredible freshness in the direct-to-camera interviews with working-class people—as Cavalcanti much later insisted, 'you can't deny that the documentary put the workers in films.'[86] At the same time, there can be no unproblematic celebration of this film simply because it does extend its social discourse to the representation of working-class figures.

The principle of montage construction is mobilized right across the spectrum of documentary film-making in the 1930s. Montage works at both a physical or emotional level in its ability to create rhythm, tempo, and momentum,[87] and at a rational level in its ability to display parallel scenes of action, to deal with the multiple, and so construct a much more extensive diegesis than classical film. These effects can be seen in *Industrial Britain* and *Coalface*, which refuse to deal simply with a single worker and present a collage of images of workers throughout Britain. *Housing Problems* equally is made up of a montage of voice-overs, direct-to-camera interviews, and primarily illustrative images (with few signs of shot-matching, the key to narrative continuity editing). And in the story-documentary *North Sea* there is a combination of both montage and continuity editing as the narrative aspect develops.

The work of Humphrey Jennings, particularly his collaborations with the editor Stewart McAllister in the late 1930s and 1940s, is perhaps the high point of this montage tradition in British documentary. *Listen to Britain* (1942), for instance, made for the Ministry of Information (MoI) at the Crown Film Unit, was just one of hundreds of war-time propaganda shorts made mostly under Government sponsorship. It is a complex, highly poetic montage of apparently discrete fragments of sounds and images of the home front at work and leisure, juxtaposed with images from the traditional iconography of pastoral England and the new iconography of the war period. The film attempts to hold these discrete fragments together as a vision of a diverse but united nation. However, the film lacks both the narrative meta-discourse of the classic narrative film, and the voice-over of the more conventional documentary, and less effort is made to exhaust the meaning of each image and sound, or to dispatch the spectator down a particular avenue of meanings.[88]

This does not mean that *Listen to Britain* lacks any organizing principle, however. On the contrary, the specificity of its mode of address is its very multivalency: what holds these particular images and sounds together is its

---

[86] 'Alberto Cavalcanti', interview, in *Screen*, 13/2 (1972), 44.

[87] These are some of the key terms of Grierson's film critical discourse—see Hardy (ed.), *Grierson on the Movies* and *Grierson on Documentary, passim.*

[88] Though note how the prologue to the film, apparently added against the wishes of the film-makers (see Vaughan, *Invisible Man*), attempts to impose a reading on the film and contain its multivalency.

diegesis—a delimited historical space, which also constitutes an ideological position. Images and sounds which do not seem initially to belong together are woven into a complex series of counterpoints and oppositions—but, although the relationship between individual shots may at first be dissociative, the larger segments of the film produce a powerful series of associations which override any sense of conflict.[89]

The image of the nation which emerges from this rich audio-visual tapestry is thus intended to promote a sense of variety and diversity rather than difference, tension, or conflict. As Malcolm Smith has suggested, the nation is presented as 'timeless moments of communion between individual and group, between past and present; different individuals and different groups they certainly are, but they hold in common an almost exactly similar experience of their group identity'[90]—or, at least, this is how the film constructs relationships between these separate entities. The final effect of the film is of unity and harmony, the holding together of difference as variety. National identity is proposed as the sum of this productive variety: the contemporary coexists with tradition (two uniformed women eat sandwiches under a classical statue; a barrage balloon is visible through the arches of the National Portrait Gallery); the rural coexists with the industrial (Army vehicles rumbling through the street of a Tudor village; aircraft spotters work in an idyllic rural setting); popular culture coexists with high culture (Flanagan and Allen sing in a factory canteen, while Myra Hess plays Beethoven to the Queen); and so on.

Listen to Britain also reworks the iconography of work familiar from so many 1930s documentaries. As in those films, images of the worker, the work process, the workplace, and the landscapes of work are strewn across the text. This iconography renews and reaffirms the 1930s tradition which aestheticizes, humanizes, and dignifies these sites of work and working bodies. But an iconography of the leisure time and space of ordinary people is also developing here—and this is a major departure from the dominant Griersonian tradition of the 1930s.

This new iconography depends upon the representation of leisure as a community activity, with an emphasis on group shots or wide shots of large masses of people (the factory canteen, the dance-hall), rather than close-ups of individuals. Music, and particularly singing, performs an integrating function—the Canadian soldiers singing on the train, the women singing in the factory, the audience singing and whistling with Flanagan and Allen, and so on. The static high-angle shot of the dance-hall, with the dancers moving through the frame, in particular seems to resonate across the films of the 1940s (*Millions Like Us* and *This Happy Breed* both have variations on this image).

[89] See Smith, 'Narrative and Ideology', 148.   [90] Ibid. 149.

Listen to Britain is also non-developmental as a text; it is not dependent upon an internal textual structure of disruption and resolution, or movement towards a new equilibrium, so much as upon a continual dispersal of significance from one image (or sound) to the next. Each image is in this sense inconsequential, and relates to the next as being parallel to it in time, and contiguous with it in the overall diegetic space of the film (Britain in war time). This, like the principle of montage construction, is another narrational strategy developed in narrative features in the documentary-realist tradition, although in *Listen to Britain* the circularity of the text (it both begins and ends by cross-cutting between images of the rural and the industrial) and the inconsequentiality of action are more marked than in most feature films. In *Listen to Britain*, the effect is one of the continuing saga of everyday life, with the disruption of the war being assumed as outside the text.

THE STORY-DOCUMENTARY

For the purposes of this study of the place of documentary in the debates about a national cinema in Britain, the most significant of the various forms of documentary practice developed in the 1930s is the story-documentary. It is not incidental that such films also received the best critical response and secured the most substantial theatrical releases and popular acclaim.[91] Most of the story-documentaries were produced by the GPO, later the Crown Film Unit, in the late 1930s and early 1940s, the period after Grierson left the GPO Film Unit—although there had been some experiments in this direction earlier. The GPO Film Unit, in its last couple of years, and the Crown Film Unit were regarded with some suspicion by other members of the documentary movement as the luxury units, and even in this context the story-documentaries were ambitious and relatively high-budget prestigious films.[92] The story-documentary was developed as part of the effort to reach a wider theatrical audience than documentary films had hitherto reached. There were two strands to this work: on the one hand, the development of a film form which non-specialist audiences might find appealing; and on the other, the attempt to secure the sort of

---

[91] See Swann, 'Grierson and GPO Film Unit', 26, 29; and Swann, *British Documentary Movement*, 70–1, 85 ff., 158–65, 172; also the comments of Mr Thurtle, Parliamentary Secretary to the Ministry of Information, in a debate on propaganda, Hansard, *Parliamentary Debates (Commons)*, 7 July 1942, vol. 381, cols. 656–8, 1941–2; Arts Enquiry, *Factual Film*, 75 ff.; also *Documentary News Letter*, 4/2 (1943), 173, on US distribution of *Target for Tonight*.

[92] See Swann, 'Grierson and GPO Film Unit', 25–6, 32; and *British Documentary Movement*, 79–80, 85, 93–4, 158–65; see also Watt, *Don't Look*, 109–10; and ch. 5, 'The Movement Divides', in Sussex, *Rise and Fall*.

theatrical distribution that might enable the films to reach these audiences. While much effort was being put elsewhere into building up a new, non-theatrical audience—that is, an audience separate from the ones built up by showmen over the last couple of decades, those involved in the production and distribution of story-documentaries hoped to work with and perhaps redefine the interests of the already established popular audience.

The form of the story-documentary developed over time by gradually increasing the degree of narrativization of more general documentary techniques such as the public gaze, montage construction, location shooting, use of non-professional actors, the iconography of work, the depiction of processes rather than events, and so on. In Harry Watt's words, the story-documentary involved 'taking actual true events, using real people, but also using "dramatic licence" to heighten the tension and the story-line.'[93] 'Experimentally speaking', Basil Wright explained in 1941,

the dramatic approach (originally signalled by *The Saving of Bill Blewitt*) was very much to the forefront. However much the conservative elements in documentary might complain it was by this time clear that the use of studio sets and reconstructions, personal stories and incidents, and actors as well, had come to stay.[94]

The most interesting examples of the story-documentary are the films of Harry Watt, whether on his own or directing in collaboration with others. *Night Mail*, for instance, adopts the loose narrative form of 'a day (or night) in the life of', with still stronger moments of narrative incident and reverse-field cutting gathered around the figure of the new postal worker being initiated into his job. The film thus narrates the story of the night mail train, but it also narrates the nation: the journey of the train from south to north, from England to Scotland, is a movement across the space of the nation (as seen from the point of view of the metropolis). It is a movement which affords a rich display of pastoral imagery. The night mail itself is also a means of networking the nation, of binding the nation together, of connecting the outer margins to the centre—crucially, it is technologies and systems of communication, the railway system and the postal system (a state organization), which are dramatized as the means of achieving this binding together, the means of keeping the national community in touch with itself.

[93] *National Film Theatre* programme note, 48; see also Watt, *Don't Look*, 101 ff.
[94] 'Realist Review', 20. The story-documentary is, of course, the forerunner of the television documentary-drama: see Caughie, 'Broadcasting and Cinema'; and Caryl Doncaster, 'The Story Documentary', in Paul Rotha (ed.), *Television in the Making* (London, 1956); Doncaster suggests, somewhat erroneously, that 'the dramatized story documentary is one of the few art forms pioneered by television', 44. In the light of recent controversies about mixing documentary and fictional devices in television programmes, one of the most remarkable things about the development of the story-documentary in film is that none of this later anxiety seems to surface here.

Several of the documentarists have gone on record testifying to the felt significance of *Night Mail* in the development of the documentary movement, and specifically of the story-documentary. Pat Jackson, for instance, recalled the reactions of the audience at an early screening of *Night Mail* at the Arts Theatre, Cambridge, and what this meant to the members of the GPO Film Unit at the time:

suddenly you see they're laughing. They're enjoying it. They're taking this as entertainment, and that, of course, changed your ideas very much. It changed immediately the idea in which you would approach a subject. To hell with commentary and stuffy old information. This idea of disseminating facts, this became immediately old hat. No, don't let's disseminate facts. Let's disseminate situations. Let's get over what we're going to say in terms of feelings, expressions on people's faces, laughter, and so on.[95]

The narrative work of *Night Mail* is extended in Watt's North Sea (1938), and *Target for Tonight* (1942), and even more so by his move to Ealing Studios, where he made narrative features such as *Nine Men* (1943)—'the purest of the pure imaginative documentaries'.[96] *Monthly Film Bulletin* commented on the latter film that it 'marks yet a further stage in the influence of the documentary on the feature film. The result comes as near to *a native style of British film-making* as anything which has yet been seen.'[97] In each of these films, there is again a juxtaposition of both continuity editing and montage techniques, and therefore of linear narrative and montage construction.

North Sea deals with the difficulties faced by the men on a small trawler caught in a storm on the North Sea, but this is in a sense a pretext designed finally to demonstrate the work of the land–sea radio network run by the GPO in securing the safety of these men. *Target for Tonight* deals with the planning and execution of a bombing raid on an enemy target during the Second World War, and the worry over the safety of one missing aeroplane, which finally limps home to base. To say that these films narrativize their action is to indicate that there is a temporal development of the diegesis, a structural movement from the definition of a goal to be achieved (the return home of the fishermen in *North Sea*, the bombing of the target and the safety of those involved in *Target for Tonight*), through various blockages to that goal, to the successful fulfilment of the goal and textual closure.

These films also try to hold together two different forms of protagonist or character: on the one hand, the typage of the documentary film (another

[95] In interview with Sussex, *Rise and Fall*, 75; cf. Anstey, 'Development of Film Technique', 250–1.
[96] 'Film of the Month: *Nine Men*', *Documentary News Letter*, Feb. (1943), 179.
[97] 10/110 (1943), 13, my emphasis.

Soviet influence)—that is, the casting of non-professional actors who bear a physical resemblance to the social type to be represented;[98] and on the other hand, the psychological realism of the narrative fiction film—that is, the progressive inscription of character with the marks of a unique individuality, the tentative filling-out of the life stories, memories, and feelings of particular characters.

What remains from the early 1930s conception of documentary is an emphasis not on the narrativization of individual desire as of central dramatic significance, but on the narrativization of public (social) processes. The power of the state is visible here, as in so many contemporaneous story-documentaries, only as the power to set in motion a chain of communication which has two functions: first, it must enable the successful completion of an act in the national interest (the securing of a haul of fish in *North Sea*; the bombing of an enemy target in *Target for Tonight*); secondly, it must be able to protect the private, sectional interests of a relatively individuated, but tight-knit community (ensuring the safety of the men of the fishing boat in *North Sea* by the actions of the land–sea radio network; enabling the safe return of the crew of the missing aeroplane in *Target for Tonight*). This same process of mapping a chain of authority as a communications network was later reworked in *Fires were Started* (1943) and *Western Approaches* (1944); again there is the image of the state as a benevolent entity, an abstraction, even, which consists in this mapping and preservation of a set of relations between different sectors of society, ensuring the smooth running of the public process.

The subject-matter of communication and the form of montage stand as metaphors for the nation in these films. The interdependence of a series of images which montage implies is equivalent to the network of relationships which a communications system achieves; together, they construct a profound sense of nationhood as interconnectedness. Both *North Sea* and *Night Mail*, for instance, present a very precise image of, first a specific local community, and finally the nation as a whole, bound together by the systems and technologies of local and mass communication: the nation is produced as a knowable community, the imagined community of the films' narrative work.

The form of earlier documentaries is retained in these films to the extent that the narrative is not organized around the point of view of a single main protagonist but employs a form of montage construction in order to map out a fuller diegesis. This world of the fiction is clearly constituted in terms of the relations between a variety of social groups or functional elements within an extensive but delimited social system. In *North Sea*,

[98] See Harry Watt's discussion of the casting of *Nine Men*, 'Casting Nine Men', *Documentary News Letter*, Feb. (1943), 179–80.

STILL 23. The nation as knowable community: a typical unglamorous group-shot of the men on board the trawler in *North Sea*.

these social groups include the women and the domestic sphere at home, the lost trawlermen at sea, their safe colleagues and employers, and the staff of the radio station. In *Target for Tonight*, we are presented with the full staff of the RAF, from messenger boy, through pilot, to top brass. There is also a very clear movement from the general to the particular in the latter film, situating the exploits and experiences of the crew of one particular bomber within the narrative of a general process, an operation requiring the interdependence of many people—metaphorically at least, situating the individual within the national, exploring the place of the individual within the nation. Central to these films, then, was what Dilys Powell described as 'the democratic feeling of community, of men [*sic*] with equal rights and responsibilities'.[99]

The contained multiplicity of interests which the story-documentary seeks to articulate demands a combination of the forms of episodic montage construction and tightly causal narrative flow, with their different systems of editing (montage and continuity, respectively). It also benefits from a combination of the distance of the establishing shot and the group shot (the public gaze) and the psychologization of the point-of-view shot (the private gaze). The spectator is therefore suspended between two forms of address, two ways of looking, two possible identifications. The public gaze of the documentary offers the possibility of a rational appraisal of particular social activities and areas of social knowledge, but it places both the characters of the diegesis and the film's spectator at a distance from and outside the political regulation of social and economic processes. On the other hand, the private looks exchanged between characters in the diegesis of the narrative fiction set up the possibility of the spectator empathetically identifying with the emotional situations of psychologically defined individuals. At the same time, the protagonist and spectator can become involved in only limited and fragmentary forms of social and domestic activity.

A public sphere and a private sphere are thus simultaneously constructed and demarcated. The role of the individual in the work of the nation becomes the role of a cog-wheel in a machine, with no control over the overall functioning of the machine. The working man of *North Sea*, for instance, is assigned a place within the national community in which his noble function is the heroic performance of manual labour (although significantly not modern, industrial, Taylorized and Fordist labour); meanwhile, women, as mothers, wives, and lovers, must stay at home and wait. The public and the private, the political and the personal, are thus effectively kept apart. There is inevitably a certain ambiguity of meaning in this interweaving of two relatively distinct forms of address, inducing some anxiety on the part of film-makers and sponsors as to whether the intended

---

[99] 'Films since 1939', 79.

message is being put across clearly enough. This anxiety can be seen surfacing in *North Sea* in the voice-over which emerges at the end of the film to bring home without any possibility of ambiguity the intended message of the film concerning the work of the land–sea radio network.

Story-documentaries were generally praised by critics of the period who saw them as truly national in their understatement and attention to 'the real thing, the real people':[100]

Watt has brought his skill [in *Nine Men*] . . . to a simple theme and has endowed it with humour and realism. The characterisation is excellent, the dialogue is masterly in its laconic understatement. One feels that justice has been done in a film to all those qualities in the British character in war-time of which we are most proud.[101]

Forsyth Hardy, one of the keenest apologists for the documentary movement, wrote of *Western Approaches*, 'Its aim was to bring alive the drama of our struggle against the U-boats. The strength of its story . . . lay in its authenticity. Here was a magnificent justification of the documentary method.'[102] Other writers were more impressed by 'the "humanization" of documentary'[103] which these films achieved, by comparison with the too austere lecturing of other types of documentary film:

Documentary is a cold word. It suggests government offices, files, research, statistics: things that we know to be desirable, but cannot approach with enthusiasm. . . . The new documentary . . . *North Sea* is more exciting, touching, dramatic and entertaining than any recent film, and its visual beauty also puts it in a class by itself. In a month of ramshackle commercialism it stands out like a lighthouse. . . . The GPO has many fine films to its credit, but none better than this, which makes you, no matter what the day's news from Berlin or Canton, proud after all of the human race.[104]

Dilys Powell wrote in similar terms:

Many of us who before the war had seen in the British documentary school an integrity and a devotion to the task which promised more than we could find in the commercial cinema, had still been chilled at times by a want of humanity, of the poetry of human life, in the documentary output. Not always: . . . *North Sea* . . . had shown the ability to bring to the screen the drama of human character.[105]

---

[100] Basil Wright, in a review of *North Sea*, *Spectator*, 6 May 1938.

[101] *Monthly Film Bulletin*, 10/110 (1943), 13, review of *Nine Men*.

[102] 'British Documentary', 57–8. The phrase 'bringing alive' was an EMB slogan; see S. Constantine, 'Bringing the Empire Alive: The Empire Marketing Board and Imperial Propaganda, 1926–33', in J. M. Mackenzie (ed.), *Imperialism and Popular Culture* (Manchester, 1986); also Hardy (ed), *Grierson on Documentary*, 49, 63, and Rotha, *Documentary Film*, 97, 113.

[103] The quotation is from Rotha's memoirs, *Documentary Diary*, 134, but the concept derived from the 1930s: see *Documentary Film*, 194.

[104] Peter Galway, *New Statesman*, 25 June 1938.   [105] *Films since 1939*, 79.

Even Watt's fellow documentarist, Basil Wright, attempted in a review of
North Sea to establish a distance from the connotations of 'this cold word,
documentary': 'Seldom has a film so poignantly revealed the inadequacy of
the word "Documentary". The dry hard flavour of the word assorts ill
with the seaspray; and with the human values of men and women, which
gives this film its greatest merit, it connects not at all.'[106] It was this matter
of real human values that was most appreciated in these films. Roger
Manvell, for instance, wrote of *Target for Tonight* that

'it illustrates processes . . . and at the same time shows us people. It does not forget
montage or the cine-eye. . . . It does not forget to dramatise the personalities of its
human material who speak and act like real people in the middle of a real job with
the RAF's flair for understatement.'[107]

If a critic like Manvell also stressed the artistic qualities of such films
(montage, the cine-eye), others, like Powell reviewing *Nine Men*, found
comparisons with American cinema more telling:

The piece has been admirably written for the screen and the acting, with its casual
understatement, could hardly be better fitted for its purpose. Do we, perhaps, miss
now and then, a touch of panache? If so the fault without doubt is not in the lack
of stars but in ourselves and in the tradition of Hollywood heroism to which we
have grown accustomed. The direction throughout is wholly discreet with a nice
mingling of documentary and fiction technique.[108]

In a similar vein, Richard Winnington praised the understatement, the
avoidance of melodrama, in *Western Approaches*, perhaps the best received of all the story-documentaries of the war period: 'the film is devoid
of heroics although it is impregnated with heroism. . . . You will not find
here the chromium-plated slickness of the commercial product'.[109] Caroline
Lejeune thought this same film 'an example of the best type of British
documentary. That is to say, it has emotion without sentimentality; it is
laconic without being off-hand; the facts have been collated with patience
and set out with fidelity.'[110] For such critics, this was praise indeed compared with what they perceived as 'the crass emotionalism of the normal
film', 'the fairy-tale atmosphere of the treatment of the average Hollywood
picture [as opposed to] the truthful nature of the new British film':[111]

The story technique [of Hollywood films] is superb . . . [and] the emotional atmosphere is nearly always 'dressed' with a certain showmanship. It makes extremely

---

[106] *Spectator*, 6 May 1938.   [107] *Film*, 1st edn., 97.
[108] *Sunday Times*, 31 Jan. 1943.
[109] *News Chronicle*, 11 Dec. 1944. See also the ch. on *Western Approaches* in Anthony
     Aldgate and Jeffrey Richards, *Britain Can Take It: The British Cinema in the Second
     World War* (Oxford, 1986).
[110] *Observer*, 10 Dec. 1944.
[111] Manvell, *Film*, 2nd edn., 25, and Jympson Harman, 'Truth and British Films', *Sight and
     Sound*, 15/57 (1946), 15–16.

effective cinema, but it seldom lives in the knowledge of the close and personal heart. It turns too easily to sentimentality, to sexual or social heroics.[112]

The comparison with Hollywood made sense too for someone within the industry like Michael Balcon: 'If a British film lacked at times the hard technical perfection of an American film (e.g. *Target for Tonight*) it was substituted and overbalanced by its human impact on its audience.'[113] But those critics who had not themselves come out of the documentary units could not wholly accept these story-documentaries when they were too close to the distanced, detached gaze and the attitude of public observation which they associated with the documentary idea. Thus, while Lejeune concurred that what was impressive about Watt's work was 'his vehement belief in the simple drama of the ordinary man', she also felt that *Nine Men* 'was a detached sort of film'.[114] In a review of the Crown Film Unit's story-documentary, *Coastal Command* (1942), she took this criticism further: while praising the 'sheer pictorial quality' of various isolated scenes, she worried over the 'unemotional approach' of the film, a characteristic of the documentary movement 'that chills me': 'there is a detachment in much of its work, an almost scandalised mistrust of showmanship, an effort, it would seem, to avoid, not only melodramatics, but any form of human appeal or persuasion.'[115]

Some films managed to strike the right balance for such reviewers. William Whitebait, for instance, a key supporter of the quality film movement of the mid-1940s, praised the Ealing film *San Demetrio, London* (1943) precisely because it adopted 'an approach less impersonal than would at one time have been conceivable in documentary circles', and felt that *Western Approaches* had surpassed the achievements of even that film.[116] What was called for was a greater stress on the individual, on story-telling, and on emotions, as Winnington suggested in his review of *Children on Trial* (1946):

This film represents the new down-to-earth style of British documentary relying . . . on a central narrative and a stressing of human values and relations rather than on a series of images for their own sakes related to each other by montage and cutting (the old fancy style of documentary).[117]

The story-documentary, starting as it did from the documentarist's side of things, did not in the end take the marriage of the documentary idea

---

[112] Manvell, *Film*, 2nd edn., 139.

[113] 'The British Film during the War', *Penguin Film Review*, 1 (1946), 69–70.

[114] *Observer*, 31 Jan. 1943.

[115] In a review of *Coastal Command* in *Observer*, 18 Oct. 1942; repr. in Caroline Lejeune, *Chestnuts In Her Lap* (London, 1947), 83; John Ellis mistakenly attributes this quotation to a review of *Target for Tonight*, in his 'Art, Culture, Quality', 33.

[116] *New Statesman*, 9 Dec. 1944, 188, also quoted in Ellis, 'Art, Culture, Quality', 33.

[117] *News Chronicle*, 7 Sept. 1946, repr. in Richard Winnington, *Film—Criticism and Caricature, 1943–53*; sel. and with introd. by Paul Rotha (London, 1975), 58; also quoted in Ellis, 'Art, Culture, Quality', 33, but mistakenly attributed to a review of *The Overlanders*.

and classical narrative techniques far enough in the direction of the latter
—hence Michael Balcon's argument that the feature film must carry on the
documentary tradition:

the potential influence of the feature film is much greater: not only does it reach
a wider audience, but since feature films by their nature must treat all problems
in terms of individual human beings, they avoid the slightly impersonal application
to 'the people' that often mars documentaries, and, therefore, bring home to the
individual human beings that make up the audience the problems in a much more
personal and impressive way.[118]

This sort of argument really represents a shift away from what the
documentarists saw as the possibility of grasping the interconnectedness of
things, the complex multiplication and interpenetration of detail which
makes up social life, and which the documentary tries to grasp through the
practice of montage. It sees authenticity, the essential truth, as residing
instead within the individual human subject, not in social relations; thus
for Lejeune, 'it is in this inner truth . . . that *Coastal Command* is lacking'.[119] The good film must somehow strike the right balance between the
detachment of the pure documentary and the melodramatics of popular
drama. Standards were being set in this period—a week after Whitebait
had reviewed *Western Approaches*, he was reviewing the immensely popular Gainsborough melodrama, *Madonna of the Seven Moons* (1944): 'Within
a week the best and worst English film of many months have made their
appearance. *Western Approaches* brought home to us how far we have
advanced in film making since the war; with *Madonna of the Seven Moons*
we slip back almost as far as it is possible to slip.'[120]

WORLD WAR II AND THE 'GOLDEN AGE' OF BRITISH CINEMA

During the War British producers have been able to provide less than
a sixth of British programme needs, but the product of their studios
has reached such a remarkable artistic standard in so many films that
it is obvious there has been a renaissance in the cinema of Britain and
that we have founded a national school which can take its place in film
history.

Roger Manvell, 1946.[121]

---

[118] 'The Feature Carries on the Documentary Tradition', *Quarterly of Film Radio and
Television*, 6/4 (1952), 353. Cf. also Manvell, 'British Feature Film', 86.
[119] *Chestnuts in Her Lap*, 83; see also Basil Wright, 'Documentary Today', *Penguin Film
Review*, 2 (1947), 40.
[120] *New Statesman*, 16 Dec. 1944, 404.
[121] *Film*, 2nd edn., 19–20.

Undoubtedly, it is the influence of realism on the British film in war-time which has given it its new and individual character and which has weaned it away from being an amateur and clumsy pastiche of its Hollywood counterpart.

Michael Balcon, 1946.[122]

Documentary is generally thought to have come of age during the war years, when it worked with a much higher public profile alongside and within the mainstream film industry and popular film culture. As a way of seeing, it became both officially and commercially sanctioned during the abnormal circumstances of war, when cinema came to be widely recognized as a powerful tool for propaganda.[123] This had, of course, been understood within certain circles for some time, and particularly by those within the documentary movement, but it was the extending of this recognition and its linkage to the documentary idea which was important. Michael Balcon, for instance, by now well established at Ealing Studios, looked back over the 1940s, and 'the documentary-cum-fiction technique that we developed [at Ealing Studios]' and suggested that 'only then we started realising the true significance of the cinema as a mass medium and the enormous power entrusted to the film makers.'[124] Balcon had, of course, long been speaking of the importance of a national cinema in one guise or another, but by the end of the war the terms in which the power of cinema was expressed—cinema as a mass medium, the responsibility of the film-maker, the importance of propaganda and documentary, and so on—had shifted far closer to the documentary discourse.

One of the functions of the propaganda machine during the war years was to create an ideological climate in which the public sphere could be represented as a sphere of national interest immediately and widely recognizable as over and above any antagonistic sectional interests; but it was also necessary that the individual citizen was in no doubt as to the importance of the assigned role which he or she must play. The national interest must be able to accommodate the private and the domestic, and the emotional capacity of the individual—if necessary, by demonstrating the irresponsibility of holding private, and particularly romantic, interests above the national interest. The individual must be allotted a place within the public sphere, must become, as it were, a full member of the public, a part of the common, national experience—at least for the duration of the war. The role of cinema in securing this consent of private citizens to the national cause became crucial. As Manvell put it, in films, 'the personal always had

---

[122] 'British Film during the War', 69.

[123] Cf. Hall, 'Social Eye'; for a somewhat cooler perspective on the impact of documentary in war-time, see Swann, *British Documentary Movement*, 150 ff.

[124] Quoted in Francis Koval, 'Sir Michael Balcon and Ealing', in *Films in 1951: Festival of Britain* (London, 1951), 58.

to be merged into the general, the story into the common mass of experience.'[125] For those attached to the documentary idea, this ideological struggle required

the documentary approach, [because] being based on the observance of reality and on many years' experience of the handling of ordinary people, [it] is in a position to give an impression of actuality to the public; and more importantly, to make the public feel that the subject dealt with is really a part of their own lives and responsibilities, and not a fictional episode divorced from their own experience.[126]

Critics such as Manvell, less exclusively attached to the documentary idea, felt that the insertion of the private into the public was achieved most successfully in those films which combined the documentary approach with the fictional. Films must be neither too distanced, which was the problem with the pure documentary, nor too personal, which was one of the perceived failings of Hollywood:

For the most part, films such as *Millions Like Us, San Demetrio London, Nine Men, The Way Ahead, Waterloo Road* and *The Way To The Stars* resolved the personal equation, and showed us people in whom we could believe and whose experience was as genuine as our own. The war film discovered the common denominator of the British people.[127]

Films such as these, emanating from the studios, sought to authenticate their fictions by drawing on the rhetoric of documentary and its connotations of responsibility and realism, and sought to articulate a sense of national community by developing a relatively complex montage structure. Hence the celebratory tone of an editorial in *Documentary News Letter* which expressed the belief that 'the war . . . in bringing into sharp focus the social function of the cinema, is leading to a re-consideration of traditional principles of story selection and treatment.'[128]

In many ways the most interesting of the war-time films which combine documentary and narrative feature modes is the first of the films listed by Manvell, *Millions Like Us* (1943), which was cited over and over again by contemporary critics and historians as central to the idea of a British national cinema in the 1940s. The film clearly draws in a variety of ways on the documentary idea and documentary practice and yet was produced by Gainsborough Pictures, a company with impeccable commercial credentials, having formerly been a part of the Gaumont-British group and now under the Rank umbrella. *This Happy Breed* (1944), with which I will be comparing *Millions Like Us*, was equally well received, but it is a much more conservative film which already begins to sever the democratic aspirations of the documentary idea from the quality feature film, and

---

[125] 'British Feature Film', in Balcon *et al.*, *20 Years*, 85.
[126] Wright, 'Realist Review', 21.   [127] Manvell, 'British Feature Film', 85.
[128] 'The Man on the Screen', 1/5 (1940), 3.

especially the melodrama of everyday life. It is these differences between the two films which interest me.

Before going on to look at these films, however, I want to explore a little further some of their conditions of existence. They were in no way isolated films, but were taken up as part of a much broader movement to establish a quality national film culture in the mid-1940s.[129] Films like *Millions Like Us* received considerable support from critics of the period, but they were also relatively popular films, especially compared to the story-documentary, and other forms of documentary film practice during the 1930s. There was a general feeling in the film culture of the period that British films generally had improved beyond all expectations. According to one report, the film trade 'discovered that whereas large sections of the public stayed away from the cinema fifteen years ago rather than see a British film, in 1945 they went to a picture for the reason that it was British.'[130]

Certainly, several British films did very well at the box-office in the war years, including the two war films *The 49th Parallel* (1941) and *In Which We Serve* (1942) (probably the most successful British film of the period). Later in the war, it was 'escapist' melodramas from Gainsborough and elsewhere which were most attractive to cinema-goers: *The Man In Grey* (1943), *Madonna of the Seven Moons* (1944), and, after the war, *The Wicked Lady* (1945) and *The Seventh Veil* (1945) all did exceptional business.[131]

During the mid-1940s, there was the first really concerted attempt to create and foster a quality national cinema that was at the same time a popular cinema. In one survey of the war years, it was argued, in a statement typical of the period, that

Before the war, it was assumed by some that imitation of Hollywood's extravagance would solve the problem [of a national cinema in Britain]. . . . But the success of films such as *Millions Like Us*, *The Way Ahead*, *Waterloo Road* and *The Way to the Stars* during the war, has shown that there is another way of overcoming Hollywood domination by producing films which reflect the British scene realistically in a way which would be impossible for Hollywood.[132]

---

[129] I discuss some other films of this type in 'Addressing the Nation: Five Films' and 'Britain's Outstanding Contribution to the Film'; see also Ellis, 'Art, Culture, Quality'.

[130] M. Epstein (ed.), *The Annual Register, 1945* (London, 1946), 341, quoted in Philip M. Taylor, 'Introduction: Film, the Historian and the Second World War', in Philip M. Taylor (ed.), *Britain and the Cinema in the Second World War* (London, 1988), 6; see also *The Bernstein Questionnaires*, 1946–7 (copies housed at British Film Institute Library, London): 96 per cent of respondents felt that British films had 'got better' since 1939 (only 26 per cent thought American films had 'got better', 56 per cent feeling they had 'not changed'); and J. P. Mayer, *Sociology of Film* (London, 1946), and *British Cinemas and their Audiences* (London, 1948).

[131] See *Kine Weekly* box-office surveys: 8 Jan. 1942, 40–1; 13 Jan. 1944, 51–2; 20 Dec. 1945, 50–1; 19 Dec. 1946, 46–7.

[132] *Factual Film*, 201.

It is clear that the critical discourse being developed by contemporary film reviewers, and reproduced in key surveys such as Manvell's *Film*, and the collection *Twenty Years of British Film*, favoured films like *Millions Like Us* which came out of the commercial sector, and which tempered the emotionally engaging psychological realism of the strong narrative film with the social responsibility and realist aesthetic of the documentary.

It would be wrong, however, to give the impression that feature films influenced by documentary were either the only or the most consistently popular types of feature films produced in Britain in the mid-1940s. Only a small proportion of the hundreds of films produced during this period could be considered to fall into this category—although significantly they are the most discussed films of the period. There were still plenty of other genre films, both British and American, in circulation at the time. An indication of this diversity can be found in a full-page advertisement billing forthcoming releases from Gainsborough Pictures in 1943. This includes stills from *Millions Like Us*, and another celebrated propaganda film, *We Dive At Dawn*, but also the popular costume drama, *The Man In Grey*, and two comedies featuring some of the biggest domestic comic performers of the period, *Miss London, Limited*, a musical comedy with Arthur Askey, and *It's That Man Again* (all 1943), featuring the team from the popular radio series of the same name.[133] Inevitably, then, the critical reputation of British films in this period rests on the perceived qualities of a relatively few actual films—including *Millions Like Us*—which are cited over and over again in both contemporary writing and subsequent histories of the period.

Another significant circumstance enabling the production of quality British films like *Millions Like Us* was the relative economic stability of the domestic film industry across the period as a whole—despite the inevitable difficulties of the war economy, and the restrictions on resources and manpower. Admissions rose steadily, and box-office takings even more dramatically; production, on the other hand, was not prolific by the standards of the 1930s—only about sixty-nine films per year were produced during the war years (compared to an average of 400 from the major American studios)[134]—but it was steady and well supported both by critics and at the box-office.

The growing power of the vertically and horizontally integrated Rank corporation and the continued strength of ABPC meant that the industry was increasingly controlled by the interests of this duopoly. Robert Murphy has suggested that 'unlike any previous British producer, Rank, with assets in excess of $200 million, had an organization as large and as powerful as the American "Big Five"'—and as early as 1943, Rank, like Gaumont-

---

[133] *Kine Weekly*, 14 Jan. 1943, 128.   [134] Taylor, 'Introduction', 6.

British some ten years earlier, began to plan its own assault on the world market, and particularly the American market.[135] At the same time, however, Rank supported the production of quality films with specifically national characteristics—that is, films which had less obvious commercial appeal in the international market. Thus, for our purposes, one of the most significant developments of the period was Rank's support for studios like Gainsborough and Ealing, as well as a number of independent film-makers, especially through the organization Independent Producers Ltd, which provided the space for *This Happy Breed*, among many other films, and which Frank Launder and Sidney Gilliat, the directors of *Millions Like Us*, affiliated to in 1944 under the company name of Individual Pictures.[136]

The various forms of state regulation of the film industry during the war years were also undoubtedly of great importance in enabling such a cinema to emerge. These forms of regulation were censorious, they were delimiting, but they also provided positive material and moral support for the development of at least a certain type of British film production in this period. Anthony Aldgate has suggested that 'the story of the British cinema in the second world war is inextricably linked with that of the Ministry of Information [MoI].'[137] This is certainly true, although Margaret Dickinson has also shown the extent to which another sector of the state apparatus, the Board of Trade, helped to shape the film industry's international and domestic economic relations.[138] The MoI sought to foster a socially responsible cinema which could produce effective propaganda; they favoured realistic films, and also encouraged the production of films which emphasized 'the democratic way of life.'[139] This of course neatly intersected with the long-standing concerns of the documentary movement—but the co-option of the documentarists into the work of the MoI was neither smooth, nor as the documentarists themselves wanted it.[140]

More generally, of course, all films produced during the war period had

---

[135] See *Kine Weekly*, 5 Aug. 1943, 5 and 14*b*; quotation from 'Rank's Assault on the American Market', in Curran and Porter (eds.), *British Cinema History*, 166.

[136] See Alan Wood, *Mr Rank* (London, 1952).

[137] 'The British Cinema During the Second World War', in Aldgate and Richards, *Britain Can Take It*, 4.

[138] 'The State and the Consolidation of Monopoly', in Curran and Porter (eds.), *British Cinema History*; see also Margaret Dickinson and Sarah Street, *Cinema and State: The Film Industry and the British Government* (London, 1985), 120 ff.

[139] From a letter from the MoI to the British Film Producers Association, reproduced in part in *Kine Weekly*, 30 July 1942, 3, 31.

[140] See Sussex, *Rise and Fall*, 116 ff.; and Nicholas Pronay, '"The Land of Promise": The Projection of Peace Aims in Britain', in K. R. M. Short (ed.), *Film and Radio Propaganda in World War II* (London, 1983). Swann, on the other hand, suggests that documentary film was taken into account from early on in the process of planning for war—but the documentarists themselves were not incorporated into the policy-making mechanisms (see *British Documentary Movement*, 150 ff).

to have the approval of the MoI, and so to some extent they were bound to the terms of the official policy of a powerful war-time state bureaucracy seeking to construct a national unity on the basis of an assumed common interest and common struggle.[141] Censorship inevitably played a major role in the war-time cinema, but recent assessments of that role suggest that censorship policy during the war actually enabled the renaissance of British cinema in this period, and especially the production of films that were perceived at the time as realist.[142]

Various institutional mechanisms were established to promote the development of films and film policy during the war. One of these was the Ideas Committee of the MoI, which brought together a variety of film-production personnel, primarily scriptwriters and directors, from both documentary and the commercial sector, as well as MoI civil servants. Vincent Porter and Chaim Litewski suggest that 'the Ideas Committee was the fount of feature film production policy. Here subjects and themes were discussed and checked against the MoI's information and propaganda policy.'[143] One aspect of the committee's deliberations was a crucial sharing of ideas between the two sectors of the production industry. Paul Rotha, for instance, suggests that a screening of his company's short documentary, *Night Shift*, at one of the committee's meetings, had a direct influence on *Millions Like Us*.[144] And an MoI memorandum, while generally fairly cool towards the documentary movement, notes with satisfaction the way in which, in early war films, 'the documentary element is made part of a dramatic story.'[145]

Once again, however, it would be wrong to promote the idea that the MoI was an ideologically watertight body acting to the letter on policies handed down directly from above. Nicholas Pronay, for instance, has shown that, despite Winston Churchill's antagonism towards the formulation of peace aims, film propaganda sponsored by the MoI consistently formulated such aims, often from a left-wing perspective. He points out that the head of the Films Division from 1940 was Jack Beddington, from

---

[141] See Frances Thorpe and Nicholas Pronay with Clive Coultass, *British Official Films in the Second World War* (Oxford, 1980), 40–4, for details of official regulation of films in war-time; also Nicholas Pronay and Jeremy Croft, 'British Film Censorship and Propaganda Policy during the Second World War', in Curran and Porter (eds.), *British Cinema History*, 152 ff.; and Vincent Porter and Chaim Litewski, 'The Way Ahead', *Sight and Sound*, 50/2 (1981), 110–111.

[142] See Pronay and Croft, 'Film Censorship'.

[143] 'Way Ahead', 110; see also Sussex, *Rise and Fall*, 140–1; and Aldgate, 'British Cinema during Second World War', 9–10.

[144] In interview in Sussex, *Rise and Fall*, 141. However, an unidentified programme note in the BFI Library file for *Millions Like Us* includes the following statement: 'Launder and Gilliat have firmly denied ever having seen *Night Shift*'.

[145] Ministry of Information Co-Ordination Committee, Sir Kenneth Clarke's paper, 'Programme for Film Propaganda', 29 Jan. 1940, PRO. INF 1/867, para. 2. ii.

a public relations background, who had very little knowledge of the commercial film industry, and that his chief adviser was Sidney Bernstein, by then a key figure in the Labour Party; together, they favoured the generally left-of-centre personnel of the documentary movement, who made 74 per cent of the films paid for by the MoI. Many of these films quite explicitly discussed the future and proposed a range of peace aims.[146]

A more spontaneous populist groundswell was also evident among the general public. A Mass Observation report of 1943 noted 'the leftward drift in political outlook which has continued at a steady rate throughout the war.' This was not, they felt, a matter of strict party political allegiance: 'so far as it has any coherent form, it is directed towards some new ideal, not yet adequately expressed in an organized way.'[147] *Millions Like Us*, although actively encouraged by the MoI, needs also be seen as part of this more spontaneous populist groundswell invoking a potentially fairly radical notion of the people, and imagining a democratic peace. In the light of these popular sentiments, adjustments had to be made by the MoI in the terms of their propaganda, and the concept of an all-inclusive 'Us' came to a certain prominence.[148] Popular mythology has it that this was the people's war, and it is this concept of the people which is mobilized in so many contemporary pronouncements, both official and unofficial. As Angus Calder has suggested, 'the concept of course was never universally accepted. But its influence over the press, the films and the radio was enormous; it shaped the rhetoric of five years of official and unofficial propaganda.'[149]

This concept of the people however tends to obscure questions of class and gender differences, while at the same time invoking them at an intuitive level.[150] How, then, do films such as *Millions Like Us* and *This Happy Breed*

---

[146] Pronay, 'Land of Promise'; also Swann, *British Documentary Movement*, 154.

[147] Mass Observation, 'Social Security and Parliament', *Political Quarterly*, 14/3 (1943), 245, 246; see also Graham Dawson and Bob West, 'Our Finest Hour?—The Popular Memory of World War 2 and the Struggle over National Identity', in Hurd, (ed.), *National Fictions*; Paul Addison, *The Road to 1945: British Politics and the Second World War* (London, 1977), 162; Angus Calder, *The People's War* (London, 1971); and Aldgate and Richards, *Britain Can Take It*, 49–51.

[148] An early poster epitomizes the problems of the initial campaigns in its implicit acknowledgement of two nations, 'Us' and 'Them': 'Your Courage, Your Cheerfulness, Your Resolution/Will Bring Us Victory'. In the wake of the disfavour shown towards such sentiments (see Ian McLaine, *Ministry of Morale: Home Front Morale and the Ministry of Information in World War II* (London, 1979), 31), the discourse was increasingly replaced by one in which 'Us' becomes an inclusive term, not an exclusive one—as in Churchill's slogan 'Let us go forward together', which was used in a later MoI poster campaign (see Ellis, 'Victory of the Voice', and Smith, 'Narrative and Ideology', 146); note also that Mass Observation published a monthly booklet under the title *Us* during 1940 and 1941.

[149] *People's War*, 159.

[150] See Graham Dawson, 'History-Writing on World War II', in Hurd, (ed.), *National Fictions*.

construct an idea of the people, and how does this relate to questions of nationhood and national identity, and class and gender identity? How do they negotiate the different understandings of 'the people' in cultural circulation at the time, and what sort of interventions do they themselves make in this debate? These are some of the questions which I will be exploring in the rest of this chapter.

NARRATING THE NATION: *MILLIONS LIKE US*, PART I

> The British feature film made great strides during the later years of the war. For many of us a foretaste of things to come was provided in 1943 by the appearance of *Millions Like Us*.
>
> Edgar Anstey, 1949.[151]

Millions Like Us is a rich and complex melodrama of everyday life about women factory workers during the war, and the family of one of those women. A *Kine Weekly* review indicates something of the panoramic scope and the collage-like texture of the film in describing it as

at one and the same time a rough sketch of working class family life in war-time, a gigantic newsreel summarising salient events on the home front since war began and a tender if ingenuous love story with an aero-engine factory employing women from all walks of life for its background.[152]

My interest in the film lies first in the way in which it narrates the nation, constructing it as a knowable and known community; secondly in the way in which this construction of a public arena inhabited by private individuals negotiates the relationship between romance and work, personal achievement and public service; and thirdly in the way in which this construction of the nation depends in large part on the use of formal devices drawn from the documentary tradition of the previous decade-and-a-half.

The film deals with a small community of people united in a common cause in which collective, social responsibility outweighs individual desires, apparently regardless of class, regional identity, and traditional gender roles.[153] In many ways, this community stands in for the nation as a whole, and the film strives to incorporate its audience into this community by

---

[151] 'Development of Film Technique in Britain', in Manvell (ed.), *Experiment in Film*, 259.
[152] 30 Sept. 1943, 16.
[153] Note also that the film draws on a variety of different cultures to stress this sense of unity-in-diversity—see for instance the use of different types of music, including both popular music-hall songs and strains of Beethoven's Fifth Symphony; there are also references to attending both classical concerts and popular films as legitimate activities for ordinary people.

means of both empathetic identification with characters and a recognition of the types on the screen as ordinary people like themselves. The individual struggles of the fiction, the personalized psychologies of the melodrama, are also placed in the real public context of contemporary history by drawing on various documentary devices.

The film began life as an MoI commission for a project which might deal with the whole of the domestic war effort;[154] in other words, it was initially conceived as a piece of propaganda within the broad outlines of official policy. The terms in which the film operates, however, and the debates in which it intervenes situate it also as part of the more spontaneous democratic populism of the period. What seems progressive about *Millions Like Us*, in the context of the political debates of the period, is the way in which it conjures up a vision of a classless society whose basis is not in the bourgeois patriarchal family but in a community which depends not upon competition but upon co-operation, and in which women and men can play an equal role—indeed, the community is dominated by women engaged in traditionally masculine operations. This vision is compromised, however, by official policy: the MoI may have been urging women into masculine occupations, and encouraging co-operation, but they were doing so on a temporary basis, for the duration of the war only, rather than seeking to encourage the possibility of more permanent social changes. The evidence of these tensions is there in the film, which thus becomes the site of an intense ideological struggle over the ideal form of the nation.

Contemporary reviewers were generally appreciative of the film on its release, praising it for what they saw as its realism. One trade paper thought it 'a mirror of modern life . . . vividly realistic as to its factory background' and that 'the attraction and charm of this Gainsborough picture lie in its down-to-earth appeal to "millions like us" '—in marked contrast to what Grierson had described as the 'garish spectacle' of Hollywood commercialism.[155] *Monthly Film Bulletin* was impressed by the way that the film 'introduce[d] a realist atmosphere and a documentary touch to life in an aircraft factory.'[156] Caroline Lejeune felt that 'you should applaud this honest, quietly-observant British film. . . . It's real',[157] while the *Manchester Guardian* enjoyed 'its warm-hearted temper . . . salted with

---

[154] See Geoff Brown, *Launder and Gilliat* (London, 1977), 108; and Sue Harper, 'The Representation of Women in British Feature Films, 1939–1945', in Taylor (ed.), *Britain and the Cinema*, 173–4; cf. letter from MoI to BFPA, reproduced in *Kine Weekly*, 30 July 1942, 3.

[155] *Today's Cinema*, 24 Sept. 1944, 8; and Grierson, 'Course of Realism', 147. The American trade paper, *Motion Picture Herald*, commented on 'the film's refreshing qualities and its sincerity and simplicity' (23 Oct. 1943, 1595); on the re-issue of the film, *Today's Cinema* referred to 'its extreme realism' (19 Dec. 1947, 11).

[156] 10/120 (1943), 133.   [157] *Observer*, 3 Oct. 1943.

spontaneous humour and strengthened by intimate realism, lapsing only at the end into starry-eyed sentiment':

Nothing more clearly marks the coming-of-age of the British cinema than its treatment of ordinary working people, especially as minor characters or in the mass. The clowns of ten years ago first became lay figures of sociological drama and then, with the war, patriotic heroes. In *Millions Like Us* they are real human beings, and the British film has reached adult maturity.[158]

For Lejeune, it was not so much the appearance of ordinary working people as its treatment of emotion and romance that distinguished the film; having sweepingly dismissed most screen romances for their lack of passion, she praises *Millions Like Us* for 'its delicate, shy love-story . . . It's not often we get a more experienced emotional job from our native studios.'[159] But it is hardly passion to which she is pointing here, as the *Monthly Film Bulletin* review suggests: 'both directors are . . . to be congratulated on the restraint which they have shown.'[160] This restraint in dealing with emotions—over and again constructed as an essentially British sensibility—is of course one of the major features of these war-time dramas.[161] Reviewers for the American trade press were equally impressed by the film's ideological project. *Variety* described it as a 'picturization of the life of the "common people"', while the *Motion Picture Herald* called it 'an English film in an English idiom'; both papers thought it should do good business on both sides of the Atlantic.[162]

For at least one section of the trade press, however, the narrative complexity of the film was a problem, since it was unlikely to meet the expectations of audiences attuned to the conventions of classic Hollywood cinema:

The overall picture is too kaleidoscopic to make significant drama. . . . The tale opens with every promise of developing into a deep and significant portrait of working-class family life but all the early characters with the exception of Celia are dropped after the first three reels. True, they are gathered up for the anti-climax—Celia's wedding is the excuse—but there appears to be little point apart from the cultivation of footage in employing such an ambitious production. . . . It has at least one story too many.[163]

Box-office potential, measured in terms of proximity to the standards of the American film, was more important to such commentators than the production of a realist national cinema. In so far as evidence exists of how contemporary audiences received the film, although it was not a huge commercial success, the annual box-office survey in this same paper later

[158] 28 Dec. 1943.   [159] *Observer*, 3 Oct. 1943.
[160] 10/120 (1943), 133.   [161] Cf. Barr, *Ealing Studios*.
[162] *Variety*, 17 Nov. 1943, repr. in *Variety's Film Reviews, 1943–1948*, vii (New York, 1983), no p. nos. given; and *Motion Picture Herald*, 23 Oct. 1943, 1595.
[163] *Kine Weekly*, 30 Sept. 1944, 16.

acknowledged it as one of several 'lively British entrants' in its first month of release.[164] Further, the mainly middle-class respondents to two contemporary surveys confirm the sentiments of the film reviewers. '*Millions Like Us*—saw it last night, and consider it the best film since *Bank Holiday*. Presents Britain and life as it is—we must have truth and integrity in our films,' wrote one, while another enjoyed the film 'because it really was true to its title. These were real people, people one knew and liked, not film actors and actresses.'[165]

As an example of the way in which the film came to epitomize a certain tendency in British cinema one can cite Anstey's comments, recalling the film some half a decade later in a discussion of the overall historical development of film technique in Britain:

It was a drama of the factory front, an examination of the emotional interplay of a group of people drawn from different levels of society and brought together for a common effort at the factory bench. Technically, it was remarkable for its use of real factory, canteen and hostel interiors, and for its naturalistic portraits of the workers portrayed. It was on the whole unsentimental and took a realistic view of the social problems involved rather than minimizing them as was then common in the more superficial forms of factory-effort propaganda. *Millions Like Us* proved to be a popular film and did something to persuade the film trade that there was a case for the documentary handling of real material even in entertainment films primarily designed to be viewed through the box-office grill.[166]

The film clearly starts from the point of view of narrative cinema, with the pleasures of fiction firmly in mind, but it also draws on documentary techniques, quite self-consciously at times, and so has some of the features of the story-documentary. The origins of the film as an official documentary about the home front are thus not without significance, and co-director Frank Launder later recalled that

With this object, we toured the country, visiting docks, farms and coastal areas, and went to war factories and works all over Britain. [But] we came to the conclusion that the best way to attract a wide public to a subject of this nature, which was what the Ministry wished, was to clothe it in a simple fictional story.[167]

---

[164] Josh Billings, 'The 1943 Box-Office Survey', *Kine Weekly*, 13 Jan. 1944, 52.

[165] Responses to the Mass Observation November 1943 directive, enquiring as to what were considered the best films of the last year, reproduced in Jeffrey Richards and Dorothy Sheridan (eds.), *Mass Observation at the Movies* (London, 1987), 238, 277; see also 241, 263, but note also that this was not one of the most frequently cited British films in the survey. See also J. P. Mayer, *British Cinemas and their Audiences* (London, 1948), who reproduces responses to a questionnaire he orchestrated through *Picturegoer* magazine; see 169, 177, 192.

[166] 'Development of Film Technique', 260; cf. *Factual Film*, 102; and Catherine de la Roche, 'Britain's Film Directors, No. 1. Frank Launder and Sidney Gilliat'.

[167] From an interview with Geoff Brown, quoted in Brown, *Launder and Gilliat*, 108.

Although this was Launder and Gilliat's first feature, they had both had long experience as script-writers for some of the most important studios and companies within the British film industry of the 1930s and early 1940s; Gilliat had also had a short stint as Associate Producer at Gainsborough Studios in 1935–6, while Launder was script editor there from 1936; they had also both worked for major American companies based in Britain. In other words, they were thorough products of the commercial industry, with no documentary training whatsoever.[168] The other senior members of the production team were similarly well-established studio personnel[169]—and the studio itself, of course, had long had a reputation for solid commercial fare. The leading players were all trained actors from the studio system, and Eric Portman was one of the most popular British stars of the period.[170]

The evidence of this commercial background can be clearly seen in the film. Several extended sequences work within what Tim Pulleine calls the 'overtly "scripted" vein of domestic comedy'—Moore Marriott, who plays the father, was a stalwart of many Will Hay comedies, several of which had been worked on by Launder or Gilliat; Pulleine also suggests that the opening scenes of the film dealing with seaside holidays directly recall an earlier Gainsborough film, *Bank Holiday* (1937), a suggestion which seems to me very pertinent, not least given that film's very favourable reception by British critics.[171] It is structurally very similar to *Millions Like Us*, and also shares with it a tendency to see working-class or lower-middle-class family life as comic, a mode which is counterbalanced by emotionally charged but carefully restrained melodrama. There is a further comic intertextual reference in the occasional appearance in *Millions Like Us* of two bumbling, Blimp-like officers, Charters and Caldicott, played by Basil Radford and Naunton Wayne. They had first appeared as characters in probably the best-known of the previous films scripted by Launder and Gilliat, Hitchcock's *The Lady Vanishes* (1938); they reappeared in the Launder and Gilliat scripted *Night Train To Munich* (1940), played in two radio series, one of which was adapted as a film, *Crooks Tour* (1940), and cropped up again in *Next of Kin* (1942).

Len England, reporting for Mass Observation, also situates *Millions Like Us* (and *This Happy Breed*) in the context of a well-established

---

[168] See ibid.; undated (c.1946) press releases on BFI microfiches for both Launder and Gilliat; de la Roche, 'Britain's Film Directors'; and entry on Launder in *Film Dope*, 33 (1985), 26–8.

[169] See Harper, 'Representation of Women', 174.

[170] See *Kine Weekly*, 13 Jan. 1944, 51; also *Bernstein Questionnaires*, 1946–7, when he was voted 8th most popular male British star (21st overall); by this time, Patricia Roc, the female lead, was also well established, being voted the 3rd most popular female British star (6th overall); see also *Kine Weekly*, 20 Dec. 1945, 51.

[171] In a review of *Millions Like Us*, *Monthly Film Bulletin*, 49 (1982), 117.

popular tradition of American and British 'family films', starring the likes
of Shirley Temple, Mickey Rooney, and Deanna Durbin; England also
mentions series such as the Hardy family films, and the Old Mother Riley
films—and, 'on a more serious plane', *Mrs Miniver*.[172]

There is then no question that the film was made as a commercial
project, by a production team with a solid commercial background. Nevertheless, there is also no doubt that Launder and Gilliat approached the
project in a documentary fashion, thoroughly researching the material
which eventually became *Millions Like Us*, attempting to authenticate the
fiction by shooting on location and building in local detail wherever possible, and using serving soldiers and airmen, and female factory workers
for various scenes.[173] The film was also shot in black and white when
colour was available; it eschews expressionistic lighting and camerawork
in favour of a primarily naturalistic *mise-en-scène*, except for a few unusually traumatic narrative moments; and in general there is a preference
for group shots over close-ups. The structure of the film recalls the documentary tradition, too, for it attempts to deal with the multiple, tracing the
lives of a number of people and situating them in the context of a popular
history of the home front up to 1943, even depicting the whole process of
manufacturing and assembling an aircraft.

This textual structure establishes a series of connections, both abstract
and concrete, expected and unexpected, through both visual and aural
links, and by means of both continuity and counterpoint. The debt to
Humphrey Jennings and others is more than evident. There is also a familiar iconography of work—and a perspective for looking at it—using high-
angle location shots of factory floors, for instance, drawn from 1930s
documentary practice. The more specific debt to Jennings is there too in
the film's iconography of the nation at war: images of St Paul's Cathedral
strangely visible through the rubble of a bomb-site; single-frame bomb
blasts and gun-fire at night silhouetting weird, surreal shapes; scenes of
urban firefighting at night; high-angle shots of a dance-hall packed with
men in uniform and women in civilian clothes; the Welsh male voice choir
which sings at a concert; and so on.

The narrative system of the film differs significantly from that of the
standard Hollywood film, and may be compared with the 'primitive' form
of *Sing As We Go*, in that it lacks the narrative refinement and economy
and the tight formal integration and goal-seeking drive of the classical film.

---

[172] 'The Film and Family Life', 13 June 1944, repr. in Richards and Sheridan (eds.), *Mass
Observation*, 292–8; the quotation is from 293.

[173] Numerous reports in the trade press stress what *Kine Weekly* called the 'authentic
detail' of the film (16 Sept. 1943, 6); see also 'Authentic Factory Settings', 21 Jan. 1943,
40; 26 Aug. 1943, 39; and 2 Sept. 1943, 13. Cf. Brown, *Launder and Gilliat*, 108; and
publicity for the film repr. in *Progress of British Films*, no author/editor (Glasgow, n.d.
[prob. 1946]), 49.

Little dramas—a variety of narrative attractions—are developed around several different individuals, but none of them is ever allowed completely to dominate the narrative interest of the entire film. The film is thus structured as a series of parallel interweaving narrative lines, a web of narrative threads, following a multiplicity of characters rather than a single consistently central narrative protagonist. The development of these narratives is episodic, often with no strong causal relationship between consecutive scenes. As such, the narrative system is able to represent precisely a community of people, rather than star individuals; it is able to develop a variety of limited egos, even if one of them, Celia, is developed into a more central and ideal ego. This vertical opening up of the horizontal linearity of the narrative, this extension of the diegetic space to embrace a multiplication of potentially redundant details, both enables the film to depict community, and creates an impression of realism—for as one commentator has suggested, 'realism is the glorification of the unessential.'[174]

The film opens with a scene which shows Britain on holiday in the last weeks of peace just before the outbreak of war. We are introduced to the various members of the respectable working-class/lower-middle-class Crowson family preparing for their summer vacation. In the film's terms, they are an ordinary family, one among millions of others just like them. The onset of war gradually disperses the family, producing also a dispersal of narrative interest which the film attempts to close off by singling out Celia, one of the grown-up daughters. She is designated a 'mobile woman' and eventually leaves home to work at an aircraft engineering factory.[175] But the other members of the family are never ignored or lost, and the foregrounding of Celia is never absolute. The obvious way of resolving the problem of dispersal in the domestic melodrama genre would be to reunite the family. That does not happen here. Instead the potential anxiety produced by the dispersal of the family is displaced by shifting the focus of attention on to the supportive community of women which develops at the factory at which Celia goes to work and at the hostel where they live. The final scene celebrates the envelopment of the individual within the all-embracing community, enabling the film to end on an image of stability and unity. The film thus deals both with the dislocation of the family in conditions of war and its substitution by community, a community in

---

[174] An unnamed mid-Victorian critic quoted in Alan Trachtenberg, *Classic Essays on Photography* (New Haven, Conn., 1980), 93. See also Barthes, 'Realistic Effect'.

[175] 'Mobile women' were those designated by the government as available for work away from home in the national interest; see Denise Riley, '"The Free Mothers": Pronatalism and Working Women in Industry at the End of the Last War in Britain', *History Workshop Journal*, 11 (1981); Harper, 'Representation of Women', 169–72, 176; Lant, *Blackout*, esp. 59 ff.; J. B. Priestley, *British Women Go To War* (London, n.d. [prob. 1943]), 7; John Costello, *Love, Sex and War* (London, 1985), 10; Calder, *People's War*, 308–10, 382–7; and Raynes Minns, *Bombers and Mash* (London, 1980), 31–41.

STILL 25. Producing the war-time community: a typical group-shot of Celia (Patricia Roc, second from left) and her work-mates in the factory canteen (*Millions Like Us*).

which each individual proves his or her worth to the team, and so by implication to the nation and the war effort.

The associative montage construction of the film enables it to deal with parallel actions without having to cut between them according to the conventions of suspense. The interruption and displacement of narrative logic, the repetition of situations, and the display of simultaneity are acceptable within the film's terms, since they suggest the unity of the nation and the routineness of everyday life. When the film does jump to parallel actions by other characters, there is rarely any real narrative motivation for such shifts of interest: the new scene is not designed to add necessary information to build up suspense or to make previous scenes comprehensible; rather, this sort of narrative dispersal enables general comments about the state of the family, or the wider community, or the nation as a whole. Thus, cut-aways to Dad at home with all his daughters away, or Celia's sister Phyllis working with the ATS, produce relatively self-contained scenes which have no impact on developments at the factory-workers' hostel. Such scenes are only very weakly motivated, if at all, within an overall interlocking system of cause and effect, and tend to function more as inconsequential gags (so once again recalling the format of the cinema of attractions). In a similar vein, when Celia and her new beau, Fred, leave the dance-hall where they have met, they pass Jenny, one of Celia's colleagues, entering the hall; the camera now follows her—not to suggest any intrigue in the relationship between the three characters, but simply to follow the parallel actions of another member of the community. The relative lack of causality and of goal-directed movement means that it is the diegetic boundaries of the family–community which define the limits of representation, as in *Listen to Britain*. Thus narrative dispersal is balanced by diegetic unity. This is in one sense no more than a specific variation on the classical narrative film's articulation of paradigmatic and syntagmatic movement, its play of repetition and difference, but it is enough of a variation to have a quite profound effect on the work of the film as a whole.

Part of the project of *Millions Like Us*, then, is to articulate a sense of the reality of everyday life in all its complexity and mundane inconsequentiality. The everyday would normally be represented in classical cinema in terms of the domestic and familial; here, however, the security of the domestic sphere of the home, the familiarity of the everyday, and the reliance upon family relationships have been destabilized by the war. The ideological goal of the narrative is the reassertion of this institution of the family which has been temporarily replaced by a wider sense of community. This means in effect regaining the conditions that allow the traditional domestic melodrama to place the family at the centre of the narrative. But this goal is impossible so long as the conditions of war continue, and a compensatory form of narrative resolution needs to be found. It is in this space, and because of the impossibility of achieving the logical goal of the narrative, that the populist celebration of community— the imagined community of the nation—emerges.

In this sense, the narrative of *Millions Like Us* does develop causally from an initial stability disrupted to a newly forged war-time stability (with contradictory aspirations for the post-war society)—but this causal development remains weak and episodic. There is also a tension between the causal development of the narrative lines which focus on particular individuals and their desires (notably Celia's story, but also other ro- mances dealt with in the course of the film) and the relatively non-causal representation of family or community life and work. There is therefore a melodramatic narrative interest for the cinema spectator, akin to the dom- inant pleasures of the Hollywood film—except that the consummation of individual desires and wish-fulfilment is effectively postponed in the na- tional interest to a post-war period. The more assertive narrative causality becomes, the more obviously classically constructed the scenes are, but this potentially tight causal development of a goal-directed narrative and the psychological development of a central hero-protagonist are constantly deflected, displaced, and marginalized by the series of narrational devices derived from the documentary form which enable it to explore more than simply the centre of the diegesis.

The vestiges of the public gaze are there in the way that the film resists invading private space with the proximity of the close-up. There are one or two exceptions to this rule, but they serve to underline what, in the film's terms, is the impossible fantasy of desire during war-time—but also its opposite, the utter tragedy of losing one's loved ones in combat. Ro- mance becomes fantasy precisely in the use of the unexpected close shot. The first occasion on which this happens is when Celia and her sister Phyllis have gone to a dance while on holiday before the war. Phyllis juggles effortlessly with four voracious young men, while the shy and innocent Celia waits for someone to approach her. Eventually, a painfully boring young man asks her to dance; while he witters away, the camera moves into a close-up of Celia—the reality of her dancing partner does not match the fantasy of her desire. In a second instance, in a scene which potentially satirizes classical cinema's romantic conventions (obviously in part for propagandist reasons), Celia has gone to the Labour Exchange to negotiate her call-up as a mobile woman. The scene opens with a long shot of Celia waiting for her interview; the camera tracks in to a soft focus close-up as dreamy romantic music wells up; there is a cut to a point-of- view shot of a WAAF poster, and a cut back to the close-up. This is sufficient motivation for a fantasy sequence depicting Celia's daydream of a romantic life in the forces first with a pilot, and then with a naval officer; meeting a landowner in the Land Army; becoming engaged to an officer when nursing him—until we finally cut back to the close-up of Celia waiting for her interview, the product of which in reality is her posting to a munitions factory.

Reality and fantasy briefly come together when Celia and Fred go out into the moonlight after their first dance, and there are big soft-focus romantically lit close-ups of both characters as they talk about their personal lives. The explicit motivation of fantasy by the use of close-ups occurs again when Fred apparently stands Celia up on a date. The camera tracks in from an oblique two-shot of Gwen and Celia to a close-up of Celia on her own; gradually superimposed over this is a romantic scene in an idyllic rural setting, in which Celia imagines Fred kissing her in the grass. There is a cut back to the close-up of a sad Celia, and then a move into another expressionist fantasy of her committing suicide. A third fantasy has a judge scolding Fred, who bursts into tears. Finally, there is a dissolve to the aeroplanes, which (unknown to Celia) contain Fred on a mission, flying overhead. Romance in war can only be a guilt-ridden fantasy, these shots suggest. The same tension is there again in a scene at the room that the newly wed couple are to occupy, and later when Celia hears of Fred's death. The close-up motivating the romantic fantasy has been replaced by its opposite, the close-up as signifier of the impossibility of romantic fulfilment during the war. The overwhelming sense of loss is compensated for in the final scene, which cuts between group shots and long shots of all the workers at the factory, and close-ups of Celia, as she is once more absorbed into the community.

DOCUMENTING THE COMMUNITY, AUTHENTICATING THE FICTION: *MILLIONS LIKE US*, PART 2

The community of *Millions Like Us* consists of representatives of a variety of class positions, regional types, accents, ages, and experiences. All characters are more or less symbolic types—some remaining no more than symbols, others being carefully rounded out psychologically to become complete, thinking, emoting subjects. The community as a whole depends upon reasonable, democratic, and co-operative forms of authority, and has the appearance of an organic unity. The relatively self-sufficient and collective nature of this social body might be seen as potentially challenging to traditional authoritarian forms of power, whether patriarchal or capitalist—but the challenge is circumscribed by a series of more conservative forces.

One such force is the traditional power relations of the bourgeois patriarchal family imposed upon the new community of the work-place, which is thereby structured like a family, with protagonists adopting the roles of father, mother, and numerous infants. Charlie Forbes, the works supervisor,

STILL 26. Escaping the war effort: the camera moves in closer to focus on Fred (Gordon Jackson) and Celia (Patricia Roc), the doomed war-time lovers of *Millions Like Us*.

is a genial but thoroughly responsible father-figure, whose parental consciousness is shared by Celia's working-class, but university-educated roommate, Gwen. The patriarchal Charlie is in the end more powerful as a public figure, given his economic status as works supervisor, while Gwen exhibits a more traditionally feminine strength in her caring qualities; that strength is very much in evidence in the closing scene of the film, when it is her efforts that win Celia back for the community.

The charmingly shy and naïve Celia and Fred seem more like sister and brother than lovers, and they lack the moral superiority, social responsibility, and experience of either Gwen or Charlie; likewise, Annie Earnshaw and Jennifer Knowles, two more of Celia's colleagues, seem like their cheeky younger sister and aloof and recalcitrant older sister respectively. The incompleteness of the Crowson family—Celia's mother is dead—is therefore replaced by the virtual completeness of this new surrogate family. More significantly, if the nation is metaphorically represented by and as the community, it too is in the end constructed like a family. The nation as one large family, uniting social groups with potentially conflicting interests, is of course central to pastoral ideology, and the urban pastoral of *Millions Like Us* clearly draws on this powerful and traditional well of nationalist sentiment. It would be wrong, however, to dismiss this family–community–nation image as irremediably conservative: it is much more ambivalent than this, with a more radical, democratic side to it as well. The overriding sense of the film is precisely this ambivalence, even contradiction, between different forces.

This sense of ambivalence, and of the containment of the potentially radical image of community, is there in the narrative work of the film too. Although it tries to deal with the multiple, it also picks out an ideal hero in Celia. While she is subsumed within the collective, like all other individuals at the factory, she is also privileged narratively and iconographically so that she stands out precisely as an individual. Moreover, her individuality, and especially her desires, are utterly conventional—a fact which has profound implications for the representation of gender roles within the film. She may have entered the public sphere as a heroic factory worker doing a man's job, but her aspirations are defined entirely in relation to the private sphere. The communal life at the hostel is clearly marked as for the duration only, and it is family life and motherhood for which Celia longs, as she and Fred plan what sort of home and what size family they will have in the future, in a scene which directly plays on thoughts of the forthcoming peace.[176] These particular wishes can never be fulfilled since Fred is killed in action over Germany—but if Celia is thereby punished for

---

[176] Cf. Sue Harper's discussion of Celia's typicality in 'Representation of Women'; also Sue Aspinall, 'Women, Realism and Reality in British Films, 1943–53', in Curran and Porter (eds.), *British Cinema History*, 280; and Lant, *Blackout*, 72–3.

pursuing individual desires during war-time, and it is the social bonds of the community (the nation) which pull Celia through in the final scene of the film, there is never any doubt that her dreams of home-making and settling down to nuclear family life have simply been postponed until after the war.

It is this tension between private romance and public duty which makes this such a powerful film. On the one hand, romance is one of the main attractions of the film; on the other, as Charlie Forbes warns Celia, 'Love may make the world go around, but it won't win the war, you know!' Later, when Celia and Fred buy train tickets for their honeymoon, she looks up at the sign that was above every ticket-seller's window at the time: 'Is Your Journey Really Necessary?' In both cases, the selfless public service ideal is translated into everyday language.

The film is ambivalent about questions of gender in other ways too. Men are always present, motivating, directing, and containing female action—and rendering women passionate. At the same time, *Millions Like Us* does validate the traditionally feminine qualities and capabilities of emotional strength, domestic order, and care for others; it does not deal with the public sphere (in this case, the masculine world of combat) at the expense of what is traditionally considered to be the realm of the feminine, the private sphere. This sphere can, perhaps, only be validated in its own more public form, the community of the work-place and the hostel, rather than in the form of the actual domestic arrangements of the Crowson family, which are so often represented as comic—but it is a validation of the private sphere all the same. In a sense the drama of the film depends upon exploring the ramifications of decisions made and actions committed in the public sphere for the personal relationships and emotional stability of those who inhabit the private sphere: the public (masculine) sphere is represented from the point of view of the personal, the domestic, the feminine.

Celia and her colleagues are also of course engaged in traditionally masculine factory work, a fact which threatens to disturb the patriarchal stability of prevailing gender relations. As an obedient public servant, however, Celia seems to perceive the factory work as no more than a temporary obstacle to her taking up her rightful role as a woman within the traditionally domestic and familial space of the private sphere. This tension between the potential democratization of gender relations and the reproduction of traditional ideologies of femininity was a prominent feature of the public debate about the role of women during the war, according to Denise Riley.[177] The government felt obliged to mobilize women for traditionally masculine tasks in the national interest, but this was counterbalanced

---

[177] 'Free Mothers'; see also Harper, 'Representation of Women', and Lant, *Blackout*.

STILL 27. 'Love may make the world go round, but it won't win the war': Celia dreams at her lathe while Gwen (Megs Jenkins) looks on (*Millions Like Us*).

STILL 28. Men are always present, motivating, directing, and containing female action: the foreman, Charlie Forbes (Eric Portman), explains the intricacies of factory labour to the new recruits from the ranks of the 'mobile women' (*Millions Like Us*).

by the promotion of images of motherhood, and especially of the woman at home nurturing her family. As we have seen, such images are hardly absent from *Millions Like Us*, with both Gwen and Celia exhibiting a natural maternalism, all the while operating lathes in an aircraft engineering factory.

Riley suggests that a central feature of the war-time discourse about the family was 'the many depictions of the family as a cellular organism in the body-politic of the state and the community. Family health was a building-block in the edifice of national health, spiritual or physical.'[178] At the centre of this image of the family–community–nation, as Christine Gledhill and Gillian Swanson have noted, is the image of the nurturing mother, who thus 'became the linchpin in conceptualising national unity': it is the maternal body which reproduces the nation, its culture, and its heritage.[179] In this context, *Millions Like Us* carefully plays off the private family (the Crowsons) against the public family (the community of the work-place and implicitly the nation): it is, then, the experience of family relations which negotiates the distance between the private and the public, between the individual and the nation. This may be a validation of the traditionally feminine, forcing the personal and the domestic into the public realm. But it also reconstructs the social—with all its divisions of class, gender, region, and so on—entirely in terms of personal relationships, subsumed under an image of benevolent motherhood.[180]

Celia is also placed very much in the centre of what might be described as the knowable class spectrum of the film. She has a Home Counties middle-class accent and is clearly from a very different background from either Annie Earnshaw, Gwen, or Fred, all of whom have regionally specific accents (northern English, Welsh, and Scottish, respectively), and the first two of whom have markedly working-class affiliations. She is also very different from Jennifer, who is defined by accent, clothes, mannerisms, previous employment, and affiliations as upper-class, a rich and rather snobbish society girl. Celia's ordinariness is thus socially very specific, *petit bourgeois* rather than working-class (however else her family may be defined). Class differences are represented primarily in terms of culture and style, and are visible in social affiliations, clothing, and certain physical attributes (the voice, gestures—the way Jennifer smokes a cigarette in a holder, for instance). This means that questions about the differential economic, social, and cultural power possessed by one or other class are rarely addressed.

The relatively autonomous community constructed in *Millions Like Us*

---

[178] 'Free Mothers', 98.
[179] 'Gender and Sexuality in Second World War Films', in Hurd (ed.), *National Fictions*, 56.
[180] See ibid., and Harper, 'Representation of Women'.

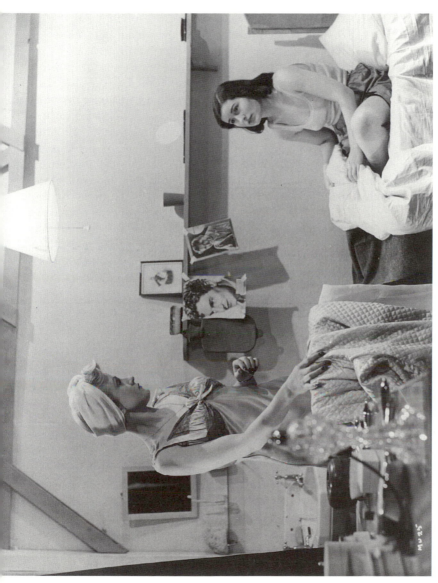

STILL 29. Straddling class differences to produce the war-time community: the glamorous middle-class southerner, Jennifer Knowles (Ann Crawford), shares a room at the factory hostel with the working-class northerner, Annie Earnshaw (Terry Randall) (*Millions Like Us*).

seems at first to be remarkably unpoliced from outside. There are few visible manifestations of a seat of real power, a ruling class which stands outside this organic and self-sufficient body—it is in this sense that Celia is in the middle of the knowable class spectrum of the film. There is a further, almost unknowable class element, however—or at least, a class that is known really only by implication. For the community clearly is regulated from outside by the state: Celia is directed into war work by the Ministry of Labour; posters at the factory urge greater output; the factory receives advance notice of the threat of an air-raid. Somewhere else, there is someone who knows, and who uses this knowledge to make decisions which affect others, including this community.

Power is thus articulated in terms of communication, as in the story documentaries—but this time by implication rather than by direct representation. The power to order and discipline the nation resides in the technological and bureaucratic means of maintaining communicative links between the many citizens of the nation and the work that is required of them in the national interest. Those who have the power to operate or activate the chains of communication are clearly outside the community itself. The nation is a self-sufficient community, it is the general public, but there is also an invisible layer of people, an élite group who somehow stand above the public sphere and have the capacity to regulate the national body.

There are two aspects of the film which threaten to undermine this somewhat conservative reading of its effects, however. First, there are the buffoonish figures of Charters and Caldicott, comic representatives of the officer class. Their singular failure to make sense of the changes taking place around them might well be read as a satire of the officer class, a satire of the exploitative privileges that were felt by many to characterize all that was wrong with the pre-war society, and all that must be changed after the war. But comedy of this sort is always double-edged, and another reading of Charters and Caldicott might suggest that buffoonery serves only to mask the real power of the officer class.

The second aspect of the film which offers some sort of comment on the nature of the class system and its relationship to a democratic society is the relationship between Charlie Forbes, the lower-middle-class northerner, and Jennifer Knowles, the upper-class southerner. The narrative has quite deliberately processed their romance as improbable—Charlie is forever disgusted by her élitist attitudes and anti-social behaviour—but it takes place all the same. The real significance of this is that the improbability of a relationship straddling such a huge class difference is directly addressed within the film. In a scene which stands out from the rest of the film by its idyllic rural setting, Charlie and Jennifer discuss their relationship. Charlie specifically stresses the peculiar circumstances of the war which have enabled the production of a community in which class differences no longer seem relevant; he fears that the community will be temporary, and that class antagonism will continue to divide the nation after the war:

'The world's roughly made up of two kinds of people—you're one sort and I'm the other. Oh, we're together now there's a war on—we need to be. What's going to happen when it's all over? Shall we go on like this, or shall we slide back—that's what I want to know. I'm not marrying you, Jennifer, until I'm sure.'

The rural setting tends to underline the fantasy of the romance, divorced from the realities of the war. The recognition that the romance may be no more than a war-time fantasy forces the spectator to move some way towards confronting the issues which Charlie is addressing. But the setting is also a traditional pastoral image of the national landscape, suggesting the timelessness of England—but also Britain—in this sense intimating to the spectator that things cannot possibly change in this environment. The question of social reform is addressed, nevertheless, and the fact that both Charlie and Jennifer seem part of the landscape, rather than at odds with it, and that their performances are entirely 'natural', suggests that such questions are themselves natural rather than extraordinary, and that some sort of social change may be sensible.[181] The scene is a profound moment of excess within the film. It raises the question of class difference, but does not offer any easy, consensual answer to it—and, although it is only a small moment in the film, it is an intriguing and memorable one all the same.

Once again, the strength of the image lies partly in its ambivalence, the necessity both to represent the nation as a responsible community and to find a place for the playing out of individual desire; to uphold the collective interest and protect the vulnerable individual. It is an articulation which offers space to both the public and the private—and in part the film offers a social history of the home front in terms of the private and personal experiences of a particular group of individuals. At the same time, an apparently more objective version of that history is presented in the film's several montage sequences, which break away from the shot-matching and point-of-view devices of continuity editing and return to the public gaze of the documentary. In this way, the authenticity and the public significance of the private traumas and achievements of Celia and the rest are continually affirmed.

There is a continuous montage thread running through the early part of the film which manages to construct a real, public history of the home front between 1939 and 1942 (the blackout, evacuation of children, men returning from Dunkirk, the removal of signposts and the mining of beaches,

---

[181] Cf. Brown, *Launder and Gilliat*, 14.

the Battle of Britain, air-raids, and so on) alongside and parallel with the individual dramas of the various characters of the film. Later, when Celia and her colleagues arrive at the factory for the first time, there is also a long documentary-style montage sequence of the complete work process involved in providing planes for the men who must fight. The sequence—a documentary within a fiction film, in effect—is presented not from the point of view of Celia and the other women, but as the objective, observational, documentary point of view of the spectator. Indeed, the women could not possibly witness the images we see. The complete sequence consists of numerous actuality shots of mainly anonymous women arriving for work at the factory by foot, bike, car, coach, and train. Sound is provided by non-diegetic music, the only diegetic sound coming in one brief insert shot of Celia and her fellow conscripts travelling in their coach.

The image dissolves into a montage of shots of the whole industrial production process, from the smelting of iron ore, through the casting of machine parts, the assembly of a bomber, to its final take-off. Again, the images are all actuality shots, dissolved together; the music track continues, but now does battle with industrial noises. Finally, without any attempt to signal this set of images as the object of a diegetic point of view, there is a dissolve to a shot of the new batch of women arriving at the factory to take up their jobs as pawns in this vast process.

These montage sequences do not operate in a classical way—they cannot be read as narrative ellipses, as means of condensing narrative information. The effect of these sequences is instead to situate the melodrama in a space—both physical and cognitive—which the spectator recognizes as real because of the resonances of the documentary devices used. These sequences are almost all confined to the first part of the film before the story of Celia's romance with Fred, and, to a lesser extent, Jenny's romance with Charlie, come to occupy the dramatic centre of the film and dominate the narrative interest. The first twenty minutes or so of the film are thus much more fragmented, much less clearly narrativized, than the latter part of the film. Initially, the sounds and images of the film are organized diegetically—that is to say, they are held in place by the limits of a historically specific diegetic space, the home front in Britain, in a manner reminiscent of *Listen to Britain*. The film subsequently shifts to a mode of representation whose organization of sounds and images, and whose production of meanings and pleasures is dependent upon a narrative meta-discourse taking hold of the film system. The film seems to declare that the individual dramas only make sense within the real historical space already established in the initial relatively unnarrativized diegesis. This more objective (because documentary) sense of history orders and situates, and therefore validates what would otherwise be the mere discourse of the film's little dramas.

There is then a continual movement between history and discourse;[182] between the public and the private; between the general and the particular; between the observational and the participatory. This movement is explicitly played out in the shift from the cinema audience being identified in the opening sequence as 'you', out there, to the cinema audience as individual members of the community which absorbs Celia and compensates for the loss of her husband at the end of the film. The film opens with a series of actuality shots of workers pouring *en masse* through the gates of a factory. The shots are combined in montage style rather than matched for continuity; the images are predominantly high-angle long shots, and/or taken with a lens with a long focal length, producing the effect of a grainy image and foreshortened perspective: all these characteristics reinforce the sense of observing the mass from a distance—and from above, from a superior position. Superimposed over these images are the credits; the final cast credit reads '—and millions like you . . .'

The second sequence of the film is again a montage of predominantly high-angle actuality shots, detailing a crowded station forecourt, a fast-moving steam train and motor coaches rushing towards the camera, a merry-go-round, a roller-coaster, a crowded swimming pool, cyclists, a girl at the seaside, and, finally, rhyming with the first shot, a long high-angle pan across a crowded beach. This is first of all an increasingly familiar iconography of the leisure of ordinary people; but it is also a familiar perspective, surveying these people from above, rendering them as an anonymous mass. An ironically nostalgic voice-over says ' "Remember that summer before the war, those gay coupon-free days when . . . you and millions like you swarmed to the sea . . . ?" '. The use of actuality shots, montage editing, the distanced observational perspective, direct address ('millions like you'), and the voice-over: these are all familiar as documentary devices, here lending the film the aura of the real.

The spectator is positioned and addressed as an observer at this stage, looking in from outside the diegesis of the film. But we are already being drawn into the diegesis in being asked to 'remember that summer', not by means of identification with an extraordinary narrative protagonist so much as by an invitation to remember a real time and place in the recent past. The way is being paved for a shift from this predominantly documentary mode of observation to a fictional world—but an authentic one—in which we can participate. The third scene of the film is shot in classical narrative style, moving from an establishing shot of a street and a house front to a series of group shots and close-ups of the Crowson family within this space, employing all the strategies of shot-matching, reverse-field cutting,

---

[182] Cf. Christian Metz, 'History/Discourse: A Note on Two Voyeurisms', *Edinburgh '76 Magazine*, 1 (1976).

and point-of-view shots. A number of characters are gradually defined as unique individuals by investing them with a set of wishes and goals—particularly the two contrasting sisters, the sweet, naïve, but responsible Celia; and Phyllis, more of a good-time girl. Now the spectator has specific points of identification and specific enigmas and dramas by which to become captivated. The film has very swiftly achieved the transition from the general to the particular, and moved the spectator from observer of the real world to participant in the drama, which has itself been validated as taking place in a real historical space. The spectators, as members of the nation whom the film addresses, are becoming almost indelibly inscribed into the community of the film; the spectator's memories are substantiated by images which give concrete evidence on which to focus—not least, the image of a typical, ordinary family chosen from among the millions.

This movement between the general and the particular is reaffirmed and restated constantly throughout the course of the film, particularly in the first half hour or so—moving, for instance, from a montage sequence of troops coming back from Dunkirk by train, to shots of Dad in the Home Guard, under a railway bridge over which the trains rattle; or moving from the montage sequence of the whole industrial process of manufacturing and assembling an aeroplane to Celia and her new colleagues arriving at the factory. The movement from the general to the particular works ceaselessly to contain the particular within the general, to insert the individual within the general community. By this means, the individuated protagonists of the fiction are not separated from the historical process, they are not removed from the public sphere. Certainly, the dominant narrative interest concerns the ways in which public events disrupt everyday domestic life and personal relationships. But these narratives also involve ordinary people participating in the public sphere, even if they are not actually present in the montage sequences which are the film's dominant means of articulating the broader sense of history. Each, in other words, does his or her bit in the public arena.

As we have seen, the narration of the film coagulates much more resolutely around a number of romances as the film progresses; but as spectators, we are punished for our fascination with these personal romances during a time of public crisis, almost as sharply as Celia is punished when she loses her husband to the war effort and an early death over Germany. Loss now becomes the dominant register, until the plenitude of community is reasserted in the final remarkable sequence.

A huge audience, standing in for the audience in the cinema, are being entertained in the factory canteen by a popular singer with a band. The camera performs a long tracking movement, and, with a series of cuts, establishes the place of Celia and her comrades in the midst of this mass of people. Celia is clearly distressed when she hears the sound of planes flying overhead, carrying with them a reminder of her loss. Gradually

Gwen, the maternal figure of the community, manages to cajole Celia into joining in with the song which by now the whole canteen are singing. It is a familiar song—the music-hall favourite, 'Waiting at the church'—which has been heard on a number of occasions previously in the film, notably at Celia and Fred's wedding. That sense of familiarity for the cinema audience is important, but the repetition of the song also serves to link the personal optimism of the wedding with the new optimism of the national community.

The shots cut between closer and closer images of Celia and the crowd around her (with brief inserts of the band). The processing of these shots is at the same time a processing of our position as spectators: we both identify with Celia's personal tragedy and are inscribed as individuals like her into this vast mass of people which make up the audience, the community, the nation. All the key characters of the work-place community are blended into the mass as a whole in the *mise-en-scène* of the group. It is a moment of intense but restrained melodrama. But the pleasure of the sequence derives also from a voluptuous sense of national unity. Loss is miraculously transformed into plenitude, but it is an unconventional plenitude from the perspective of classical cinema, as a Mass Observation respondent suggested at the time: 'no attempt is made to give the film a conventional happy ending, which makes the film seem more realistic.'[183]

The nation which *Millions Like Us* constructs in its mode of address is never homogenous and coherent, however much it struggles to achieve a sense of unity. The film conjures up an image of community as a progressive, classless, co-operative social formation—but that community also takes on the form of the family, with its patriarchal structures of power and authority, reworking difference as mere variety. The film constructs an image of a post-war society which might be organized on the basis of community—and yet it privileges those characters whose aspirations for the future include the family in its present form—that is, characters who articulate no desire for change. There is a populist representation of 'the people', which seems progressive in that it does indeed depend on the narrative centrality of ordinary people, working people—but it is a respectable, lower-middle-class position which is finally privileged within this social formation of ordinary people, an emphasis which is only achieved at the expense of erasing the visibility of the state and the ruling classes.

A CONSERVATIVE POPULIST VISION OF THE NATION: *THIS HAPPY BREED*, PART I

This Happy Breed is another self-consciously nationalist piece of cinema, another melodrama of everyday life and ordinary people. Like *Millions*

[183] Quoted in Richards and Sheridan (eds.), *Mass Observation*, 278.

Like Us, it speaks to the nation, about the nation. A David Lean–Noël Coward collaboration adapted from Coward's play of the same name, it tells the story of the Gibbonses, a lower-middle-class family who live in the suburbs of London. Again, there are several narrative threads dealing with the various trials and tribulations, romances, and arguments attaching to each member of the family over the twenty-year period between the two world wars, as the children grow up, marry, and leave home. These private narratives are placed in the broader public context of a popular history of the nation over this same period, presented in montage sequences inserted into the gaps between the episodes in the private drama: 'On this simple basis is built a Coward pictorial history of England's ordinary folk be-tween the wars—historically superficial, but sometimes touching deep emotion and handling simple sentiment with the deftness of which Coward is a supreme master.'[184]

The film was a major box-office success and received as warm a recep-tion from most of the critics of the period as had *Millions Like Us*.[185] This 'British film of remarkable quality' was taken up as yet further evidence of the growing strength of the national cinema.[186] Even parts of the American trade press saw it as 'a tribute . . . to the new excellence of endeavour which inspires Britain's picture makers.'[187] One reviewer, William Whitebait, linked the film directly to *Millions Like Us*:

The number of good films about English life has been mounting up; *Millions Like Us, The Demi-Paradise*, quite recently, have explored the unexplorable; and with *This Happy Breed* we shall no longer be able to keep up any pretence of not knowing ourselves. It would be hard to overpraise the skill, the feeling, and the enhanced fidelity of this film.[188]

---

[184] *Monthly Film Bulletin*, 11/125 (1944), 54. The film is in many ways a sequel to *Cavalcade* (1933), the Hollywood adaptation of another Coward play, which offers a similarly popular social history of Britain between 1899 and 1932, presented in a very similar format.

[185] The film was designated best British entry of 1944 in *Kine Weekly*'s annual box-office review (11 Jan. 1945, 44–5); see also refs. to its popularity by several critics: Lejeune, *Observer*, 27 Aug. 1944; Whitebait, *New Statesman*, 21 Oct. 1944; and Manvell, 'British Feature Film'.

[186] Winnington, *News Chronicle*, 27 May 1944.

[187] *Motion Picture Herald*, 27 May 1944, 1910. But cf. the *Variety* review (7 June 1944, repr. in *Variety's Film Reviews, 1943–1948*, no p. nos.), which complained about the 'dingy . . . drab . . . ugliness' of the settings and the 'leisurely tempo': 'the film needs drastic cutting.' Such criticisms of the lack of Hollywood-style spectacle and fast-moving narrative recall the American criticisms of *Comin' Thro' The Rye* and make a telling contrast to all those comments that this was British cinema at its best, and a realistic representation of its subject-matter.

[188] *New Statesman*, 27 May 1944. Whitebait's enthusiasm for the film is indicated by the fact that he devoted another column to it after a second visit some five months later (*New Statesman*, 21 Oct. 1944).

'Knowing ourselves': this is typical of the way the film was taken up as a realistic impression of the ordinary life of the nation, with numerous of the middle-class critics of the quality daily and weekly press somewhat condescendingly celebrating the fact that 'this film about the suburbs has gone out into the suburbs, and the suburbs have taken it to their hearts.'[189] What evidence there is of contemporary (middle-class) audience reception tends to confirm this view: 'I liked it because it was about ordinary people very much like ourselves,' proffered one Hampstead schoolgirl.[190]

The trade press had kept up a steady commentary about the film while it was in production, repeatedly stressing the efforts made to create a realistic impression of contemporary English life,[191] and in the subsequent reviews, critics duly noted the documentary influence: 'Mr Coward and his colleagues have excelled in the exact observation of ordinary speech and behaviour,' suggested Lejeune.[192] But the key to *This Happy Breed*'s critical success was the way in which it was felt to have superseded the perceived coldness of the documentary idea: '[it] is not just a photographic and microphonic record of suburban life. If it were, nobody would care to see it. Art does not consist in repeating accurately what can be seen and heard around us,' claimed Lejeune, while Whitebait argued that 'Not only is *This Happy Breed* true to life, to emotions as well as exteriors, but here [in the opening shot of the film] is the camera magic woefully lacking from so many documentary-inspired stories.'[193]

It was these moments of magic, these 'instants of poetry' which distinguished the film from the mere document: 'A Mass Observation report on "Sycamore Road, Clapham" would no doubt provide us with the same detail, exhibited under glass; Mr Coward sees it very much alive.'[194] The film is superior not only to documentary but also to the standards of the Hollywood film:

In point of photography and direction and acting few recent films from America . . . have approached it. This technical confidence, accompanied by a native

---

[189] Lejeune, *Observer*, 27 Aug. 1944.

[190] One of the respondents to the audience survey conducted by Mayer, *Sociology of Film*, 71; see further comments on 72, 91–3, 97–8, 101–2, 122; *This Happy Breed* was 'the most quoted film in our essays and interviews, always liked for its "realism"' (105). The film is again frequently mentioned in a subsequent study by Mayer, *British Cinemas*, but there were just as many approving citations for the critically despised *Madonna of the Seven Moons*.

[191] See e.g. *Kine Weekly*, 15 Apr. 1943, 35; 6 May 1943, 26; and 15 July 1943, 19.

[192] *Observer*, 27 Aug. 1944; cf. similar comments in American reviews, e.g. *Motion Picture Herald*, 27 May 1944, 1909–10, and *Variety*, 16 Apr. 1947, repr. in *Variety's Film Reviews*, 1943–1947, no p. nos. On the other hand, the British fan magazine, *Picturegoer*, more downmarket than the likes of Lejeune, thought the picture 'all very completely Noël Coward . . . It's a matter of opinion as to whether you can wholly believe in their particular environment or not' (5 Aug. 1944, 12).

[193] *Observer*, 27 Aug. 1944; *New Statesman*, 21 Oct. 1944.

[194] *New Statesman*, 21 Oct. 1944, and Whitebait, *New Statesman*, 27 May 1944.

warm honesty and an increasing sureness in the defining of atmosphere, marks the progressiveness of the British cinema as opposed to the backward trend of Holly-wood, gripped in a deadly paralysis of self-imitation.[195]

This was a national cinema, but it was also a serious, responsible, and intelligent cinema. The marks of this cinema, despite the derisory criticisms of the documentary idea, were its restraint, its sense of reserve—once more elevated to a national characteristic during the war period, and here being used to praise the acting, the emotional quality of the film, and even its use of colour—'so discreet that one almost loses sight of it':[196]

The flavour of *This Happy Breed*, with its accumulation of clichés and small touches, is as subdued as the admirable Technicolor . . . Miss Celia Johnson's per-formance is a miracle of unstressed vitality and charm that makes one wonder how English audiences can ever have wept over a pasteboard Miniver.[197]

The distinction which Whitebait makes here between the Hollywood melodrama of *Mrs Miniver* (1942) and the down-to-earth qualities of *This Happy Breed* can be seen as an attempt to mobilize a true sense of national identity, over against Hollywood's vision of Englishness. The effort is there too in another of Whitebait's revealing comments—note the effortless slip-page from British to English: 'with *This Happy Breed* and *Millions Like Us* and *The Way Ahead*, British films after the war should have their chance of becoming what we should all like them to be—English.'[198] *This Happy Breed*'s Englishness is however much less ambiguous in its con-servatism than *Millions Like Us*, suggesting a domestication and contain-ment of the documentary idea as it is embodied in the latter—a fact which is signalled most obviously in the use of colour film rather than black and white.[199]

The film is still very much concerned with the state of the nation and the national character, exploring family life as a metaphor for the national life: 'the Gibbonses are a large family: they are found all over the British Isles . . . the special quality of [this film is that it] finds in a house in a row the symbol of a nation'.[200] As this comment implies, the representation of

---

[195] Winnington, *News Chronicle*, 27 May 1944; cf. Manvell, 'British Feature Film', 94.
[196] Whitebait, *New Statesman*, 27 May 1944; cf. Winnington, *News Chronicle*, 27 May 1944, and *Kine Weekly*, 13 Jan. 1944, 173.
[197] Whitebait, *New Statesman*, 21 Oct. 1944; *Motion Picture Herald* also compares the film to *Mrs Miniver*, 27 May 1944, 1909.
[198] *New Statesman*, 21 Oct. 1944.
[199] It is the same conservatism which pervades those two other 'well-remembered' Coward–Lean collaborations of the 1940s, *In Which We Serve* (1942) and *Brief Encounter* (1945).
[200] Lejeune, *Observer*, 27 Aug. 1944. Cf. the trade paper *Today's Cinema*'s description of the Gibbonses as a 'typical British suburban family', adding that 'in the whimsical philosophies of old man Gibbons, the sturdy courage of his wife and the superficial bickerings of the family, we sense something of those qualities characteristic of the

the nation in *This Happy Breed* should again be seen in terms of urban pastoral: the imagined community of the nation is an extended family, organic, self-sufficient, knowable unto itself—even in the context of a massively urbanized and heavily populated environment. The film seeks to establish this image by focusing primarily on the relationships which exist between the members of one family (and one set of neighbours); but it also tries to make the metaphorical relationship between individual family and the nation as a whole as solid and as visible as possible by developing the history of the family alongside a history of the recent national past.

The shots which open and close the film are also crucial in establishing in as fluid and seamless a way as possible the relationship between the family, the knowable community, and the nation. The first shot of the film is a high-angle panoramic shot of London; the camera pans across this landscape, moves down towards a particular, immaculately ordered neighbourhood, then one street within this neighbourhood, and eventually the house in which the action is set. The camera continues to move in through the window of the house, down the stairs, to the front door, which the Gibbons family are just entering for the first time.[201] The final scene of the film shows, from inside the house, the Gibbons now leaving the house for the last time, and shutting the door behind them; virtually the same movements with which the film had opened are now repeated in reverse as the camera leaves the particular detail and places it once more within the general view of the city.

Another feature which the film shares with *Millions Like Us* is speculation as to the form the nation should take after the war. *This Happy Breed* comes down very firmly on the side of stability, or at the very least, gradual evolution, but it certainly does not suggest the radical social change which Charlie Forbes stands for in *Millions Like Us*. There is a major narrative difference from the latter film which is significant here: *This Happy Breed* situates itself outside the war, in the inter-war years of peace, partly in order to be able to foreground the family so conclusively, but also to be able to place a complete family at the centre of the narrative. The narrative place of *This Happy Breed* is resolutely the home, and its

nation in general' (28 Apr. 1944, 44); also *Kine Weekly*: 'an average English family' who 'live in an ordinary little house, but it is the sort of house that is one of the bulwarks of England' (13 Jan. 1944, 173); *Manchester Guardian*: 'an essential "photo" for John Bull's family album' (27 May 1944); and the American magazine *Time*: 'Coward's proud and loving tribute to the unbreakable British backbone' (7 July, 1947).

[201] It is not actually one shot, of course, but the impression that it is only serves to underline the ideological implications of the scene. Compare the opening shots of *Sing As We Go*, and another melodrama of everyday life, *The Bells Go Down* (1943); see also my discussion of the use of high-angle panoramic shots of the city in British new wave films of the late 1950s and early 1960s, in Higson, 'Space, Place, Spectacle'.

STILL 40. Making houses into homes: the Clthman awaiting outside for the front in The Uninvited...

protagonists are, in the end, all members of one extended family, which enables the film to establish the family as the stable and secure cornerstone of the nation in peace-time.

This Happy Breed thus loses the potentially progressive sense of community found in *Millions Like Us* by placing the family and the home firmly at the centre of the narrative. The tendency was there in *Millions Like Us*, but *This Happy Breed* follows it through to its logical conclusion. Thus the film returns again and again to scenes of the family gathered together for moments of celebration—a wedding, Christmas, or just a pot of tea. The family and the home exist as a secure, stable, virtually unchanging sanctuary from the hectic and threatening outside world. This narrative focus on the family and the home also reaffirms woman's place as firmly within the domestic sphere, her role being to transform house into home. The figure of the mother—and there are few more ideal mothers than Ethel Gibbons—is thus placed once again right at the heart of the nation-as-family.[202] All the hesitations and equivocations of *Millions Like Us* around this issue are lost, as is the potentially quite radical story of the 'mobile women', involved in traditionally masculine occupations away from the home. While there may be an overriding sense of this work being only for the duration of the war in *Millions Like Us*, *This Happy Breed* explicitly shows women in their place, in the home, and never releases them from it. The film is, in this way, able to acknowledge the strength of women in processing the domestic sphere and maintaining the home—and thereby the nation—but in the film's terms, the discourse of women is constructed as both trivial and comic; the invitation is to laugh at, rather than to laugh with the women and their domestic quarrels. The image of the mother is thus no more than symbolic for the nation as a whole; outside the domestic space, within the public sphere, she has no real power.

Where *Millions Like Us* quite self-consciously plays on progressive forces within the conjuncture, *This Happy Breed* tends to close down those very issues. Both films confront historically specific ideological and political problems of national life, and both work to forge some sort of unity of the popular forces of the moment. While neither film attempts to be class-specific, they both aim to construct a popular consensus outside class distinctions, above class antagonisms. But, if *Millions Like Us* directly questions the stability of that consensus in Charlie and Jennifer's hilltop discussion about the future, *This Happy Breed* posits it as the natural and essential product of the national character; it seeks to articulate national character as the backbone of England–Britain, as a timeless quality forged in the past.

This Happy Breed is thus decidedly nostalgic for the settlement, the

---

[202] See Gledhill and Swanson, 'Gender and Sexuality', 61.

STILL 31. Homely England: the private sphere as a female space (*This Happy Breed*). Aunt Sylvia (Alison Leggatt) butters the cat's paws while Gran (Amy Veness) pours a cup of tea.

STILL 32. Homely England: Ethel Gibbons (Celia Johnson), her daughters Queenie (Kay Walsh) and Vi (Eileen Erskine), and more tea (*This Happy Breed*).

security, and the stability which it finds in its representations of inter-war domestic arrangements and family life; it may propose that this should be the social basis for the post-war world, but it also seems to suggest that such a society belongs only to fond memory. The film is invested with a powerful sense of loss throughout its course, but particularly in the closing moments. This is achieved narratively, in the gradual dispersal of the family via marriages, deaths, and the final move to a new flat, the relentless emptying of the home that has been so carefully and lovingly established. It is there too in the constant knowledge that this film, which so carefully sets itself up as taking place in the aftermath of the war to end all wars, is actually being watched while a new war is being waged. This sense of loss in relation to the plenitude of the family in peace-time is finally brought home as the narrative moves towards a close just as this new war opens. It is achieved too in the camerawork, in its preference for the distance of the medium shot and the group shot, rather than the proximity of the close-up, and in the way that, on a number of occasions at the end of a sequence, the camera pulls back to an extreme long shot, as if the image, and the time that it documents, were fading from memory.

This Happy Breed has a similar narrative form to *Millions Like Us*. Once again, there are several interweaving plots, and many of its scenes are markedly inconsequential—as an American critic put it, 'it hardly has any story; there is much talk and the directors have taken great pains in centring their attention on characterisations.'[203] In many ways, this film provides the model for the British low-life television soap opera, and as in soap opera a lot of the narrative work is carried in talk, with much cutting between interlocutors to provide visual interest. Most of this talk is deliberately mundane, deliberately trivial—that is, it is not narratively developed. But this insignificance is of course precisely its significance: it foregrounds the everyday, the detail of national life, over against the extraordinary fantasies of Hollywood, while the understatement, the non-narrativization, the redundance of the detail create a profoundly realistic effect.[204] The film remains very restrained for the most part, with the most dramatic and eventful incidents taking place off-screen, providing the motivation for yet more talk. In one particularly poignant example of this narrational strategy, the camera stays on a long shot of an empty room in which incongruously joyful music plays on a radio, while Vi tells her parents off-screen that their son and daughter-in-law have been killed in

---

[203] *Motion Picture Herald*, 19 Apr. 1947, 3586. Cf. *Time*: 'the real meat of *This Happy Breed* is in the many plotless little human studies' (7 July 1947); and *The New York Times*: 'Although it flows evenly and temperately with no exciting or spectacular ups and downs, it has a quiet charm and gentle penetration of human nature which should give it wide appeal. The story is mild and episodic . . .' (14 Apr. 1947, 24).

[204] See Barthes, 'Realistic Effect'.

a car crash (an event which has itself of course not been seen in the film); in other words, the tragedy of the moment is conveyed by the self-consciously empty room. Other dramatic or spectacular incidents are taken up in the montage sequences of public life which constitute almost a separate diegesis to that of the family and its home.

Formally, *This Happy Breed* shares some characteristics with *Listen To Britain*, since there is no central disruptive force which sets the narrative of the film in motion; rather, as in the case of the Jennings and McAllister film, and to a lesser extent *Millions Like Us*, it is organized around the 'day in the life of' format—although in this case it is twenty years in the life of a family. There is no real narrative enigma to be solved in the film—the family is already intact, in place, at the start of the film—and instead, there is a multiple series of almost self-contained episodes or dramas to be completed. In so far as there is any narrative enigma at all, it is situated outside the film, in terms of the course of the on-going war—we cannot determine the real ending of the film until we know the outcome of the war.

Although there is a certain linearity to the text, it is also noticeably episodic, circular, and repetitive, which can imply not so much the development of a narrative across time, as a sense of timelessness and a refusal to move forward, once more invoking a nostalgic relation to the drama. Repetition is there, for instance, in the ceaseless reworking of numerous similar 'trivial' domestic situations and personal relationships, without any of these being developed into a substantial narrative trajectory. The circularity—another form of repetition, of course—is particularly evident in the reverse rhyming of the ending with the beginning, discussed above. Movement is the natural flow of time, and closure is thus the poetic closure of turning full circle, the end of an era, time running out, rather than the resolution of disrupted forces, the fulfilment of a wish, or the achievement of a goal.

This suggests that it is not so much a strong, causally motivated narrative linearity which organizes the work of the film, but once again the diegetic space of the family and the home (and the nation, at least metaphorically) which binds together the various disparate dramas of the film. If there is a sense of time passing in the narrative of the family, it is achieved above all only by the device of the montage sequences; but running against this experience of temporality is the opposite experience of timelessness, of lack of development, of time standing still. The synchronic placing and relating of events and people within the family is then explored diachronically in the context of historical progress. The latter is a narrative of the nation—but it too is marked by a lack of causality, given the way in which the montage sequences are built up out of a series of discrete moments from the recent national past. The procedure is akin to that of *Comin' Thro' The Rye*: a sort of sampling of heritage space, a rummage through the diegesis of national history.

Millions Like Us may be repetitive too, and it may be marked by a sense of loss at times. But it rarely looks back further than 1939, while its ending, and several aspects of the main body of the text, are also decidedly optimistic and forward-looking. *This Happy Breed*, on the other hand, does not really seem to know how to imagine post-war society at all. It has no profound vision of the future, it can only return nostalgically to the beginning of the cycle, as if it wants time to stand still, as if to imply that things should continue as they were before, while at the same time recognizing that this cannot be. Whitebait, for instance, felt that

we sense an end to things when the house finally empties. The family life of the Gibbonses, we may feel, with its loyalties and ailments, its jokes and idols, will never return; and as likely as not Sycamore Road, Clapham, copped it in the Blitz. The film isn't tragic, however, because the English are not a tragic people.[205]

The observation is accurate: the film revels in nostalgia, not tragedy—and, as we have seen, nostalgia can be a vital component in the formation of national identity. There is really only one aspect of the film which looks beyond this nostalgia for an untroubled and mundane family life. It is interesting that this is also the one area in which the script allows for the development of a more substantial and causally moving narrative line which threatens to break out of the circularity of the text. This narrative focuses on the individual desires of one of the daughters of the family, Queenie, who finds the domesticated life of suburbia utterly unfulfilling, and runs off to France with a married man. This emphasis on the individual and her desires puts Queenie at odds with the responsibility of the family—just as, in *Millions Like Us*, individual desire was at odds with the needs of the community and the nation. In a conventional Hollywood melodrama, it would surely have been Queenie who was of most narrative interest; in *This Happy Breed*, however, her desires are always marked off as deviant and problematic. We are never in any doubt that the unity and stability of the home and the family are the real sources of wisdom, emotional truth, and moral strength, and it is inevitable that Queenie will eventually return to the fold, as she does, safely married to the boy next door. The figure of Queenie potentially offers a profound critique of everything that the film stands for, in her desire for something more than the familiarity of everyday life, the burden of domestic labour, and the claustrophobic repressions of the family. But in the end her difference is contained and defused.

This Happy Breed is resolutely on the side of the social, albeit a social

[205] *New Statesman*, 27 May 1944.

formation which is understood in terms of a highly self-contained and heavily demarcated private family life. The diegetic space of the film is relatively wide, inhabited by several significant characters forming a network of social relations, rather than dominated by an individual hero-protagonist. Queenie's story can thus never be developed to its full melodramatic potential, since it is constantly displaced by another line of narrative interest.

The most telling critique of the film comes, significantly, from the documentarist Edgar Anstey:

> It is a brilliant and a bewildering piece of work. It can report on the contents of the cupboard under the stairs at 17, Sycamore Road, Clapham—the gas-meter, the soda-syphon and the ironing board—with documentary meticulousness and a warm intimacy; it can supply us with dialogue really appropriate to the four-handed folding of sheets in the back-garden or to the drying of summer crockery, and yet, for all its shrewd observation of detail, it apparently can see no sense or meaning in the whole phenomenon.[206]

Although Anstey's desire for sense and meaning may in part reveal a conventional patriarchal dissatisfaction with and lack of interest in the domestic,[207] as well as a desire for a rational rather than an emotional account, it does seem valid to suggest that the film can offer nothing more than a rather camp fascination with the details of the lives of the lower classes. Another critic, Dilys Powell, argued that:

> the suburban family in their suburban house are presented with warmth and sympathy; but is the sympathy too resolute? Should not the observation be a trifle less benevolent, the defence of the ordinary man a trifle less condescending. . . . I find in *This Happy Breed* a tendency . . . to stand well away and, however admiringly, point; Coward is here not so much the artist as the patron.[208]

The film is very much defined by this detached bourgeois point of view which, in this sense at least, places it very firmly within the documentary-realist tradition. *This Happy Breed* simply renews the pastoral concern to dignify the common people—and once again does so from a perspective which is fascinated by the exotic trivia of this other class, whom it can patronize, and with whom it can sympathize because they too are human, but who in the end must remain at a distance.

It is perhaps for this reason that '*This Happy Breed* adduces no evidence

---

[206] *Spectator*, 2 June 1944.

[207] He also thought the film 'lacking in virility' (ibid.).

[208] *Sunday Times*, undated review of *This Happy Breed*, on BFI Library microfiche. See also Powell, 'Films since 1939', 88: 'the approach is . . . detached; look, the film seems to be saying, look at these unassuming people, see of what heroic metal they are framed! There is even a touch of patronage now and then; Coward is here not speaking with his characters, but about them.' Cf. Coward's defence of the play from similar criticisms, in *Play Parade*, iv (London, 1954), quoted in Raymond Mendler and Joe Mitchenson, *Theatrical Companion to Coward* (London, 1957), 265–6.

of better times to come', as Anstey goes on to point out.[209] The nostalgia is precisely for the apparent stability of class difference and deference, so that the film cannot possibly entertain any more democratic settlement. It seeks to reaffirm the pre-war social place of ordinary people, and to identify the public sphere of politics as separate from, but a frustrating impingement on, the private domestic sphere of the family and the home. It does remain a populist film, and the Gibbons family define themselves as ordinary people, just as the iconography of the film conventionally marks the diegetic world of their home as ordinary rather than glamorous or exotic, but it is a much more conservative populism than that of *Millions Like Us*, lacking its (tentative) optimism and its (ambivalent) exploration of alternative social formations.

THE PUBLIC SPHERE AS SPECTACLE: *THIS HAPPY BREED*, PART 2

The most conservative aspect of *This Happy Breed* is the way in which a public history of the recent national past is written into the private story of a family—in other words, the way in which the montage sequences are woven into the narrative web of the film. These sequences—the only occasions in the film on which we leave the Gibbons family home[210]—are made up of a series of discontinuous fragments of activity from the public arena, mostly depicting concrete manifestations of political power and political struggles: the Victory marches at the end of World War One, the British Empire Exhibition of 1924, the General Strike, a British fascist haranguing the crowds at Speakers Corner, crowds cheering Chamberlain on his return from Munich, and so on. There is also a series of newspaper headlines, radio announcements, and street hoardings giving information of important political moments—the end of the General Strike, news of the Nazi successes in the 1933 elections, news of the 1935 General Election in Britain, the death of one king and the abdication of another, a 'Get Your Gas Mask Now' poster, 'Peace in Our Time', and so on.

These sequences are marked off from the rest of the film, and from the everyday domestic life of the family, by the repeated use of not only a different system of editing and subject-matter, but also a different use of music. Thus, the montage sequences are accompanied by extra-diegetic music, and often lack dialogue, whereas in the private drama of the family,

---

[209] *Spectator*, 2 June 1944.
[210] There are in fact several occasions when we see the Gibbons family gathering outside the front of their house—but this is part of the home, for all intents and purposes. There is also one scene of Frank and Ethel Gibbons in Hyde Park which does not initially seem to be part of a montage sequence; however, the sequence does eventually take on the characteristics of other montage sequences.

dialogue is pervasive, and there is no extra-diegetic music. There is also a brief passage of harp music at the beginning and end of most of the sequences[211] which, by Hollywood conventions, would signal the entry of the fiction into a fantasy world, a dream, or a flashback, which is indeed the way in which we are invited to relate to this public, political arena. It is almost a fantasy world, quite separate from the private world of the family. One of the sequences shows the family and their neighbours in the crowds watching but not participating in the Victory celebrations, for instance; another shows them visiting the Empire Exhibition. Later, Vi (one of the daughters) talks of wanting to 'go and watch the crowds cheering' after Chamberlain's return from Munich; in other words, she wants not to participate in the political celebration but to look at it from the position of a spectator. The public sphere is thus reproduced as spectacle, something upon which the fascinated spectator can gaze from a distance.

The montage sequences of course serve to authenticate the 'people's history' of the Gibbons family, and to invoke the wider dimensions of public life and the national community of which they are just one small part. But the processing of the montage sequences within the fiction serves also to separate these ordinary people and their private lives from the public arena of Politics and History, to separate them from the public sphere, in which, it implies, they have no part.[212] The spectacle of the public sphere may provoke emotional crises in the home, but it has no real social or political impact on its inhabitants.

'The national and the international background', as one reviewer noted, 'is seen always from the point of view of this single home'.[213] Important though such a perspective may be, it does at the same time effectively block any recognition of the nature of class interests, or the role of ordinary people in the relations of power. By focusing so resolutely on the family and the home and by foregrounding domestic affairs, class power as an issue or a problem is obscured from view. In so far as power is explored at all, it is entirely in terms of personal relationships, in which, of course, patriarchy is taken for granted. The film thus reaffirms the ordinary person's deference to, if at times slight unease with, the traditional

---

[211] The harp music is not in fact used at the start of every such sequence, nor is non-diegetic music ever-present in all the montage sequences. There are also occasional brief shots accompanied by non-diegetic music which are neither strictly part of montage sequences, nor part of the family life; they serve to indicate a temporal ellipsis.

[212] Cf. John Keane's discussion of the nature of the bourgeois public sphere, or civic culture, as he calls it: 'The civic culture . . . comprises an eclectic mixture of meaningful beliefs in privacy, pre-modern deference, and the orientation to active political involvement. The "democratic citizen" is called on to pursue contradictory goals; he or she must be involved, yet not involved; active, yet passive; influential, but deferential' (*Public Life and Late Capitalism*, 103).

[213] Powell, undated review in *Sunday Times* (from microfiche in BFI Library).

STILL 33. Observing the public sphere: Reg Gibbons (Robert Newton), his wife Ethel, and his neighbour Bob Mitchell (Stanley Holloway) watch the Victory Parade at the end of the First World War (*This Happy Breed*).

forms of political and social power. It is this deference which Tom Nairn has argued is central to the dominant ideology of Englishness, the populist mythology which holds 'not a belief that the People can do anything, in the last resort, but the conviction that popular aspirations will always, in the end, be attended to up there.'[214]

At a time when the end of the Second World War was in sight, *This Happy Breed* uses an allegory about the aftermath of the First World War to address its audience as a people who have played their part in the public, international struggles during the extraordinary events of the war period. It suggests, however, that those same people must now return to their real concerns: the domestic, the everyday, the trivial. The film opens with a voice-over which states, documentary-style, that in 1918 'hundreds and hundreds of houses are becoming homes once more'. The implication is that now, with the Second World War moving towards a close, the urgent task once more facing the ordinary people is home-making, replacing the family at the heart of the peace-time society, and woman at the heart of the family.

Various members of the family do make occasional forays into the public arena, but this serves only to reinforce the effective separation of the public and the private. In the General Strike montage, Frank Gibbons is seen working as a blackleg, driving a bus; he justifies his participation by arguing that it is the precious stability of the nation which is under threat. As he says to his son, 'It's up to us ordinary people to keep things steady.' While this does show a member of the family participating in political struggle, it is significant that it is the male head of the household whom we see intervening; when this montage sequence of the strike dissolves back to the private sphere, a teapot is placed on an Evening News bulletin announcing the end of the strike, and the women are seen gossiping and doing the housework: Gran, speaking from the point of view of Victorian values, roundly condemns the strike, Sylvia goes to wash some socks, and Mum clears the table. The strike is over, and normal family life can resume. The scenes of the strike are far less dramatic than the row which ensues between the women at home.

Reg, Frank's son, and Sam, his communist-sympathizing friend, have meanwhile joined the strikers, but, in a number of ways, this involvement is marked as deviant within the film's dominant discourse. First, the views which we have of the strike are always from outside, from a distance—notably in a high-angle shot of a demonstration. The spectators in the cinema are thus never placed by the camera as participants in the strike, but always as observers of it. Secondly, in conversation, Reg and Sam's involvement in the strike is dismissed as mere youthful hotheadedness.

---

[214] *The Break-Up of Britain* (London, 1981), 296.

STILL 34. Observing the public sphere: the General Strike of 1926—with the camera situating the cinema audience as spectators of rather than participants in this public, historical event (*This Happy Breed*).

STILL 35. Queenie and her lover dance their exhibition Charleston (*This Happy Breed*).

Thirdly, there is a significant play on position and point of view when Frank Gibbons decides to have a talk about politics with his temporarily deviant son. In one shot, Dad explains with good common sense that problems arise from human nature, not from governments and systems; Reg is in the foreground, and Dad is only visible under his arm. Reg replies that human nature would change if everyone started with an equal chance, loses his temper, and sits down facing the camera, completely blocking out any view of his father; momentarily, his point of view, his position, wins the day. But then Dad continues, in very reasonable fashion; he stands up, so becoming once more visible, and the camera follows him as he moves away—it is his point of view which dominates. Finally, the two of them are resolved in shot together as authoritative father and once more deferential son. It is by devices such as these that difference is contained, and the deviant reduced—or elevated—to ordinariness.

In the next montage sequence (roughly 1927–1928–1929), we are shown the second daughter, Vi, at her wedding to Sam—in other words, the public manifestation of a private romance, and the institutional means of containing Sam's communist excesses, transforming him into an ordinary person. Later, Vi and Sam are shown visiting a cinema to see the latest 'all talking, all singing, all dancing sensation', *Broadway Melody* (1929)—which serves to confirm the place of the spectator in the cinema watching *This Happy Breed* as the same as that of the ordinary people of the fiction: primarily spectators of rather than participants in the public arena.

In between these two moments, we do, however, see the erring daughter, Queenie, precisely participating in this public arena and in consequence being transformed herself into a spectacle: she is shown doing an exhibition Charleston with her current lover, a married man, having won a dance competition. The audience at the dance-hall gaze at her, while the audience in the cinema are afforded the privilege of a soft-focus close-up as she takes pleasure in being the object of the gaze. It is this escape from the private claustrophobic insularity of the family into the exotic, glamorous—and now eroticized—public arena, this crossing of boundaries, which constitutes the extent of her transgression. But in the context of the rest of the film, this scene serves to label her pleasure as irresponsible, and to confirm the dangers of entering the public arena and thereby leaving the safety and security of the home.

The overriding emphasis of *This Happy Breed* is a resolute separation of discourse and history: the series of montage sequences constitute an apparently objective, real history, a meta-discourse which places and processes the mundane discourses of the ordinary people. The episodic narrative of the family consists mainly of gossip, reminiscence, uninformed and brief discussions of public events, family arguments, the occasional restrained love scene—in each case, within the film's terms, inconsequential trivia, mere discourse, in relation to the important and real events of the history over which they have no control.

There are of course occasions when explicitly political views are voiced within the confines of the domestic space, but the most outspoken of these occasions serves once again to underline the improbability of the public sphere having any real bearing on the private dramas of the family. The setting is Christmas 1925, and Sam, a communist at the time, is addressing the rest of the young people. It is a set-piece speech, both within the world of the fiction, in that he is standing up and speaking in knowingly formal terms, and in terms of how the scene is constructed filmically. It is also a potentially powerful speech, noting in no uncertain terms the nature and extent of class difference in contemporary society. But this power is undermined in various ways. First, he is constantly interrupted by 'trivial' and uninformed comments from the women present, the gist of which is that politics are irrelevant to the everyday. But secondly, his speech seems particularly melodramatic within a text which favours restraint; in its performance, it is too evidently a speech, it is obtrusive, rather than knitted into the discourse of the film, such that the ordinariness of the women seems much more the position of audience empathy. They are down-to-earth where he is over the top. It is thus the (deliberate) obviousness of the performance which separates it from the rest of the film as deviant.

This Happy Breed's narrative of national history situates it at the meeting-point of the heritage film and the documentary idea, where the latter is understood as a means of detailing an alternative heritage of the common people—'such people with their gaiety and fortitude, are indeed the "happy breed" of Shakespeare's sceptred isle.'[215] Although the public events of national significance in *This Happy Breed* are presented as contemporaneous with the everyday experiences of the Gibbons family, they are represented as history to the spectators of the film. The particular form of this (re)presentation plays out precisely the terms of the heritage impulse as explored in Chapter 3. In one of the works drawn on there, Michael Bommes and Patrick Wright argue that 'National Heritage appears to involve nothing less than the abolition of all contradiction in the name of a national culture: the installation of a spectacular display in which "the past" enters everyday life.'[216]

The refusal to explore the class position or the gender relations of the ordinary people at the centre of *This Happy Breed* is precisely this abolition of contradiction; at the same time, the difference between the quiet domesticated home and the lavish parade of public history for the cinema spectator serves to install 'the past' as a spectacular display within the everyday:

[215] *Today's Cinema*, 28 Apr. 1944, 34.   [216] 'Charms of Residence', 264.

At the ideological level, 'heritage' involves the extraction of history—of the idea of historical significance, process and potential—from everyday life and its re-staging and display in particular coded sites, images and events. . . . In order to become spectacular, something which one can stand outside and then re-connect with in regular acts of appreciation—history must be completed and fully accomplished. As a process which is fully accomplished, history, with all its promise of future change and development, is closed down and confined entirely to what can be exhibited as the 'historic past'.[217]

This is exactly the procedure which *This Happy Breed* adopts in order to impose a pre-war vision of the nation, its people, and its political formation, on the prospective post-war period. The public sphere has been absorbed into the popular culture of the ordinary people as another form of cinematic spectacle. But rather than this being the democratization of cinema, of public life, and of everyday life, it is instead the transformation of democracy into an image-commodity. The spectators of the film, far from being absorbed through it into the public sphere as participants, are offered a place precisely as spectators both of the national past and of contemporary politics. As *Today's Cinema* put it, 'here, then, is memory-stirring spectacle and drama, all subtly introduced as backgrounds to the compelling domestic theme.'[218] History as *aide-mémoire*, familiar and comforting, helps us to place the narrative of the family, but it is rarely of narrative significance in itself; rather, the national past, national identity even, exists as an exotic, compelling, fascinating spectacle.

CONCLUSIONS

Millions Like Us and *This Happy Breed* are key texts in the formation of a relatively distinctive British film genre, the melodrama of everyday life. Although I have stressed the differences between the two films, there are clearly enough shared characteristics, not only in these films but in others of the period too, for the term genre to be applied with confidence. The genre is formed out of diverse cultural traditions, but in particular, the incorporation of certain features of the documentary idea into the conventions of the domestic melodrama to produce a brand of fiction film which purports to deal realistically with life in contemporary Britain. The particular articulation of the public and the private in these films makes it possible for them to construct a very powerful image of the nation as a secure and self-sufficient community. In the context of the political debates of the period and the push towards democratic social reforms in the post-war period, *Millions Like Us* comes across in the end as ambivalent.

---

[217] Ibid. 289–91.   [218] 28 Apr. 1944, 34.

Questions of class and gender are certainly raised in the course of the film in an often quite challenging way, but they are always circumscribed by more conservative forces within the culture. In *This Happy Breed*, these more conservative forces have themselves become the dominant character-istics of the text. Where *Millions Like Us* tries to hold together the public and the private, the broad scope of history and the detail of discourse, *This Happy Breed* tends to separate them, and consequently to separate ordin-ary people from the public sphere. *Millions Like Us* can, on the contrary, show ordinary people doing their bit for the nation, it can leave the do-mestic sphere, and show the world of work, and it can articulate a more profound sense of community, one which is much greater, and more in-clusive, than the extended *petit bourgeois* family of *This Happy Breed*.

This Happy Breed's conservatism derives in part from the way in which it also draws on certain tendencies in the heritage genre as well as the documentary idea. There may be a potential democratization of those tendencies in the effort to stage the heritage of the common people, but this is undermined by the film's conservative nostalgia, its suggestion that nationhood, Englishness, is a timeless and invariant category. *Millions Like Us* also draws on the traditions of urban pastoral, but it does so more ambivalently, suggesting that a different social formation is at least possi-ble within that tradition, even if it cannot make a conclusive statement about that formation in the end.

The genre which these two films represent has a central place in ortho-dox historical accounts of British cinema: the critical discourses which have dominated intellectual film culture in Britain since the 1920s have preferred and promoted this genre of films above all other British films. It is in many ways perverse to describe these films in generic terms, for what has been celebrated in them has been their distinctiveness, their unique-ness, their difference from mere formulaic popular cinema. Certainly, there are particular characteristics of the films which are regularly noted in reviews and histories, but this is rarely done in order to establish them as genre films. In fact, these noteworthy characteristics are seen not so much as the recurring icons or themes of a filmic tradition, but first as indisput-able signs of Englishness, as markers of national identity, and secondly as necessary signs of quality. This quality is always more than national, and comes to assume a universal status: this is what constitutes good art.

If these films are discussed collectively, that discussion tends to be in terms of movements and auteurs, rather than in terms of genres. Move-ments thus come to occupy the high ground of national cinema, unlike genres which are merely variations on the debased culture of popular cinema. Yet it would be very fruitful to discuss these films in terms of genre, and to look at the transformations in that genre as it comes to terms with changing historical circumstances. I do not have the space to do this in any detail, but I do want to indicate what such a history would look like.

One aspect of such films which is rarely discussed in the more conventional histories is the proximity of these films to popular melodrama, and in particular to the woman's film. The woman's film is associated above all with the feminine. It is addressed primarily to female spectators; it operates in the space of the home, the family, personal relationships, and romances; it foregrounds emotions over either rational thought or aggressive action; it often seeks to articulate a female point of view, and to explore the vicissitudes of female desire and fantasy.[219] All this would seem to fit ill with the more self-consciously masculine realm of documentary and its world of work, of dignified manual labour, placed within a rational framework.[220] Yet it is the traditions of the woman's picture and the documentary on which the genre draws most heavily—and all of the above features can be found in both *Millions Like Us* and *This Happy Breed*. Indeed, the trade press specifically noted that the former film at least had 'terrific feminine appeal'.[221]

How does the contemporary critical discourse respond to these features? There are three points worth noting here. First, the home is not remarked upon as a feminine space, but as a national metaphor. The response to *This Happy Breed* in particular is to read the Gibbons family home as a bulwark of the nation; implicit here is the symbolic figure of the mother— that is, an ideal version of the feminine—as the centre-point of the family– community–nation, but this symbolism is rarely dwelt upon in the critical discourse. Secondly, if a female point of view is articulated, it is admired not because of its femininity, but because of its humanity, in an abstract, generalized, universal sense; the point of view is significant for its sincerity, its emotional truthfulness, its mature balancing of desire and responsibility. This leads on to the third point: it is not emotionality or romance as such which is admired in these films, but the restraint with which it is handled.

It is perhaps this last fact above all else which enables the critical discourse to avoid the issue of popular melodrama in these films. They may occupy the thematic territory of the woman's film, but these films tend to underplay melodramatic effect. The potentially excessive characteristics of

---

[219] See Christine Gledhill (ed.), *Home Is Where The Heart Is: Studies in Melodrama and the Woman's Film* (London, 1987); and Mary Ann Doane, *The Desire to Desire: The Woman's Film of the 1940s* (London, 1987). On the woman's film and British cinema of the 1940s, see Aspinall, 'Women, Realism and Reality'; Pam Cook, 'Melodrama and the Woman's Picture', in Aspinall and Murphy (eds.), *Gainsborough Melodrama*; Lant, *Blackout*; and Marcia Landy, *British Genres: Cinema and Society, 1930–1960* (Princeton, NJ, 1991).

[220] See Colls and Dodd, 'Representing the Nation'.

[221] *Kine Weekly*, 30 Sept. 1943, 16.

melodrama, its overblown qualities, the passionate intensity, even hysteria, with which it deals with the subjective, are constantly offset by the details of realism. It is films like *Madonna of the Seven Moons* which are melodramatic in these terms, not *Millions Like Us*, or *This Happy Breed*, which seek always to authenticate their fictions and to understate—or even parody—the pleasures of fantasy. *Mise-en-scène*, camerawork, performance, and use of music are all tastefully restrained. What is excessive about these films is the emphasis on the social, not the exploration of the subjective. The potential melodramatic intensity of any particular drama is constantly displaced by shifting focus to another drama. Individuals are present in these dramas as representatives of the social, and their capacity to resist social responsibility by pursuing an individual wish is explored less than their capacity to play an allotted part within a consensual social formation. Indeed, the most melodramatic moment in *Millions Like Us* is probably the ending, which is a celebration of the pleasures of community, not a moment of individual romantic fulfilment. The social constantly exceeds the boundaries of any particular narrative line. Melodrama is there, but it is the melodrama of consent, not the melodrama of wish-fulfilment.

The consolidation of this genre of British cinema in the mid-1940s was due in no small part to the peculiar ideological conditions of the Second World War. These circumstances enabled a remarkable convergence of the modes of melodrama and documentary. Paradoxically, they also laid the foundations for the consequent marginalization of British documentary proper. Post-war documentary film-making is overwhelmingly involved in the refinement of the public gaze in the form of the instructional and scientific documentary, and tends to lose the contact it briefly had with certain sections of the mainstream cinema.[222]

By about 1946, the melodrama of everyday life seems to have completely absorbed the documentary idea and to have incorporated it into its own project, appropriating what it needed for its own ends and discarding the rest. The story-documentary form, for instance, had been almost entirely fused with the narrative film-making of Ealing Studios and others in the mid- and late 1940s. Documentary devices and strategies were by now so completely and seamlessly absorbed by and integrated into the dramatic conventions of the narrative that they were no longer visible as such. In other words, by this time, the narrative feature film had regained its pre-war position centre-stage within the film culture, establishing the norm: this is once more what cinema is about, it is cinema.

Documentary film-making as such still had a place—but it seemed much more confined to that place, with little impact on cinema and film culture as a whole. The boundaries between documentary and narrative feature

---

[222] See e.g. the debates in the later issues of *Documentary News Letter*.

films seemed much more clearly marked. There was no longer such a sense of each practice borrowing from the other. Certain documentary films still gained a fairly high film cultural profile, but by 1946 documentary was being discussed much more in terms of a truly public cinema, addressing and engaging in the public sphere in ways quite distinct from the commercial film industry. The discourse about documentary was then firmly about its function as a public information system, reaching a mass public audience through distribution networks established by the state during the war. The energies of documentary film-makers were directed towards two key involvements in the public sphere during the period of post-war reconstruction: first, the attempt to consolidate public subsidies for educational film production and distribution; and secondly, involvement in the international arena, through UNESCO, attempting to use documentary films to promote the cause of international understanding, peace, communication, and democracy. As such documentary had been wrested a long way from debates about the art of cinema to become an official public information service.

The most visible and most critically acclaimed aspect of documentary-realist film-making in the period between the end of the war and the mid-1960s was therefore narrative feature film-making, in the form of the melodrama of everyday life. There was still a tradition of attempting to explore contemporary social problems, using the moral perspective developed by the documentary movement of the 1930s, tempered by the humanism of the most influential film critics of the 1940s. It was the latter, however, which tended to mark the new direction of quality cinema. The dominant critical discourse within the intellectual film culture of the immediate post-war period can be summarized as follows.[223]

The ideal narrative form was felt to be a strong, solid, economic, and energetic narrative, with the emphasis on narrative continuity and clear motivation, rather than a montage of stories, or episodic development. The image was important: cinema was above all a visual story-telling medium, and the best cinema adopted a rhythmic visual narration—but never to the extent of indulging in gratuitous spectacle, exceeding the narrative requirements. Thus most of the contemporary critics found the crafted and atmospheric visuals of *Great Expectations* (1946) a perfect embodiment of what cinema was capable of in this department. Well-developed characters with a strong personality were considered more important than stars, who were no more than displays of types. Characters must be integral narrative

---

[223] This summary is based on a reading of all the British film periodicals held at the BFI Library for 1945–1947, including *Film Forum, Contemporary Cinema, Sight and Sound, Monthly Film Bulletin, Film, Film Quarterly, Penguin Film Review*, etc.; also reviews on microfiche for individual films, notably *Great Expectations* and *The Captive Heart*; see also Ellis, 'Art, Culture, Quality'.

elements, and marked by emotional integrity and sincerity. Thus *Great Expectations* was praised for its 'solid, credible and richly detailed people you know and care about'.[224] Narrative situations should be clearly dramatized and staged, and developed in terms of point-of-view structures, rather than montage or the public gaze of documentary, and diegetic dialogue should be favoured over extra-diegetic commentary—where a voice-over is used, it should be subjectified; the voice of authority should be privatized.

Great Expectations is an interesting example in this case, since it was directed by David Lean, and, like *This Happy Breed*, straddles both the melodrama of everyday life and the heritage genre. Its concern with the predicaments of class, its focus on ordinary people, and its general restraint situate it in the former category, while the fact that it is an adaptation of a literary classic links it to the heritage impulse. It was also a great critical success. *The Sunday Express*, for instance, wrote:

In *Great Expectations* surely the last doubter will see what we, who have been signalling the advance of British film, have been making all the fuss about. Here is a picture which is British to the backbone yet belongs proudly to the cinema of the world. For beauty, good taste and intelligence, for dramatic and emotional content, and expert polish in every department, it is beyond nationality. In brief a classic.[225]

The *Daily Mirror*'s comments are revealing, too: 'It is more than a triumph for British films. It is an open proof that a film can satisfy every technical and "highbrow" requirement and still provide outstanding popular entertainment.'[226] What was particularly admired in this film was what was seen as the film's emotional truth, its sincerity, and its integrity; critics revelled in the aesthetic experience which it offered them, delighting in the moral value of a human story, by contrast with documentary's perceived coldness. This is of course no more than a strengthening of certain developments already there in earlier periods. As the genre of the melodrama of everyday life—and the quality British film more generally—shifted away from documentary, so the relationship between the public and the private was renegotiated. In *Great Expectations*, for instance, it is psychologically rounded protagonists who are at the centre of the narrative, and it is their private dramas of romance, success, and individual freedom which are played up. The film was not taken up as melodrama, however, but as quality cinema. This meant in part trying to construct an audience for a cinema which was differentiated from popular cinema, comparable to Hepworth's project in the early 1920s. It required a discerning audience, but in order to survive, it also had to be a mass audience. This paradox was resolved in the discourse of the period with the assumption that the

[224] Stephen Watts, *Sunday Express*, 15 Dec. 1946.   [225] Ibid.
[226] Noel Whitcomb, 3 Jan. 1947; see also other reviews on BFI Library microfiche.

emotional integrity of a film like *Great Expectations* had a universal quality which would appeal to all audiences. What this really means is that the
class perspective of the public gaze had been absorbed into the subjectivity
of the film's central protagonists: simple folk like Pip and Joe Gargery can
express complex moral truths. They are bourgeois subjects in the guise of
ordinary people. Ideally, the private emotions, the tastes, and the interests
of the bourgeois subject are transformed into a responsible and common
public experience, accessible and desirable to all classes. Art, with its civil-
izing function, can enable this transformation to take place.

Great Expectations can again be read as a parable about ordinariness,
and about the ideal national identity. It tries to establish a secure centre-
ground, against which are contrasted various more excessive positions.
The core of the film, its narrative and moral centre, and its preferred figure
of identification, is the moderate, undemonstrative, sensible, middle-class
Pip. The characters of Magwitch, Joe, Miss Estella, and Miss Havisham
are, by contrast, marginal figures, representatives of undesirable excesses,
in one direction or another, of Pip's moral sensibility.

Joe Gargery may be the salt of the earth, common humanity, but he is
parodied for his excesses in this mode. Magwitch's problem is precisely his
roughness. Miss Havisham and Estella are parodies of the aristocratic
sensibility. Pip also occupies this position of snobbishness temporarily,
when his bourgeois values are not properly tempered by Joe's simple sincerity. The other characters all represent grotesque spectacles which constantly push us back towards the centre-ground of Pip, and his private
(bourgeois) sensibility.

This privatization of the documentary attitude—the shifting of the bourgeois gaze from outside the narrative space, looking in, to inside the narrative space, as the gaze of the central protagonist—eventually led towards
the realms of art cinema. But there were other strands to the melodrama
of everyday life and other ways of exploring the nature of the national
community in the post-war period. By the late 1940s it had become increasingly difficult to represent the nation as a tight-knit knowable community, a difficulty which is particularly apparent in the films produced by
Ealing Studios. A number of films, including *Passport to Pimlico* and
Whiskey Galore (both 1949), go to great lengths to reproduce the war-
time conditions of siege and insularity and to assert and explore the idea
of community, represented by a proliferation of narrative protagonists and
a multiplication of incidental narrative lines.[227]

Other films take it for granted that the network of interrelations which
make up a community are already in place and go on to explore the
possibility—or danger—of its deconstruction by the intrusion of violent

---

[227] See Barr, *Ealing Studios*; and Ellis, 'Made in Ealing'.

and erotic forms of individual desire. Good examples of this tendency can be found in *It Always Rains on Sunday* (1947) and *The Blue Lamp* (1950). The potentially violent dismantling of the assumed community can be understood in terms of an increasing anxiety about the relations between the public and the private, and about the emergence of a new social category, the delinquent youth of *The Blue Lamp*. The image of the family–community–nation had become a generic convention, full of melodramatic potential. It could constitute the narrative buffer to the young delinquent individual. It could be exploited for the tension it created between individual desire and social responsibility. But it was rarely any longer a powerful image of secure social cohesion or moral and political consensus. The ending of *The Blue Lamp* is interesting in this respect. The delinquent murderer of a policeman is rounded up by a collective effort which relies on the interconnectedness of a communication system (the tic-tac men at a race course) and the discipline of the police force. Even so, the film cannot quite contain the energy and vitality of Dirk Bogarde's performance as the young criminal, while the crowd at the stadium where he is captured remains a crowd, and does not become a knowable community. The community is thus reserved for small disciplined pockets (the police force); it can no longer command the consent of the national community as a whole.

In the late 1950s and early 1960s, there was a further transformation and renewal of this genre. The pleasures of the new wave films derive from the ways in which a single central narrative protagonist transgresses the parameters of the family–community–nation.[228] The regional emphasis of films like *Saturday Night and Sunday Morning* (1960) also to some extent challenges the sense of a hegemonic nationality. In these films, there is a marked intensification of psychological realism and a deeper attention to the articulation of character and individuality. The community now constitutes the backdrop, the setting for the exploration of the psychological complexity of the (usually young working-class male) protagonist. Both the community of the neighbourhood, and its most domestic form within the genre, the family, have become intrusions on the private (sexual) life of the individual—now the hero of the film.

The relations between the elements of the genre have almost been turned upside down in the period between the 1940s and the 1960s. In 1943, in *The Bells Go Down*, a petty criminal eventually saves the life of his old enemy, the local policeman, and both individuals are enveloped by the folds of the community. In *The Blue Lamp*, the police force itself is the centre of the community, both its ideal image, and that which regulates the community. Troubling the community is a new form of criminality: a

[228] See Hill, *Sex, Class and Realism*.

delinquent and recklessly individualistic criminality with no sense of moral responsibility, and a dangerous threat to the fabric and well-being of the community. By 1962, in *The Loneliness of the Long Distance Runner*, the petty criminal has become the hero, while the police and borstal staff, as the official managers of the community, are constructed as threats to the integrity of the individual. By this time it is much more the individual who is at the centre of the narrative, and around whose somewhat irresponsible acts the narrative gathers momentum. In a sense Dirk Bogarde's psychopathic juvenile delinquent of *The Blue Lamp* has become the central protagonist, the (anti-) hero of *The Loneliness of the Long Distance Runner*. This shift is even clearer in *Saturday Night and Sunday Morning,* where the image of the family is now much more in the background. While it is still able to offer some sustenance to the individual, the family is already also something of a stifling burden to the energies of the young working-class male. Similarly, the community of the neighbourhood and the workplace has become claustrophobic and debilitating rather than warm and cosy, a source of conflict and tension rather than the microcosm of the united nation.

The new wave films acknowledged the separation of the individual from key political decision-making processes of society, and used the generic form to explore this social gulf as much in psychological terms (alienation as a state of mind) as in sociological terms. In the end, it does seem that social relations are marginalized in favour of personal relations. As such, the formal strategies of the genre are newly inflected towards the exploration—if not fulfilment—of individual desires. The narratives are resolutely organized around a single central protagonist, a single psychology and subjectivity, and no longer require a multiplicity of plot lines. While this lends a stronger causal movement to the narrative, the goals of that movement are defined as much in terms of broad character development as in terms of concrete achievements. Vestiges of montage construction remain, both in the relatively episodic structures to the narratives, and in the numerous montage sequences of some of Tony Richardson's films, notably *A Taste Of Honey* (1961) and *The Loneliness of the Long Distance Runner.*

Montage no longer constructs a common public sphere of social existence, but is directed towards the articulation of a private personal experience. Thus *Saturday Night and Sunday Morning* has a relatively episodic narrative structure not because it tries to hold together a variety of aspects of the same sphere, but because it deals with loosely connected moments in the development of a character. Similarly, the montage constructions of certain sequences in Richardson's films produce a poetic experience of a state of mind—for instance, the montage of shots of the canal which a melancholy Jo walks beside in *A Taste of Honey,* or the montage of shots of the countryside as an ecstatically free Colin goes running in *The Lone-liness of the Long Distance Runner*. In other words, the function of montage construction has shifted from spatial metaphors (the construction of a broad inclusive diegesis) to temporal metaphors (the self-conscious elision of real time), and from an articulation of the look of the documentary, the public gaze, to the privatized look of the narrative protagonist—that is, from an objective statement of commonality and universality, to a subjective impression of experience. It is this establishment of an intensified psychological realism which seems as remarkable in these films as their attempt to foreground working-class protagonists.

While these films seem to be offering a working-class perspective by foregrounding the working-class protagonist and his or her privatized gaze, there is still a lingering sense of the bourgeois class looking at this working-class other from a position of superiority. This tension is most evident in the difference between the subjective point of view of the narrative character (the working-class victim) placed within the city, and the spectacular authoritative point of view which momentarily recurs throughout these films, from a position outside and above the city ('That Long Shot of Our Town From That Hill', as one jaded critic put it[229]). This latter point of view is effectively the position of wish-fulfilment (heavily inscribed in the realist genre), the position to which the victim who desires to escape must aspire.

---

[229] J. Krish, *Society of Film and TV Arts Journal*, Spring 1963, 14, quoted in Higson, 'Space, Place, Spectacle', 2, which discusses this class perspective in the new wave films in much more detail.

Constructing a National Cinema in Britain: Some Conclusions

My starting-point in this book was the dominant presence of Hollywood in British cinema since at least the First World War. The construction of a national cinema in Britain inevitably involves coming to terms with this presence. British cinema has done that in various ways: by competing with Hollywood on its own terms and in its own markets; by colluding with Hollywood in the distribution and exhibition of American films in the British market; by trying to protect British producers from the immense power and penetration of the American film industry; and by various forms of product differentiation. It is this question of product differentiation which is of most interest in the end and which has been my central concern in the preceding chapters. Even so, the case-study method has enabled me to capture something of the cultural and economic diversity of British cinema across several decades. Thus, although I have had much to say about the formation of intellectual film culture in Britain and its role in promoting particular types of cinema, there has also been the space to explore some aspects of popular cinema. In other words, I have tried to show how both the critically valued and the critically despised—as well as the critics themselves—have played their part in constructing a national cinema in Britain.

There have been some surprising overlaps—the figure of Michael Balcon moves through all of the case-studies, for instance. His first feature film as producer was *Woman to Woman*, the hit of late 1923 and early 1924 with audiences and critics, British and American. This film represented a very different strategy from that adopted by Hepworth in his search for an English idiom with the contemporaneous *Comin' Thro' The Rye*. By the mid-1930s, Balcon was Head of Production at one of the biggest British corporations and centrally involved in their attempt to break into the American market. *Evergreen* and *Woman to Woman* share a great deal, since they both aspire to the standards of the classical Hollywood film as a means of competing in the domestic and export markets with the best of American cinema. By the 1940s, however, Balcon had moved to Ealing Studios where he was involved in a rather different strategy, the attempt to make distinctively British films on a small scale, gaining much from the convergence of documentary and feature modes in the peculiar circumstances of the Second World War. In many ways, Balcon became a spokesperson for this version of national cinema during the 1940s.

The strength of the cinematic forms examined in the various case-studies can be seen in the fact that the same forms and industrial strategies have dominated British cinema in recent years—with the exception of popular genre production, which has not had a place in the straitened circumstances of British film-making since the mid-1970s. As far as the other strategies are concerned, Goldcrest attempted to break into the American market in the mid-1980s with expensive international films like *Revolution* (1985); films like *My Beautiful Laundrette* and *Letter to Brezhnev* (both 1985), on the other hand, represent a renewal of the modestly budgeted documentary-realist tradition and the melodrama of everyday life; and the heritage film has been one of the most heavily exploited areas of British art cinema in the last decade-and-a-half with films like the Merchant-Ivory productions of *A Room With A View* (1985) and *Howards End* (1991).

The latter area of recent British film production may be seen as a relatively conservative and nostalgic attempt to turn away from contemporary realities and seek an image of national stability in some golden age of the past. Inevitably, those golden ages (notably the age of the Raj) were already crumbling and could not offer the pure and untainted image of national identity that was perhaps desired, but this is very much offset by the way in which these films display the attractions of the heritage, including the heritage of cinema, with its own conventions of artistry and glamour.[1]

In the contemporary melodramas of everyday life, meanwhile, the image of a consensual national community has been lost, fragmented into so many local communities. The centralizing forces of a film like *Millions Like Us*, with its inclusive, all-embracing vision of Englishness as achieved community, have been displaced by an attempt to articulate various different social identities, to represent the ethnic, sexual, regional, gender, and class differences around which community and identity have been formed in contemporary Britain. While the most powerful international forces move in the direction of global markets and cultures, the independent sector of British film production, at least, has pushed towards a construction and recognition of many specific public spheres, rather than a single, universal public sphere.

This raises the question of whether such films can still usefully be understood as the products of a national cinema, or whether the national in national cinema always invokes the myth of consensus—which such films as *My Beautiful Laundrette* show up precisely as myth. What is important about such films is that they refuse over-arching visions of national identity

---

[1] See Higson, 'Re-presenting the National Past: Nostalgia and Pastiche in the Heritage Film', in Lester Friedman (ed.), *Fires Were Started: British Cinema and Thatcherism* (Minneapolis/London, 1993).

and stress those other senses of identity and belonging which have always criss-crossed the body of the nation, and which often cross national boundaries too. Perhaps it is more important in this context to call for the renewal of feminist cinema, or black cinema, or gay cinema rather than to call for the renewal of British cinema.[2]

Films made in Britain today have to come to terms with the cultural inheritance of British cinema history one way or another. How best to describe the film culture which contemporary British cinema inherits? In summarizing the conclusions of the previous chapters, I want to pick out three ways in which British films seem different from those of classical Hollywood. First, I will look at the way in which films from very different sectors of the industry have imagined the nation. Secondly, I will offer some generalizations about the distinctive stylistic characteristics of the films and filmic traditions which have been examined. And thirdly, I will speculate on the cultural construction of distinctiveness and otherness in relation to these films and traditions.

IMAGINING THE NATION

The first point to note here is the extent to which cinema has been used as an apparatus for narrating the nation as a stable entity with a strong sense of its own identity and its past achievements, and for securing an image of the nation as a knowable, organic community. The nation becomes a body of people marked in their diversity, but even more marked in their interconnectedness. The films I have analysed achieve this image precisely by foregrounding some form of community, often the community of the family. This stress on the plural, on the social, on what Grierson called the cross-section, thus sets such films against the individualist ethic of classical Hollywood cinema. The community of the nation is very often imagined from the point of view of pastoralism, the dominant mobilizing myth of the British people. The populism of this myth can be rural or urban, it can be forward-looking or nostalgic—what is shared is the mobilizing of an image of the nation as one large family whose common concerns ride above any sectional interests. Both the heritage film and the documentary-realist film attempt to document and authenticate this image of the nation. The heritage film constructs a sense of an invariant and spectacular national past, which is above all a modern past, imagined from the point of view of the present. The documentary-realist film tends to foreground the contemporary formation of the nation.

---

[2] For a contrary view, see John Hill, 'The Issue of National Cinema and British Film Production', in Duncan Petrie (ed.), *New Questions of British Cinema* (London, 1992).

The ideological function of British cinema as a national cinema is thus to pull together diverse and contradictory discourses, to articulate a contradictory unity, to play a part in the hegemonic process of achieving consensus and containing difference and contradiction. The cinematic apparatus does not simply reflect or express an already fully formed and homogeneous national culture and identity, as if it were the undeniable property of all national subjects. It actively works to construct subjectivity by privileging a limited range of subject positions which thereby become naturalized or reproduced through the work of cinema itself as the only legitimate positions of the national subject.

Central to this image of the nation as a knowable community with a known history is the particular way in which the public (the national) is related to the private (the individual subject). Heritage films, popular genre films like *Sing As We Go*, and films influenced by the documentary idea, are all in one way or another marked by a dual perspective of distance and closeness. On the one hand, there is the observational gaze of one who is outside the narrative space, separate from that which is being observed. On the other hand, there is the participatory stance, the perspective which shares the imagination of the protagonists. The distinction between these two gazes, these two opposed (but often co-present) ways of relating to the drama of the film, suggests in the end a distinction between class perspectives. Given that these perspectives will often embody different interests, the sense of the nation as an unstratified community, with an apparently coherent and shared set of interests, begins to fall apart. Thus the community is inclusive, but it also has the exclusivity of an institution which distinguishes between them and us, between the onlookers and the surveyed, between one class and another. Power in these films is so often the power to look, to be able to survey. Cinema is an apparatus for looking, it is a communication system, and as such does not simply represent the community but regulates it.

Certainly, there are changes over time in the nature of the public sphere and in who can rightfully occupy a place within that sphere. In *Comin' Thro' The Rye*, the lower classes are virtually invisible, present only as the servants of the upper classes (and either deferential or untrustworthy). There is no representation of the lower classes as having their own collective interests. *Comin' Thro' The Rye* can be understood as the exhibition of a class sure of its own identity, and sure that this identity is the essence of Englishness—except that the class is already becoming culturally debased, the exhibition already nostalgic. For the distanced perspective of *Comin' Thro' The Rye* is also of course the voyeuristic perspective of the heritage tourist, nostalgically seeking out this mythical English identity.

By the time of *Sing As We Go*, under the influence of a strong tradition of popular pleasures, the lower classes can be represented both collectively and individually. But the crowd is still caught in the same dual perspective. The crowd can be fun, it is to some extent knowable, it can be participated in; but it is still in part terrifying, grotesque, something from which one must keep a respectable distance. The documentary idea is haunted by this same anxious fascination, and the task of the documentary film is, in a sense, to dispel the popular and the trivial in order to prepare the crowd for responsible citizenship: it is a question of disciplining the lower classes before they can enter the public sphere.

In *Millions Like Us*, however, the crowd has finally become knowable—it is, precisely, millions of people like us. The development of the melodrama of everyday life from then on effectively focuses on a single figure from the crowd, an ordinary person, but one whose simplicity and ordinariness are the result of having absorbed bourgeois values, of having been humanized, civilized.

THE DISTINCTIVE STYLISTIC CHARACTERISTICS OF BRITISH CINEMA

The versions of British cinema that I have examined are the products of a series of dialogues—with Hollywood, with popular and élite indigenous cultural traditions, with notions of the people, and so on. The result of these dialogues is the development of various distinctive stylistic characteristics. I will concentrate on three aspects here: modes of narration, types of looking, and uses of space. It is these characteristics which enable the films under discussion to articulate the particular image of the nation which I have explored above.

The difference between the classical Hollywood film and the British heritage film, the popular musical-comedy and the documentary-realist film, is in part narrational. These filmic traditions typically refuse the rigours of classical narrative integration in favour of what by comparison seems a more 'primitive' narrational form. It is characterized by episodicism, by multiple, interweaving narrative lines, and by a diegesis which above all displays its attractions. This is a national cinema, then, which displays the multiple attractions of the nation. What is really distinctive about British cinema is the narratively excessive, those aspects which in various ways go beyond strictly narrative requirements: the various attractions of Englishness, the authenticity of the national, the pictorial, and the pastoral, even the carnival of *Sing As We Go*. On another level, the culture of montage—as well as Hepworth's aesthetic of the shot—also exceeds the limits of narrative linearity.

The dramas of these various films are also very often narrated as if from outside the narrative space, which of course relates to the distinctive mode of looking in these films, the stress on the distanced and objective point of view, the outsider's view, looking in from outside the diegesis, rather than the subjective point of view of classical cinema's narrative protagonists. It is a type of looking which (re)defines what is public and what private, and which monitors and reproduces the relations between classes. It is a type of looking which can take in the display of the public past, or the dignity of the common labourer, the objective visibility of the nation and its people. But it is also a type of looking which finds the other class fascinating and exotic, whether it is the crowd of the carnival, or the ordinary people in the domestic sphere of *This Happy Breed*.

This distanced look is also more decorous, more restrained, than the engaging look of the classical film, and it relates more easily to a diegesis which is filled with detail, which foregrounds characterization and atmosphere over action. The films under examination are decidedly not primarily action-oriented.

The construction and use of space in these films is also different from classical Hollywood. It is a much more exhibitionist space, whether it is the display of the national past and pastoral England (heritage space), or the performance space of carnival, or the urban pastoral of the broad diegesis of the people in the melodrama of everyday life. The particularly extensive diegesis of these films, coterminous with the episodic and multiple narratives, is precisely a perspective on public space, on social space, and of course on national space, rather than the private space of the classical romantic hero. It is the limits of the diegesis which mark the boundaries of the national community. And as we have seen, there is always the play on the spectator being both inside and outside this space, both a participating member of the community, and a superior onlooker.

THE CULTURAL CONSTRUCTION OF DISTINCTIVENESS

Nationalism is about drawing boundaries, about marking an inside and an outside. The process of constructing national identity is thus a continual process of negotiating these limits. Film culture also seeks to identify and define others in relation to the ideal national cinema. The documentary-realist tradition comes to occupy that ideal position, and Hollywood, of course, becomes the most significant 'other' within the intellectual film culture. Yet a British film like *Evergreen* seeks to erase the boundary between the British and the American, to refuse this designation of otherness, and to become Hollywood.

Comin' Thro' The Rye, on the other hand, occupies an ambivalent position in the cultural debates of the 1920s. It is both the ideal British cinema, and the other, the too-theatrical, the old-fashioned, the uncinematic, and so on.

Sing As We Go also occupies an ambivalent position. It is the enemy within, the vulgar mass culture, the grotesque low other of the ideal British cinema, from one point of view. Above all, it was felt by many commentators to be incapable of coming to terms with the political realities of the period. But it does have a critical perspective on the nation and its people, and Dean did attempt to transform it into a serious, quality film, a culturally respectable film. However, as we know, he could not resist the fascination with the popular which Gracie Fields represents.

National cinema is, then, a profoundly complex issue, and in the end it cannot be reduced only to the consideration of the films produced by and within a particular nation-state.[3] It is important to take into account the film culture as a whole, the overall institution of cinema, and in particular to address the whole question of consumption, which I have only been able to touch on here.

Another study would need to take into account in a much more comprehensive way the whole range of films in circulation within a nation-state—including American and other foreign films—and how they are taken up at the level of exhibition. In the present era, of course, films are in circulation and on display in a variety of ways—in multiplexes, in art-house cinemas, on video and via the various forms of broadcast and cable television, and so on—but they are also present and recycled in popular culture intertextually, as icons, reference-points, standards, and pastiches.

It would also be useful to be able to take into account the whole range of sociologically specific audiences for different types of film, and how these audiences use these films in particular exhibition circumstances. That is to say, we need to take into account the historically constituted reading practices and modes of spectatorship and subjectivity, the mental machinery and relative cultural power or readerly competences of different audiences. But we also need to take into account the experience of cinema in a more general cultural sense: the role of marketing and audience expectation; the reasons why particular audiences go to the cinema, and the pleasures they derive from this activity; the specific nature of the shared social and communal experience of cinema-going, differentiated according to class, race, gender, age, and so on; the role of television (and video) in mediating and transforming the experience of cinema; and the different experiences offered by the various types of theatrical exhibition spaces.

It is worth remembering that, from the point of view of economic historians such as Douglas Gomery, film industries marked by a high degree

---

[3] The following section draws on material used in *Screen*, 30/4 (1989), in my article 'The Idea of National Cinema'.

of horizontal and vertical integration can be seen as no more nor less than highly diversified cinema circuits, where production is a necessary high-risk service industry, and where cinemas are as much luxurious sites for the consumption or advertising of commodities other than films, as they are sites for the fantasy experience of watching films.[4]

An analysis of national cinema in these terms would also need to take into account the range of and relation between discourses about films circulating within that cultural and social formation and their relative accessibility to different audiences. Crucial amongst these discourses is the tension between, on the one hand, those intellectual discourses which insist that a proper national cinema must be one which aspires to the status of art; and on the other hand, those more populist discourses where, in effect, the idea of good entertainment overrides questions of art or nationality. This latter discourse suggests that a cinema can only be national, and command a national-popular audience, if it is a mass-production genre cinema, capable of constructing, reproducing, and recycling popular myths on a broad scale, with an elaborate, well-capitalized, and well-resourced system of market exploitation. Again, the role of television must be taken into account as one of the agents which generates, sustains, and regulates film cultures and renders discourses about the cinema more or less accessible.

To explore national cinema in these terms means laying much greater stress on the point of consumption and on the use of films (sounds, images, narratives, fantasies), than on the point of production. It involves a shift in emphasis away from the analysis of film texts as vehicles for the articulation of nationalist sentiment and the interpellation of the implied national spectator, to an analysis of how actual audiences construct their cultural identity in relation to the various products of the national and international film and television industries, and the conditions under which this is achieved. Films may articulate a sense of national community, but the audience at a specific cinema may constitute their own community of resistance against that articulation.

This is not of course to renounce all interest in cultural production as opposed to consumption, nor to assume that all types of cinema are to be encouraged because it is how audiences use texts which makes them socially functional. But in the present climate, I would rather call for a socialist cinema, or a green cinema, or a feminist cinema than for the renewal of British cinema.[5]

---

[4] See Douglas Gomery, *The Hollywood Studio System* (London, 1986); also *Shared Pleasures: A History of Movie Presentation in the United States* (London, 1992). On film reception more generally, see Janet Staiger, *Interpreting Films: Studies in the Historical Reception of American Cinema* (Princeton, NJ, 1992).
[5] I am again taking issue with Hill, 'Issue of National Cinema'.

Appendix: Credits and Plot Synopses

COMIN' THRO' THE RYE

Credits

Director:	Cecil Hepworth
Production company:	Hepworth Picture Plays
Distribution:	Ideal Films
Script:	Blanche MacIntosh
	from the novel by Helen Mathers
Camera:	Geoffrey Faithfull

Starring: Alma Taylor (Helen Adair), Shayle Gardner (Paul Vasher), Eileen Dennes (Sylvia Fleming), Ralph Forbes (George Tempest).

Other players: James Carew (Colonel Adair), Gwynne Herbert (Mrs Adair), Francis Lister (Dick Fellows), Christine Rayner (Jane Peach, the maid), Henry Vibert (Mr Tempest), Nancy Price (Mrs Titmouse, an acquaintance of Sylvia's), John MacAndrews (Simpkins, the butler), Margaret Armstrong (Alice Adair, Helen's sister).

GB, 1923/4, U certificate, black and white.

Trade shown in an incomplete form on 13 Nov. 1923.
Premièred (in its complete form) on 25 Jan. 1924.
General release 26 May 1924.

Length: the most complete copy of the film currently available is the National Film Archive (London) Viewing Copy, which is 6,769 feet (5 reels); however, the end of the film reviewed in 1924 is missing from this print. *Bioscope*, 31 Jan. 1924, 55, gives the length of the film which was trade shown as 6 reels, while the censors passed the film at 7,900 feet (*Kine Weekly*, 14 Feb. 1924, 86). This suggests that the NFA print is still missing one reel, or 1,131 feet.

Plot synopsis

Seed-time. Helen Adair is the youngest daughter of Colonel Adair, a Victorian gentleman, and owner of Silverbridge Manor. The house and various members of the family are introduced. As a girl in her early teens, Helen plays with her friend and neighbour George Tempest, who is in love with her. Her father chastises her and punishes her, but she is obviously resilient and full of life.

'Close to the Manor House lived Sylvia Fleming, generally believed to be the Most Heartless Little Flirt in the Whole County' (intertitle). Sylvia meets a lover, Dick Fellows, outside her house, but is evidently concerned that someone else will see them together. Paul Vasher arrives, and greets Dick, who is evidently a friend, and discusses the next day's steeplechase in which Dick is riding. Paul and Sylvia leave Dick, and go inside, where he proposes marriage to her. Outside, Dick resolves to go inside and likewise declare his love for Sylvia. He is very surprised to find Paul and Sylvia together. Sylvia indicates to him to keep quiet about their affair, unseen by Paul.

'The next day, Dick rides purposefully for disaster' (intertitle). At the weigh-in for the steeplechase, Dick nervously fingers a letter and pockets it. Dick rides recklessly, is thrown from his horse and killed. Paul, who has run to the scene of the 'accident', finds the letter which has fallen on the ground, and puts it in his pocket without thinking. Later, alone, he reads it—it is a letter from Sylvia, breaking off her affair with Dick—and realizes that Dick has taken his own life because of Sylvia's flirtatious treatment of him.

Helen and George are playing outside, and Helen, pressed by George, promises to marry him when she is 18, provided she doesn't meet a better contender. Helen hides, and inadvertently overhears Paul explaining to Sylvia that he can no longer marry her, because of her actions.

Helen is walking in the rye-field close to Silverbridge Manor when she unexpectedly meets Paul, who is enchanted by her innocence. He leaves for Rome on business.

Summer. Three years later, Paul returns to Silverbridge and takes a walk through the rye-field, where again by chance he meets Helen.

Helen is invited to a house party by her sister. Paul has also been invited to the party, as has Sylvia. Helen and Paul immediately strike up a close relationship. They walk through the gardens and play croquet, where Sylvia flirts with Paul but is snubbed by Helen. Sylvia plots to win back the affections of Paul, and plants her maid on the staff at Silverbridge Manor.

Paul and Helen arrange to meet again at their spot in the rye-field. They become engaged. Helen explains to a heartbroken George that she can no longer marry him. Paul announces that he must again travel to Rome. He is overheard by the maid, who informs Sylvia where he will be staying in Rome. Before leaving for Rome, Paul and Helen say goodbye at the same old place in the rye-field. They kiss and part. By chance, George turns up just after Paul has left and, being a perfect gentleman, comforts a sad Helen. Paul turns and sees them together in the distance, but thinks nothing of it.

Paul arrives at his hotel in Rome, and is followed out there by Sylvia. The maid intercepts Paul's and Helen's letters to each other, and passes them on to Sylvia. A mysterious announcement (the work of Sylvia) appears in *The Times*, indicating that George and Helen have married. George resolves to go out to Rome and explain that the announcement is false. Helen, disconsolate, goes back to the old spot in the rye-field.

In Rome, Sylvia forges a letter to Paul from Helen, giving details of the 'marriage'. Paul receives the letter and is astonished by its contents, recalling that he had seen George with Helen as he left for Rome. Sylvia bursts into his room, and tries to comfort him. Distraught, he pushes her away, and goes to a bar, where the sight of another romantically involved couple inspires him to go back and seek solace with Sylvia. The next day, at Sylvia's bidding, they are married in Rome.

George arrives in Rome and explains to Paul that the announcement of a marriage between himself and Helen is false, and points the finger at Sylvia, who sinks to the ground having been revealed. Paul packs to leave for England immediately.

Harvest. Back at Silverbridge, Paul, who has just returned, meets Helen at the rye-field, now harvested and barren. They embrace, but he falls to his knees and explains what has happened. Helen insists that he return to Sylvia to live as husband and wife, for her sake. He leaves her, and she sinks to the ground, desolate.

Three years later, Sylvia and Paul have had a son, but relations between them are extremely strained. At a garden party at the vicarage, 'the Inevitable Meeting Occurs' (intertitle): George and Helen sit together, and are joined unexpectedly by the Vashers. Helen snubs Sylvia, but Sylvia follows her, and confronts her aggressively in the gardens, vowing to further humiliate her by humbling her pride.

Later, at home, Sylvia is taken ill. Paul visits Helen and tells her that Sylvia is dying, and has asked to see Helen. Against her will, Helen goes to meet her, and Sylvia asks for her forgiveness. The child, Wattie, comes in, and Helen is clearly taken by him, hugging and kissing him. Helen says 'For the child's sake, I will forgive you, and will come to see you sometimes' (dialogue title).

A few weeks later, Sylvia has recovered, but is unrepentant. She writes to Helen, asking her if she would look after Wattie while she and her husband go away for a week or two. Paul delivers the letter to Helen, who is playing with Wattie at Silverbridge Manor (she is the only person to show any affection towards the child). A title tells us that 'Unconsciously, Paul's son filled a gap in Helen's life.' Helen reads the letter, and hugs Wattie.

Here the NFA Viewing Copy abruptly ends. *Bioscope*'s review of the completed film (31 Jan. 1924, 55) yields further that the child has a very serious illness and dies in his parents' absence. *Bioscope* also notes that Helen and Paul 'are, quite properly, too Victorian to have the courage of their passion' (ibid.). Sylvia presumably does not die of her illness ('Most picturegoers . . . would have liked to see Sylvia punished with a severity befitting her altogether un-Victorian behaviour', ibid. Neither does she die in the novel). *Kine Weekly* notes that 'The hero of *Comin' Thro' The Rye*, having discovered the treachery of the woman who parted him from the girl he loves in order to win him as her own husband, dies fighting for his country, while the girl . . . is left to face the world with only the memory of an ideal' (31 Jan. 1924, 41), and the *Variety* review tells us that 'the closing scene of the picture shows the heroine reading a letter that her beloved has died as a brave soldier on the field of action' (31 Dec. 1924, repr. in *Variety's Film Reviews, 1921–1925*, ii (New York, 1983), no p. nos.); while *Bioscope* notes that 'Mr Hepworth has had the courage to retain the 'unhappy ending'—a decision which is well-justified' (31 Jan. 1924, 55).

SING AS WE GO

Credits

Producer/Director:	Basil Dean
Production company:	Associated Talking Pictures
	(shot at Ealing Studios, and on location in Blackpool)
Distribution company:	ABFD
Script:	J. B. Priestley,
	with continuity by Gordon Wellesley
	from an original story by J. B. Priestley
Lyrics:	Harry Parr-Davis
Camera:	Robert Martin
Design:	J. Elder Wills
Editor:	Thorold Dickinson

Starring: Gracie Fields (Grace Platt), John Loder (Hugh), Dorothy Hyson (Phyllis). Other players: Stanley Holloway (policeman), Maire O'Neill (fortune-teller), Lawrence Grossmith (Sir William Upton), Frank Pettingell, Morris Harvey, Ben Field, Oliver Sloane, James R. Gregson.

GB, 1934, U certificate, 80 mins., black and white

Trade show: 7 Sept. 1934; released: 29 Oct. 1934.

Plot Synopsis

During the Depression, Greybeck Mill is forced to close down, throwing all its employees out of work. Grace Platt is one of the employees and is asked by the rest of the workforce to speak to Hugh Phillips, the Assistant Manager, about the possibility of continuing rehearsing the show they were intending to put on. In Hugh's office, they decide there's no point in going on. Hugh says he'll miss Grace. Outside, in order to keep spirits up, Grace leads the workforce in a rousing chorus of 'Sing as we go', as they march out of the factory gates.

Grace returns home. She lives with her Uncle Murgatroyd and his wife, and numerous clocks, none of which work: a hangover from Murgatroyd's trade, which he no longer practises. A small boy comes to fetch a clock left there some years earlier. Meanwhile, Hugh is on the phone to his father, who tells him about Sir William Upton, who has developed an artificial silk process which they might be able to exploit at the mill. Hugh resolves to find Sir William.

Uncle Murgatroyd and his friend Ezekiah, both the worse for drink, return home to Grace, where they have 'a bit of a do', with beer, tripe, and a burlesque song, 'Thora', from Grace. Murgatroyd's wife arrives back unexpectedly, Ezekiah makes a swift exit, and the other two are scolded for such merry-making. When Grace lets on that she is out of work, her Aunt tells her she might be able to get a job with a friend of hers who runs a boarding-house in Blackpool. Grace resolves to go there the next day, by bike, to save money.

On her way to Blackpool, Grace gets into various scrapes and meets various eccentric characters, including a policeman. She starts work as a maid at Mrs Clotty's boarding house, where she meets Gladiola, a young woman who adores

American film stars and boasts that she has five boyfriends. Fed up with verbal and physical abuse from Mr Parkinson, a notorious client of Mrs Clotty's, she tips a bowl of rhubarb over his head and is given the sack.

At the Labour Exchange, she is told of a job selling Crunchy-Wunchy toffee, which doesn't start for a few days, and also of a forthcoming bathing beauty contest. At the registration desk for the competition, she meets the beautiful and young Phyllis and decides there is no point in entering the competition after all. They strike up a friendship, and Phyllis invites Grace to share her lodgings, which are run by an Irish clairvoyante with an oriental accent, Madame Osiris, who also takes to Grace. Masquerading as the clairvoyante, who is not feeling well, Grace tells the fortunes of three customers, the second of whom is the policeman whom she had met earlier; the third customer lets on that there may be a job going as a song-plugger, since she has split up with her man who runs the outfit.

Meanwhile, Hugh is searching for Sir William, who has also gone to Blackpool. He follows him there.

Grace goes to the song-pluggers, and is an immediate success, singing 'Just a catchy little tune'. Phyllis and Hugh meet in the crowd while watching Grace perform, and are clearly attracted to one another. Grace is just about to be offered the job, when the lady-friend returns.

Hugh and Phyllis have become good friends, but are unable to find Grace, who has a mysterious job. They go to the Pleasure Beach, arriving—unknown to them— at the same time as Sir William Upton. They argue about the morality of the bathing beauty contest, and go on various rides. In a sideshow, they discover Grace performing as a Human Spider. By a series of mishaps, Grace bursts into a neigh-bouring Wild West sideshow, whose players give chase to her, with the policeman joining in. By chance, Grace rides on the Ghost Train with Sir William, but then is chased again. Eventually escaping from the Pleasure Beach, she bumps into Sir William again; when he introduces himself, Grace immediately takes command of the situation.

Later, she is selling toffee on the Promenade, when Murgatroyd and Ezekiah go by in the Staghunters' parade, which is followed by a convention at the Winter Gardens. They all meet again at the bathing beauty contest, which is won by Phyllis as Miss London. Phyllis celebrates in a bar with several men, having too much to drink. Elsewhere, Hugh is meeting with Sir William to discuss plans for developing the artificial silk process at Greybeck Mill. Back in Blackpool, Grace is searching for Phyllis, who is due to appear with the runners-up at the Tower Ballroom. Grace looks for her in the bar, at the zoo, and eventually finds her at the circus, where she manages to fall into the ring, which has become a swimming pool. Drenched, she drags Phyllis to the Ballroom, but due to a series of misun-derstandings, the bedraggled Grace is revealed on the stage each time in place of the three bathing beauty contest winners. In order to calm the crowd down, she sings 'Little bottom drawer'.

Returning home, she finds Phyllis drunk with a much older man. She sends Phyllis off to bed, but before she can get rid of the man, Hugh turns up looking for Phyllis. Grace pretends the man is with her, and that they are both drunk, so covering for Phyllis. Hugh leaves, disgusted at Grace's behaviour. The man is ejected as Murgatroyd and Ezekiah arrive to see Grace. It turns out that Murgatroyd and Madame Osiris are old friends. Grace tells Ezekiah that she has just lost the only man she ever loved, and they sing a romantic song, which is briefly picked up by the policeman, who is also drunk, below their window.

The next day, Grace sees Hugh and Phyllis off at the station. Hugh leaves a message for her with the policeman: the Mill is re-opening, and Grace is to be Welfare Officer. The town of Greybeck and the factory are shown coming back to life, and Grace leads the workers in through the gates, again singing 'Sing as we go'.

EVERGREEN

Credits

Director:	Victor Saville
Production company:	Gaumont-British
	(shot at Shepherd's Bush Studios)
Distribution company:	Gaumont-British
Producer:	Michael Balcon
Scenario:	Marjorie Gaffney; adapted by Emlyn Williams from the C. B. Cochran stage musical by Lorenz Hart and Benn Levy
Dialogue:	Emlyn Williams
Songs:	Lorenz Hart and Richard Rodgers
Additional songs:	Harry M. Woods
Camera:	Glen MacWilliams
Art Director:	Alfred Junge
Editor:	Ian Dalrymple, Paul Capon
Musical Director:	Louis Levy
Sound recordist:	A. F. Birch
Costumes:	Borleo
Dances and ensembles:	Buddy Bradley

The Gaumont-British Orchestra conducted by Bretton Byrd

Starring: Jessie Matthews (Harriet Green/Harriet Hawkes), Sonnie Hale (Leslie Benn), Betty Balfour (Maudie), Barry Mackay (Tommy Thompson).
Other players: Ivor MacLaren (Marquis of Staines), Hartley Power (Treadwell), Patrick Ludlow (Lord Shropshire), Betty Shale (Mrs Hawkes), Marjorie Brooks (Marjorie Moore).

GB, 1934, A certificate, 90 mins (British trade show, 92 mins; American release, 82 mins), black and white.

Trade show: 23 Apr. 1934; released: 10 Sept. 1934.

Plot synopsis

Harriet Green, a famous Edwardian music-hall star, is giving her farewell performance at the Tivoli Theatre in London to a large and admiring audience—she is retiring from the stage to marry the Marquis of Staines. Later at a celebration dinner, her friend Maudie, who had been performing with her, announces her engagement to Lord Shropshire, much to the distaste of another friend, Leslie Benn. The dinner is interrupted by Harriet's dresser, Mrs Hawkes, who tells Harriet that a former lover wants to see her. Harriet knows that this means blackmail and abruptly leaves the dinner, much to the surprise of the other guests. She confronts the former lover, Treadwell, by whom she had borne a daughter that no one knows about. Rather than go through further blackmail, she decides to disappear (to South Africa) without telling her intended husband, leaving Mrs Hawkes to bring up her daughter.

The action is then picked up some years later in 1934, when the daughter,

Harriet Hawkes, also a performer, turns up for an audition as a chorus girl. The show for which she is auditioning is being directed by Leslie Benn, now well established in this role. A young publicity agent, Tommy Thompson, annoys Benn, who calls off the rehearsal and audition before Harriet has even had time to be looked at. Tommy and Harriet console each other and by chance meet again outside a well-known agent's office. Maudie, now Lady Shropshire, turns up at the office, and presents herself to her old friend Benn who is with the agent. On leaving, she is startled to see Harriet, who is the spitting image of her mother, whom she hasn't seen since the night she left a score and more years earlier. Tommy sees some potential here and the three of them go off together. They hatch a plan to present Harriet as her own mother, as if she hasn't aged (hence 'evergreen', 'the star who never grows old') and invite Benn to sample the surprise.

Together, they put on a show to re-launch 'Harriet Green', with Mrs Hawkes and others coaching Harriet in her mother's mannerisms. Harriet performs 'Springtime in your heart', an elaborate production number, which takes the audience back through the music and dance styles of 1934, 1924, 1914, and 1904. The show is a great success, and the press and audience seem convinced by the stunt, especially when the now aged Marquis of Staines turns up and apparently (mis)recognizes the daughter as the woman he was once to marry, and Tommy, who is by now quite fond of Harriet, as the illegitimate child mentioned in a letter many years previously. All the same, they are all very worried about being found out and being charged with fraud and impersonation.

Meanwhile, Treadwell turns up again, threatening blackmail once more, and has to be bought off.

Rehearsals start on a new show, 'Harriet Gilbert and Son'. The Marquis apparently falls in love with 'Harriet Green' once more and proposes marriage to her again. But Tommy and Harriet have also fallen in love, and are finding it a great strain having to present themselves in public as mother and son. The strain is exacerbated when the Marquis buys them an exotic art deco house, 'so that you can look after your mother', only for Treadwell to turn up yet again demanding more money. In the house alone, they are unable to relax, and Harriet puts on a song-and-dance performance for herself.

Finding it impossible carrying on like this, Tommy and Harriet separately resolve to end the charade. Tommy refuses to pay Treadwell more money, in the hope that he will then give the game away. On the opening night of the new show, Harriet reveals the truth to the Marquis, who is not surprised, explaining that he had seen through the stunt from the start but had gone along with it because he admired their nerve. After a couple of successful numbers of the new show, Harriet pushes another performer out of the way and takes her place in an exuberant solo dance, clearly performing in a way that no one of her supposed age could. She rips off her clothes down to her underclothes and tears off her wig, all the while furiously tap-dancing. The audience become restless and cries of 'Fraud!' are heard. At the end of the dance, she laughs at the audience, to sounds of booing and jeering.

The curtain falls, and Benn comes out to try to appease the audience. He is joined by Tommy, who wins them over by complaining that 'I've been in love with her for weeks and had to go about London calling her Mummy.' Benn tells the whole story to a now forgiving audience, and Tommy brings Harriet back on stage. The explanation is taken up in court, where they are being tried for defrauding the public. The defence lawyer argues that there was no fraud because Harriet actually fulfilled the promise made to audiences. The case is clinched when she is heard to sing as well as her mother as captured on a 'phonographic reproduction', and the defendants are found not guilty.

The film ends with a production number from another show, with Harriet again singing 'Springtime in your heart'. In the finale, she is joined on stage by Tommy, who kisses her hand on which is now their wedding ring.

MILLIONS LIKE US

Credits

Scriptwriters/Directors:	Frank Launder and Sidney Gilliat
Producer:	Edward Black
Production company:	Gainsborough Pictures
	(Islington Studios; Maurice Ostrer in charge of production)
Distribution company:	General Film Distributors (GFD)
Camera:	Jack Cox, Roy Fogwell
Editor:	R. E. Dearing, Alfred Roome
Musical director:	Louis Levy
Art director:	John Bryan

Starring: Patricia Roc (Celia Crowson), Eric Portman (Charlie Forbes), Ann Crawford (Jennifer Knowles), Gordon Jackson (Fred Blake).

Other players: Megs Jenkins (Gwen), Moore Marriot (Dad), Terry Randall (Annie Earnshaw), Joy Shelton (Phyllis Crowson), Basil Radford (Charters), Naunton Wayne (Caldicott), Bertha Wilmott (as herself, performing 'Waiting at the church').

GB, 1943, U certificate, 103 mins., black and white.

Trade Show: 22 Sept. 1943; public première: 10 Oct. 1943; general release: 15 Nov. 1943 (re-released early 1948).

Plot Synopsis

During the credits, anonymous crowds are seen leaving work at various factories. A voice-over asks: 'Remember that summer before the war, those gay, coupon-free days . . . and you and millions like you swarmed to the sea . . . ?' There is a montage sequence of people holidaying.

Summer 1939. Widower Jim Crowson and his grown-up children prepare to leave the family home for the annual summer holiday. It is all very cosy; Dad chats over the fence with a neighbour, the younger daughter Celia leaves the cat with his wife. The family eventually arrive at the usual guest-house in Eastgate, on the coast. In the evening, the elder daughter, Phyllis, and Celia go to a dance, where Phyllis is soon dancing with a variety of dashing young men; Celia is much shyer, however, and is eventually asked to dance by a very boring man. She is not happy.

War is declared, and various typical scenes from the early part of the war are depicted. Two officers, Charters and Caldicott, are shocked to find their first-class compartment on a train taken over by a crowd of children being evacuated. Dad is on guard for the Home Guard, as trains rattle back from the coast filled with soldiers returning from Dunkirk. At home, he is embarrassed to have to salute the young man in uniform whom Phyllis is kissing on the doorstep. The family is gradually broken up as duty calls. By 1942 Tom is in the army, fighting in north Africa. His wife, who is living with the Crowsons, with their two young children, gets her old job back. Elder sister Phyllis joins the ATS, much to the chagrin of her father.

There are more typical scenes from the early years of the war. Charters and

Caldicott lay mines on a beach and discuss the plight of a man whose valet has been evacuated; he hasn't dressed himself for thirty years.

Later, Dad is annoyed again to find Phyllis, back home on leave, cuddling in the front room with a Polish officer. There is a family row, and everyone gets very upset as the family is torn apart by the war. The shy younger sister, Celia, is designated a 'mobile woman', which worries her father, because there will be no one left at home to look after him. At the Labour Exchange, she day-dreams about joining the Land Army, or becoming a nurse, and of having romantic liaisons with various officer-types. The reality is that she is detailed to factory work, operating a lathe in a munitions factory making parts for aircraft, in the town of Stockford.

Celia leaves home and meets up with several other new conscripts, including the maternal working-class Welshwoman, Gwen Price, the disdainfully well-to-do society girl Jennifer Knowles, and the young working-class northerner, Annie Earnshaw. The women are drawn from all classes, all regions, and all walks of life, but there is a strong sense of community and of caring for each other at the factory and the hostel where they live. They are very impressed by the standards of the hostel. Jenny and Annie share a room, and discover they have very different standards about the most simple things.

There is a montage of scenes depicting the work involved in the production of aeroplanes. Gwen and Celia are seen arriving at the factory for the first time. The women are shown round, then go through a training course in which Celia does very well, but Jennifer cannot take such work seriously.

Phyllis is seen working on the lorry which she drives. She talks of her younger sister.

Celia and the others are set to work in the factory under works supervisor Charlie Forbes. He sums up Jennifer as an attractive, spoiled woman, and proceeds to 'break' her, but in so doing, they become somewhat begrudgingly attracted to one another. Celia enjoys her work and is very good at it. A group of young RAF men from a local airfield are shown round the factory; one of them is an old friend of Jennifer's; another is a shy Scottish air-gunner, Fred Blake, who takes a shine to Celia. Later, the RAF and the factory hostel staff arrange a joint dance and hundreds of uniformed men are bussed in to liven up the otherwise tedious works dance.

Fred and Celia renew their acquaintance and become romantically involved. Jennifer meanwhile snubs Charlie by dancing with the doctor, rather than him. Later, however, she learns to respect him, and they too become romantically involved.

Back at work, Celia is day-dreaming. Charlie tells her that 'Love may make the world go round but it won't win the war'. There is an air-raid at the factory. A newly keen Jennifer tries to impress Charlie by carrying on working, but he carries her to the air-raid shelter.

Fred apparently stands Celia up on a date to attend a classical concert. Celia is upset and fantasizes various dreadful happenings. It later transpires that Fred had been on a raid, and couldn't tell Celia. The next day, he waits outside the factory for the annoyed Celia; he explains what happened, and suggests that they go for a quiet country drink. The pub however is full of soldiers, and in this unromantic setting, he proposes to her. They become engaged.

At home, Dad clearly cannot look after himself; the house is filthy, there is a mountain of washing up, and he is living on fish and chips.

Phyllis, driving her lorry, muses about her daft younger sister.

At the factory canteen, the women discuss Celia's plans for her honeymoon. The wedding is attended by her sister Phyllis, with a French officer in tow, and her father. Fred and Celia leave by train for their honeymoon. Charters and Caldicott eat sandwiches in a crowded train. Fred and Celia arrive at Eastgate, which is now very much a war-zone; the old guest-house is billeting soldiers, who are amused to see the young couple arrive. After the honeymoon, Fred and Celia return to their respective duties. Fred finds a room for them to rent, and they begin to lay plans for the future and discuss where they will live and how many children they will have. Back at the factory, some time later, Celia is informed that Fred has been killed in action over Germany.

Out in the country for a picnic, Charlie and Jennifer decide to postpone their marriage until they know what the post-war world holds for them, and how their class difference will be treated outside the special conditions of war.

The distraught Celia lives out her memories in the rented room. At lunch at the factory canteen, among a vast crowd who are being entertained by Bertha Wilmott and her band singing 'Waiting at the church', Celia is coaxed by Gwen into joining in the singing, and becoming part of the community again. Aeroplanes fly overhead.

THIS HAPPY BREED

Credits

Director:	David Lean
Producers:	Noël Coward, Anthony Havelock-Allan
Production company:	Two Cities/Cineguild
Distribution company:	Eagle-Lion
Script:	Noël Coward, with David Lean, Anthony Havelock-Allan, Ronald Neame, from the play by Noël Coward
Camera:	Ronald Neame
Editor:	Jack Harris
Art director:	C. P. Norman
Music:	Muir Mathieson
Sound:	C. C. Stevens

Starring: Celia Johnson (Ethel Gibbons), Robert Newton (Frank Gibbons), Kay Walsh (Queenie Gibbons), John Mills (Billy Mitchell).
Other players: Stanley Holloway (Bob Mitchell), Amy Veness (Mrs Flint), Alison Leggatt (Aunt Sylvia), John Blythe (Reg Gibbons), Eileen Erskine (Vi Gibbons), Guy Verney (Sam Leadbitter), Merle Tottenham (Edie), Betty Fleetwood (Phyllis), Laurence Olivier (narrator).

GB, 1944, A certificate, 111 mins., Technicolor.

Trade show: 27 Apr. 1944; public première: 29 May 1944.

Plot Synopsis

Frank Gibbons has returned home from the First World War, and with his wife Ethel and the rest of the family they move into a house in Clapham. Ethel's elderly mother and Frank's sister, Sylvia, live with them. They arrive at the empty house and start to settle in; the women make a pot of tea and immediately get involved in various forms of domestic labour; this is their lot for most of the film. Their next-door neighbour, Bob Mitchell, comes to welcome them and interrupts a coy kiss. Frank recognizes him as an old comrade and they have a drink. Frank tells Bob that he has a job at a travel agency, selling tours of the battlefields.

The Gibbonses and the Mitchells watch the Victory Parade. A few years later, the families visit the Empire Exhibition. Billy Mitchell, Bob's son, is in the navy, and is dating Queenie; they walk arm-in-arm. The kids prefer the pleasures of the fairground to the exhibition itself.

Christmas 1925. The kids are eating together in the dining room. Reg's friend, Sam, who has communist sympathies, makes a speech against poverty and injustice. Queenie makes fun of him, and talks to her friend Phyllis.

Billy comes round from next door; he is due to go away on a tour of duty in the navy that evening, and wants to say goodbye to Queenie. They talk about marriage, but Queenie says she wants too much, and it wouldn't be fair on Billy. She bursts into tears. Billy is naturally disappointed, and, on leaving the house, asks Frank to put in a good word for him whenever he can. Aunt Sylvia sings at the piano; the others have to grin and bear it, but Ethel and Frank manage to escape to the quiet of the kitchen. They talk about Sam and his political views. Frank as usual is very reasonable.

In the 1926 General Strike, Frank is seen driving a bus, with Bob working as conductor. The strike finishes, the women argue, and the men return home, drunk, singing 'Rule Britannia': 'We've saved the country from the horrors of bloody revolution.' Ethel quietens them down. Reg has not been seen for some time and eventually arrives home with a head injury; he and Sam have been at a demonstration in Whitechapel Road. Vi is very angry with Sam, whom she has been dating, for leading her brother astray. She says she never wants to see him again.

Frank resolves to try and talk some sense into his son. He is very reasonable, and eventually wins Reg round to his way of thinking: 'It's up to us ordinary people to keep things steady.' Political principles are eventually reduced to a family conflict.

Sam and Vi get married in 1928.

Queenie is seen dancing an exhibition Charleston with her lover, a married man.

Sam and Vi go to see *Broadway Melody* at the cinema in 1929; they complain that they can't understand the American accents. Once married, Sam has become very respectable and has lost his left-wing views. Frank reads a newspaper which has news of Nazi election successes in Germany.

On the morning of Reg's marriage to Phyllis, Dad has a man-to-man talk with his son, and speaks of the morality of marriage and the family. Later, as they wait for the car to take them to the church, there is a terrible family row, with everyone getting at everyone else. Sylvia has turned to spiritualism, and is now very happy, but Gran provokes her into an argument. Queenie says she won't marry Billy, who is upset; she admits there is another man. Queenie rows with her parents.

Queenie eventually decides to leave home and runs off to Marseilles with a married man. She leaves a note for her parents. Frank and Bob come home drunk from a comrades' reunion. Ethel tries to keep them in order. She finds the note from Queenie, disowns her, and refuses to have her name mentioned in the house. Vi comes round with the news that Reg and Phyllis have been killed in a car crash. Frank and Ethel are shattered.

1935. A fascist is seen lecturing at Speakers' Corner. The Conservatives win the 1935 election, which pleases Frank and Bob. Telephone wires are rigged up. The death of the king is announced. The new king abdicates. Gran has died; Edie the maid has got married and no longer works for the Gibbonses; Queenie has been away for three years.

Billy arrives back from a tour of duty, and comes to visit Frank and Ethel. He tells them he has news of Queenie—indeed, he has brought her home, and they have got married. Ethel tearfully welcomes back her daughter.

Queenie has a baby; she and her mother walk through a park in which trenches are being dug. The country is preparing for war once more. Vi and Sam have come round; they announce that they are going to go and watch the crowds cheering Chamberlain on his return from Munich. Frank argues that appeasement is an unsuccessful policy; Sylvia accuses him of being a war-monger.

Bob, now a widower, comes round to say goodbye: he is moving into the country. Frank and Bob recall some of the events of the last twenty years and discuss the possibility of another war. Queenie leaves on a liner to meet Billy in Singapore, and Frank and Ethel look after the baby.

On the eve of war, Frank and Ethel move out of the house where they have lived for twenty years, and go to live in a flat. The removal van arrives and the house is once more empty and full of echoes, as it had been twenty years earlier; Frank and Ethel walk out of the front door, with Queenie's baby.

Filmography

This list of all films cited in the text includes the following details: title of film; year of initial release, followed by year of release in Britain, if different; director; production company. All films are British-made black-and-white narrative features, unless indicated otherwise. Fuller details of films discussed at length in the main text are given in the preceding Appendix.

Film	Date	Director, production company; other details.
Aunt Sally	1933	Tim Whelan, Gainsborough.
Autumn Crocus	1934	Basil Dean, ATP.
Bank Holiday	1937	Carol Reed, Gainsborough Pictures.
Bells Go Down, The	1943	Basil Dearden, Ealing Studios.
Blue Lamp, The	1949	Basil Dearden, Ealing Studios.
Captive Heart, The	1946	Basil Dearden, Ealing Studios.
Catherine the Great	1934	Paul Czinner, London Films.
Cavalcade	1932, 1933	Frank Lloyd, Fox; USA.
Chariots of Fire	1981	Hugh Hudson, Enigma/20th C-Fox; colour.
Children on Trial	1946	Jack Lee, Crown Film Unit; documentary.
Coalface	1935	Alberto Cavalcanti, GPO Film Unit; documentary.
Coastal Command	1942	J. B. Holmes, Crown Film Unit; documentary.
Comin' Thro' The Rye	1916	Cecil Hepworth, Hepworth Manufacturing Company; silent.
Comin' Thro' The Rye	1924	Cecil Hepworth, Hepworth Picture Plays; silent.
Crooks' Tour	1940	John Baxter, British National Films.
Demi-Paradise, The	1943	Anthony Asquith, Two Cities.
Drake's Love Story	1913	Cecil Hepworth, Hepworth Manufacturing Company; silent.
Drifters	1929	John Grierson, New Era, for Empire Marketing Board; documentary; silent.
Enough To Eat	1936	Edgar Anstey, Frank Sainsbury, Gas Light and Coke Co; documentary.
Escape!	1930	Basil Dean, ATP.
Evergreen	1934	Victor Saville, Gaumont-British.
Fires Were Started	1943	Humphrey Jennings, Crown Film Unit; documentary.
First a Girl	1935	Victor Saville, Gaumont-British.

Film	Date	Director, production company; other details.
Flying Down To Rio	1933, 1934	Thornton Freeland, RKO; USA.
Footlight Parade	1933, 1934	Lloyd Bacon, Warner Bros; USA.
42nd Street	1933	Lloyd Bacon, Warner Bros, USA.
49th Parallel	1941	Michael Powell, Ortus.
Gangway	1937	Sonnie Hale, Gaumont-British.
Ghost Goes West, The	1935	René Clair, London Films.
Golddiggers of 1933	1933	Mervyn Leroy, Warner Bros; USA.
Good Companions, The	1933	Victor Saville, Gaumont-Welsh-Pearson.
Great Expectations	1946	David Lean, Cineguild.
Housing Problems	1935	Edgar Anstey/Arthur Elton, Gas Light and Coke Co.; documentary.
Howards End	1991	James Ivory, Merchant-Ivory Productions.
In Which We Serve	1942	Noël Coward/David Lean, Two Cities.
Industrial Britain	1933	Robert Flaherty/John Grierson, Empire Marketing Board; documentary.
It Always Rains On Sunday	1947	Robert Hamer, Ealing Studios.
It's Love Again	1936	Victor Saville, Gaumont-British.
It's That Man Again	1943	Walter Forde, Gainsborough Pictures.
Jack Ahoy!	1934	Walter Forde, Gaumont-British.
Java Head	1934	J. Walter Ruben, ATP.
Jew Süss	1934	Lothar Mendes, Gaumont-British.
Lady Vanishes, The	1938	Alfred Hitchcock, Gainsborough Pictures.
Letter to Brezhnev	1985	Chris Bernard, Yeardream/Film Four International/Palace; colour.
Listen To Britain	1942	Humphrey Jennings/Stewart McAllister, Crown Film Unit; documentary.
Loneliness of the Long Distance Runner, The	1962	Tony Richardson, Woodfall Films.
Look Up and Laugh	1935	Basil Dean, ATP.
Lorna Doone	1934	Basil Dean, ATP.
Love, Life and Laughter	1934	Maurice Elvey, ATP.
Loyalties	1933	Basil Dean, ATP.
Madonna of the Seven Moons	1944	Arthur Crabtree, Gainsborough Pictures.
Man in Grey, The	1943	Leslie Arliss, Gainsborough Pictures.
Man of Aran	1934	Robert Flaherty, Gainsborough Pictures.
Man with a Movie Camera, The	1929	Dziga Vertov, VUFKU; USSR; documentary; silent.
Metropolis	1926, 1927	Fritz Lang, Ufa; Germany; silent.
Midshipman Easy	1935	Carol Reed, ATP.

Film	Date	Director, production company; other details.
Millions Like Us	1943	Frank Launder/Sidney Gilliat, Gainsborough Pictures.
Miss London Limited	1943	Val Guest, Gainsborough Pictures.
Mist In The Valley	1924	Cecil Hepworth, Hepworth Picture Plays; silent.
Mrs Miniver	1942	William Wyler, MGM; USA.
My Beautiful Laundrette	1985	Stephen Frears, Working Title/SAF Productions, for Channel 4; colour.
Next of Kin	1942	Thorold Dickinson, Ealing Studios.
Night Mail	1936	Harry Watt/Basil Wright, GPO Film Unit; documentary.
Night Shift	1942	Jack Chambers, A Paul Rotha Production; documentary.
Night Train to Munich	1940	Carol Reed, Twentieth Century Productions.
Nine Men	1943	Harry Watt, Ealing Studios.
No Limit	1935	Monty Banks, ATP.
North Sea	1938	Harry Watt, GPO Film Unit; documentary.
Overlanders, The	1946	Harry Watt, Ealing Studios.
Passport to Pimlico	1949	Henry Cornelius, Ealing Studios.
Private Life of Henry the 8th, The	1933	Alexander Korda, London Films.
Queen of Hearts	1936	Monty Banks, ATP.
Rainbow Dance	1937	Len Lye, GPO Film Unit for PO Savings Bank; documentary; colour.
Revolution	1985	Hugh Hudson, Goldcrest; colour.
Room With a View, A	1985	James Ivory, Merchant-Ivory Productions; colour.
Sally In Our Alley	1931	Maurice Elvey, Associated Radio.
San Demetrio, London	1943	Charles Frend, Ealing Studios.
Saturday Night and Sunday Morning	1960	Karel Reisz, Woodfall Films.
Saving of Bill Blewitt, The	1937	Harry Watt, GPO Film Unit; documentary.
Scarlet Pimpernel, The	1934	Harold Young, London Films.
Secret Agent, The	1936	Alfred Hitchcock, Gaumont-British.
Secrets of Nature	1919–33	Series of shorts produced by H. Bruce Woolfe, Percy Smith, and Mary Field; British Instructional; documentary.
Seventh Veil, The	1945	Compton Bennett, Theatrecraft/Sydney Box/Ortus.

Film	Date	Director, production company; other details.
Sheba	1919	Cecil Hepworth, Hepworth Picture Plays; silent.
Sing As We Go	1934	Basil Dean, ATP.
South Riding	1938	Victor Saville, London Films.
Stars Look Down, The	1939	Carol Reed, Grafton.
Target for Tonight	1941	Harry Watt, Crown Film Unit; documentary.
Taste of Honey, A	1961	Tony Richardson, Woodfall Films.
There Goes The Bride	1932	Albert de Courville, Gainsborough/British Lion.
This Happy Breed	1944	David Lean, Two Cities/Cineguild; colour.
Three Men in a Boat	1933	Graham Cutts, ATP.
Tol'able David	1921, 1923	Henry King, First National; USA; silent.
Top Hat	1935	Mark Sandrich, RKO; USA.
Trade Tattoo	1937	Len Lye, GPO Film Unit; documentary; colour.
Turkey Time	1933	Tom Walls, Gaumont-British.
Waltzes From Vienna	1934	Alfred Hitchcock, Tom Arnold.
Waterloo Road	1944	Sidney Gilliat, Gainsborough Pictures.
Way Ahead, The	1944	Carol Reed, Two Cities.
Way to the Stars, The	1945	Anthony Asquith, Two Cities.
We Dive at Dawn	1943	Anthony Asquith, Gainsborough Pictures.
Western Approaches	1944	Pat Jackson, Crown Film Unit; documentary; colour.
Whiskey Galore!	1949	Alexander Mackendrick, Ealing Studios.
Whom The Gods Love	1936	Basil Dean, ATP.
Wicked Lady, The	1945	Leslie Arliss, Gainsborough Pictures.
Woman of Paris	1923, 1924	Charles Chaplin, United Artists; USA; silent.
Woman to Woman	1923	Graham Cutts, Balcon-Saville-Freedman; silent.

Bibliography

The bibliography is divided into the following sections:

1. British Film Institute materials
2. Newspapers, magazines, trade press and other trade publications, etc.
3. Books
4. Periodical articles, conference papers, occasional papers, dissertations, etc.

1. British Film Institute Materials

British Film Institute Library cuttings files and microfiches on individual films and personalities.
Aileen and Michael Balcon Special Collection.
Basil Dean Special Collection.
The Bernstein Questionnaires (audience polls carried out in 1928, 1932, 1934, 1937, and 1946–7, at the Granada cinemas).
Evergreen, Pre-production script.
Evergreen, Press Book.
Sing As We Go, 'Blue Script', a draft script for the film, dated 15 May 1934.
This Happy Breed, script and Press Book.

Please note: most references to film reviews dated 1933 or later from daily and weekly British newspapers and magazines, excluding specialist publications such as the trade press, have been drawn from cuttings kept on microfiche at the British Film Institute Library; these cuttings do not provide page numbers.

2. Newspapers, Magazines, Trade Press and Other Trade Publications, etc.

The Bioscope
Cinema Quarterly
Close Up
Contemporary Cinema
Daily Film Renter
Documentary News Letter
Eastern Daily Press
Film (c.1946)
Film Daily Yearbook, 1935
Film Form
Film Forum
Film Lovers Annual, 1933–4
Film Miscellany
Film Quarterly
Film Survey
Film Weekly

The Fortnightly
Kinematograph and Lantern Weekly
Kinematograph Weekly
Kinematograph Yearbook
Monthly Film Bulletin
The Motion Picture Herald
The Motion Picture Studio
Movie
The New York Times Film Reviews (New York, 1970)
Penguin Film Review
Pictures and Picturegoer
Picturegoer
Picture Show
Screen International
Sequence
Sight and Sound
The Times
Today's Cinema
Variety .
Variety's Film Reviews (New York, 1983)
World Film News

3. *Books*

ADDISON, PAUL, *The Road to 1945: British Politics and the Second World War* (London, 1977).
AITKEN, IAN, *Film and Reform: John Grierson and the Documentary Film Movement* (London, 1990).
ALDGATE, ANTHONY, 'Comedy, Class and Containment: The British Domestic Cinema of the 1930s', in James Curran and Vincent Porter (eds.), *British Cinema History* (London, 1983), 257–71.
—— and RICHARDS, JEFFREY, *Britain Can Take It: The British Cinema in the Second World War* (Oxford, 1986).
ALTMAN, RICK (ed.), *Genre: The Musical* (London, 1981).
ALVARADO, MANUEL, 'The Documentary Enterprise: Realism and Convention', in Elizabeth Cowie (ed.), *BFI Production Board Catalogue, 1977–78* (London, 1978), 24–8.
ANDERSON, BENEDICT, *Imagined Communities: Reflections On The Origin And Spread of Nationalism* (London, 1983).
ANDERSON, LINDSAY, 'Get Out and Push', in Tom Maschler (ed.), *Declaration* (London, 1957), 155–78.
ANDREW, DUDLEY, 'Family Diversions: French Popular Cinema and the Music Hall', in Richard Dyer and Ginette Vincendeau (eds.), *Popular European Cinema* (Routledge, 1992), 15–30.
ANSTEY, EDGAR, 'Development of Film Technique in Britain', in Roger Manvell (ed.), *Experiment in Film* (London, 1949), 234–65.

—— 'The Regional Life of Britain as Seen through British Films', in Roger Manvell (ed.), *The Year's Work in the Film, 1950* (London, 1951), 44–9.

ARMES, ROY, *A Critical History of British Cinema* (London, 1978).

ARTS ENQUIRY, *The Factual Film* (London, 1947).

ASPINALL, SUE, 'Women, Realism and Reality in British Films, 1943–1953', in James Curran and Vincent Porter (eds.), *British Cinema History* (London, 1983), 272–93.

—— and MURPHY, ROBERT (eds.), *Gainsborough Melodrama* (London, 1983).

ATKINSON, G. A., 'A Foreword', in Harold Weston, *The Art of Photoplay-Writing* (London, 1916), 7–11.

AUTY, MARTIN and RODDICK, NICK (eds.), *British Cinema Now* (London, 1985).

BAKHTIN, MIKHAIL, *Rabelais and His World* (Cambridge, Mass., 1968).

—— *Problems of Dostoyevsky's Poetics* (Manchester, 1984).

BALCON, MICHAEL, *A Lifetime in Films* (London, 1969).

—— LINDGREN, ERNEST, HARDY, FORSYTH, and MANVELL, ROGER, *Twenty Years of British Film, 1925–45* (London, 1947).

BARKER, ERNEST, *National Character and the Factors in its Formation* (London, 2nd edn. 1928 [1st pub. 1927]).

BARNOUW, ERIK, *Documentary: A History of the Non-Fiction Film* (New York, 1974).

BARR, CHARLES, *Ealing Studios* (Newton Abbot, 1977).

—— 'Introduction: Amnesia and Schizophrenia', in id. (ed.), *All Our Yesterdays: 90 Years of British Cinema* (London, 1986), 1–29.

—— (ed.), *All Our Yesterdays: 90 Years of British Cinema* (London, 1986).

BARRETT, MICHÈLE, CORRIGAN, PHILIP, KUHN, ANNETTE, and WOLFF, JANET (eds.), *Ideology and Cultural Production* (London, 1979).

BARRELL, JOHN, *The Dark Side of the Landscape: The Rural Poor in English Painting, 1730–1840* (Cambridge, 1980).

BARRY, IRIS, *Let's Go To The Movies* (New York, 1972 [1st pub. 1926]).

BARTHES, ROLAND, 'The Third Meaning', in *Image-Music-Text*, essays sel. and trans. by Stephen Heath (London, 1977), 52–68.

BAZIN, ANDRÉ, *What Is Cinema?*, i, ii, essays sel. and trans. Hugh Gray (London, 1967, 1972).

—— *Jean Renoir* (New York, 1973).

—— *Orson Welles: A Critical View* (London, 1978).

BENNETT, TONY, 'A Thousand and One Troubles', *Formations of Pleasure* (London, 1983), 138–55.

—— 'Popular Culture and Hegemony in Post-War Britain', in *Politics, Ideology and Popular Culture*, Open University Popular Culture course booklet, Unit 18 (Milton Keynes, 1982), 5–29.

—— 'Hegemony, Ideology, Pleasure: Blackpool', in Tony Bennett, Colin Mercer, and Janet Woollacott (eds.), *Popular Culture and Social Relations* (Milton Keynes, 1986), 135–54.

—— and DONALD, JAMES, 'Postscript to Block 2', in *The Historical Development of Popular Culture in Britain*, Open University Popular Culture course booklet, Units 7 and 8 (Milton Keynes, 1981), 79–85.

—— MERCER, COLIN, and WOOLLACOTT, JANET (eds.), *Popular Culture and Social Relations* (Milton Keynes, 1986).

BETTS, ERNEST, *The Film Business* (London, 1973).

BEVERIDGE, JAMES, *John Grierson, Film Master* (New York, 1978).

BHABHA, HOMI K. (ed.), *Nation and Narration* (London, 1990).

BOARD OF TRADE, *Minutes of Evidence taken before the Departmental Committee on Cinematograph Films*, i, ii (London, 1936).

BOMMES, MICHAEL and WRIGHT, PATRICK, ' "Charms of Residence": The Public and the Past', in Richard Johnson *et al.* (eds.), *Making Histories: Studies in History-Writing and Politics* (London, 1982), 253–301.

BORDWELL, DAVID, *Narration in the Fiction Film* (London, 1985).

—— STAIGER, JANET, and THOMPSON, KRISTIN, *Classical Hollywood Cinema* (London, 1985).

BREWSTER, BEN, 'Deep Staging in French Films, 1900–1914', in Thomas Elsaesser with Adam Barker (eds.), *Early Cinema: Space, Frame, Narrative* (London, 1990), 45–55.

BROOKER, PETER and WIDDOWSON, PETER, 'A Literature for England', in Robert Colls and Philip Dodd (eds.), *Englishness: Culture and Politics, 1880–1920* (London, 1986), 116–63.

BROOKS, PETER, *The Melodramatic Imagination* (New Haven, Conn., 1976).

BROWN, GEOFF, *Launder and Gilliat* (London, 1977).

BURCH, NOËL, *Correction Please, or How We Got Into Pictures* (London, 1979).

—— 'A Primitive Mode of Representation?', in Thomas Elsaesser with Adam Barker (eds.), *Early Cinema: Space, Frame, Narrative* (London, 1990), 220–7.

CALDER, ANGUS, *The People's War* (London, 1971).

CAUGHIE, JOHN, 'Broadcasting and Cinema: Converging Histories', in Charles Barr (ed.), *All Our Yesterdays: 90 Years of British Cinema* (London, 1986), 189–205.

CHANAN, MICHAEL, 'The Emergence of an Industry', in James Curran and Vincent Porter (eds.), *British Cinema History* (London, 1983), 39–58.

CHANEY, DAVID, 'Public Opinion and Social Change: The Social Rhetoric of Documentary and the Concept of News', in Elihu Katz and Tamas Szecsko (eds.), *Mass Media and Social Change* (London, 1981), 115–36.

—— and PICKERING, MICHAEL, 'Authorship in Documentary: Sociology as Art Form in Mass Observation', in John Corner (ed.), *Documentary and the Mass Media* (London, 1986), 29–44.

CHRISTIE, IAN (ed.), *Powell, Pressburger and Others* (London, 1978).

—— *Arrows of Desire: The Films of Michael Powell and Emeric Pressburger* (London, 1985).

CLARK, JON, HEINEMANN, MARGOT, MARGOLIES, DAVID, and SNEE, CAROL (eds.), *Culture and Crisis in Britain in the Thirties* (London, 1979).

COLLS, ROBERT, and DODD, PHILIP (eds.), *Englishness: Culture and Politics, 1880–1920* (London, 1986).

CONSTANTINE, STEPHEN, 'Bringing the Empire Alive: The Empire Marketing Board and Imperial Propaganda, 1926–33', in Mackenzie, J. M. (ed.), *Imperialism and Popular Culture* (Manchester, 1986), 192–231.

COOK, PAM, 'Melodrama and the Woman's Picture', in Sue Aspinall and Robert Murphy (eds.), *Gainsborough Melodrama* (London, 1983), 14–28.

CORNER, JOHN (ed.), *Documentary and the Mass Media* (London, 1986).

COSTELLO, JOHN, *Love, Sex and War* (London, 1985).

COWARD, NOËL, *Play Parade*, iv (London, 1954).

COWIE, ELIZABETH (ed.), *BFI Production Board Catalogue, 1977–78* (London, 1978).

CRAFTON, DONALD, 'Pie and Chase: Gag, Spectacle and Narrative in Slapstick Comedy', in Eileen Bowser (ed.), *The Slapstick Symposium* (Brussels, 1988), 49–59.

CURRAN, JAMES and PORTER, VINCENT (eds.), *British Cinema History* (London, 1983).

DAVIS, FRED, *Yearning For Yesterday: A Sociology of Nostalgia* (New York, 1979).

DAVY, CHARLES, 'Postscript: The Film Marches On', in id. (ed.), *Footnotes to the Film* (London, 1938), 303–22.

—— (ed.), *Footnotes to the Film* (London, 1938).

DAWSON, GRAHAM, 'History-Writing on World War II', in Geoff Hurd (ed.), *National Fictions: World War II in British Films and Television* (London, 1984), 1–7.

—— and WEST, BOB, 'Our Finest Hour?—The Popular Memory of World War 2 and the Struggle over National Identity', in Geoff Hurd (ed.), *National Fictions: World War II in British Films and Television* (London, 1984), 8–13.

DEAN, BASIL, *Mind's Eye* (London, 1973).

DICKINSON, MARGARET, 'The State and the Consolidation of Monopoly', in James Curran and Vincent Porter (eds.), *British Cinema History* (London, 1983), 74–95.

—— and STREET, SARAH, *Cinema and State: The Film Industry and the British Government, 1927–1984* (London, 1985).

DICKINSON, THOROLD and DE LA ROCHE, CATHERINE, *Soviet Cinema* (London, 1948).

DOANE, JANICE and HODGES, DEVON, *Nostalgia and Sexual Difference* (New York, 1987).

DOANE, MARY ANN, *The Desire to Desire: The Woman's Film of the 1940s* (Basingstoke, 1987).

DODD, PHILIP, 'Englishness and the National Culture', in Robert Colls and Philip Dodd (eds.), *Englishness: Culture and Politics, 1880–1920* (London, 1986), 1–28.

DONCASTER, CARYL, 'The Story Documentary', in Paul Rotha (ed.), *Television in the Making* (London, 1956), 44–8.

DRUMMOND, PHILIP, DUSINBERRE, DEKE, FIELD, SIMON, HEIN, BIRGIT, LE GRICE, MALCOLM, and REES, AL, *Film as Film: Formal Experiment in Film, 1910–1975* (London, 1979).

DURGNAT, RAYMOND, *A Mirror for England* (London, 1970).

DYER, RICHARD and VINCENDEAU, GINETTE (eds.), *Popular European Cinema* (Routledge, 1992).

EAGLETON, TERRY, *Walter Benjamin, or Towards a Revolutionary Criticism* (London, 1981).

EISENSTEIN, SERGEI, 'Dickens, Griffith and the Film Today', in id., *Film Form* (New York, 1949), 195–255.

—— *Film Form* (New York, 1949).

ELLIS, JOHN (ed.), *Screen Reader 1* (London, 1977).

—— *Visible Fictions* (London, 1982).

ELSAESSER, THOMAS, 'Vincente Minnelli', in Christine Gledhill (ed.), *Home Is Where The Heart Is: Studies in Melodrama and the Woman's Film* (London, 1987), 217–22.

—— *New German Cinema: A History* (London, 1989).

—— with BARKER, ADAM (eds.), *Early Cinema: Space, Frame, Narrative* (London, 1990).

—— 'The Continuity System: Griffith and Beyond—Introduction', in eid. (eds.), *Early Cinema: Space, Frame, Narrative* (London, 1990), 293–317.

EMPSON, WILLIAM, *Some Versions of Pastoral* (London, 1968 [1st pub. 1935]).

EPSTEIN, M. (ed.), *The Annual Register, 1945* (London, 1946).

FEUER, JANE, 'The Self-Reflexive Musical and the Myth of Entertainment', in Rick Altman (ed.), *Genre: The Musical* (London, 1981), 159–74.

—— *The Hollywood Musical* (London, 1982).

FIELDS, GRACIE, *Sing As We Go* (London, 1960).

Films in 1951: Festival of Britain (London, 1951).

FLUEGEL, JANE (ed.), *Michael Balcon: The Pursuit of British Cinema* (New York, 1984).

FORGACS, DAVID and NOWELL-SMITH, GEOFFREY (eds.), *Antonio Gramsci: Selections from Cultural Writings* (London, 1985).

FOUCAULT, MICHEL, *The Archaeology of Knowledge* (London, 1974).

FRIEDMAN, LESTER (ed.), *Fires Were Started: British Cinema and Thatcherism* (Minneapolis and London, 1993).

GARVIN, PAUL L. (ed. and trans.), *A Prague School Reader on Esthetics, Literary Structure and Style* (Washington, DC, 1964).

GENETTE, GÉRARD, 'Verisimilitude and Motivation', xeroxed typescript in University of Kent Library, trans. of 'Vraisemblance et motivation', *Figures II* (Paris, 1969).

GERNSHEIM, HELMUT with GERNSHEIM, ALISON, *The History of Photography* (London, 1955).

GLEDHILL, CHRISTINE (ed.), *Home Is Where The Heart Is: Studies in Melodrama and the Woman's Film* (London, 1987).

—— and SWANSON, GILLIAN, 'Gender and Sexuality in Second World War Films— A Feminist Approach', in Geoff Hurd (ed.), *National Fictions: World War Two in British Films and Television* (London, 1984), 56–62.

GLOVERSMITH, FRANK (ed.), *Class, Culture and Social Change, A New View of the 1930s* (Brighton, 1980).

GOMERY, DOUGLAS, *The Hollywood Studio System* (London, 1986).

—— *Shared Pleasures: A History of Movie Presentation in the United States* (London, 1992).

GRAMSCI, ANTONIO, 'Concept of "National-Popular" ', in David Forgacs and Geoffrey Nowell-Smith (eds.), *Antonio Gramsci: Selections from Cultural Writings* (London, 1985), 206–12.

GRIERSON, JOHN, 'The Course of Realism', in Charles Davy (ed.), *Footnotes to the Film* (London, 1938), 137–61.

GUBACK, THOMAS H., *The International Film Industry* (Bloomington, Ind., 1969).

GUNNING, TOM, 'The Cinema of Attraction: Early Film, its Spectator and the Avant-Garde', in Thomas Elsaesser with Adam Barker (eds.), *Early Cinema: Space, Frame, Narrative* (London, 1990), 56–62.

HABERMAS, JÜRGEN, *The Structural Transformation of the Public Sphere: An Inquiry into a Category of Bourgeois Society* (Cambridge, 1989).

HAMPTON, BENJAMIN, *The American Film Industry* (New York, 1970 [1st pub. 1931]).

HARDY, FORSYTH, 'The British Documentary Film', in Michael Balcon, Ernest Lindgren, Forsyth Hardy and Roger Manvell, *Twenty Years of British Film, 1925–1945* (London, 1947), 45–60.

—— (ed.), *Grierson on Documentary* (London, 1979 [1st pub. 1946]).

—— (ed.), *Grierson on the Movies* (London, 1981).

HARPER, SUE, 'The Representation of Women in British Feature Films, 1939–45', in Philip M. Taylor (ed.), *Britain and the Cinema in the Second World War* (Basingstoke, 1988), 168–202.

HARTOG, SIMON, 'State Protection of a Beleaguered Industry', in James Curran and Vincent Porter (eds.), *British Cinema History* (London, 1983), 59–73.

HEATH, STEPHEN (ed. and trans.), *Image-Music-Text* (London, 1977).

—— 'Narrative Space', in id., *Questions of Cinema* (London, 1981), 19–75.

—— *Questions of Cinema* (London, 1981).

HEBDIGE, DICK, *Hiding in the Light* (London, 1988).

—— 'Towards a Cartography of Taste, 1935–1962', in id., *Hiding In The Light* (London, 1988), 45–76.

HEPWORTH, CECIL, *Animated Photography: The ABC of the Cinematograph* (London, 1897).

—— *Came The Dawn: Memoirs of a Film Pioneer* (London, 1951).

HIGSON, ANDREW, 'Addressing the Nation: Five Films', in Geoff Hurd (ed.), *National Fictions: World War II in British Films and Television* (London, 1984), 22–6.

—— ' "Britain's Outstanding Contribution to the Film": The Documentary-Realist Tradition', in Charles Barr (ed.), *All Our Yesterdays: 90 Years of British Cinema* (London, 1986), 72–97.

—— 'Film-Europa: Dupont und die britische Filmindustrie', in Jürgen Bretschneider (ed.), *Ewald André Dupont: Autor und Regisseur* (Munich, 1992), 89–100.

—— 'Re-presenting the National Past: Nostalgia and Pastiche in the Heritage Film', in Lester Friedman (ed.), *Fires Were Started: British Cinema and Thatcherism* (Minneapolis and London, 1993), 109–29.

—— '[The] Way West', in Jörg Schöning (ed.), *London Calling* (Munich, 1993).

HILL, JOHN, 'Ideology, Economy and the British Cinema', in Michèle Barrett, Philip Corrigan, Annette Kuhn and Janet Wolff (eds.), *Ideology and Cultural Production* (London, 1979), 112–34.

—— *Sex, Class and Realism: 1956–63* (London, 1986).

—— 'The Issue of National Cinema and British Film Production', in Duncan Petrie (ed.), *New Questions of British Cinema* (London, 1992), 10–21.

HOBSBAWM, ERIC, 'Introduction: Inventing Traditions', in Eric Hobsbawm and Terence Ranger (eds.), *The Invention of Tradition* (Cambridge, 1983), 1–14.

—— and RANGER, TERENCE (eds.), *The Invention of Tradition* (Cambridge, 1983).

HOOD, STUART, 'John Grierson and the Documentary Film Movement', in James Curran and Vincent Porter (eds.), *British Cinema History* (London, 1983), 99–112.

HOUSTON, PENELOPE, *The Contemporary Cinema* (Harmondsworth, 1963).

HOWKINS, ALUN, 'The Discovery of Rural England', in Robert Colls and Philip Dodd (eds.), *Englishness: Politics and Culture, 1880–1920* (London, 1986), 62–88.

Humphrey Spender—Worktown—Photographs of Bolton and Blackpool, Taken for Mass Observation, 1937/38, exhibition catalogue, Gardner Centre Gallery, University of Sussex, Brighton, 1977.

HURD, GEOFF (ed.), *National Fictions: World War Two in British Films and Television* (London, 1984).

JAKOBSON, ROMAN, 'Concluding Statement: Linguistics and Poetics', in Thomas A. Sebeok (ed.), *Style in Language* (Cambridge, Mass., 1960), 350–77.

—— 'On Realism in Art', in Ladislav Matejka and Krystyna Pomorska (eds.), *Readings in Russian Poetics* (Ann Arbor, Mich., 1978), 38–46.

JEANCOLAS, JEAN-PIERRE, 'The Inexportable: The Case of French Cinema and Radio in the 1950s', in Richard Dyer and Ginette Vincendeau (eds.), *Popular European Cinema* (Routledge, 1992), 141–8.

JOHNSON, RICHARD, MCLENNAN, GREGOR, SCHWARZ, BILL, and SUTTON, DAVID (eds.), *Making Histories: Studies in History-Writing and Politics* (London, 1982).

JORDAN, MARION, 'Carry On . . . Follow that Stereotype', in James Curran and Vincent Porter (eds.), *British Cinema History* (London, 1983), 312–27.

KAMENKA, EUGENE, 'Political Nationalism: The Evolution of the Idea', in id. (ed.), *Nationalism* (London, 1976), 3–20.

—— (ed.), *Nationalism* (London, 1976).

KANN, MAURICE, 'Hollywood and Britain—Three Thousand Miles Apart', in Charles Davy (ed.), *Footnotes to the Film* (London, 1938), 185–202.

KARDISH, LAURENCE, 'Michael Balcon and the Idea of a National Cinema', in Jane Fluegel (ed.), *Michael Balcon: The Pursuit of British Cinema* (New York, 1984), 43–73.

KEANE, JOHN, *Public Life and Late Capitalism: Towards a Socialist Theory of Democracy* (Cambridge, 1984).

KEATING, PETER (ed.), *Into Unknown England: Selections from the Social Explorers* (London, 1976).

KERMODE, FRANK, *English Pastoral Poetry* (London, 1952).

KLINGENDER, FRANCIS and LEGG, STUART, *Money Behind The Screens* (London, 1937).

KRACAUER, SIEGFRIED, *From Caligari To Hitler* (Princeton, NJ, 1966 [1st pub. 1947]).

KUHN, ANNETTE, 'British Documentary in the Thirties and "Independence": Re-Contextualising a Film Movement', in Don MacPherson (ed.), *Traditions of Independence: British Cinema in the Thirties* (London, 1980), 24–33.

KULESHOV, LEV, 'Americanism', 1st pub. 1922, reproduced in trans. in Richard Taylor and Ian Christie (eds.), *The Film Factory: Russian and Soviet Cinema in Documents* (Cambridge, Mass., 1988), 72–3.

LANDY, MARCIA, *British Genres: Cinema and Society, 1930–1960* (Princeton, NJ, 1991).

LANE, BARRY (ed.), *Pictorial Photography in Britain, 1900–1920* (London, 1978).

LANT, ANTONIA, *Blackout: Re-inventing Women for War-time British Cinema* (Princeton, NJ, 1991).

LEJEUNE, CAROLINE, *Cinema* (London, 1931).

—— *Chestnuts In Her Lap* (London, 1947).

LERNER, LAURENCE, *The Uses of Nostalgia* (London, 1972).

LEVACO, RON (ed. and trans.), *Kuleshov on Film: Writings of Lev Kuleshov* (Berkeley, Calif., 1974).

LINDGREN, ERNEST, 'The Early Feature Film', in Michael Balcon, Ernest Lindgren, Forsyth Hardy and Roger Manvell, *Twenty Years of British Film, 1925–45* (London, 1947), 13–28.

LORE, COLDEN, *The Modern Photoplay and its Construction* (London, 1923).

LOVELL, ALAN and HILLIER, JIM, *Studies in Documentary* (London, 1972).

LOW, RACHAEL, *The History of the British Film, 1914–1918* (London, 1950).

—— *The History of the British Film, 1918–1929* (London, 1971).

—— *The History of the British Film, 1929–1939: Documentary and Educational Films of the 1930s* (London, 1979).

—— *The History of the British Film, 1929–1939: Film-Making in 1930s Britain* (London, 1985).

MACFARLANE, BRIAN, 'A Literary Cinema? British Films and British Novels', in Charles Barr (ed.), *All Our Yesterdays: 90 Years of British Cinema* (London, 1986), 120–42.

MACKENZIE, JOHN M. (ed.), *Imperialism and Popular Culture* (Manchester, 1986).

MCLAINE, IAN, *Ministry of Morale: Home Front Morale and the Ministry of Information in World War II* (London, 1979).

MACPHERSON, DON (ed.), *Traditions of Independence: British Cinema in the Thirties* (London, 1980).

MANVELL, ROGER, *Film* (London, 1st edn., 1944; rev. and enlarged edn., 1946).

—— 'The British Feature Film from 1940 to 1945', in Michael Balcon, Ernest Lindgren, Forsyth Hardy and Roger Manvell, *Twenty Years of British Film, 1925–45* (London, 1947), 81–96.

—— (ed.), *Experiment in Film* (London, 1949).

—— (ed.), *The Year's Work in the Film, 1950* (London, 1951).

MARRIS, PAUL (ed.), *Paul Rotha* (London, 1982).

MASCHLER, TOM (ed.), *Declaration* (London, 1957).

MATEJKA, LADISLAV and POMORSKA, KRYSTYNA (eds.), *Readings in Russian Poetics* (Ann Arbor, Mich., 1978).

MATHERS, HELEN, *Comin' Thro' The Rye* (London, 1907 [1st pub. 1875]).

MATTELART, ARMAND, DELCOURT, XAVIER, and MATTELART, MICHÈLLE, *International Image Markets* (London, 1984).

MATTHEWS, JESSIE, *Over My Shoulder* (London, 1974).

MAYER, J. P., *Sociology of Film* (London, 1946).

—— *British Cinemas and their Audiences* (London, 1948).

MEDHURST, ANDY, 'Music Hall and British Cinema', in Charles Barr (ed.), *All Our Yesterdays: 90 Years of British Cinema* (London, 1986), 168–88.

MELLOR, DAVID, 'Patterns of Naturalism: Hoppé to Hardy', in *The Real Thing: An Anthology of British Photographs, 1840–1950* (London, 1975), 25–35.

MENDLER, RAYMOND and MITCHENSON, JOE, *Theatrical Companion to Coward* (London, 1957).

MERCER, COLIN, 'That's Entertainment: The Resilience of Popular Forms', in Tony Bennett, Colin Mercer, and Janet Woollacott (eds.), *Popular Culture and Social Relations* (Milton Keynes, 1986), 177–95.

METZ, CHRISTIAN, *Film Language* (New York, 1974).

MILES, PETER and SMITH, MALCOLM, *Cinema, Literature and Society: Elite and Mass Culture in Inter-war Britain* (London, 1987).

MILIBAND, RALPH and SAVILLE, JOHN (eds.), *Socialist Register 1973* (London, 1974).

MINNS, RAYNES, *Bombers and Mash* (London, 1980).

MORRIS, LYNDA and RADFORD, ROBERT, *The Story of the Artists International Association, 1933–1953* (Oxford, 1983).

MOULES, JOAN, *Our Gracie: The Life of Dame Gracie Fields* (London, 1983).

MOYNE COMMITTEE, *Cinematograph Films Act, 1927: Report of a Committee Appointed by the Board of Trade* (London, Cmd. 5320, 1936).

MUKAROVSKY, JAN, 'Standard Language and Poetic Language', in Paul L. Garvin (ed. and trans.), *A Prague School Reader on Esthetics, Literary Structure and Style* (Washington, DC, 1964), 17–30.

—— 'The Esthetics of Language', in Paul L. Garvin (ed. and trans.), *A Prague School Reader on Esthetics, Literary Structure and Style* (Washington, DC, 1964), 31–69.

MULHERN, FRANCIS, *The Moment of Scrutiny* (London, 1981).

MURDOCK, GRAHAM and GOLDING, PETER, 'The Political Economy of Mass Communications', in Ralph Miliband and John Saville (eds.), *Socialist Register 1973* (London, 1974), 205–34.

MURPHY, ROBERT, 'Rank's Attempt on the American Market, 1944–9', in James Curran and Vincent Porter (eds.), *British Cinema History* (London, 1983), 164–78.

—— 'British Film Production, 1939–1945', in Geoff Hurd (ed.), *National Fictions: World War II in British Films and Television* (London, 1984), 14–17.

—— *Realism and Tinsel: Cinema and Society in Britain, 1939–1948* (London, 1989).

NAIRN, TOM, *The Break-up of Britain* (London, 1981).

NOWELL-SMITH, GEOFFREY, 'But do we Need it?', in Martin Auty and Nick Roddick (eds.), *British Cinema Now* (London, 1985), 147–58.

OAKLEY, CHARLES, *Where We Came In: The Story of the British Cinematograph Industry* (London, 1964).

ORBANZ, EVA, WILDENHAHN, KLANS, HOOD, STUART, and ALLEN, JIM, *Journey To A Legend and Back: The British Realistic Film* (Berlin, 1977).

PERRY, GEORGE, *The Great British Picture Show* (London, 1974).

PETRIE, DUNCAN (ed.), *New Questions of British Cinema* (London, 1992).

PIRIE, DAVID, *A Heritage of Horror* (New York, 1973).

POTTS, ALEX, ' "Constable Country" Between the Wars', in Raphael Samuel (ed.), *Patriotism: The Making and Un-making of British National Identity. iii. National Fictions* (London, 1989), 160–86.

POWELL, DILYS, 'Films since 1939', in Arnold Haskell, Dilys Powell, Rollo Myers, and Robin Ironside, *Since 1939: Ballet, Films, Music, Painting* (London, 1948), 57–95.

PRIESTLEY, J. B., *English Journey* (London, 1934).

—— *Rain Upon Godshill* (London, 1941).

—— *British Women Go To War* (London, n.d. [c.1943]).

Progress of British Films (Glasgow, n.d. [c.1946]).

PRONAY, NICHOLAS, ' "The Land of Promise": The Projection of Peace Aims in

Britain', in K. R. M. Short (ed.), *Film and Radio Propaganda in World War II* (London, 1983), 51–77.

—— and CROFT, JEREMY, 'British Film Censorship and Propaganda Policy during the Second WORLD WAR', in James Curran and Vincent Porter (eds.), *British Cinema History* (London, 1983), 144–63.

PUDOVKIN, V. I., *Film Technique* (London, enlarged edn., 1933).

QUINLAN, DAVID, *British Sound Films: The Studio Years, 1928–1959* (London, 1984).

RICHARDS, JEFFREY, *The Age of the Dream Palace* (London, 1984).

—— 'National Identity in British Wartime Films', in Philip M. Taylor, *Britain and the Cinema in the Second World War* (London, 1988), 42–61.

—— and ALDGATE, TONY, *Best of British: Cinema and Society 1930–1970* (Oxford, 1983).

—— and SHERIDAN, DOROTHY (eds.), *Mass Observation at the Movies* (London, 1987).

ROBINSON, DAVID, 'United Kingdom', in Alan Lovell (ed.), *The Art of the Cinema in Ten European Countries* (Strasburg, 1967), 197–229.

ROBINSON, H. P., *The Elements of a Pictorial Photograph* (New York, 1973 [1st pub. 1896]).

ROLLINS, CYRIL and WAREING, ROBERT, *Victor Saville* (London: National Film Archive booklet, n.d.).

ROTHA, PAUL, 'A Survey of Recent Film Literature in Britain', *The Year's Work in the Film, 1949* (London, 1950), 77–85.

—— *Documentary Film* (London, rev. and enlarged 3rd edn., 1952 [1st pub. 1936]).

—— (ed.), *Television in the Making* (London, 1956).

—— *Documentary Diary: An Informal History of the British Documentary Film, 1928–1939* (London, 1973).

—— Essays Selected by, *Richard Winnington, Film—Criticism and Caricature, 1943–1953* (London, 1975).

—— *The Film Till Now* (London, rev. and enlarged edn., 1977 [1st pub. 1930]).

RYALL, TOM, *Alfred Hitchcock and the British Cinema* (London, 1986).

SALES, ROGER, *English Literature in History, 1780–1830: Pastoral and Politics* (London, 1983).

SALT, BARRY, *Film Style and Technology: History and Analysis* (London, 1983).

SAMSON, JEN, 'The Film Society, 1925–1939', in Charles Barr (ed.), *All Our Yesterdays: 90 Years of British Cinema* (London, 1986), 306–13.

SAMUEL, RAPHAEL (ed.), *Patriotism: The Making and Un-making of British National Identity*, i–iii (London, 1989).

SCANNELL, PADDY, 'The Media and the Public Sphere', in Peter Golding, Graham Murdock, and Philip Schlesinger (eds.), *Communicating Politics* (Leicester, 1986), 37–53.

—— ' "The Stuff of Radio": Developments in Radio Features and Documentaries before the War', in John Corner (ed.), *Documentary and the Mass Media* (London, 1986), 1–26.

—— and CARDIFF, DAVID, 'Serving the Nation: Public Service Broadcasting before the War', in Bernard Waites, Tony Bennett, and Graham Martin (eds.), *Popular Culture Past and Present* (London, 1981), 161–88.

SEBEOK, THOMAS A. (ed.), *Style in Language* (Cambridge, Mass., 1960).

SHORT, K. R. M. (ed.), *Film and Radio Propaganda in World War II* (London, 1983).

SHOWALTER, ELAINE, *A Literature Of Their Own: British Women Novelists From Brontë to Lessing* (London, 1978).

SMITH, ANTHONY D., *Nationalism in the Twentieth Century* (Oxford, 1979).

SMITH, MALCOLM, 'Narrative and Ideology in *Listen To Britain*', in Jeremy Hawthorn (ed.), *Narrative from Malory to Motion Pictures* (London, 1985), 145–57.

SORLIN, PIERRE, *The Film as History: Re-staging the Past* (Oxford, 1980).

SPOTO, DONALD, *The Dark Side Of Genius: The Life of Alfred Hitchcock* (London, 1983).

STAIGER, JANET, *Interpreting Films: Studies in the Historical Reception of American Cinema* (Princeton, NJ, 1992).

STALLYBRASS, PETER and WHITE, ALLON, *The Politics and Poetics of Transgression* (London, 1986).

SUSSEX, ELIZABETH, *The Rise and Fall of British Documentary: The Story of the Film Movement Founded by John Grierson* (London, 1975).

SWANN, PAUL, *The British Documentary Film Movement, 1926–1946* (Cambridge, 1989).

TAYLOR, JOHN, 'Pictorial Photography in Britain, 1900–1920', in Barry Lane (ed.), *Pictorial Photography in Britain, 1900–1920* (London, 1978), 9–32.

TAYLOR, JOHN RUSSELL (ed.), *The Pleasure Dome: The Collected Film Criticism of Graham Greene, 1935–1940* (Oxford, 1980).

TAYLOR, PHILIP M., 'Introduction: Film, the Historian and the Second World War', in id. (ed.), *Britain and the Cinema in the Second World War* (London, 1988), 1–14.

—— (ed.), *Britain and the Cinema in the Second World War* (London, 1988).

THOMPSON, KRISTIN, *Exporting Entertainment: America in the World Film Market, 1907–1934* (London, 1985).

THORNTON, MICHAEL, *Jessie Matthews: A Biography* (London, 1974).

THORPE, FRANCES and PRONAY, NICHOLAS, with COULTASS, CLIVE, *British Official Films in the Second World War* (Oxford, 1980).

TRACHTENBERG, ALAN, 'Introduction', in id. (ed.), *Classic Essays on Photography* (New Haven, Conn., 1980), 7–13.

—— (ed.), *Classic Essays on Photography* (New Haven, Conn., 1980).

TUDOR, ANDREW, *Theories of Film* (London, 1974).

TULLOCH, JOHN, *Australian Cinema: Industry, Narrative and Meaning* (Sydney, 1982).

VAUGHAN, DAI, *Portrait of an Invisible Man: The Working Life of Stewart McAllister, Film Editor* (London, 1983).

WATT, HARRY, *Don't Look At The Camera* (London, 1974).

WESTON, HAROLD, *The Art of Photoplay-Writing* (London, 1916).

WIENER, MARTIN J., *English Culture and the Decline of the Industrial Spirit, 1850–1980* (Cambridge, 1981).

WILDENHAHN, KLAUS, 'Approaches to the Legend', in Eva Orbanz, Klaus Wildenhahn, Stuart Hood, and Jim Allen, *Journey To A Legend and Back: The British Realistic Film* (Berlin, 1977), 11–23.

WILLEMEN, PAUL, 'On Realism in the Cinema', in John Ellis (ed.), *Screen Reader 1* (London, 1977), 47–54.

WILLIAMS, ALAN, 'The Musical Film and Recorded Popular Music', in Rick Altman (ed.), *Genre: The Musical* (London, 1981), 147–58.

WILLIAMS, RAYMOND, *Marxism and Literature* (Oxford, 1977).

—— 'British Film History: New Perspectives', in James Curran and Vincent Porter (eds.), *British Cinema History* (London, 1983), 9–23.

—— *The Country and The City* (London, 1985).

WINCHESTER, CLARENCE (ed.), *The World Film Encyclopaedia* (London, 1933).

WOOD, ALAN, *Mr. Rank* (London, 1952).

WOOD, LINDA, *British Films, 1927–1939* (London, 1986).

WRIGHT, BASIL, *The Long View: A Personal Perspective on World Cinema* (London, 1974).

—— *The Use of the Film* (London, 1948).

WRIGHT, PATRICK, *On Living In An Old Country: The National Past in Contemporary Britain* (London, 1985).

Year's Work in the Film, 1949, The (London, 1950).

4. Periodical Articles, Conference Papers, Occasional Papers, Dissertations, etc.

ANDERSON, BENEDICT, 'Narrating the Nation', *Times Literary Supplement*, 13 June 1986, 659.

ANDERSON, PERRY, 'Components of the National Culture', *New Left Review*, 50 (1968), 3–57.

BADDER, DAVID and BAKER, BOB, 'Thorold Dickinson' (interview), *Film Dope*, 11 (1977), 1–21.

BALCON, MICHAEL, 'The British Film during the War', *Penguin Film Review*, 1 (1946), 66–73.

—— 'The Feature Carries on the Documentary Tradition', *Quarterly of Film, Radio and Television*, 6/4 (1952), 351–3.

BARTHES, ROLAND, 'The Realistic Effect', *Film Reader*, 3 (1978), 131–5.

BLAKESTON, OSWELL, 'British Solecisms', *Close Up*, 2 (1927), 17–23.

BROWNING, H. E. and SORRELL, A. A., 'Cinemas and Cinema-Going in Great Britain', *Journal of the Royal Statistical Society*, 117/2 (1954), 9–170.

BURCH, NOËL, 'Porter or Ambivalence', *Screen*, 19/4 (1978–9), 91–105.

—— 'Film's Institutional Mode of Representation and the Soviet Response', *October*, 11 (1979), 77–96.

—— 'Narrative/Diegesis: Thresholds, Limits', *Screen*, 23/2 (1982), 16–33.

BUSCOMBE, EDWARD, 'Film History and the Idea of a National Cinema', *Australian Journal of Screen Theory*, 9–10 (1981), 141–53.

CASTLE, HUGH, 'Attitude and Interlude', *Close Up*, 7/3 (1930), 184–90.

CAUGHIE, JOHN, 'Progressive Television and Documentary Drama', *Screen*, 21/3 (1980), 9–35.

CHANEY, DAVID and PICKERING, MICHAEL, 'Democracy and Communication: Mass Observation, 1937–1943', *Journal of Communication*, 36/1 (1986), 41–56.

COLLS, ROBERT and DODD, PHILIP, 'Representing the Nation: British Documentary Film, 1930–45', *Screen*, 26/1 (1985), 21–33.

CROFTS, STEPHEN, 'Re-conceptualizing National Cinema/s', *Quarterly Review of Film and Video*, 14/3 (1993), 49–67.

CUBITT, SEAN, 'Introduction: Over the Borderlines', *Screen*, 30/4 (1989), 2–8.

DAVIES, GILL, 'Teaching about Narrative', *Screen Education*, 29 (1978–9), 56–76.

DE LA ROCHE, CATHERINE, 'Britain's Film Directors, 1. Frank Launder and Sidney Gilliat', *Our Time*, Dec. (1946), 101–3.

DONALD, JAMES, 'How English is it? National Culture and Popular Literature', *New Formations*, 6 (1988), 31–47.

ELLIS, JOHN, 'Made in Ealing', *Screen*, 16/1 (1977), 78–127.

—— 'The Institution of Cinema', *Edinburgh '77 Magazine*, 2 (1977), 56–66.

—— 'Art, Culture and Quality: Terms for a Cinema in the '40s and the '70s', *Screen*, 19/3 (1978), 9–49.

—— 'Victory of the Voice', *Screen*, 22/2 (1981), 69–72.

—— 'The Literary Adaptation: An Introduction', *Screen*, 23/1 (1982), 3–5.

ELSAESSER, THOMAS, 'Images for England (and Scotland, Ireland, Wales . . .)', *Monthly Film Bulletin*, 51 (1984), 267–9.

—— 'Chronicle of a Death Retold: Hyper, Retro or Counter-Cinema', *Monthly Film Bulletin*, 54 (1987), 164–7.

EVANS, MARY and MORGAN, DAVID, 'Class and Ideology in the 2nd World War', *Red Letters*, 16 (1984), 33–47.

EVERSON, WILLIAM K., 'Jessie Matthews', *Films in Review*, 26/10 (1975), 579–96.

'Frank Launder', *Film Dope*, 33 (1985), 26–8.

GRIERSON, JOHN, 'Documentary (1)', *Cinema Quarterly*, 1/2 (1932), 67–72.

—— 'Documentary (2): symphonies', *Cinema Quarterly*, 1/3 (1933), 135–9.

—— 'The Documentary Producer', *Cinema Quarterly*, 2/1 (1933), 7–9.

GUNNING, TOM, 'Building an Ending: Vitagraph Films and the Cinema of Narrative Integration', a paper for the festival of Vitagraph screenings at Pordenone, autumn 1987.

HABERMAS, JÜRGEN, 'The Public Sphere: An Encyclopaedia Article (1964)', *New German Critique*, 1/3 (1974), 49–55.

HALL, STUART, 'The Social Eye of Picture Post', *Working Papers in Cultural Studies*, 2 (1972), 83–119.

—— 'Cultural Identity and Cinematic Representation', *Framework*, 36 (1989), 68–81.

HANSEN, MIRIAM, 'Co-operative Auteur Cinema and Oppositional Public Sphere: Alexander Kluge's Contribution to *Germany in Autumn*', *New German Critique*, 24–5 (1981–2), 147–84.

HARMAN, JYMPSON, 'Truth and British Films', *Sight and Sound*, 15 (1946), 15–16.

HARPER, SUE, 'A Note on Basil Dean, Sir Robert Vansittart and British Historical Films of the 1930s', *Historical Journal of Film Radio and Television*, 9/2 (1989), 191–7.

HARRISSON, TOM, 'The Fifty-Second Week: Impressions of Blackpool', *Geographical Magazine*, 6/6 (1938), 387–404.

HARTOG, SIMON, 'L'histoire exemplaire de la G-B', *Film Échange*, 13 (1981), 47–62.

HEATH, STEPHEN, 'Film and System: Terms of Analysis', *Screen*, 16/1 and 16/2 (1975), 7–77 and 91–113.

—— 'Questions of Property: Film and Nationhood', *Ciné-tracts*, 1/4 (1978), 3–11.

HEPWORTH, CECIL, 'What to Learn from "the Pictures" ' (interview), *Snapshots*, July (1924), 139–40, 162.

HIGSON, ANDREW, 'Critical Theory and "British Cinema"', *Screen*, 24/4–5 (1983), 80–95.

—— 'Space, Place, Spectacle', *Screen*, 25/4–5 (1984), 2–21.

—— 'The Discourses of British Film Year', *Screen*, 27/1 (1986), 86–110.

—— 'Saturday Night or Sunday Morning: British Cinema in the Fifties', *Ideas and Production*, 9–10 (1989), 141–60.

—— 'The Idea of National Cinema', *Screen*, 30/4 (1989), 36–46.

—— and NEALE, STEVE, 'Introduction: Components of a National Film Culture', *Screen*, 26/1 (1985), 3–8.

HILLIER, JIM, LOVELL, ALAN, and ROHDIE, SAM, 'Alberto Cavalcanti' (interview), *Screen*, 13/2 (1972), 36–53.

HOHENDAHL, PETER, 'Jürgen Habermas: "The Public Sphere" (1964)', *New German Critique*, 1/3 (1974), 45–8.

HONRI, BAYNHAM, 'Cecil M. Hepworth—His Studios and Techniques', *British Journal of Photography* 15 and 22 Jan. 1971, 48–51 and 74–79.

HUNTER, WILLIAM, 'The Art-Form of Democracy?', *Scrutiny*, 1/1 (1932), 61–5.

JAMESON, FREDERIC, 'Post-Modernism, or the Cultural Logic of Late Capitalism', *New Left Review*, 146 (1984), 53–92.

JEFFERY, TOM, 'Mass Observation: A Short History', Occasional Papers no. 55, Centre for Contemporary Cultural Studies (University of Birmingham, 1978).

KERR, PAUL, 'Classic Serials: To Be Continued . . .', *Screen*, 23/1 (1982), 6–19.

KLUGE, ALEXANDER, 'On Film and the Public Sphere', *New German Critique*, 24–5 (1981–2), 206–20.

KNIGHT, ERIC, 'The Passing of Hollywood', *Cinema Quarterly*, 1 (1933), 216–18.

KRAMER, PETER, 'The Double Standard of Classical Hollywood Cinema', a paper presented at the Society for Cinema Studies Conference, 29 June–3 July 1988.

KUHN, ANNETTE, ' "Independent" Film-Making and the State in the 1930s', *Edinburgh '77 Magazine*, 2 (1977), 44–55.

—— 'The Camera I: Observations on Documentary', *Screen*, 19/2 (1978), 71–83.

—— 'Desert Victory and the People's War', *Screen*, 22/2 (1981), 45–68.

MACCABE, COLIN, 'Realism and the Cinema: Notes on some Brechtian Theses', *Screen*, 15/2 (1974), 7–27.

MACFARLANE, BRIAN, 'Novel into Film—Transfer and Adaptation: the Processes of Transposition', Ph.D. thesis (University of East Anglia, 1987).

McINTYRE, STEVE, 'National Film Cultures: Policies and Peripheries', *Screen*, 26/1 (1985), 66–76.

MACPHERSON, KENNETH, 'As is', *Close Up*, 1 (1927), 5–15.

Mass Observation, 'Social Security and Parliament', *Political Quarterly*, 14 (1943), 245–55.

METZ, CHRISTIAN, 'History/Discourse: A Note on Two Voyeurisms', *Edinburgh Magazine*, 1 (1976), 21–5.

MORDEN, TERRY, 'The Pastoral and the Pictorial', *Ten : 8*, 12 (1983), 18–25.

MORLEY, DAVID and ROBINS, KEVIN, 'Spaces of Identity', *Screen*, 30/4 (1989), 10–34.

MUELLER, JOHN, 'Fred Astaire and the Integrated Musical', *Cinema Journal*, 24/1 (1984), 28–40.

MULVEY, LAURA, 'Visual Pleasure and Narrative Cinema', *Screen*, 16/3 (1975), 6–18.

MURPHY, ROBERT, 'A Rival to Hollywood? The British Film Industry in the Thirties', *Screen*, 24/4–5 (1983), 96–106.

NEALE, STEVE, 'Triumph of the Will—notes on documentary and spectacle', *Screen*, 20/1 (1979), 63–86.

—— 'Art Cinema as Institution', *Screen*, 22/1 (1981), 11–39.

—— 'Melodrama and Tears', *Screen*, 27/6 (1986), 6–22.

NICHOLS, BILL, 'Documentary Theory and Practice', *Screen*, 17/4 (1976–7), 34–48.

NOWELL-SMITH, GEOFFREY, 'Gramsci and the National-Popular', *Screen Education*, 22 (1977), 12–15.

—— 'Popular Culture', *New Formations*, 2 (1987), 79–90.

PAWLING, CHRIS, 'George Orwell and the Documentary in the Thirties', *Literature and History*, 4 (1976), 81–93.

PORTER, VINCENT and LITEWSKI, CHAIM, 'The Way Ahead', *Sight and Sound*, 50/2 (1981), 110–16.

RILEY, DENISE, ' "The Free Mothers": Pronatalism and Working Women in Industry at the End of the Last War in Britain', *History Workshop Journal*, 11 (1981), 59–118.

ROHDIE, SAM, 'History and Film', BFI Education Advisory Service/Society for Education in Film and Television Seminar Paper (1973).

ROSEN, PHILIP, 'History, Textuality, Nation: Kracauer, Burch, and some Problems in the Study of National Cinemas', *Iris*, 2/2 (1984), 69–83.

ROWSON, SIMON, 'A Statistical Survey of the Cinema Industry in Great Britain in 1934', *Journal of the Royal Statistical Society*, 99/1 (1936), 67–129.

(SAVILLE, VICTOR), 'A Life in Films' (interview), *BFI News*, 3 (1973), 4.

SCANNELL, PADDY, 'Public Service Broadcasting and Modern Public Life', *Media, Culture and Society*, 11/2 (1989), 135–66.

SCHLESINGER, PHILIP, 'On National Identity: Some Conceptions and Misconceptions Criticised', *Social Science Information*, 26/2 (1987), 219–64.

SWANN, PAUL, 'The Selling of the Empire: The EMB Film Unit', *Studies in Visual Communication*, 9/3 (1983), 15–24.

—— 'John Grierson and the G.P.O. Film Unit, 1933–39', *Historical Journal of Film Radio and Television*, 3 (1983), 19–34.

THOMPSON, KRISTIN, 'The Concept of Cinematic Excess', *Ciné-tracts*, 1/2 (1977), 54–63.

TURNER, BRYAN S., 'A Note on Nostalgia', *Theory, Culture and Society*, 4 (1987), 147–56.

VINCENDEAU, GINETTE, 'Community, Nostalgia and the Spectacle of Masculinity', *Screen*, 26/6 (1985), 18–38.

WILLEMEN, PAUL, 'In Search of an Alternative Perspective: An Interview with Armand and Michelle Mattelart', *Framework*, 26–7 (1985), 54–62.

WILLIAMS, RAYMOND, 'A Lecture on Realism', *Screen*, 18/1 (1977), 61–74.

WOLLEN, PETER, 'Cinema/Americanism/the Robot', *New Formations*, 8 (1989), 7–34.

WRIGHT, BASIL, 'Realist Review', *Sight and Sound*, 10/38 (1941), 20–1.
—— 'Documentary Today', *Penguin Film Review*, 2 (1947), 37–44.
WYETH, PETER and MacPHERSON, DON, 'The Third Front', *Sight and Sound*, 47/3 (1978), 143–5, 185.

Index